Jack Harris
Australian Golfer Extraordinaire

Jack Harris
Australian Golfer Extraordinaire

David Lunt

Copyright © 2015 David Lunt

All rights reserved. No part of this publication may be reproduced, stored in retrieval system or transmitted in any form or by means without the prior written permission of the copyright owner. Inquiries should be made to the publisher.

First published by David Lunt 2015
Revised edition 2018

Unless otherwise stated, photographs and newspaper articles are from Jack Harris's personal collection or kindly provided by the PGA of Australia. Every attempt has been made to locate copyright holders for material used in this book and I apologise if any infringement has taken place. Any person or organisation that may have been overlooked or misattributed or who believe they own copyright to material in this book may contact the author / publisher.

Cover Design   JD Creative Designs

Typeset by BookPOD Pty Ltd

Typeset in Garamond Premier Pro and ITC Avant Garde Gothic

National Library of Australia Cataloguing-in-Publication entry

Creator: Lunt, David, author.

Title: Jack Harris Australian golfer extraordinaire / David Lunt.

ISBN: 9780646932736 (paperback)

Subjects: Harris, Jack, 1922-2014.
Golfers--Australia--Biography.
Golf--Australia--History
Golf--Tournaments--Australia--History.

Dewey Number: 796.352092

Dedication

For Jack and Grace

John Bruce "Jack" Harris
8 December 1922 – 22 August 2014

Author's Note: This book was virtually completed before Jack's passing. He had received various copies of the manuscript throughout the process. I have not gone through the book and changed the parts which refer to Jack still being with us.

Should any profit from the sale of this book accrue, it will be donated in its entirety to the Doncaster Rotary Club for use at their discretion on community service assistance projects.

Contents

Dedication v
Introduction ix
Forewords xi
Preface xv
About the Author and How the Book Came to be Written xvii

Chapter 1
Pre-Second World War Days 1

Chapter 2
The Second World War Days 11

Chapter 3
Post War Years 21

Chapter 4
City Golf Schools 25

Chapter 5
The Keysborough Days 33

Chapter 6
Jack Harris Tournament Playing Record 49

Chapter 7
From Paupers to Princes? 63

Chapter 8
Brotherly Love 87

Chapter 9
Jack Harris the Teacher 95

Chapter 10
Exhibition Matches 115

Chapter 11
Australian Open and Australian PGA 119

Chapter 12
King of Victoria.. 129

Chapter 13
British Open, Here We Come!.. 141

Chapter 14
Caddies.. 165

Chapter 15
When Is a Rule Not a Rule?... 177

Chapter 16
Characters of the Game and the John McEnroe of Golf................ 183

Chapter 17
Best Ever World Golfers... 189

Chapter 18
Best Ever Australian Golfers.. 201

Chapter 19
Amateurs and Professionals... 223

Chapter 20
Sorrento and the Non-Playing Years.. 233

Chapter 21
Knights and Dames... and Other Baubles....................................... 243

Chapter 22
Wattle Park Days... 251

Afterword 261

The Final Chapter... 263

Postscript 267

Acknowledgments... 269

References.. 273

Appendix I
Norman von Nida (14 Feb 1914 – 20 May 2007)........................... 405

Introduction

This is the previously untold story of John Bruce 'Jack' Harris, an Australian golfer who played tournament golf for twenty-five years between 1946 and 1971. Throughout that period Jack Harris was consistently ranked in the top five or six professional golfers in Australia even though he was essentially a club professional and leading Victorian golf teacher. He had more than 90 tournament wins and played in over 485 events. Late in his career he even played a few times against Jack Nicklaus, the world's best ever golfer.

In 1960 Jack Harris shot 282 in the Victorian Open Championship to equal the long standing course record at the Metropolitan Golf Club (GC) which had been set by the legendary American golfer Gene Sarazen at the 1936 Australian Open. He also played against many other world golfing superstars like Arnold Palmer, Gary Player, Bobby Locke and Sam Snead when they visited Australia during the 1950s and 1960s.

He is an Australian PGA Life Member and an inaugural inductee into the Victorian Golf Hall of Fame with six Victorian PGA titles, a Victorian Open and many more tournaments to his credit. In the process he broke almost forty course records.

Despite his achievements, the name of Jack Harris is perhaps not so well known outside golfing circles as some of his more recognised Australian contemporaries. These included household names like Peter Thomson, Kel Nagle and Norman von Nida.

Jack was a very humble, softly spoken and unassuming man. It is hoped by highlighting in this book details of his impeccable playing and teaching record that the situation can be somewhat rectified and more people can be made aware of his outstanding achievements. This is a story which was crying out to be told and is long overdue.

The post-war era from 1946 to 1971 was a very exciting time to be a professional golfer. During this twenty-five year period the professional golfing scene in Australia and around the world started to rapidly change and the emergence of the modern day touring professional was seen. Jack

Harris and his peers were pioneers for that change. Why such a major transition in golf took place at this point in history will be fully explained in this book.

Forewords

I first met Jack in 1960 at a function held by the Sportsman's Association of Victoria in his honour; probably as a good luck gesture as we farewelled him prior to his trip to England where he was to take on the golfing world. Ted Whitten (arguably the best Australian Football player of all time), Jack Collins (Footscray champion full forward and Footscray team of the Century inductee), Jim Miller (Footscray Club President), Walter Lindrum (World Professional Billiard Champion) and myself, presented Jack with Ted Whitten's famous number three Footscray jumper.

Jack was thrilled as he has always been a very keen Footscray/Western Bulldogs supporter. He had grown up near the Western Oval and had even sold records (programs) on match days as a boy. Jack was a good friend of both Jack Collins and Ted Whitten who both admired him greatly.

It was great to meet Jack again recently to reminisce about the old days. We spoke about growing up in the Western Suburbs, wagging school to play golf, about old friends, our careers in sport and even about the 2014 form of the Footscray/Western Bulldogs Football team. He is still the quiet unassuming person he has always been.

This book will bring back special memories for those golfers who were able to follow Jack's career, be coached by him or just fortunate enough to enjoy his company as they played a round of golf together.

It has been a great honour for me to acknowledge the life and career of Jack Harris, a champion golfer and a great man. I am sure you will enjoy reading about his remarkable golfing career.

John Schultz – Footscray Footballer, Australian Football Hall of Famer and 1960 Brownlow Medallist
August 2014

Jack Harris

Jack Harris was one of the greats of our game and his contribution to the PGA of Australia and the game of golf was significant.

A leading tournament professional through the 1940's to 1960's and respected club professional, Jack will be remembered as a generous man who made a positive impact on the lives of many.

Jack secured over 80 tournament wins in his career, including a record six Victorian PGA Championship titles, and the tournament trophy is now named in his honour – the Jack Harris Cup.

Not only was Jack a great golfer and tournament winner, who played alongside the likes of Peter Thomson, Kel Nagle and Frank Phillips, he was also a dedicated teacher, mentor and PGA Member.

Jack was the Club Professional at the Keysborough Golf Club for 16 years and also spent 15 years at the Sorrento Golf Club where he taught thousands of golfers.

Jack's achievements have been recognised in many ways, he received Life Membership of the PGA in 2001 followed by inaugural induction to the Victorian Golf Hall of Fame in 2011.

Greatness was one of the traits of Jack Harris and although Jack is no longer with us, his memory will live on through the Victorian PGA Championship.

Brian Thorburn
Chief Executive Officer
PGA of Australia

Tim Moore from PGA of Australia presents Jack Harris with his Victorian Golf Hall of Fame Award. Jack Harris first joined the PGA of Australia in 1940 and became a Life Member in 2001.

In July, 2011 Jack Harris was an inaugural inductee into the Victorian Golf Hall of Fame, along with five other Australian greats of the game. Seated is Miss Burtta Cheney MBE. Standing are (left to right) Jack Harris, Paul Bachli representing his late father Doug Bachli, Flo Grimwade representing her late father Ivo Whitton, Peter Thomson AO CBE and Bob Shearer. (Photographs courtesy of the PGA of Australia)

Preface

After this book had been first published in early 2015 a significant amount of new information about the tournament playing days of Jack Harris continued to emerge. As a result, details of a 120 more tournaments / purses played have been included in the tournament record pages and in the reference section. Attempts have also been made to rectify errors and omissions made in the first edition as far as possible.

About the Author and How the Book Came to be Written

My name is David Lunt. I am a seventy-year old Lancastrian who has lived in Melbourne since emigrating here from the UK in 1983 with my wife Kathleen and four children: Jennifer, Jonathan, Susanna and Richard. How does the son of an English blacksmith come to write a book about Jack Harris, one of Australia's greatest post war golfers?

Let's start at the beginning. For those interested in useless trivia, the surname Lunt dates back to the days when the Vikings were raping and pillaging in England over a thousand years ago. These Vikings were most likely the Norwegian Vikings who were drummed out of Ireland by the equally pugilistic Irish. They fled across the Irish Sea and landed on the Fylde coast just a few miles north of Liverpool.

I have never had an ancestry DNA test done but I am aware that knowledge in this area has expanded rapidly in recent years. Recent studies have actually suggested that both the Romans and the Vikings left very little DNA trace in the blood of modern day Britons. Apparently, the Anglo-Saxons who came after the Romans but before the Vikings, had a much bigger impact.

The world of male Y chromosomes, haplogroups, haplotypes, mitochondrial DNA and polymorphisms certainly sounds very interesting. However, I think I may give it a miss and just continue to believe that I really do have some Viking blood in me. After all, why risk letting the truth spoil a good story?

There is even a small village in that area which rejoices in the name of Lunt. The name Lunt was derived from the pre-seventh century Norse Viking word *lunder* which means a group of trees. My ancestors came from that region. The Royal Birkdale golf course (GC) where Peter Thomson won two of his British Opens is not many miles away. Also in the same vicinity is the Royal Lytham and St Annes GC where *el buen caballero* Severiano Ballesteros had one his most memorable victories.

My earliest sporting recollections were following the fortunes of Burnley Football Club and also of a great Australian cricketer called Bill Alley. He was the paid professional playing for Colne in the Lancashire League between 1948 – 1953. And despite all the famous world cricketers who played in that League over the years, such as Sir Viv Richards, Sir Clive Lloyd, Shane Warne just to name a few, Bill Alley is still the only man in history to score over 1000 runs per season EVERY year he played. After he left Colne he played for Blackpool where he achieved the distinction of being the highest paid cricketer in the world up to that point in time. But he was still not done. At age 38 he played County cricket for Somerset and during his time there he became one of only eight cricketers in English County cricket history who scored over 3000 runs in one season. A record which of course still stands in 2018. How Bill Alley was never picked to play for Australia still puzzles me.

Although I loved cricket and football, my interest in golf had also been awakened at a fairly early age. As an eleven or twelve-year old schoolboy, I had somehow discovered that I could earn a bit of pocket money by caddying at the nearby Colne GC Club. I caddied regularly for a local mill owner called Mr Hardaker who played golf a few times every week with a doctor whose name escapes me – after all, it was almost sixty years ago! Mr Hardaker used to give me half a crown each time I caddied and I thought I was the bee's knees! I didn't learn much about golf from Mr Hardaker although I did quickly learn what a slice was. I spent much of my time scaling the dry stone walls which surrounded the golf course boundary, searching for wayward golf balls in the tall meadow grass of the adjoining farmland. Even when I did find the golf ball, I discovered that it wasn't worth the trouble. This was because the glancing blow which had caused it to slice over into the meadow had inevitably inflicted a large cut or *smile* into the soft balata cover which rendered the ball unfit for further play.

It wasn't long, however, before education and work commitments became top priorities. Golf had to take a back seat and the early fascination which had been awakened, remained dormant for a while. I was educated at Colne Grammar School before studying polymer physics and polymer chemistry at John Dalton College in Manchester. In those days, Lancashire was dominated by the cotton industry. The industry, however, started to dwindle rapidly when English manufacturers of weaving and spinning machinery began selling their wares in far-flung places like India and Pakistan. Even though Lancashire mill owners themselves were paying pitifully low wages, labour costs in these countries were much lower. Very soon, cheap finished cotton goods were being imported from Asia and the writing was on the wall. I decided fairly early on that the cotton industry was not for me. When an opportunity arose for the position of junior laboratory assistant at the local oil seal and O-ring manufacturing company, I thought it sounded interesting. The job involved dealing with fancy names such as acrylonitrile butadiene, polychloroprene and fluoroelastomer, all of which seemed pretty exotic to someone as impressionable as myself so I jumped in. However, this job started to become less exciting when I received my first week's wage of two pounds, three shillings and four pence – that was less than five dollars per week! Wow, I was well on my way to being the next Kerry Packer! Or as Eddie Murphy in the film *Coming to America* said, Soon I'll be on the fries...and that's when the big bucks start rolling in.

A few years later, I quickly made friends with Ivan Hipperson, another junior laboratory assistant at the oil seal company. He was also interested in golf so we decided to jointly invest in a half set of second hand golf clubs which cost five pounds between us. When I say half set, this is me using some poetic licence. There were seven clubs in the bag but each was a different brand. Some had metal shafts and some even had hickory shafts. There were no woods in the bag, just six irons and a putter. However, it was good enough to get us going and we soon started thwacking balls around the local Nelson public golf course. We only had one bag of clubs so we could never play together. In addition, we never had any golf lessons; we just read a few golf instruction books and away we went. I broke ninety on my first ever game. Since I never knew how to do it properly, my technique sadly didn't improve over the years.

My course management skills, however, did improve with age. My score also improved when it eventually dawned on me that to propel a golf ball one doesn't need big strong muscles, only decent swing rhythm. This, for me, meant having a forward swing about three times faster than my backswing. Even at age seventy I can still regularly shoot less than my age off the stick on the short par sixty-four Wattle Park public course. And when I say 'off the stick' I mean that literally because I often just play *one* club only over the full round, the driver. I use it for all tee shots, for all fairway shots and – because of my dodgy eyes – I even putt with it.

There is nothing new about using the driver for both driving and putting. The very first British Open which was held in 1860 at Prestwick GC was won by Willie Park Sr from Musselburgh. Willie was reputed to be a long hitter and just like yours truly, he used the same club to drive and putt with. It was obviously very effective for him. He won four British Opens and also came runner-up four times. What goes around comes around I suppose?

Over the years, I have had five holes in one and two of these were made using the driver. I do generally carry a sixty-four-degree lob wedge in the bag to get out of greenside bunkers with. However, I found out that the best way to play bunkers is not to get in them in the first place. Consequently many of my rounds are completely bunker-free and the lob wedge is mostly redundant. I am happy to report that the original half set of clubs has long since gone and the driver, I mostly use nowadays, is a super modern technology club with a head the size of Western Australia.

When studying polymers in Manchester, I was also lucky to meet a Yorkshire man called Mike Shaw who was enrolled in the same study course. We often played golf together and I eventually became lifelong friends with Mike and his wife, Joyce. When Mike's studies ended, he became the Technical Manager at Dunlop's Golf ball division in the UK. Mike used to keep me supplied with freebie Dunlop 65 golf balls which had some lines marked on them in Biro pen ink from laboratory tests carried out. He also gave me good insights into the importance of the dimple pattern, the number of dimples and the depth of the dimple on golf ball performance. All these items were patented by the various golf ball manufacturers and were fiercely guarded secrets. He also told me that the biggest problem when manufacturing those old technology wound golf balls was to keep the small paste-filled ball absolutely in the dead centre of the overall ball during manufacture. This was not always achieved and consequently many of the old balls had a built-in bias. Dunlop 65s used by top golf professionals such as Tony Jacklin were pre-selected. The balls were rolled down a chute along a straight line marked on the flat slate bed of a snooker table. Any balls that curved slightly away from the line were not selected for the pros. Those were sold to average punters like me. Our studies at John Dalton College also taught us all about the materials used to manufacture golf balls.

In golf balls of that era, the main polymer used on the inside of the balls was natural rubber. This was the elastic thread which was wound around a small rubber ball in the centre which was filled with a barium sulphate paste. For the botanically minded natural rubber comes from the *Hevea Brasiliensis* tree. For the chemically minded, it is called cis-1, 4-polyisoprene which has a base molecular unit consisting of five carbon atoms and eight hydrogen atoms. Most of the golf ball covers in those days were made from gutta percha (balata) which chemically is trans-1, 4-polyisoprene, although towards the end of the era the tougher cut resistant ionomer resin covers had started to appear.

Balata has the same number of carbon and hydrogen atoms as natural rubber but arranged in a slightly different molecular configuration. Natural rubber is a crystallising polymer. That means it does not require reinforcing fillers in order to obtain high tensile strength and modulus. Hence in a golf ball of those days the elastic thread was just a vulcanised gum stock with high tensile strength, high elongation at break and high rebound resilience. Here endeth the testicle lesson! (Well, it was about balls!)

While all this oil seal making and polymer studying was going on in the UK during the late 1950s to mid-1960s, I did not know it at the time, but a Melbourne-based professional golfer called Jack Harris was coming towards the end of what had been a remarkable tournament playing career. Indeed, it was only after my family and I had lived in Melbourne for twenty-seven years that in 2008, I met Jack Harris, then aged eighty-seven, for the first time at Wattle Park golf club. I also often sat with him over coffee. Over a period of weeks and months I started to learn from Wattle Park's teaching professional Trevor Hollingsworth that Jack Harris had been a good tournament golfer and had also been an outstanding golf teacher. I still didn't know just how good he had been until one day my attention was drawn to a new photograph on the wall of the pro shop. This showed Jack Harris being inducted as a Legend into the Victorian Golf Hall of Fame at a ceremony held at the world famous Melbourne Cricket Ground (MCG) in 2011. The blurb under the photo mentioned that Australian PGA Life Member Jack Harris was one of six inaugural inductees into the Victorian Golf Hall of Fame. These included five times British Open winner Peter Thomson, former Australian Open winner Bob Shearer, renowned amateur lady golfer Ms Burtta Cheney and two other top amateurs, Doug Bachli and Ivo Whitton. It was only then that I realised Jack Harris must have been an exceptionally good golfer.

Over the next few years and over many cups of coffee with Jack, I gradually heard more and more about his tournament playing exploits and stories about many of the world's golfing greats he had played with and against. These included Peter Thomson, Kel Nagle, Norman von Nida, Eric Cremin, Frank Phillips, Sir Bob Charles, Gary Player, Sam Snead, Bobby Locke, Arnold Palmer, Bruce Crampton, Bruce Devlin, Billy Dunk, Ossie Pickworth, Art Wall Jr, Tommy Bolt and on more than one occasion, Jack Nicklaus, the world's best ever golfer. Even a NAGA golfer like myself knows that this short list of golfing legends has won somewhere around fifty-two of golf's major championships between them. I am sure that any regular golfer will be familiar with the acronym, *NAGA*. However, for the uninitiated I can spell it out:

Not A Golfer's A---hole.

Put simply, it means that I am a pretty ordinary golfer.

That said, I can hardly lay claim to being the world's worst ever golfer. That honour must surely go to the legendary 'professional golfer' Maurice Flitcroft who played in the 1976 British Open qualifying event at Formby. Royal Birkdale where the British Open proper was held that year is just a few miles down the road. Maurice was another Lancashire boy from Barrow-in-Furness with a great sense of humour. His record first round score of 121 (forty-nine over par) in the Formby qualifier will never be beaten. His biography *Phantom of the Open* published in 2010 and written by Scott Murray and Simon Farnaby is hilarious. Alternatively, just Google 'Maurice Flitcroft' and read about his amazing golfing career. The bit in the story about Maurice's gas oven is an absolute classic! The 1976 British Open was also the year that the late great Severiano burst on to the world golf scene. Seve only came second that year but already we knew that a new star had been born.

Apart from stories about all these great golfers who Jack Harris played both with and against, I also heard lots of stories about famous celebrities he had taught or maybe played with in exhibition matches. Unfortunately, however, I don't think that Jack Harris ever had the pleasure of playing with the irrepressible Maurice Flitcroft.

For some time, Trevor Hollingsworth and I had been telling Jack Harris that he really should write his biography because he has such a great story to tell. I half-jokingly said to Jack one day, 'Why don't I write your story for you?' To my surprise and great delight he replied, 'OK, go ahead.' That is how this book came about. The problem was I didn't know anything about writing books. But I thought, what the hell, I don't know anything about playing golf either but that doesn't stop me from pulling out my Big Bertha several times a week!

For many years, I harboured the thought in the back of my mind that I would like to try my hand at writing a book but I never settled on a subject until this opportunity presented itself.

It has been an honour and a privilege to write this book for Jack Harris. Every person I consulted or spoke with during the research work on this book confirmed the view I have personally held for a long time now: that Jack Harris is a gentleman in every sense of the word. Jack, I thank you for allowing me to delve into just about every aspect of your wonderful golfing career. I never saw you play when you were at your peak. Nevertheless, I felt like I was actually there at many of your big golf tournaments by virtue of the hundreds of newspaper tournament reports which I have read and re-read many times during my research.

This is not so much a book about golf; it is just a beautiful love story. The love of his beautiful wife Grace who shared Jack's passion for over fifty-five years and the love he has for his children, his grandchildren and his great grandchildren. And naturally the love he continues to have for the great game of golf for nigh on eighty years, and still counting!

Chapter 1

Pre-Second World War Days

Jack Harris was born in West Footscray, a suburb of Melbourne, Australia on 8 December, 1922. He was the third son of John and Marion Harris. They lived at 59 Wales Street in Footscray. John's ancestry went back to Somerset in South West England and Marion's went back to Scotland. John worked as a foreman in the sheet metal department of HV McKay Pty Ltd which, at the time, was the largest manufacturing operation in Australia. They made combined harvester machines and a very wide range of agricultural implements. Because the company was so big and employed almost three thousand people, its founder Hugh Victor McKay decided that he would build a whole new town just to house his employees. He named the model town Sunshine Estate after the brand name of his very successful combined harvester, Sunshine. The 'Estate' part was eventually dropped and it became known as just Sunshine, the name of the suburb which survives to this day. Mr McKay actually got the idea of building a model town for his employees from a similar project which had started in the UK in the 1880s at Port Sunlight on the Wirral near Liverpool. In that case Lever Bros (now Unilever), a very large soap manufacturing business employing over three thousand people at its peak, built the town and named it after their most popular brand of cleaning agent, Sunlight.

HV McKay used to export their combined harvesters all over the world. Before Jack was born, his dad John had actually spent two years working for the company in Argentina teaching the Argentinos how to use their machines. From what Jack's dad told him later, apparently many of the Footscray VFL team of that era also worked at HV McKay.

As anyone who lives in Melbourne knows, AFL football is an absolute religion. From these very early days Jack Harris became, and has always remained, a loyal Bulldog supporter. As a young boy, Jack used to sell football programmes outside the ground before games. This allowed him to get into the ground and watch the games for free. When he lived in Footscray, he attended Kingsfield Junior School and many of his classmates played for the Footscray Football Club when they got older.

During the early 1900s, The Sunshine Combined Harvester machine manufactured by HV McKay's at their Sunshine factory. A shipment of Sunshine Harvesters being loaded on to a sailing ship bound for Argentina

One of the vivid memories Jack has from the HV McKay days was going on company employee picnic days. As a young boy in the 1920s he would often go sailing on Port Phillip Bay with his mum and dad on a paddle steamer called the *Weeroona* which had been built in Glasgow, Scotland in 1910. The *Weeroona* made regular sailings between Port Melbourne and the resorts of Mornington and Sorrento. This vessel didn't end its days until the end of the Second World War when, from all accounts, it was finally scrapped in Sydney. It had been purchased earlier in 1942 by the US Navy who had intended to refit her as a convalescent and accommodation ship.

Over time, HV McKay Pty Ltd merged with other companies and eventually ended up as part of Massey Ferguson, the tractor people. Anyone interested to learn more about the fascinating HV McKay story should visit Museum Victoria in Nicholson Street, Carlton where thousands of documents, old photos and even equipment relics can be found. Even a complete set of HV McKay employment records can be found at the Australian Trade Union Archives held in the University of Melbourne.

The *Weeroona* paddle steamer which operated a daily service between Port Melbourne and the Mornington Peninsula in the 1920s

Life in Australia during the 1920s was pretty cushy and the general standard of living was high. At least it was until the Great Depression which began with the Wall Street stock market crash of October 1929. Australia was hit by the crash very badly; unemployment averaged twenty-three per cent from 1930 to 1934 and peaked at thirty per cent in 1932. This was higher than most other industrialised countries and only Germany was worse. Many people in Australia were living in the street and lots of men left the big cities and went into the countryside looking for any old job they could find in the agricultural sector. Hardly any married women worked in those days - it was generally accepted that the menfolk had to be the bread winners for the family and the women stayed home to look after the children.

The eighth prime minister of Australia from 1923 to 1929 had been Stanley Bruce who later became Viscount Bruce of Melbourne and in 1954 became the first Australian to be elected captain of the Royal and Ancient (R&A) Golf Club of St Andrews. Bruce was replaced by James Scullin as PM in 1929 but the Depression caused a split in the Labor government of the day. As a result, Prime Minister Scullin lost his seat in 1932. No other sitting Prime Minister lost his seat after that until John Howard was ousted from Bennelong by former journalist Maxine McKew in 2007. Joseph Lyons of the United Australia Party replaced James Scullin as prime minister in 1932 and the economy started to improve.

It was around this time that John Harris left the employment of HV McKay. He had actually moved home sometime before then with his family to a poultry farm called *Early Morn* in the small suburb of Heatherton very close to Kingswood GC. John had been running the poultry farm as well as commuting each day to Sunshine from Clayton train station to work at HV McKay's. Heatherton in those days was a very small countrified suburb. Even today it has a very low population for a metropolitan suburb. In the 2011 census there were only 2768 residents in Heatherton.

I don't suppose that it ever entered John's or son Jack's heads at the time, but Heatherton just happens to be located in the very epicentre of the famous Melbourne sand belt golf courses. From where Jack's family lived in Heatherton it is possible to drive in about fifteen minutes or less to many of Australia's best golf courses including Commonwealth, Huntingdale, Keysborough, Kingston Heath, Kingswood, Long Island, Metropolitan, Peninsula, Riversdale, Rossdale, Royal Melbourne, Southern, Spring Valley, Victoria, Woodlands, Yarra Yarra and many more. Some of these are also listed in the *Golf Digest* website top 100 World golf courses. In such an environment, it is hardly surprising that young Jack Harris gravitated towards a golf career at an early age.

Jack was about eight years old when the family moved to Heatherton and was attending the local primary school. The parents of one of his school friends, Paddy Smith, had a pig farm nearby. Paddy's elder brother, Martin Smith, was at that time an assistant golf professional at Kingston Heath GC where Ernie Wood was the club professional. Through Paddy, Jack learned that it was possible to earn some pocket money by caddying at Kingston Heath GC so it wasn't long before he went there to check it out. The problem was Jack Harris was quite small at that age and just a slip of a lad. He was told that he wasn't yet big enough to carry a heavy golf-bag around the golf course. So for the next year or so, all they allowed him to do was to go and pick up the golf balls which Ernie Wood's pupils had hit during their lessons. By the time he had left Heatherton primary school and started high school in Dandenong, he had filled out a bit and his caddying career had begun. Ernie Wood had started as golf professional at Kingston Heath in 1925 and he stayed there for thirty-five years until he finally retired in 1960.

Jack often caddied for Dr Elliot True and it was this gentleman who presented Jack with his first ever golf clubs: six hickory-shafted second hand clubs in a bag. Jack's reward for caddying was a two shilling ticket. The caddie master at Kingston Heath took three pence and that left Jack with one shilling and nine pence for the afternoon's work. In those days there were Caddie Championships and young Jack Harris played in several of these while he was still at Dandenong High School.

On one particular occasion he was invited to play in the under fifteen Caddie Championships at Riversdale GC. The problem was that the event was held on a school day afternoon. Consequently, Jack got his mother to write a letter to give to the headmaster inventing some excuse as to why he couldn't attend school that day. Imagine Jack's surprise and embarrassment when he played in the event only to discover that his headmaster was a member at the Riversdale GC and was present at the course during the Championship! For the record, Jack won the Caddie Championship and from that time onwards he knew that all he wanted to do in future was to play golf.

Jack was still only about fifteen years old when his formal education finished and he left high school for good. He started work in 1937 as assistant to golf professional Colin Campbell at Patterson River GC. He recalls that his first ever weekly wage was the princely sum of fifteen shillings and sixpence (less than two dollars per week) and each week he handed this over to his mum. Certainly his travelling expenses and lunch money each week cost more than this so he surely got all of it back and more besides!

Jack Harris's first ever win. The Under 15s Caddie Championships at Riversdale GC in 1935

Colin Campbell was Jack's first official golf teacher. However, the truth was that Jack had already more or less taught himself how to play golf even before he went to Patterson River. He had done this when he was a caddie at Kingston Heath by just carefully watching and listening to what Ernie Wood was telling his pupils before mimicking how Ernie himself hit the ball. All Colin had to do then was to fine-tune what was already a very fine golf swing. As we will see later, it wasn't long before the pupil very quickly surpassed his teacher in golfing achievements.

Before the end of the decade, Jack Harris had moved twice. He did a bit of golf teaching with Colin Campbell at Long Island GC before that golf course was taken over by the Army to provide accommodation for soldiers during the Second World War. He also spent a short time at Yarra Yarra GC in 1939 as assistant to club professional Arthur Spence.

It was while he was at Yarra Yarra GC in 1939 that Jack had the unique experience of meeting the legendary US lady golfer, Babe Didrikson Zaharias. She was in Australia at the time with her husband George Zaharias, a famous American wrestler, to do a series of exhibition matches.

On 3 July, 1939 Babe Didrikson played at Yarra Yarra GC against Arthur Spence, the Yarra Yarra club pro, and Charlie Connors, the Victorian PGA champion, in an exhibition match. They played off the men's tees and Babe shot a two under par 72 against the then par of 74. She was said to have easily outdriven both men on many of the holes! Jack remembers vividly shaking hands with George Zaharias. He told me that George was not really very tall, even compared to Jack who was only five feet seven inches in old money. However, his grip was so strong that he almost broke Jack's fingers!

Babe Didrikson had earlier competed as an athlete in the 1932 Olympic Games in Los Angeles where she won two gold medals (javelin and eighty metres hurdles) and one silver medal (high jump). In both the javelin and hurdles events, she created new Olympic and World records. She also tied for the gold medal place in the high jump but was relegated to silver because she apparently went over the bar head first which was not done in those days.

She began playing golf in 1935, turned pro after the Second World War in 1947 and died prematurely age forty-five in 1956. During the intervening nine years she won an incredible forty-one times on the US LPGA Tour. Didrikson had also been born to Norwegian immigrant parents and no doubt had some Viking ancestry, just like me.

In August 1939, Jack Harris had his first taste of big time golf. As a sixteen year old, he caddied for Arthur Spence in the Australian Open at Royal Melbourne GC. In the same tournament, Jim Ferrier retained the title while playing as an amateur, which he had also won the previous year at Royal Adelaide GC. Martin Smith, the brother of Jack's school friend Paddy Smith, tied for runner-up alongside Norman von Nida and Arthur Spence finished fortieth. Arthur had won the Queensland PGA title in 1926 and he was the golf professional at Yarra Yarra from 1929 to 1966.

Before the 1939 Australian Open actually took place, there had been some controversy when the above-mentioned Babe Didrikson applied for entry into the competition to play alongside the men. She was not very happy when her application was turned down. Martin Smith by this time had become the club professional at the Northern GC and remained there until 1950.

When Jack Harris had been at Long Island GC he had applied for junior membership to the PGA. News of his acceptance into the PGA as a junior member was eventually received in a letter dated June 1940, six months before his eighteenth birthday.

In less than one week after the 1939 Australian Open had finished (August 24-26), the Second World War began on 1 September, 1939.

The career of Jack Harris and many other aspiring young pre-war golfers was put on hold for the next five or six years. During this time Jack served in the Australian Army in Darwin and Borneo.

Sadly many of the young men who went away to war did not return. And even many of those who did return came back too badly injured or too badly mentally scarred to be able to resume their careers.

In that respect Jack was one of the lucky ones. He was able to resume his career after the war despite missing a critical period in his development. And as we will see in later chapters he was still able to reach a level where he could perform just about as well as any golfer in the world on his day.

Professional Golfers' Association
VICTORIAN SECTION

CHAIRMAN:
A. LE FEVRE
ROYAL MELBOURNE GOLF CLUB
BLACK ROCK, S.9
PHONE: XW 2600

HON. SECRETARY:
D. C. WHILLANS
CHELTENHAM GOLF CLUB
CHELTENHAM, S.22
PHONE: CHELTENHAM 567

26th June 1940.

Mr. J.B. Harris,
Long Island Golf Club,
FRANKSTON.

Dear Jack,

I have much pleasure in informing you that, at the last meeting of the executive of the above association, your application for Junior Membership was agreed to.

You will, in due course, receive from Mr. G. Naismith, the Hon. Treasurer, an account for subscription due.

In welcoming you as a member of the P.G.A. we trust you will have a long and pleasant connection with the association.

Yours faithfully,

D C Whillans
Hon. Secretary.

Letter accepting Jack Harris into the PGA as a junior member in 1940.

Chapter 2

The Second World War Days

After the 1939 Australian Open, big golf tournaments in Australia did not resume until 1946. However, quite a few exhibition matches were played during this period by golfers who did not go to war because they were too old or had some prior health condition which kept them out of the action. These matches were arranged to raise funds for the War Effort or the Red Cross and other similar organisations.

In England however, not even Adolf Hitler could stop the mad keen golfing fanatics from playing their regular club golf. Some golf clubs even drew up some special temporary war time rules to cover any unexpected situation.

For example in 1940, according to an article in *The Times* newspaper of the day, during the Battle of Britain, the Richmond Golf Club in Surrey had a war time golf rules list as follows:

1. Players are asked to collect Bomb and shrapnel splinters to save these causing damage to the mowing machines.

2. In competitions, during gunfire, or while bombs are falling, players may take cover without penalty for ceasing play.

3. The positions of known delayed-action bombs are marked by red flags placed at reasonably, but not guaranteed safe distance therefrom.

4. Shrapnel / and /or bomb splinters on the Fairways, or in bunkers within a club's length of a ball may be moved without penalty, and no penalty shall be incurred if a ball is thereby caused to move accidentally.

5. A ball moved by enemy action may be replaced, or if lost or destroyed, a ball may be dropped not nearer the hole without penalty.

6. A ball lying in a crater may be lifted and dropped not nearer the hole without penalty.

7. A player whose stroke is affected by the simultaneous explosion of a bomb may play another ball from the same place. Penalty, one stroke.

Further research on this set of temporary rules also suggested that the rules had been written by B L Edsell, the club secretary of St Mellons Golf and Country Club in Monmouthshire. So there is obviously some doubt about where they actually originated from. Wherever they came from we can be sure that they were written by someone with a typical British sense of humour! The old British TV comedy programme *Dad's Army* immediately springs to mind. I bet that Captain George Mainwaring was a good golfer!

I'm not sure if similar temporary rules were also applied in Australia – it would not surprise me if they were. After all, golf fanatics are golf fanatics the world over! A bunch of nutters, if you ask me!

However, not all golf clubs were able to keep on playing through the war. Some, like Long Island GC and Peninsula GC, were taken over by the Defence Forces as temporary accommodation for a rapidly expanding military force and also for the big influx of US military personnel who were based in Australia. Even the famous Melbourne Cricket Ground was lost to the cause – there was no cricket or football played on it for the next three years.

In Sydney, at the Australian GC, Kensington, the Army put an anti-aircraft battery on the short course and in 1942 the US forces took over the club house.

Elsewhere, the famous Augusta National GC in Georgia, where they play the US Masters tournament, became a farm to help alleviate war time food shortages in the USA.

Many golf clubs struggled for financial reasons because most of the menfolk members were off at war and their membership subscriptions were suspended. Golf equipment and especially golf balls were in short supply.

From the start of the war on 1 September, 1939 until 2 September, 1945 when the war officially ended, more lives were lost than in any other conflict in the history of mankind.

Although 1939 was the acknowledged start date in Europe, hostilities in the Asia Pacific region had started even earlier. Japan, who had grand designs of building their own Empire, was at war with China from 1937. That year an estimated three hundred thousand Chinese civilians were murdered by Japanese soldiers in the Nanking Massacre.

Of course everyone knows about the Holocaust in Germany and German occupied territories where approximately six million Jews were murdered in the notorious concentration camps.

But at the end of the war even this large number was only a small fraction of the total people who lost their lives. No one knows the exact number of lives lost but there are various estimates which range from sixty to eighty-five million of which thirty-eight to fifty-five million (more than sixty per cent) were said to be civilians.

History tells us much about what the UK and USA were doing during the war through famous names such as Sir Winston Churchill, Dwight D Eisenhower and Franklin D Roosevelt. But in reality these two countries lost relatively few lives compared to many others. Total American and British lives lost were estimated to be just under one million. This is a mind-blowingly high number but maybe not when one considers that the Soviet Union lost 21-28 million, China lost 10-20 million, Germany lost 7-9 million, Poland lost 5-6 million, Indonesia (Dutch East Indies) lost 3-4 million, Japan lost 2-3 million and India lost over one million. Poland was probably the most to suffer because they lost almost seventeen per cent of their entire population. By comparison, Australia only lost approximately forty thousand five hundred lives during this major conflict. John Curtin was the prime minister who guided Australia through most of this difficult period and from all accounts did a very good job.

During the war, Jack Harris was a sapper (a soldier of the engineer corps) in the Australian Army. For much of the early part of the war he was based in the north part of Australia near Darwin. His job was to help defend Australia from the threat of invasion by the Japanese who had steadily been overcoming their neighbours in SE Asia. Darwin was subjected to sixty-four air raids by the Japanese over the period starting on 19 February, 1942 and ending 12 November, 1943 and there was significant loss of life. By 1943, the year I was born, there were 110,000 Australian Defence personnel based in or around Darwin.

Guard duty for sapper Jack Harris (second left) in 1943

As if the war was not bad enough, the 1944 bush fires in Victoria destroyed millions of acres of grassland and half of the state's stud sheep perished. There were drought conditions right across Australia. Wheat production fell to one third of the pre-war levels. Thousands of cattle died because there was no feed or water for them. Despite all this, Australia still managed to feed its population and also help feed the Allied troops in the Asia Pacific struggle.

The Japanese invaded Borneo in early 1942. But in mid-1945, General Douglas MacArthur, Commander-in-Chief of Allied forces in the South West Pacific area, decided that Australian Forces should be involved in the liberation of Borneo. (John Curtin had earlier made the crucial decision to give full control of the Australian Forces to MacArthur.)

Jack Harris was part of 9th Division which was sent to Labuan Island in Brunei Bay, North West Borneo. The strategic plan was to secure Brunei Bay so that it could be used as an advanced naval base. They also had to capture the oilfields and the natural rubber plantations which were both important commodities which had to be taken out of Japanese hands.[1] Many Australians were killed in this operation. I have deliberately not questioned Jack very much about his time in Labuan Island. I know that many atrocities were committed by the Japanese in Borneo and other places in Southeast Asia so the last thing I wanted to do was to stir up any bad memories.

Jack and his favourite Borneo girlfriend "Mrs OFTEN" in 1945

As for yours truly, I was just a little boy enjoying my second birthday on 6 August, 1945. My blacksmith grandad was making a wooden cart for a local farmer in the village of Trawden, Lancashire and I was helping him with my toy hammer to add the finishing touches before it was delivered. I was blissfully oblivious to the fact that, 12,000 miles away in a Japanese city called Hiroshima, another *Little Boy* was about to change the whole course of the Second World War. On that day, the Americans dropped the first

---

1   Natural rubber was needed for golf ball manufacture so Jack was doing his best to rectify the golf ball shortage back in Australia!

atomic bomb with devastating effect. Three days later on 9 August, 1945 they dropped another atomic bomb, *Fat Man,* on the city of Nagasaki. By 15 August, 1945 it was all over. The Japanese had surrendered and signed the official Instrument of Surrender on 2 September, 1945.

Meanwhile, back in Heatherton, at the Early Morn poultry farm, Jack Harris's mum, Marion, was also doing her bit to help the war effort. She was the honorary Secretary of the Sixth Australian Cavalry Regiment Auxiliary. Ninth Division de-mobilised from October 1945 until the last unit of the Division disbanded in May 1946. It was sometime during this period that Jack Harris was finally de-mobilised from the army and was able to resume his golfing career. While Jack was back in Melbourne waiting to be discharged, he was based at Watsonia Barracks and he recalls that during this short period he was ordered to conduct town patrols in Melbourne's CBD area. Just for the record, 9th Division was the most highly decorated of the four AIF Divisions during the war. Seven of its members received the Victoria Cross. Ninth Division lost 2732 men killed in action across all the various campaigns they took part in.

> **MEMORIAL TO PADRE**
> A movemnet is in progress to commemorate the work of the late Padre Leslie Cula, who died while on service in New Guinea. The organisers wish to contact all former members of the 8th Australian Cavalry Regiment, AIF, and Mrs J. Harris, Early Morn, Grange rd, Heatherton, S22, honorary secretary, will appreciate assistance of parents and relatives, who are requested to forward the present addresses of former members of the regiment.

The Argus Monday 7 May 1945

Jack Harris was obviously unable to play any golf while he was helping to drive the Japanese out of Borneo. However, two interesting events happened during his time in Borneo which later had an influence on his future golfing career.

He had not been in Labuan Island very long when one day his company commander asked him what he did in civilian life back in Australia. When Jack told him that he was a professional golfer, the commander replied 'That's interesting! Ossie Pickworth is over there in the next camp.' 'Who the hell is Ossie Pickworth?' asked Jack. At that stage Jack had not heard of Ossie Pickworth, an up and coming young New South Wales (NSW) golf professional at Manly GC just before the war started. Manly GC was founded in 1903 and is one of Australia's oldest clubs. Ossie at that time was assistant to Alf Chitty the Manly GC professional. Even before the war started he had tasted serious success when he beat Eric Cremin in the Assistants' Professional Championship at Villard.

Although Jack didn't know it then, he and Ossie were to become good friends and to have many future battles of their own on golf courses all over Australia in the fifteen year period following the war. However, they never actually met each other when they were on Labuan Island.

The other significant occurrence was that Jack's commanding officer in Labuan Island was a Colonel Gyngell. After the war, this gentleman played a big part in shaping Jack's future golfing career as will be explained in the next chapter.

Apart from Jack Harris and Ossie Pickworth, many other Australian pre-war golfers also lost several years from their careers. For example, Norman von Nida was in the Australian Army. Kel Nagle was a gun sergeant in Darwin and New Guinea. Bert Clay had been a POW during the war and couldn't even hold a golf stick when he returned. Ron Harris was a prisoner of war for over three years in the notorious Japanese-controlled Changi prison (Selarang Barracks) in Singapore. About eight hundred prisoners of war died in Changi during the Japanese Occupation of Singapore.

But perhaps the star of them all was Dan Cullen[2], a West Australian golfer who had moved to a club professional role in NSW. Dan was a

---

2   Dan Cullen passed away on 27th January 2016 aged 101. It just happened to be on my brother's birthday. In July 2015 he was awarded the Légion d'honneur medal for wartime services. This is the highest military decoration bestowed by the French and would be their equivalent to the Victoria Cross. The Légion d'honneur was established in 1802 by Napoleon Bonaparte.

bomber pilot during the war flying Lancaster bombers over Germany. The Lancaster was a four-engine heavy bomber, most of which were built by Avro at Chadderton near Oldham in Greater Manchester just down the road from where I later studied polymer chemistry and polymer physics in the early 1960s.

From stories which I have read, I understand that Dan flew an incredible thirty-three bombing missions over Germany during the war and survived them all. The Lancaster bomber was the plane which was used by 617 Squadron in Operation Chastise, aimed at destroying the dams of the Ruhr Valley as featured in the famous epic *Dam Busters* film. A problem with the Lancaster bomber was that in the case of being hit by enemy fire the escape hatch was relatively small compared to other war planes and was difficult to get through while wearing a parachute. On problem flights, it had been shown that only fifteen per cent of a Lancaster's crew was able to bail out in time successfully in case of emergency. Luckily Dan never had to bail out – otherwise he would have been in a lot of strife because he was a very big man. Jack Harris told me that Dan was once asked by a newspaper reporter how he managed to handle the pressure of playing in big time golf tournaments. Dan's reply was something like this: there is no pressure playing golf. Real pressure is when you are flying a Lancaster bomber over Germany and the enemy is trying to shoot you out of the sky. Some of the guys who can be seen frequently chucking their golf clubs into the bushes when they miss a putt or stomping around cursing should maybe reflect on this?

The amazing story of this particular war hero doesn't end there. In 1977, Dan Cullen DFC, at the ripe old age of sixty-four qualified for the British Open at Turnberry. That year he was celebrating his fiftieth year as a professional golfer. He had to battle through qualifying rounds against several hundred international players but nevertheless, he won the battle and lived his dream. He didn't make the cut for the final two rounds but he didn't finish last either. He shot 161 for the first two rounds and managed to beat two old super-stars in Bobby Locke and Henry Cotton. He was only a few shots behind Jack Newton and Sandy Lyle who both shot 155 and also missed the cut that year.

Charlie Snow, Mt Lawley pro in WA, was in the AIF (Second Australian Imperial Force). He was a POW after being taken prisoner at Alamein. By chance he returned to Perth at the end of July, 1945 on the same ship as fellow West Australian golfer, Dan Cullen. Dan had been awarded the DFC for his part in the attack on Frederickshafen in April, 1944.

Sadly some of the Australian pre-war golf professionals did not return from the war. One of these was Don Walker from Heidelberg GC who was killed in action with the RAAF. Jack Harris was very proud to have won the annual Don Walker Memorial purse in 1952.

Needless to say many of the American golfers who Jack Harris played against after the war also saw plenty of action during the Second World War. Lloyd Mangrum was maybe the superstar in this regard. He was on the front lines with General Patton's Third Army and won two Purple Hearts and four battle stars. Tommy Bolt, Ed Oliver and Jack Fleck were also in the thick of it. Although Jack Harris never played against him, it is also worth noting that forty-two years old Bobby Jones also landed at Normandy with a gun in his hand.

While frustrated golfers such as Jack Harris, Norman von Nida, Kel Nagle, Dan Cullen and many others were up to their necks in muck and bullets in Germany, Labuan Island, New Guinea and Darwin during the war, at least one budding young golfer didn't have those problems. Peter William Thomson was busy back in Melbourne sharpening up his game and getting ready to take on the golfing world after the war had finished. Peter had been born on 23 August, 1929 and was only about ten years old when the war started. His years of extra practice over and above what many of the others had been able to muster proved to be most invaluable as will be revealed in the later chapters.

According to *The Age*, 9 July 1946, Jack Harris was officially de-mobilised from the Army that week after serving for five and a half years. Less than three months later he was already competing in the Australian Open championship at Royal Sydney GC. He finished tied 35th out of 120 qualifiers.

Chapter 3

Post War Years

The Best Thing That Ever Happened in Jack's Life

It was a typical steamy hot summer day in Melbourne and Jack Harris was just embarking on the task of trying to resurrect his golfing career after the long Second World War interlude.

It was not long since his discharge from the Army and he was strolling down the main street of the Port Phillip bayside suburb of Mordiallac. He was with another budding young professional golfer called Norm Taylor, who was down in the big smoke from the country town of Mildura, when they decided that they needed an ice cream to cool down. No sooner had they placed their order in the ice cream parlour than in walked two nice looking girls. Quick as a flash, young Jack piped up to the girl behind the counter, 'better make that four!'

One of the girls, a bit of a looker, was a young lass called Grace McGregor. As the surname suggested, her parents had been immigrants from Scotland. Interestingly enough, Jack's mother Marion, also had a similar Scottish heritage. Her maiden name was McColl.

Jack had been away at war for several years and there were not too many good looking girls to be found in the jungles of Borneo. Consequently, he could have been excused if his technique for chatting up girls had been a bit rusty. However, this proved not to be the case and he was back on the horse very quickly. When Grace asked him what his name was and what he did for a living, the old survival plan kicked in immediately. 'My name is Jack Murphy,' replied Jack. 'I'm a bottle washer down at the local dairy.'

Apart from being a smooth talker, Jack Harris was also a very handsome, well-dressed young man. He could have told Grace anything. He could have told her that he was an airline pilot or even a brain surgeon, but typical of the man, he didn't want to big note himself. This was a trait Jack Harris has never lost. Nearly seventy years have passed since that lucky day in Mordialloc and he still steadfastly refuses to talk himself up despite all the fantastic achievements in his golfing career.

It turned out that Grace, who had been born in nearby Oakleigh on 26 January, 1926, was a waitress at the Metropolitan GC and later at the Kingwood GC where her mother was the manageress. She even had an interest in playing golf herself and had also taken some golf lessons from Horrie Boorer, the Metropolitan GC professional. Horrie had tied eighth place in the 1933 Australian Open, the year Lou Kelly won it. In later years Jack Harris played a lot of exhibition matches with Horrie's two brothers, Jack and Lenny, who were also golf professionals.

Jack still chuckles to himself when he recalls that Grace used to tell him that he too should take up playing golf and she even gave him some basic golf lessons on how to grip the club and address the golf ball. But still Jack did not reveal to Grace what his true profession was or what his real name was.

Grace Harris (second left) plays with friends at Riversdale GC.

Jack and Grace continued to see each other a few times after that chance meeting but for quite a while he remained incognito and was known to Grace only as *Jack Murphy*.

A few months later however, Jack's cover as Jack Murphy was well and truly blown out of the water. Grace had seen an advertisement on the club house wall at Metropolitan GC for an exhibition match to be played at Yarra Yarra GC to raise funds for the Good Friday Melbourne Royal Children's Hospital Appeal. Because of her interest in golf, she decided to go along as a spectator and to support the worthwhile cause.

By coincidence, Jack Harris was playing in that exhibition match along with Arthur Spence, the Yarra Yarra GC professional, Ossie Pickworth, the reigning Australian Open Champion and Eric Cremin, the reigning Victorian PGA Champion. They had just putted out on the eighteenth and were doing the customary handshakes as they walked off the green headed for the nineteenth hole. Suddenly this beautiful young girl emerged out of the crowd and came walking towards them. It was Grace McGregor. She had recognised Jack Murphy! Will the real Jack Harris please make himself known? The game was up and the rest is just history!

That day £137 was raised for the Royal Children's Hospital Fund from collection at the gate, birdie holes and auction of the balls used in the match. Ossie and Arthur defeated Eric and Jack by three and two in the match play format. Jack Harris and his golfing partner may have lost the match that day but Jack ended up winning something much more precious: a perfect match for life!

Over the next two or three years their relationship continued to blossom but without the hitherto deception. Jack and Grace were married at a church in Burke Road, East Malvern in 1950. They had their wedding reception at Kingswood golf club, spent their honeymoon in Melbourne and set up their first home at a modest little place in Bayswater. Their first daughter Marilyn was born in 1952 and her sister Christine came along in 1955.

For the next fifty years or more, Jack and Grace were inseparable until she sadly passed away in 2002. Grace was always very supportive of Jack's golfing career especially in the dark days when he would lose a tournament which he was positioned to win. In turn, Jack was always very proud of the fact that although he never made a fortune out of playing or teaching golf, he nevertheless was able to always be the sole bread winner. He provided a good life for the family and Grace never had to work again after they married.

Jack and Grace on their wedding day in 1950.

Jack and Grace never travelled outside of Australia together. In fact, the only time Jack went overseas apart from his war time days in Borneo was in 1960 when Keysborough Golf Club paid for his trip to England to play a few tournaments and also try to qualify for the British Open. Jack recalls that he found this trip very hard because it stretched over several months and he missed Grace and the girls so much. There were no emails, no Skype and no webcams in those days and even ordinary telephone calls were sometimes difficult and very expensive.

It is with a bit of a tear in his eye that Jack often tells me that Grace and the girls was the best thing which ever happened to him. Just thinking about it also sends me searching for the box of Kleenex tissues.

Theirs was a beautiful love story lasting fifty-five years. Sadly, Grace was not around to see Jack receive his well-deserved recognition in 2011 when he was one of the inaugural inductees into the Victorian Golf Hall of Fame during a ceremony at the MCG along with five other golfing legends including Peter Thomson AO, CBE and Bob Shearer. She would have been so proud of him.

Chapter 4

City Golf Schools

In the years immediately after the Second World War, Jack Harris managed to hook up again with his original teacher, Colin Campbell. However, it wasn't in a golf course situation.

At that time Colin had a teaching school and driving range located at the very top of an office block tower in Melbourne's CBD, the Manchester Unity Building. Even when Jack was not based at a golf course, he was still able to be competitive in major tournaments like the Ampol and pick up useful prize money. The Grand Opening night for the Manchester Unity Golf School was the first week in November, 1947. Miss McCarthy, a Collins Street business girl, was the first ever pupil there.

Jack and Colin taught there for a while until one day they realised that golf balls were sometimes being hit straight through the driving nets and dropping down into the street twelve storeys below. Obviously that was a dangerous situation and someone could end up being badly injured with a golf ball so the school was quickly shut down.

Bob Spencer, Colin Campbell's nephew, was also working as a teaching assistant with Colin and Jack in the Manchester Unity School and also later in the Hartley's sports store. Bob was later to become Jack's assistant pro at Keysborough GC and subsequently took over the head pro job when Jack left. Bob eventually retired from Keysborough in the mid-1990s after over thirty years' service.

In 1946 there were at least five so-called golf schools in the city of Melbourne. These included Hartley's sports store in Flinders Street; the Melbourne Sports Depot (MSD), an eight storey building at the corner of Bourke and Elizabeth Streets; the Leviathan Sports Department on the corner of Swanston and Bourke Streets, and the Myer Emporium. Some of these had been selling golf equipment and offering golf lessons from the 1920s.

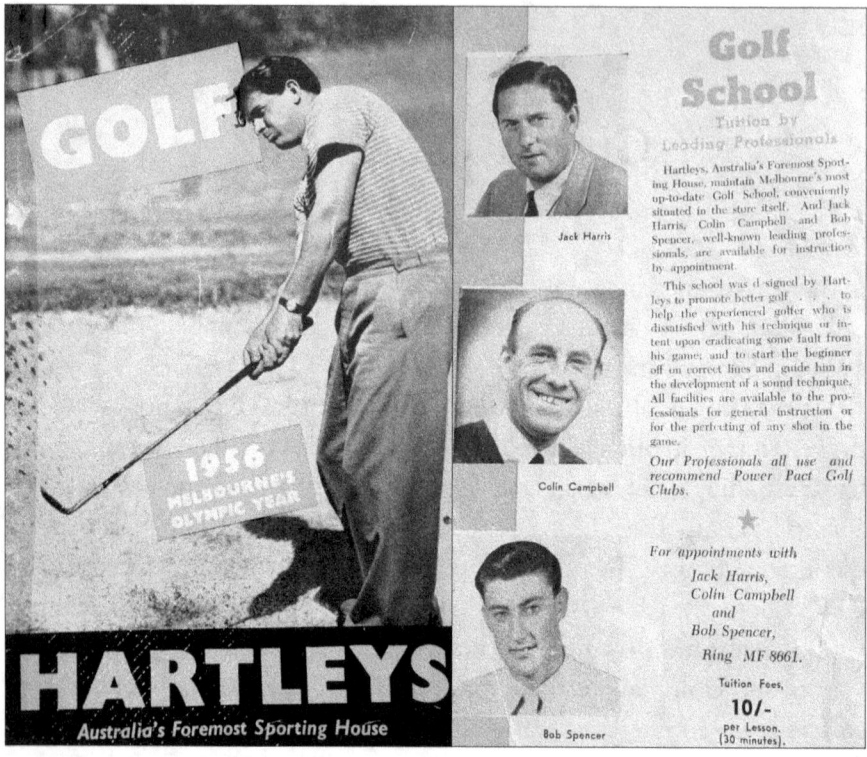

Jack Harris, Colin Campbell and Bob Spencer work in the Hartley's Sports Store in Flinders Street in the city of Melbourne in 1950

Many of the big names in golf during this era actually started off their careers working at one of these stores. George Naismith, the 1937 Australian Open champion used to be a teacher at the MSD before he went to Riversdale GC.

In 1950, Jack's old mate from the Heatherton pig farm, Martin Smith, also had a city school in the Metropole arcade. Martin had been joint runner-up in the 1939 Australian Open alongside Norman von Nida. In June 1950, thieves cut a hole in the glass door of his school and stole twenty golf clubs, a golf-bag and three umbrellas.

In 1927 the Leviathan Store alone had up to five professionals attending on different days to give teaching lessons. Amongst these were Ernie Wood who later became the club pro at Kingston Heath GC and Arthur Le Fevre the 1921 Australian Open champion who was also the pro at Royal Melbourne GC. Leviathan was offering golf sets for sale in 1933 for fifty-nine shillings and sixpence. These sets included a Spalding wood, a mid-iron, a mashie and a putter, a golf bag, a box of tees and one golf ball! Arthur's brother, Ernest Le Fevre was also a teacher in the 1920s and 1930s at the Myer Emporium Golf School. Ray Wright started at Hartley's sports store in 1950 as a twenty-one year-old teaching pro. Ted Naismith had a golf school in Lonsdale Street.

In 1950, the cost of a golf lesson at Hartley's sports store was ten shillings for a thirty-minute lesson but a new Slazenger All Weather golf grip cost nineteen shillings fitted. Jack, Colin and Bob were teaching flat out sometimes for ten hours per day. They were especially busy on weekends because most people had to work during the week. It was possible to buy a golf bag and half a set of clubs at Hartley's in 1950 for nineteen Guineas (fewer than twenty pounds or less than forty dollars). It appears that the cost of golf lessons in those days was very cheap relative to the cost of both golf grips and golf sets – or maybe it was the golf equipment which was expensive? A new All Weather golf grip cost almost twice as much as a thirty-minute lesson in 1950. In 2014, however, the cost of a new golf grip is about twelve dollars fitted compared with a lesson at fifty dollars per thirty minute session. Maybe rubber was still in fairly short supply in 1950 and there was a supply and demand factor at play?

Not being based at an actual golf course was not really an ideal situation for Jack Harris to find himself in. At a crucial time in his career development, from the age of eighteen to twenty-four, he had had to put everything on hold and do his bit for King and Country. Then from about 1946 to 1950, until he was about twenty-eight years old, he was either at Manchester Unity Building or at Hartley's sports store teaching by hitting into driving nets off rubber mats. He had no proper putting greens to practice on except maybe some felt carpet and no sand bunkers to practice in. In fact, apart from when he played in tournaments during this period, the only bunkers he had probably seen for about ten years were the air raid bunkers he had to dive into for protection when the Japanese were bombing Darwin!

If he was not too tired after a long week of teaching, he could spend some time at an actual golf course on Sundays and get in some decent practice. How anyone could possibly prepare themselves to reach the tournament playing level he ultimately reached, when the first ten years or so were either lost or effectively wasted, is beyond me.

How Jack could, from 1947 onwards, go on to win six Victorian PGAs, finish runner-up in the Victorian PGA eight times and win a Victorian Open is simply mind blowing. Apart from this, he made the cut in fifteen of his sixteen Australian Open appearances. He also won an Adelaide Advertiser tournament and performed consistently well in all the big money events of the day. These included the Ampol, Coles, Speedo, Wills Classic, Mobilco and McWilliams Wines. Several of these wins were while he was still working at Manchester Unity or at Hartley's sports store.

Golf clubs seemed pretty cheap in 1950 but maybe not when the average weekly wage in those days was less than ten pounds

It was 1950 when things really started to happen for Jack Harris. Up until that point, Keysborough GC had been just one of several clubs which operated at the Albert Park public golf course in the city. However, all these clubs were kicked out of Albert Park just prior to 1950. Luckily, Keysborough GC eventually found the site where they are today and built a new course. The club captain of the Keysborough GC at that time was a gentleman called Max Gyngell, the same Max Gyngell who had been Jack Harris's commander in the Army in Labuan Island in Borneo!

Jack was still working at Hartley's Sports Store when, over a cup of coffee, Max offered the job of professional and assistant professional at the new Keysborough GC to the dynamic duo, Colin Campbell and Jack Harris. As soon as the new club house and pro shop were completed they moved there. Colin, however, didn't stay very long. He decided to take up an offer to work as a golf teacher on cruise ships sailing between Australia and the USA.

That left Jack in full charge as golf pro at Keysborough GC. And he stayed there for the next seventeen years which effectively covered his entire tournament playing career. Colin Campbell's nephew, Bob Spencer, was appointed as Jack's assistant. After Bob had learned the ropes with Jack, he left Keysborough GC in 1956 and took up the position of golf professional at Elsternwick GC. However, when Jack left Keysborough GC, Bob returned to replace Jack in 1966 and stayed there until his retirement in 1996.

GOLF SCHOOL

Tuition by Leading Professionals

Hartleys, Australia's Foremost Sporting House, maintain Melbourne's most up-to-date Golf School, conveniently situated in the store itself. Jack Harris, Colin Campbell and Bob Spencer, well-known leading professionals, are available for instruction by appointment.

This school was designed by Hartleys to promote better golf—to help the experienced golfer who is dissatisfied with his technique or intent upon eradicating some fault from his game, and to start the beginner off on correct lines and guide him in the development of a sound technique. All facilities are available to the professionals for general instruction or for the perfecting of any shot in the game.

For appointments with Jack Harris, Colin Campbell and Bob Spencer, ring MF 8661.

Tuition Fees, 10/- per Lesson (30 minutes).

Wow! Golf grips were very expensive in 1950 compared to the cost of a golf lesson.

Jack Harris

Cremin 4 Up After First 18 Holes
By J. M. DILLON

FINAL DAY

Eric Cremin (NSW), 35-year-old National Open Champion and tournament specialist, after 18 holes in the final of the Victorian Professional Championship at Yarra Yarra today, was four up on Jack Harris, 25, Victoria's most promising post-war professional.

PRO GOLF FINALISTS

Cremin left Harris off at the first by missing a four-footer, cross bunker at the second, he four-footer to lose the hole.

After a magnificently clean shot from a number seven iron from casual water in a fairway cross bunker in the second, he chipped in weakly with a number eight iron and missed a four-footer.

Each got a four at the 325-yard third, where Harris had a nine-footer for a win, but missed.

After 3s at the short fourth, Cremin sliced a drive to the 427-yard fifth, cleverly cut the wood up to the green, chipped on, and got a four, while Harris, bunkered, took five.

RECOVERS

In spite of a bad slice from the sixth tee to the fifth fairway, Cremin won the sixth to be one up. Harris, after a long drive down the middle of the fairway, was short with a high pitch and eventually missed a three-footer.

A great recovery to two feet from the pin from a bunker near the green of the 427-yard 7th by Harris was the feature of halving 4's there.

After a brace of big woods on the 528-yard 8th, each played a high spectacular pitch, but Harris missed his six-footer, while Cremin with a two-footer, got a birdie four to be two up.

Harris at the 473-yard 9th, got his first birdie, and from the edge of the green he ran in to 18in. With a four, he reduced his deficit to one hole. Approximate figures for the first nine were: Cremin, 454,344, 445—37. Harris, 444,355,454—38.

PICKED UP

The match was squared at the 10th where Cremin hooked his drive to an unplayable spot and gave up. Harris was on in 2, 18 feet from the flag.

Harris made a good save at the 192 yards 11th when he holed a 9-footer after being bunkered short. He missed a 3-footer to lose the 12th. At the 452 yards 13th Cremin chipped to 3 feet, holed the putt for a birdie 4 and was 2 up.

Cremin cut his drive at the 14th, but was on in 2 for a halving 4. Each hooked his tee shot at the short 15th and

ERIC CREMIN (LEFT) AND JACK HARRIS, the two finalists in the Victorian professional golf championship, shaking hands before they started their match at Yarra Yarra today.

CREMIN TAKES GOLF TITLE
By JACK DILLON

Eric Cremin, Australia's most 'titled' golfer added another major title to his National Open,

Jack Harris and Eric Cremin contest the Victorian PGA final in 1949 at Yarra Yarra GC. Eric came out on top on that occasion.

In 1949 while Jack was still at Hartley's sports store he reached his first Victorian PGA final at Yarra Yarra GC where he played Eric Cremin a NSW pro. Jack lost that particular final but he managed to reverse the tables many times in subsequent matches against Eric.

After leaving Hartley's Sports store in late 1949 and in the few months before the new Keysborough GC facility was ready, an interesting sidetrack arose for Colin Campbell and Jack Harris.

Earlier, in April 1948, Sorrento GC on the Mornington Peninsula had appointed their first ever full time golf professional, an English gentleman by the name of Sam Walsh. Sam was already in his mid-50s at that time but in 1948 he fought his way through to the final of the Victorian PGA Championship final which was held that year at the Commonwealth GC. To this day I believe that Sam is the oldest player ever to reach the final of that event at fifty-six years of age. The Victorian PGA was a match play event in those days. Sam played the reigning Australian Open winner Ossie Pickworth in this final, who had only narrowly beaten Jack Harris in the semi-final. Ossie Pickworth went on to easily beat Sam Walsh in the final.

However, there is another twist to this story. In July 1949, less than one year after this final, Sam Walsh sadly died of stomach cancer. Jack Harris remembers going to pay him a visit when he was in hospital. Sorrento GC needed a temporary golf professional until they could find a new replacement for Sam, so Colin Campbell and his trusty young assistant Jack Harris stepped into the breach from December 1949 to April 1950. During this period Colin was paid the princely sum of two pounds per week by the club as a retainer. It was only when I was doing some research into this story that I uncovered something totally unexpected.

Sam Walsh had been born in the North of England in the early 1890s. He had apparently been a North of England golf champion before he moved to Australia. Just imagine my surprise when I learned that Sam had been born in the tiny village of Trawden in Lancashire. This was the very same Trawden where I was raised and where my ninety-one year old mother and my younger brother and his wife still live! It was also the same Trawden I have returned to thirty-six times since I emigrated from the UK to Australia in 1983.

Even today Trawden is far too small to have its own golf course. From what I could find out, Sam had actually crossed over the border from Lancashire into Yorkshire to play his early golf at Baildon GC which is close to both Leeds and Bradford in West Yorkshire. Baildon GC is a moorland course which was designed back in 1896 by Tom Morris, the early British Open legend. In more recent times Baildon's most famous son was Gordon Brand who ran second to Greg Norman in the 1986 British Open at Turnberry in South Ayrshire.

After Jack and Colin had left Hartley's store in late 1949, the position at the store was taken up by twenty-one year old Ray Wright. He stayed there until 1954 when he opened up his own golf school in 1954 on the seventh floor of the Softgoods Building in Flinders Lane. That didn't last long however and by 1955 he was the club professional at Cheltenham GC.

Jack Harris remained the pro at Keysborough GC from 1950 until 1966. He then ran his own golf school in Chapel Street, St Kilda before eventually returning to Sorrento GC in 1983 where he remained as their longest serving pro until his retirement in 1996 at age seventy-four.

Chapter 5

The Keysborough Days

Jack Harris and Ossie Pickworth fighting one of their many battles.

Jack Harris extricated himself from the city golf school environment in about 1950. Soon after that, as the club professional at the newly built Keysborough GC, he was able to start making serious improvements to his already prodigious natural golfing ability.

Being based at an actual golf club instead of at an indoor driving range meant that when he did have a few minutes spare time to practice he was hitting off grass instead of rubber mats. He was aiming at real targets and could study his ball flight which you could not do in those days when hitting into a net. These days it is different. With modern camera and computer technology and devices such as *Swing Tip Analyser*, virtually every part of the golf swing can be looked at wherever you are.

He could also practice putting on an actual putting green and practice bunker shots in all kinds of real life situations. The improvement in Jack's game was virtually immediate and in 1950 he won his first Victorian PGA when he beat his old friend and foe, three times Australian Open champion, Ossie Pickworth, at Kingston Heath GC.

34 Jack Harris

```
                    COMMONWEALTH OF AUSTRALIA
                    POSTMASTER-GENERAL'S DEPARTMENT
                         TELEGRAM

HEARTIEST CONGRATULATIONS ON YOUR MAGNIFICENT VICTORY ALL VERY
PLEASED HERE KEEP IT UP BEST OF LUCK - H W JOSEPH HARTLEYS

         CONGRATULATIONS ON YOUR WONDERFUL WIN FROM THE
         PRESIDENT AND COMMITTEE TORQUAY GOLF CLUB
         ---FRED VARY

         MANY CONGRATULATIONS ON GREAT WIN---GEOFF BRASH

CONGRATULATIONS   ON WONDERFUL   EFFORT
                                      JOAN  AND RON MCPHERSON

HEARTIEST CONGRATULATIONS  AND FURTHER GOOD LUCK FROM---JOE
LLOYD AND FAMILY

         Congratulations on your excellent win
                                    Fred & Irene Reeves
```

Well done Jack on first Victorian PGA title in 1950

The benefit of being able to practice properly on an actual golf course had been well demonstrated immediately after the Second World War by none other than Ossie Pickworth. Ossie was the guy Jack heard about, but didn't know, when he was in Labuan Island in Borneo. After the war, Ossie had been able to go straight back to Manly GC in Sydney where he had been before the war started. In less than one year after his discharge from the Army, Ossie, not having even swung a club for the past six years or so, incredibly won his first Australian Open title in 1946. He repeated the feat again in 1947 and 1948 and to this day remains the only man in history to win three consecutive Australian Opens. Not even Jack Nicklaus, Gary Player, Greg Norman or Peter Thomson managed to do that.

After winning his third title in 1948 Ossie moved to Victoria from New South Wales and became the club pro at the Royal Melbourne GC. From that point onwards, over the next decade or more, Ossie Pickworth and Jack Harris became good friends. They played against each other very frequently and even played together in many exhibition matches at golf clubs throughout Victoria promoting the game of golf. At first Ossie held the whip hand but eventually Jack got his act together and was able to reverse the tables on many occasions.

Jack and Ossie shake hands after Ossie had just won the £200 Spalding Bowl in 1947 at Kingston Heath GC

At least Old Father Time was on Jack's side. Although Jack lost several years because of the war and was effectively only really starting his career at age twenty-seven or twenty-eight, the war had an even bigger impact on Ossie's golfing longevity. He was almost five years older than Jack having been born in January 1918; at the start of the 1950s he was already well into his thirties. Ossie had married his wife Lorna in 1942 and in a very quirky coincidence, just like Jack Harris, he married a waitress with a Scottish surname: McDougall. Quite a few other golfers like Naismith, Kelly, Bolger and Martin Smith, who had all performed exceptionally well before the war, were even older than Ossie Pickworth. They were most likely robbed of a few more possible Australian Opens had they been able to play in the 1939-1945 period.

As far as Keysborough GC was concerned, Jack had all the normal responsibilities of a club professional. He was paid a small retainer by the club but most of his income had to come from giving lessons and running the pro shop where he sold golf equipment and golf balls. He also did custom golf club fitting and golf club repair for the members. Overall, all these duties were just the nuts and bolts of what his main function at the club was. Essentially, he was there to help attract and retain new members to the club. Jack was acutely aware of what the main objective was and he took this responsibility very seriously. He had great success at this side of his job and the Keysborough GC flourished while he was there and continued to do so seventeen years later after his assistant Bob Spencer had taken over.

When it came to Jack being away from the club to play in Australian tournaments, Keysborough GC were quite supportive – presumably because any success he had reflected on the club in some way. However, most of the smaller tournaments he played in were local Victorian events. He only travelled interstate to play in the Australian Opens or in the bigger tournaments such as the Ampol, Wills Classic, Speedo, Adelaide Advertiser, McWilliams Wines and Pelaco. He didn't often travel interstate to play in events like the New South Wales Opens or the Queensland Opens because the prize money was small and was much less than what he could earn by staying home teaching. When he did travel interstate the club helped him with his travel expenses. This was somewhat different to what the Queensland and New South Wales club pros did. They regularly travelled to Victoria to play in the Victorian PGA, the Victorian Open and even many of the smaller purse events.

As far as travelling to tournaments within Victoria was concerned, early on in the piece, Jack had bought an old second hand Dodge from Colin Campbell's brother Bob who was also a golf pro at Ballarat. When he won his first big tournament, the Adelaide Advertiser in 1952, he kicked the Dodge into touch, splashed out and bought a brand spanking new Morris Minor. When travelling to New South Wales, Western Australia, Queensland or Tasmania they would generally fly. However, sometimes when going to Sydney, several Victorian pros would all drive up together so that they had a car to use when they got there.

Travelling to play in overseas tournaments was however a different proposition. Right from the start Jack had decided that it would be very difficult to try to earn a living by just playing tournament golf. Purses at small tournaments were very meagre and only the top few players in any competition received any reward at all. Prize money in Europe was somewhat better than in Australia but when travel and several months of accommodation costs were taken into account, the sums still didn't add up. Jack got confirmation of this through his friend and foe, Ossie Pickworth.

In 1950, Ossie went over to Europe to play in the British Open. He also played in several smaller tournaments in the UK and on the continent, and had a few good finishes which included winning the Irish Open which was played that year at the Royal Dublin links at Dollymount. Ossie beat fellow Australian, Norman von Nida. Needing a birdie four to win on the eighteenth hole, Ossie romped home with a magnificent eagle three. When he returned to Melbourne, Ossie was reported in the newspapers as saying that even though playing wise his trip had been reasonably successful it was not profitable. Although Ossie had finished third on the British Order of Merit in 1950, his expenses for the trip were £1400 and his prize money had only been £1300! That year he qualified for the main event at the British Open but didn't make the cut for the last two rounds finishing fifty-ninth and missing the cut by four strokes. He played in the British Open again in 1953 with almost the same result: missing the cut and coming in fifty-fourth.

Not for the first time Jack Harris and Ossie Pickworth, the Borneo boys, at the start of yet another battle.

It may have been around this time that a journalist asked Jack why he did not go and play in overseas tournaments. Jack told him that he couldn't because he was too much 'under the thumb at home.' In fact he went on to say that 'I am so far under the thumb that only my golf shoes are still poking out!' Good one, Jack! Nice try, but we don't believe you. The truth is that when you did eventually go over to England to play in the British Open in 1960, you were missing Grace and the girls so badly even before you arrived there. By the time you had only arrived in Calcutta on the outward journey you already wanted to come home!

Jack loses Victorian PGA final at Amstel GC to Ossie Pickworth.

The prize money in the USA, just like now, was higher than in either Europe or Australia. However, travel and accommodation expenses were still a big item. There were also far more very good golfers on the US circuit chasing the goodies. One Australian golfer who did have success in the USA during that period was Jim Ferrier. After winning the 1938 and 1939 Australian Opens as an amateur, he turned pro and after the war played mostly in the USA winning several PGA events and a US Major.

Later on, in the 1950s, the Asian golf circuit started to develop and tournaments began to spring up in Hong Kong, Philippines, Malaysia and Singapore. Many of the NSW and QLD pros such as Eric Cremin, Norman von Nida and Frank Phillips, began to play regularly in these but Peter Thomson was the only Victorian golfer of that era who frequently went overseas. He no doubt also travelled more than any other golfer in Australia. Maybe even more than von Nida who had mostly been the trailblazer. Of course the New Zealand Open had been also going for a long time by then. One of Jack Harris's first big matches was in the 1949 Victorian PGA Championship final at Yarra Yarra GC where he lost (five and four) to Eric Cremin. Sadly in 1973 at only sixty years of age, Eric Cremin collapsed and died while playing golf at the Singapore Island Country Club.

What it really amounted to in those days was, if you wanted to be just a touring professional instead of a club professional, you needed to have rich parents or a rich sponsor, or both. Or you could just decide that you and your family could live on the smell of an oily rag and go for it. As far as Jack was concerned, it was a no brainer. He decided almost from the start that travelling to play in overseas golf tournaments was not for him. To be honest, I don't even think that the poor prize money of the day was the main driver for his decision. Nor was it because he didn't think he was good enough to compete at the highest level. I suspect the real reason was that Jack was just a simple family man who loved his wife and kids and he just didn't want to be away from them for many months at a time.

Having made this decision, it then just became a balancing act. Jack had to generate most of his income from teaching golf and running his pro shop but in between, he still had to find enough time to practise for some of the big tournaments he competed in. This was not easy to do. Most golfing gurus will tell you that if you want to improve your golf game you should find yourself a good teacher and do lots of practice. You should also play with players better than yourself and go to big tournaments to watch how the top players do it. In both cases you should let your subconscious mind take over. If this is true then surely the reverse must have some credibility? If you spend many hours each day teaching the average Joe Hacker and watching them hook, slice, push, pull, top and shank (especially shank!) surely it cannot be good for your own game? I did ask Jack Harris what effect this had on his own game but he just played it down. Obviously, as the record shows, he did manage to find a way to cope with it and still win a lot of tournaments. He must have had a way of switching his subconscious mind off.

There were many Australian club pros of that period who were trying to do the same balancing act. One such club pro was Brian Twite who was a talented young British pro who had been at the prestigious Sunningdale GC in the UK. He came to Australia in 1955 and took up the club pro job at Metropolitan GC. In a newspaper interview which Brian gave around that time, he said that he just couldn't find enough practice time in between the very long teaching hours to keep his game sharp enough to regularly succeed in tournament play. In 1963, at the age of forty-one, Jack Harris shot 273 when he won his sixth Victorian PGA title at Long Island GC. Brian, who was about five years younger than Jack, shot 325 which was fifty-two strokes behind Jack. This little anecdote is included not to suggest that Brian was a poor player. It merely serves to highlight how outstanding Jack Harris must have been when it came to balancing the teaching side of golf with the tournament playing side. In fact, very deservedly, in early 2013, Brian Twite was honoured by the Governor General in the *Australia Day Honours* list. He received the Medal of the Order of Australia (OAM) for his outstanding services to golf in Australia.

Maybe Jack Harris was just one of those lucky guys who could play great golf without practicing for eight hours a day? In fact, from what Jack's assistant, Bob Spencer, told me, this was very much the case. Bob told me that a typical preparation by Jack Harris for a big tournament was to spend the four or five days before the tournament just flat out teaching. On the day before the tournament started he would go out onto Keysborough GC and play a few holes with three of the high handicap club members or anyone who just happened to be there looking for a game. When he did arrive at the tournament to play, he didn't hit buckets of balls with every club in the bag like all the top pros do today. He would just roll his shoulders forwards and backwards a couple of times, have a few air swings with a club, light up a cigarette to warm his hands and then nonchalantly smack one straight down the middle. Maybe I got the sequence wrong – the chances are he lit up the cigarette first! How could he win so many tournaments just doing that? The mind boggles! I asked Jack if this was an accurate description of how he used to prepare and he told me that it was exaggerating a little but more or less correct. The teaching part was spot on. However, he did admit that he was not a golfer who liked to practice a lot or to do an extensive warm up. He didn't like to hit lots of balls in his warm up because he 'preferred to keep all [his] energy for the match'. He never hit his driver during any warm up period. He also had a habit of not hitting any of his least favourite clubs in the warm up because he didn't want to take the risk of hitting a bad shot and then go into the round with a negative thought.

Bob Spencer also told me that Jack was not renowned as being a great putter and I had previously also heard the same story from other people. However, when his playing record is dissected and actual scores are examined it must surely be concluded that Jack wasn't a bad putter either. He may not have been the best putter around. He may not have been as proficient with the putter as the world's best ever putter, Old Baggy Pants himself, Bobby Locke or as Eric Cremin when he was on a roll. However, I don't believe that Jack Harris could have won the Varley trophy for low scoring average several times if he had been a bad putter. An example of this was in 1957 when over nineteen tournaments he averaged 70.9 shots per round. Only one golfer in Australia did better that year; Frank Phillips who averaged 70.61 shots. We should bear in mind that in those days many courses were rated par 73, 74 or even 75. Sure Jack Harris may have missed a few crucial putts at critical points in a round but he was not *Robinson Crusoe* in that regard.

An interesting comparison with Jack Harris's Australian scoring average in 1957 can be made with that of Norman von Nida for 1947. According to the *Adelaide News*, 16 October, 1947 von Nida was the top money earner on the British Tournament circuit that year. He had won over £3000 for the season and over the fifty-eight rounds of golf he had played, he had averaged 71.25 shots per round. The next best in England that year was the Welsh Ryder Cup player, Dai Rees, who had averaged 71.91 per round. Maybe Jack Harris really did know how to play golf?

I suspect that Jack's reputation as a questionable putter may have dated back to the days between 1946 and 1950 when he was working in a City

Golf School environment. Obviously in this period of his career, even if he did any putting practice at all, it would have been only straight putts on a flat carpet. He would not had any opportunity to practice uphill putts, downhill putts and big breaking putts on sloping or two tiered greens which would have varied in speed from day to day. Carpet putting is essentially at the same speed every day and while it can be argued that it is better than nothing, it is far from ideal.

So it is perhaps fair to say that in those early years after the war during Jack's putting was not as good as it may have been even though he did play quite a lot of tournaments and still had plenty of success. A good example where this lack of proper putting practice cost Jack Harris was in the Victorian Close Championship at Yarra Yarra GC in 1949 when he was still working at Hartley's sports store.

Peter Thomson won this event with a three under par 293 over seventy-two holes (76, 73, 72, 72). Jack Harris finished second with a 301 (74, 73, 79, 75). The third round was a disaster for Jack when he three putted five greens. Jack's last round of 75 which was only one over par doesn't look too bad but it doesn't tell the full story. According to the match report in the *Argus* newspaper July 30, 1949, in the last round Jack played magnificent from tee to green and 'his long game was perfect'. He was reported to have been shooting for birdie from an average of six feet on each of the last eighteen holes but never sank a single one. Thankfully, from 1950 until the end of his tournament playing days, he was located at an actual golf course where when he did have a few spare minutes he was able to practice putting on proper greens. As would be expected his number of three putt greens reduced dramatically during that period and his number of tournament wins soared.

In the early days at Keysborough GC, after they had moved from Albert Park to where the club is today, working conditions were pretty rough and ready. Colin Campbell and Jack Harris had to put up with makeshift temporary accommodation as far as the pro shop facilities were concerned. After Colin left to go working as a golf instructor on cruise ships, Bob Spencer joined Jack. The situation had still not improved very much and Bob recalls that there were lots of deadly poisonous snakes on the Keysborough course. In those days when players strayed away from the normal fairways the rough was like elephant grass. The snakes often used to get cut to pieces in the mowing machines when they were trimming the first cut off the fairways. According to Bob, the record was apparently thirteen dead snakes in one day! Bob remembers one day the Keysborough cat caught a small brown snake and brought it into the pro shop. Both Jack and Bob had never moved so fast in their lives. They were up on the table top in a flash. Apparently Jack in particular was not very fond of snakes!

The performance by Jack Harris as a tournament player from the late 1940s to the mid-1960s was truly remarkable. Of all the top Australian golfers of that era, Jack Harris was most likely the only one without overseas tournament experience. He only played against overseas golf stars when they came to Australia. This was only a few times each year and in any given event there may have been just a handful of overseas players. Norman von Nida had played many times over in Europe. Peter Thomson, right from the start of his career played just about everywhere. Argentina, Brazil, Canada, USA, South Africa, New Zealand, UK and all over Europe and throughout Asia. Kel Nagle played often in Europe and later in his career had quite a lot of success in the USA. Eric Cremin went over to Europe and also played in Asia. And later people like Frank Phillips, Bruce Devlin, Bruce Crampton, Billy Dunk and a host of others also travelled frequently. Even Ossie Pickworth, who didn't travel anywhere near as much as the ones mentioned so far, still travelled much more than Jack Harris and made a few golfing trips in Europe. There is no doubt that these overseas experiences helped to battle harden all these players most of whom had quite a lot of success on the international scene as well as in Australia.

Jack Harris won most of his tournaments in Victoria. Unlike most of his interstate contemporaries such as Eric Cremin, Kel Nagle or Frank Phillips, he generally didn't travel interstate to play in the other State Opens or State PGA Championships or any of the smaller purse tournaments. This was because the prize money was too small and even if he had won, it would not have covered his travel expenses and lost teaching revenue. Apart from one solitary occasion when he competed in the Queensland Open and finished fourth, Jack only travelled interstate for the Australian Open or for the bigger money tournaments such as the Pelaco, Wills Classic, Ampol and Coles.

On the other hand, NSW professionals the likes of Kel Nagle, Eric Cremin, Norman von Nida and Frank Phillips were frequent visitors to Victoria to play in the Vic Open, Vic PGA and even in many of the smaller purse events. They clearly had some assistance from either the NSW PGA or from their clubs which enabled them to do this. By doing this Nagle, Cremin, Phillips and other interstate plunderers were able to significantly boost their Australian PGA tournament playing record. Had Jack Harris also played more interstate events such as the NSW Open, he too would have undoubtedly added considerably to his Australian PGA tour victories tally. He frequently beat all the above mentioned interstate players when they came to Victoria.

One of the chief reasons NSW golfers may have travelled more than players from other states during that period may have been due to the poker machine influence in that state. Poker machines had started to appear in NSW in the 1930s. They were not actually fully legalised in NSW until 1956 but despite frequent bans, there were constant loopholes which clubs and hotels exploited, so in practice they were in common usage long before 1956. According to *The Sydney Morning Herald*, (SMH) December 14, 1952, after the 1939 ban, fruit machines were 'tolerated' in non-proprietary clubs but banned in proprietary clubs. Non-proprietary meant that the profits went to all club members and not to an individual. After the ban in 1939 an article in the SMH mentioned that many suburban and country clubs were claiming that their revenue had been seriously affected by the ban and they were campaigning for the ban to be lifted. Even Royal Canberra GC had pokies in 1939. Yet another article in the SMH dated 1969 mentioned that since World War II there had been a revolution in Sydney's golf courses since the introduction of pokies. Randwick GC had pokies in the 1950s and all the clubs based along the River Murray on the NSW side had pokies. In the SMH dated 1962 it mentioned that a dozen Sydney clubs or more will start the season with improved club and course facilities. These clubs included Pennant Hills GC, Moore Park GC and even Pymble GC where Kel Nagle was the professional. It seems highly likely that the NSW professionals were financially supported in those days by their clubs which allowed them to do far more travel throughout Australia than their counterparts from other states. Golfers such as Kel Nagle, Frank

Phillips, Norman von Nida and Eric Cremin were to be found at all times at any golf tournament / purse anywhere in Australia. Even discounting their jaunts overseas to play in Europe, America, Asia and New Zealand, they played four or five times more events each year than Jack Harris, just within Australia.

Bear in mind that we are not talking chicken feed. From its beginnings in the early 1930s the NSW poker machine industry had grown to 73 billion dollars by 2015. Which means that over $7 billion is lost on machines in NSW ever year. I don't know just how much of this was grabbed by golf clubs but it would certainly not be insignificant. NSW still has more than 50% of all poker machines in Australia.

By contrast, poker machines were not legalised in Victoria until 1994 when Premier Joan Kirner unleashed the scourge. Even with this relatively late start, over $2.5 billion is lost on poker machines in Victoria each year and this grows sharply every year. While prestigious clubs in Victoria such as Royal Melbourne GC and Victoria GC do not need to succumb to the easy money grab, there are plenty of Victorian clubs who have seized the opportunity. And these clubs are not all located in the country. In 2014/2015 Box Hill GC made over $2 million from their pokies, Kooringal GC over $4 million and Amstel over $6 million. Golf Clubs such as Port Arlington, Mildura, Clifton Springs, Eastwood, Benalla, Robinvale, Mansfield, Numurkah, Bacchus Marsh, Ballarat, Foster and Cobden, all do very nicely thank you from poker machines.

The extra money which came to NSW golf clubs from the poker machine source during the immediate post war period, and continuing after the war, undoubtedly made a significant contribution to the development of golf and golfers in that state. Not only would the NSW players of that period get more help from their clubs when it came to travelling expenses but it was also very obvious that there were far more purse events held at NSW clubs (and bigger purses) for them to play in. Victorian golfers like Jack Harris or WA golfers like Les Nichols, were definitely at a serious disadvantage compared to their NSW cousins.

When nearly at the end of his career, Keysborough GC did eventually sponsor Jack on a trip to Europe in 1960 when Jack was thirty-eight years old. It was a kind of reward for all the great work he had done to help build up the Keysborough GC. He played in a few tournaments in the UK and tried to qualify for the British Open. He also played in the French, Dutch and German Opens.

It was Jack's first overseas trip apart from when he was in Borneo during the war. He was away from Australia for several months and he missed Grace and the kids terribly. He played quite well while he was away and picked up cash from most events but did not win any tournaments.

However, during the three months he was overseas he was able to concentrate just on playing or practicing golf and not having to teach every day. This extra practice, plus playing on different courses against many of the top European pros, did wonders for Jack's game and his confidence.

When he returned to Australia, between 1960 and 1963, he saw the benefits of the overseas experience and of the extra practice, because, at over forty years of age, he won three more Victorian PGAs and a Victorian Open and also had several seconds and a third in these events. His Victorian PGA win at Keysborough GC in 1961 was memorable because he beat two British Open winners (Peter Thomson and Kel Nagle) and four Australian Open winners (Peter Thomson, Kel Nagle, Eric Cremin and Frank Phillips). His Victorian PGA win at Long Island GC in 1963 was also memorable when he beat four times British Open winner Peter Thomson by twelve strokes.

His Victorian Open win in 1960 on the tough Metropolitan GC was no less impressive when he beat double Australian Open winner Frank Phillips, Billy Dunk and Bruce Crampton. Gary Player had won the Victorian Open in 1959.

Jack never told me about the win at Long Island. I found out the results when I was troving through newspaper articles. After I had discovered this particular result I decided to ask Jack about it. I just said to him, 'tell me about Long Island, Jack.' I was fully expecting him to give me a blow-by-blow account of how he had hammered the much younger Peter Thomson there, a guy who was at the peak of his form. Thomson had already won four British Opens and still had maybe his greatest British Open win in 1965 to come when he beat both Jack Nicklaus and Arnold Palmer. But all I got from this very modest man was 'Oh yes, I used to do some teaching there just before the war.' End of conversation! I was absolutely gob-smacked!

Even after this purple patch, Jack Harris remained competitive. He was runner-up in the Victorian PGA on two more occasions. He was just two strokes behind Alan Murray at Woodlands GC in 1965 and in 1969 he lost to Geoff Parslow in a play-off at Waverley GC.

Apart from his unequalled record in the Victorian PGA of six wins and eight times runner-up, Jack also performed remarkably well in the Australian Open over a twenty-year period.

He also had dozens of wins or good performances in smaller tournaments and purse events such as Croydon Open, Penfold–Bromford purse, Dunlop purse, Slazenger purse, Victorian closed, The Liquor Industry purse, Riverside and Tasmanian Tyre Service purse, the Woodlands Open and many more too numerous to detail here.

It was after the Riverside tournament that the White City Greyhound Meeting in Launceston started to name each of their races after one of the golfers in the tournament. They had the Jack Harris Stakes, the Peter Thomson Stakes and the Ossie Pickworth Stakes. Jack never knew at the time that this was happening. I came across old newspaper reports of the meetings.

However, in June 1966, Jack Harris's time at Keysborough GC club came to an end and Bob Spencer returned from Elsternwick GC and re-joined Keysborough GC to take over from Jack on July 1, 1966. Jack Harris played one last tournament, the Victorian PGA in 1969, while he was at his St Kilda Golf School, before he threw the clubs into the garage and bowed out of playing tournament golf.

Chapter 6

Jack Harris Tournament Playing Record

Professional wins (90) including **eight PGA Tour of Australasia** wins. (Six **Victorian PGA** wins, one **Victorian Open** and one **Adelaide Advertiser**) from **485 Tournaments / purses**

1936	**1st Under 15s Victorian Caddie Championship**
1937	**1st Assistants Championship**
1938	T8 Victorian Assistant Professionals Championship **1st Kew 36-hole Handicap**
1940	24th Major-General HW Grimwade purse
1941	T10 Dunlop Cup, T9 Kingswood GC purse, T7 Kingston Heath purse, 8th Major-General HW Grimwade purse, **1st Huntingdale Four-ball**
\multicolumn{2}{l	}{End 1941 – Mid 1946 Jack Harris served in the Army during the Second World War. Refer Chapter 2 for more details.}
1946	23rd Huntingdale purse, 4th Royal Sydney purse, **35th Australian Open**, 12th Adelaide Advertiser, 5th Paterson River purse, 2nd Kingswood purse, 8th Victorian PGA, 1st Victorian PGA Foursomes
1947	T3 ACT Four ball, 11th ACT Open, 25th Royal Canberra purse, T12 Ampol, 11th Victoria purse, 8th Dunlop Cup, 17th Brisbane purse, 2nd Spalding Bowl, 8th Amstel purse, 27th Victorian PGA, 13th Slazenger purse, **9th Victorian PGA Foursomes**, T7 Woodend purse, 4th Kingswood purse

1948	**T6 Kingswood Pro-Am, T5 Adelaide Advertiser, 15th Ampol**, 4th Wally Frazer, 1st Yarra Yarra Open, **T3 Victorian Close, T4 Victorian PGA Foursomes**, T7 Spalding Bowl, T3 Slazenger purse, T2 Amstel purse, 2nd Vicars Shield, **15th Australian Open**, 2nd Croydon Open, **T3 Victorian PGA**, T8 Ampol
1949	**6th Victoria Open Scratch, T31 McWilliams Wines, 5th Adelaide Advertiser**, 1st Victoria purse, T11 Don Walker Memorial, **2nd Victorian Close**, 5th Dunlop Cup, **T3 RSL Tournament, 1st Victorian PGA Foursomes, 1st RSL Team Tournament**, 3rd Slazenger purse, T9 Metropolitan purse, **2nd Victorian PGA**, T10 Ampol, 4th Chesterfield purse, T5 Riversdale purse
1950	T8 Findlay Cup, 1st Spalding Bowl, T5 Victoria Open Scratch, **T40 McWilliams Wines, T10 Adelaide Advertiser, T5 Yarra Yarra Pro-Am**, 3rd Penfold-Bromford purse, T2nd Slazenger purse, 5th Don Walker Memorial, **T7 Silver King**, T11 Dunlop Cup, 1st Amstel purse, 2nd RSL State, T6 Torquay purse, **T9 Victorian Close**, T1 Woodend purse, T4 Waverley purse, T2 Victorian Open Provincial, **1st Victorian PGA Foursomes, 1st Victorian PGA**
1951	T3 Chesterfield purse, T9 Spalding purse, **T12 McWilliams Wines**, T2 Yarra Yarra Open, **T3 Adelaide Advertiser**, T4 Peter Scott purse, 1st Penfold-Bromford purse, T14 Kingswood purse, 20th Lakes Open, 4th Rossdale purse, 2nd Slazenger purse, **4th Victorian Close**, 2nd Dunlop Cup, 1st Amstel Show Day purse, 10th Metropolitan purse, **1st Vicars Shield, 4th Australian Open**, 9th Australian PGA, 8th Major-General HW Grimwade purse, T11 Silver King, 8th Kingswood purse, T9 Don Walker Memorial, 7th Victorian Provincial Open, **2nd Victorian PGA Foursomes**, 3rd Rossdale purse, T9 Victorian PGA

1952	T7 Spalding Bowl, **T4 McWilliams Wines, 1st Adelaide Advertiser**, T4 Kingswood purse, 1st Royal Canberra Four-ball, **2nd ACT Open, 3rd ACT purse**, 2nd 3AW Sportsman's, 1st Penfold-Bromford purse, 2nd Slazenger purse, **T5 Mobilco Machinery**, 1st Vicars Shield, T12 Lake Karrinyup purse, **4th Australian Open**, 3rd Mount Yokine Fourball, 1st Chesterfield purse, 1st Don Walker Memorial, 1st Amstel purse, 3rd Dunlop Cup, **T9 Victorian PGA, 1st Victorian Close**, T22 Ampol, 1st Varley Trophy, **13th Advertiser Special Open, T16 Ampol**
1953	2nd Patterson River purse, 2nd Peter Scott purse, T2 Cheltenham purse, **3rd Victorian PGA Foursomes, T2 Latrobe purse**, 22nd **McWilliams Wines, 10th Adelaide Advertiser,** 2nd Yarra Yarra Open, T4 Long Island purse, 1st Woodlands Coronation, 1st Victorian Open Provincial, **4th Victorian Close**, 4th Chesterfield purse, **T3 Victorian PGA**, T11 Amstel purse, T5 Don Walker Memorial, **T8 Ampol**, T6 Royal Melbourne purse, 1st Vicars Shield, **T12 Australian Open, T9 Australian PGA**, 7th Riverside purse, **1st West-Victorian Open, T4 Cheltenman purse**, 1st Keysborough
1954	1st Findlay Cup, 1st Williamstown purse, T3 Uncle Bob's, 1st Yarra Yarra Open, T4 Latrobe purse, **2nd Peninsula 9-hole purse, 2nd Peninsula 18-hole purse,** 2nd **Peninsula 27-hole purse, 4th Queensland Open**, T5 Victoria Park purse, T6 Royal Queensland purse, **T2 Victorian Close,** T1 Woodlands Open, **T7 Commonwealth purse, T2 Liquor Industry purse,** T4 Rossdale purse, **2nd Victorian PGA,** T6 Kooyonga purse, 2nd Vicars Shield, **T9 Australian Open,** T4 Chesterfield purse, 3rd Geelong ULVA purse, T6 Kingswood purse, T1 Amstel purse, 5th Williamstown purse, **T5 Australian PGA**, 6th St Michaels purse, **T3 Ampol**, 2nd West Victorian Open, 3rd Patterson River purse, **6th Ampol**, T6 Don Walker Memorial, 5th Riverside / Tasmanian Tyre, T7 Long Island purse, 1st Kew purse

52 Jack Harris

1955	1st Albert Findlay Cup, T1 Keysborough purse, **T5 Victorian PGA Foursomes**, 2nd Yarra Yarra Pro-Am, T2 Kingswood Centenary Cup, **2nd Victorian PGA**, T1 Latrobe purse, T5 Gailes purse, **2nd Vicars Shield, M/C Australian Open**, T2 Woodlands Open, T2 West-Victorian Open, 1st Liquor industry purse, T5 Northern purse, 2nd Long Island purse, M/C Speedo, T7 Roselands purse, 2nd Williamstown purse, 4th Amstel purse, 2nd RSL, 3rd Lions Club purse, T2 Spring Valley purse, **T5 Pelaco, 2nd Patterson River purse**, T13 East-Victorian Open, T13 Don Walker Memorial, **T4 Ampol**, T7 Riversdale purse, 2nd Cranbourne purse
1956	T3 Rossdale purse, 1st Findlay Cup, T2 Kingswood Four-ball, T7 Yarra Yarra Open, **T6 Adelaide Advertiser, 2nd Victorian PGA**, 1st Eastern Four-ball, T1 Liquor Industry, T1 Latrobe purse, 1st Woodlands Open, T2 North-East Open, T4 Warracknabeal purse, 2nd West-Victorian Open, 3rd Long Island purse, **T15 Australian Open**, 1st Williamstown purse, 2nd Chesterfield purse, **T10 Speedo**, 4th Croydon purse, T6 Peninsula 18-hole purse, 2nd Peninsula 9-hole purse, T2 Amstel purse, **T11 Pelaco, T3 Ampol**
1957	2nd Oscar Mayer Portsea purse, 2nd Anglesea purse, **12th Victorian PGA Foursomes, T12 Adelaide Advertiser**, 1st Yarra Yarra Open, T4 Rotary Club purse, **1st Victorian PGA**, 7th Latrobe purse, 3rd Woodlands purse, T6 North-East Victorian Open, T2 South-West Victorian Open, 1st Liquor Industry purse, 1st Chesterfield purse, **T11 Ampol, T6 Pelaco, T8 Australian Open**, T8 Spring Valley purse, T9 Australian PGA, T10 Keysborough purse, **T7 Croydon Lawn Patrol**

1958	1st Anglesea purse, **2nd Victorian PGA**, T7 Rossdale purse, 1st Yarra Yarra Open, **6th Adelaide Advertiser**, T4 Green Acres purse, T1 Rossdale Testimonial, T3 Woodlands Open, 2nd North-East Victorian Open, **3rd Lakes Open**, T5 South-West Victorian Open, 1st Liquor Industry purse, **T5 The Grange Ampol, T13 Kooyonga purse, T14 Australian Open**, T5 Australian PGA, 9th Goulburn Valley Open, 4th Bendigo Ampol, 1st Northern purse, **T10 Pelaco**, T4 Don Walker Memorial, 2nd Spring Valley purse, **3rd Victorian Open**, T7 Hawthorn Rotary Club purse, 1st Keysborough purse, 1st Victorian PGA Foursomes
1959	4th Yarra Yarra Open, **5th Adelaide Advertiser**, T1 Mount Lofty purse, 1st Green Acres purse, T5 Kooringal purse, **1st Victorian PGA**, T1 Woodlands Open, 1st Yarrawonga Open, 2nd South-West Victorian Open, **9th Australian PGA Foursomes, T8 Australian Open**, T9 Australian PGA, **T15 Victorian Close, 2nd Dallas Brooks Mixed Open**, 1st Cranbourne purse, **T6 Victorian Open, T21 Ampol**, T2 Keysborough purse, **T5 Pelaco, 13th Northern purse, T3 Coles, T6 Coca Cola**, 1st Victorian PGA Foursomes
1960	**1st Victorian PGA, 1st Victorian PGA Foursomes**, T1 Yarra Yarra Easter Open, **T11 Penfold-Swallow, M/C Daks, T16 Yorkshire Evening News**, 30th Bowmaker, DNQ British Open, T24 French Open, T14 Dutch Open, T21 German, Open, 3rd Barham Border Open, T2 Cohuna purse, T4 Royal Fremantle purse, **T11 Australian Open**, 1st 3AW purse, **5th Standard Triumph**, 1st Kooringal purse, **T3 Coles, 1st Victorian Open**, 1st Keysborough purse, **2nd Victorian Close**, 1st Northern purse, 5th Beauty Bath Ware Manufacturers purse
1961	**1st Victoria purse, 3rd Victorian Foursomes**, T4 Yarra Yarra Open, 2nd Green Acres purse, 1st Woodlands Open, 3rd Yarrawonga Open, 1st Liquor Industries purse, T2 South-West Victorian Open, 1st Henderson purse, T10 PGA Jubilee Foursomes, T2 Massey Park Pro-Am, **3rd Victorian Open, 13th Wills Classic, 6th Australian Open, 1st Victorian PGA**, T9 Australian PGA, **1st Victorian Close**, T3 Don Walker Memorial

Year	Results
1962	2nd Kingston Heath purse, 3rd Yarra Yarra Open, 3rd Keysborough Mixed Foursomes, **2nd Victorian PGA Foursomes**, T7 Woodlands Open, T9 Yarrawonga Open, 1st South-West Victorian Open, T4 Fairways Club purse, **T12 Adelaide Advertiser, T13 Wills Masters, T12 Australian Open, 15th Amstel purse,** 4th Southern purse, **T5 Victorian Open, T9 Australian PGA, 1st Victorian Close, T6 Victorian PGA**
1963	**2nd Commonwealth Pro-Am, T5 Victorian Foursomes, T1 Keysborough purse,** T2 Yarra Yarra Open, 4th Metropolitan purse, T2 Yarra Yarra Pro-Am, **1st Victoria Pro-Am,** T3 Woodlands Open, 2nd Yarrawonga Open, T3 Rossdale Pro-Am, 1st Barham Border Open, T7 Amstel purse, **30th Wills Masters,** 5th Victorian Open, T3 Latrobe purse, T16 Liquor Industries purse, **1st Victorian PGA**
1964	**T5 Victorian PGA Foursomes,** T8 Yarra Yarra Open, T8 Colvan Pro-Am, T1 Woodlands Open, T13 Yarrawonga Border Open, **1st Liquor Industries purse, 1st Royal Melbourne purse, 3rd Barham Border Open, T8 Victorian Open, 8th Victorian PGA,** 1st Van Cooth Celebrities, T5 Medway Open, **T17 Wills Masters, T28 Australian**
1965	T4 Commonwealth Pro-Am, T2 Metropolitan Pro-Am, 2nd Colvan Pro-Am, T18 Yarra Yarra Open, T4 Liquor Industries purse, 1st Woodlands Open, T7 Yarrawonga Border Open, 2nd Victoria purse, **T2 Victorian PGA, T14 Victorian Open,** 1st Keysborough purse, T12 Southern Pro-Am, T22 Medway Open, **T11 Australian PGA, 3rd Victorian Close**
1966	T3 Colvan Pro-Am, T8 Yarra Yarra Open, T3 Liquor Industries purse, T6 Woodlands Open, **6th Victoria purse, T21 Victorian Open,** T34 Wills Masters, 3rd Waverley Pro-Am, 10th Victorian PGA
1967	**T10 Victorian Open, 2nd Victorian PGA Foursomes,** T2 Colvan, T10 Yara Yarra Open, T12 Woodlands Open, 5th Yarrawonga Open, T3 Barham purse, **T17 Australian Open,** 2nd Southern purse, **T11 Australian PGA, T11 Victorian Close, T4 Victorian PGA**

Year	Results
1968	**2nd Victorian PGA Foursomes**, T3 Colvan, T11 Woodlands Open, **4th Yarrawonga Open**, 2nd Royal Melbourne purse, 3rd Liquor Industries purse, M/C Australian PGA, **2nd Victorian PGA**
1969	**55th Victorian Open, T7 Sunshine Open, T5 Victoria purse**, T15 Eastwood Open, **T44 Dunlop International, T9 Victorian Close**, T1 Niblick-Corfam purse, **2nd Victorian PGA**
1970	T7 **Riversdale Pro-Am, T31 Victorian Open**, T6 Yarra Yarra Open, T7 Medway purse, T6 Woodlands Open, T7 Patterson River Pro-Am, **T9 Victorian Close**, T6 Rothmans Pro-Am, **T4 Victorian PGA**
1971	**T4 Yarra Yarra Open**, T9 Victoria purse, T5 Eastwood Open, **T33 Wills Masters, T26 Victorian Close**, T12 Heidelberg Open, T5 Rothman's Pro-Am, **8th Victorian PGA**
1972	**T30 Victorian Open, T5 Victorian PGA Foursomes**, T2 Eastwood Open, M/C Dunlop International, **T6 Victorian PGA**
1973	**T12 Chrysler Classic qualifier, T8 Rothmans Pro-Am**
1977	**2nd Victorian PGA Foursomes, T4 Colvan Pro-Am**
1979	**11th Citizens Watch Seniors**

Playing Record Abbreviations Used:

M/C Missed Cut
T Tied Result
DNQ Did Not Qualify

Please note that this table was constructed entirely from old newspaper articles, from data on the Australian PGA website and also from Wikipedia information. It is not claimed to be a complete record and inevitably will contain errors and omissions. Refer to the "References" section at the back of this book for validation of these records.

What stands out from Jack's tournament record is the remarkable consistency over a twenty-five year period. For those who like numbers it can be summarised as follows.

Finishing place	Number of times	Percentage
1st	90	18.6%
2nd	83	17.1%
3rd	47	9.7%
4th	42	8.7%
5th	37	7.6%
6th	25	5.2%
7th	22	4.5%
8th	21	4.3%
9th	20	4.1%
10th	14	2.9%
11th	13	2.7%
12th	13	2.7%
13th	10	2.1%
14th	4	0.8%
15th	6	1.2%
16th	3	0.6%
17th	3	0.6%
Other	32	6.6%
	485	

In summary	
Won	19%
Top Three	45%
Top Five	62%
Top Ten	83%
Top Fifteen	92%

I am not a golf statistician but to my eyes this record looks pretty amazing! Few club based professional golfers of that period, without international playing experience, came close to what Jack Harris achieved.

But there were three other golfers who could really be described as 'the Jack Harris's' of their States. One was Reg Want, a Queensland golfer, who won eight State PGA titles plus one State Open title. Another was Les Nichols, a Western Australian golfer who did the same thing in that state. Neither of these players ever played overseas. Neither travelled much outside of their state to play, particularly Les. Reg did a few interstate events in his early days.

The third was Murray Crafter of South Australia who won six South Australian Opens, eleven South Australian PGAs and overall 123 professional wins. Murray did play in Europe in 1960 but, like Jack Harris, it may have been his only overseas venture.

All three of these golfers finished higher than Jack Harris on the all-time list of PGA Tour of Australasia wins. But it must be said that in his very long career of over thirty years, Jack Harris never played in the state PGAs or state Opens of South Australia, Western Australia or New South Wales. He only played once during all that time in the Queensland Open and never in their state PGA. Had he done so he would have surely picked up a few, just as Ossie Pickworth, Kel Nagle, Eric Cremin, Frank Phillips, Peter Thomson and Norman von Nida did.

It must also be considered that in those days Western Australia, Queensland and South Australia were much weaker golfing states compared with either New South Wales or Victoria. These states never did well in the annual inter-state Vicars Shield contest which was invariably won by NSW or Victoria because they didn't have the strength in depth to form strong teams.

Jack Harris was always ranked ahead of Want, Nicholls and Crafter on the best players in Australia ranking list. Jack also had a better Australian Open record and generally did better in the big money tournaments like the 1956 Ampol.

Not only did Jack Harris have no international playing experience throughout the vast majority of his tournament playing days but he was also the least travelled of all the top golfers even within Australia. Of the 485 events listed he played well over 80% of these in the state of Victoria.

It may seem like close to 500 tournaments / purses is a lot of events for a club-based teaching professional to play in. But bear in mind that this was over a very long period, starting before 1940 and ending in about 1978, albeit with close to six years lost due to war. When averaged out across so many years, Jack Harris played far fewer tournaments that his better-known contemporaries such as Pickworth, Thomson, Nagle, von Nida, Phillips,

Cremin etc. All these players boosted their Tour of Australasia wins and purse wins in general by frequent travel throughout Australia, and apart from Ossie Pickworth, in New Zealand as well. For example, the all-time leader of the Tour of Australasia win list, Kel Nagle, had over 60% of his 61 wins outside of his home state of NSW. After Jack Harris, Ossie would have been the least travelled of all the top guys. But Ossie did play in North America a couple of times and he did have two cracks at the British Open and play other tournaments in Europe at that time, in addition to playing in the inaugural Canada Cup in Montreal. Ossie also travelled throughout Australia much more than Jack.

It should also be noted that Jack Harris played in many one round purses. Also, for most of his playing career the two-rounds events were played in one day and the four-round events were played in two days. This meant that the time away from his club, Keysborough, was minimised.

The way golf was set up in Australia in those days, Jack Harris could still find himself playing against any of the top Australian golfers even in a small purse event. I guess this just doesn't happen these days. In 2018, reigning British Open champions generally do not even play in the Australian Open unless they are guaranteed big appearance money. Whereas Jack could often come across two British Open champions and five or six Australian Open champions playing in any old nondescript event.

Despite a relative lack of big tournament experience, Jack Harris, against all odds, still managed to rack up many impressive wins against his better-known opponents. Pickworth, Thomson, Nagle, von Nida, Cremin and Phillips had six British Opens, sixteen Australian Opens and sixteen Australian PGAs between them. A home based, virtually full-time teaching professional had no right to be spanking the likes of these guys ... but he often did!

Jack Harris made quite a habit of breaking course records in the Victorian Close Championship

With such an impressive tournament playing record it is not surprising that Jack Harris created many course and tournament records along the way. Below are some of the records which he equalled or broke. Again this is almost certainly not a complete list.

Jack Harris Course Records

Year	Score	Golf Course	Year	Score	Golf Course
1949	68	Victorian Close Championship at Woodlands GC	1957	278	Victorian PGA at Croydon GC (Tournament Record)
1950	70	Silver King £500 at Long Island GC	1957	67	Woodlands GC purse
1950	70	Amstel purse at Amstel GC	1957	139	Easter Open at Yarra Yarra GC (Two Round Record)
1950	68	Victorian Provincial at Ballarat GC	1957	70	Anglesea GC purse
1951	70	Victorian PGA Foursomes at Long Island GC (playing with Colin Campbell)	1957	65	West Victorian Open at Warrnambool GC
1952	68	Australian Open at Lake Karrinyup GC	1958	68	Victorian Close at Geelong GC
1952	65	Vicars Shield at Lake Karrinyup GC	1958	68	Victorian PGA at Latrobe GC
1952	68	Victorian Close at Woodlands GC	1958	68	Anglesea GC purse
1952	62	Victorian Close Championship at Ballarat GC			
1953	66	Exhibition Match at Maffra GC	1959	62	Mount Lofty GC purse (Included 28 on back nine. Jack's lowest ever nine-hole score!)
1953	70	Victorian PGA at Commonwealth GC			
1953	68	West Victorian Open at Horsham GC			
1953	65	Albert Park purse at Albert Park GC	1959	65	South West Victorian Open at Warrnambool GC
1953	70	Exhibition Match at Sale GC	1959	66	Pelaco tournament at Victoria
1954	68	Kew GC purse	1960	282	Victorian Open at Metropolitan
1954	68	West Victorian Open at Horsham GC	1960	70	Kooringal GC purse GC
1954	76	Williamstown GC purse	1960	67	Victorian Open at Metropolitan GC (Previous record of 68 set by Peter Thomson)
1954	67	Tasmanian Tyre Services purse at Riverside GC	1961	65	Victorian PGA at Keysborough GC
1956	68	Lawn Patrol at Croydon GC	1961	65	South West Open at Warrnambool GC
1956	69	Victorian PGA at Long Island GC	1961	62	Victorian Close at Midlands GC
1956	141	Victorian PGA at Long Island GC (Two Round Record)	1961	69	Woodlands GC Open
1956	197	South West Victorian Open at Warrnambool GC (Tournament Record)	1961	68	Henderson purse at Rosebud GC
1956	68	Speedo Tournament at Victoria GC	1963	66	Victorian PGA at Long Island GC
1956	70	Albert Finlay Cup at Victoria GC (18th hole had recently been lengthened by 30 yards)	1965	69	Victorian PGA at Woodlands GC

The list of Jacks course records should be viewed bearing in mind that very few of the top golf courses on which he played were rated par 72 or below during the 20-year period after World War II.

Most of them were above that and some of them significantly so as can be seen from the following table.

Golf Course Par Rating					
Golf Course	Year	Par Rating	Golf Course	Year	Par Rating
Amstel	1950	73	Northern	1958	73
Amstel	1955	71	Northern	1960	73
Ballarat	1950	71	Northern	1970	73
Barham	1967	73	Patterson River	1954	73
Bell Park Links	1954	72	Patterson River	1962	74
Box Hill	1950	68	Patterson River	1970	73
Box Hill	1964	70	Riversdale	1949	73
Commonwealth	1947	76	Riversdale	1969	73
Commonwealth	1950	76	Riverside	1952	72
Commonwealth	1963	74	Royal Adelaide	1952	74
Commonwealth	1973	73	Royal Adelaide	1959	72
Cottesloe	1952	72	Royal Melbourne	1947	75
Cranbourne	1955	74	Royal Melbourne	1949	75
Cranbourne	1959	74	Royal Melbourne	1956	73
Croydon	1948	73	Royal Melbourne (East)	1963	74
Croydon	1957	70	Royal Melbourne (East)	1968	74
Croydon	1967	72	Royal Melbourne (West)	1968	73
Eastwood	1972	72	Royal Queensland	1954	75
Gailes	1954	75	Southern	1951	73
Glenelg	1950	73	Southern	1967	73
Green Acres	1959	73	Spring Valley	1957	72
Green Acres	1965	71	The Australian	1950	71
Huntingdale	1948	77	Victoria	1948	75
Huntingdale	1952	75	Victoria	1949	76
Huntingdale	1959	75	Victoria	1956	73
Huntingdale	1966	75	Victoria	1959	73
indooroopilly	1954	73	Victoria	1961	73
Keysborough	1961	73	Victoria	1963	73
Keysborough	1965	73	Victoria	1971	72
Kingston Heath	1951	76	Waratah	1950	71
Kingston Heath	1958	74	Warrnambool	1957	68
Kingston Heath	1962	74	Waverley	1950	73
Kingswood	1954	74	Waverley	1968	72
Kingswood	1958	74	Woodlands	1952	73
Kingswood	1963	74	Woodlands	1957	73
Kooyonga	1954	74	Woodlands	1965	73
Lake Karrinyup	1952	73	Woodlands	1968	73
Long Island	1940	76	Yarra Yarra	1950	74
Long Island	1947	75	Yarra Yarra	1955	73
Long Island	1963	73	Yarra Yarra	1957	73
Long Island	1971	71	Yarra Yarra	1967	73
Maffra	1953	72	Yarra Yarra	1969	73
Metropolitan	1950	76	Yarra Yarra	1971	72
Metropolitan	1960	74	Yarrawonga	1959	73
Metropolitan	1968	74	Yarrawonga	1968	74
Mt Lofty	1959	68	Yeerongpilly	1949	73

Chapter 7

From Paupers to Princes?

Being a professional golfer in Australia in the pre-war and immediate post war years may have sounded like a glamorous profession. However, very few golfers in that era were destined to become rich.

I suspect that most if not all professional golfers when they start out do so with the dream of playing in big tournaments. But when it sinks in that even though they have reduced their handicap to scratch and still have almost zero chance of winning a big tournament, I am sure there is a lot of soul searching that needs to be done. By this time they have no doubt already invested several years of their time and money into chasing the dream. Several years which could have been spent training to be a pharmacist, an architect or a plumber may have been wasted.

Australian golfers who get past that point and who learn how to consistently string together sub-par rounds have to deal with the fact that there are not enough big tournaments played in Australia. Therefore, they must inevitably look elsewhere. This can mean an enormous amount of travelling and time away from their family or can mean re-locating the family unit overseas somewhere. Not every individual can adjust to this. No matter how brilliant they are at actually playing golf and even if the golfers themselves can adjust, the rest of the family may not be able to feel comfortable in their new surroundings.

Prior to the Second World War, only a handful of golfers ventured overseas to play. Joe Kirkwood, who won the Australian Open in 1920, two years before Jack Harris was born, was an early trail-blazer.

Kirkwood played in the British Open and performed exceedingly well with several top ten finishes. He later played in the USA but even though he won some tournaments he could not survive on the very poor prize money on offer in those days. Consequently, he teamed up with the legendary Walter Hagen. They toured the world doing exhibition matches and Kirkwood also became very famous for doing trick shots.

In the 1930s after Lou Kelly and Bill Bolger had both won Australian Opens, they both went over to the USA to play some tournaments along with George and Ted Naismith and some other NSW pros. Unfortunately, it was a very short tour and not at all profitable.

The most successful of the early Australians to play regularly overseas was probably Jim Ferrier. After winning the 1938 and 1939 Australian Opens as an amateur, he turned pro and after the war played more or less exclusively in the USA. He had a fair degree of success winning many PGA tour events and a US Major. Ferrier was in fact the first ever Australian golfer to win a Major tournament. He would not have been super rich but he would have had a very comfortable living. His most successful time on the US PGA tour was between 1946 and 1951. During that period he hovered around fifth on the earnings list and averaged approximately US$16,000 per year in prize money.

Norman von Nida was also one of the early pioneers to tour overseas. He played before and after the war in England and also on the Asian tour. He won three Australian Opens and plenty of tournaments on the British circuit but he did not win any overseas majors or any PGA tour events. Like Jim Ferrier, he would have been very comfortable.

Throughout the 1950s most of the players who regularly finished in the top ten in Australian tournaments were also travelling overseas to play including von Nida, Thomson, Nagle, Pickworth, Cremin and Phillips. Jack Harris was the notable exception. He never travelled outside of Australia during that peak period of his career. There were plenty of other Australian club professionals who also never travelled outside of Australia but none who managed to accumulate such a great playing record as Jack Harris.

In the year that Jack Harris left school and started work as an assistant pro, the total US Masters purse was US$5000 and the winners share was US$1500. This is quite a tidy sum when one considers that Jack Harris, as a fourteen year old, was paid only fifteen shillings and six pence per week in 1936. The average adult male weekly wage in Australia in 1936 was four pounds, one shilling and seven pence. So as an assistant golf professional, Jack was paid only about twenty percent of an adult wage.

Peter Thomson was travelling extensively as soon as he turned professional to just about every place on earth where he could find a golf tournament being played. When he won his five British Open golf championships the prize money for the winner was as follows:

1954	£750	(£937 Australian)[3]
1955	£1000	(1250)
1956	£1000	(1250)
1958	£1000	(1250)
1965	£1750	(2187)

If we forget about travelling expenses, income tax and caddie fees, this is still over two years' average wages in Australia in 1955 before tax or maybe one year's salary for a management job.[4] But a big chunk of this would quickly disappear if the golfer had to pay for his own travelling and accommodation expenses.

Another way to look at the British Open winner's cheque for say 1955 is to compare this with the price of a Rolls Royce Silver Cloud. In 1955 a Silver Cloud cost about £5000 so a golfer would need to win five British Opens to buy one Rolls Royce ignoring tax and travel costs. If this is compared to the prize money offered in the 2013 British Open the winner received £945,000 and a Rolls Royce Phantom costs about half of that. In other words, the money from just *one* British Open in 2013 can buy *two* Rolls Royce cars.

We can also compare the two periods by looking at the average wage to prize money ratio. In 2013 the British Open winner's cheque was equivalent to about thirty-three years average Australian workers wage whereas in 1955 the winner's cheque was only about thirty-six month's salary for the average worker!

---

3 The Australian pound had been pegged at 0.80 English pounds since December 1931. It didn't change until decimal currency was introduced into Australia on 14 February, 1966. At that time the Aussie dollar was de-valued. An English pound was suddenly worth two Australian dollars instead of 1.25 Australian pounds.

4 Average wage was only about ten Australian pounds per week.

Since 1950 the average wage of a worker in Australia has gone up about one hundred times but the average British Open winners prize has gone up about one thousand two hundred and fifty times.

This can easily explain why the top golfers these days who are winning major tournaments or even regular PGA tour events don't bother with mundane possessions like buying Rolls Royces. These days they go for luxury yachts or maybe even their own Lear jet!

Talk about golfers going from paupers to princes! At least as far as the top golfers are concerned. For the less successful however, being a professional golfer in 2013 is still a very tough gig, just as it was in Jack Harris's day.

It is safe to say that Peter Thomson was the most successful Australian golfer during the period when Jack Harris played. However, the prize money he won during that early phase of his career would not have put him in the mega-rich category. Later in his career, Peter Thomson played on the US Seniors Tour with significantly more success than he had earlier enjoyed on the regular US tour. The Seniors Tour is undoubtedly where he eventually won most of his prize money.

In fact, Thomson's best year on the Seniors Tour was in 1985 when he won six out of twenty-two events and topped the Money List that year with earnings of $386,724. In 1987 Thomson's career earnings on the Seniors Tour had been $955,718. He also branched out into golf course design and that too would have been 'a nice little earner,' as Arthur Daly of TV's *Minder* fame would have said.

The Antipodean star on the Senior Tour from that era was in fact New Zealander Sir Bob Charles. However, he was only just getting started on the Seniors Tour around the time Peter Thomson was finishing. By as late as the year 2000 he had career earnings on that tour of just over eight million dollars. But even Sir Bob doesn't get close to all-time leader on the Seniors Tour after the 2013 season, Hale Irwin, who by then had amassed $26.75 million.

The problem in Jack Harris's days was that in most tournaments only the top few golfers won any worthwhile cash. The prize money did not go all the way down the list of golfers who made the cut like it does today. For example, in 1962 the total purse in the Victorian Open was £1500 and only the top twelve received anything at all. A year earlier, when Jack Harris won the £500 Henderson purse at Rosebud the first prize was only £150.

Another problem was that although there was a scattering of smaller local tournaments throughout the year which Jack and his peers could play in, big tournaments in Australia were few and far between. Nevertheless Jack Harris won more than his fair share of the smaller events and he was nearly always in the mix for the big tournaments. So at least he was picking up some purse money on a regular basis to help supplement his teaching income.

Many of the smaller purses such as the Woodend were only £50 or £100 and only the top three or four players received any money. Even the tournaments sponsored by the big sporting companies Dunlop, Spalding and Slazenger only offered £200 purses. The bigger money tournaments like the Ampol, McWilliams Wines, Advertiser, Mobilco, Pelaco, Speedo, Coles and Wills Classic did increase the total prize money into the £2500 to £5000 range. These tournaments were often staged in a cluster around October / November but at least the prize money stretched a bit further down the playing list. For example the £2500 McWilliams Wines purse in 1952 gave £600 to the winner, £300 to the runner-up, £200 for third, £132 for fourth and £91 for sixth. This still left about half of the total purse money to be distributed in smaller lots to the players down the field.

The Ampol and McWilliams Wines were the biggest money events in the early 1950s and both these events regularly attracted some foreign players. The visiting American stars who played in the Ampol tournaments also received appearance money in addition to competing for the prize money. On top of their higher US Tour earnings this definitely made them relatively wealthy compared to their poor Australian golfing cousins. The British Ryder Cup players who often came during that period were also presumably paid appearance money.

From a prestige point of view I suppose that the Australian Open Championship was the tournament every Australian golfer wanted to win. However, this event did not offer the biggest prize money. When von Nida won it in 1953 he only won £150. When Frank Phillips won it in 1957, the winner's cheque was still only £250.

On the other hand, tournaments such as the Ampol, Pelaco, Coles, McWilliams Wines, Adelaide Advertiser and Wills Classic were somewhat more lucrative.

In 1952 von Nida won £650 for winning the McWilliams Wines tournament and Ossie Pickworth received £300 for second place. Even Jack Harris got £132 for tied fourth alongside Ryder Cup player and 1951 reigning British Open winner Max Faulkner.

In 1952 the Ampol total purse was £3000. The top four place getters all won more than the 1957 Australian Open winner (£650, £450, £350 and £300 respectively). In 1954 the first place prize in the Ampol had increased from £625 to £1500. Jack Harris tied third in that event which was won by US player Dutch Harrison, so he most likely won £500 or £600.

In 1955 the first prize in the Pelaco tournament was £1000. Peter Thomson was the winner on that occasion. Jack Harris was fifth and so no doubt also had another worthwhile pay day.

However, it wasn't until the late 1960s before five figure golf purses started to appear in Australia with tournaments like the Dunlop International.

From all the above, it will be very easy for the reader to understand that it would have been nigh on impossible for a golf professional in Jack Harris's day to survive on prize money alone if he only played Australian tournaments. Bearing in mind that every golfer who ever played the game always lost many more tournaments than he won.

There were two big game changers which happened on Jack Harris's watch which eventually had a massive impact on the whole golfing scene, particularly on players' earning potential as tournament prize money sums began to increase.

The first was the advent of television (TV). Most ordinary working class folk in England bought their first small black and white TV with a twelve-inch screen in 1953, just in time to watch Queen Elizabeth II's coronation. In Australia the driver behind the introduction of TV was the 1956 Melbourne Summer Olympics. The first sporting event to be telecast live in Australia was the 1956 Pelaco golf tournament from the Lakes GC in Sydney. The first time the Australian Open golf was shown live on TV was in 1957 when Frank Phillips won at Kingston Heath. Jack Harris tied for eighth that year but still ahead of former Australian Open winners Eric

Cremin and Norman von Nida as well as an up and coming young Bruce Devlin. I guess the biggest breakthrough for golf with TV in Australia came in 1975 when full time colour TV rapidly burst on to the scene, having been introduced as early as 1967 in a limited way. In the USA the move from black and white to colour TV had already happened earlier and the transition was more or less complete by 1968.

The second big game changer was the appearance of Mark McCormack's IMG Sports Management group in the USA in about 1960. IMG had first signed up Arnold Palmer and quickly followed with Jack Nicklaus and Gary Player. Colour TV was already very common in the USA by the time the 'Big Three' started to dominate the scene. Within two years of starting up in the USA, IMG were already present in Australia. A 1962 newspaper report mentioned that Mark McCormack had offered a guaranteed £4500 each to Ted Ball, Bruce Devlin and Alan Murray to play on the US circuit. In Jack Harris's day none of the golf pros had a management team looking after their interests. If you were lucky you may have a rich tycoon such as Kerry Packer who could bankroll you but most pros were, effectively, on their own.

As TV viewing rights and management group participation developed, the tournament prize money started to significantly improve from the early 1960s onwards. But all this was mostly too late for Jack Harris. He was already about forty years old and was approaching the end of his playing career.

Overseas, especially in the USA, film stars and famous celebrities such as Bob Hope and Bing Crosby started to play golf and this also helped to further promote the game.

It was not until the late 1970s that the concept of a Seniors Tour started to appear in Australia and even early 1980s before the US Senior Tour took off. Unfortunately, Jack Harris and most of his peers missed out on that as well.

If big changes were happening on the golfing scene during Jack Harris's time, it was all relatively minor compared to what was happening in the world at large. In the twenty-five years after the Second World War ended, from 1945 up to 1970, the changes in the world political scene were enormous. Moreover, those changes were the greatest in Australia's part of the world. One by one all the countries in the Asia Pacific region which had been ruled by a Western government gained their independence. India, Malaysia, Singapore, Burma, Pakistan and Bangladesh all broke out of the

British Empire. Indonesia freed itself from the Dutch and the Philippines from the USA. France let go of Vietnam, Cambodia and Laos. Hong Kong was an oddball. It had been occupied by the Japanese from 1941 to 1945 but after they had been sent home it remained a British Colony until 1997 when sovereignty was transferred back to the Chinese.

All these changes facilitated the growth of golf in many of those countries. Jack Harris would not have directly witnessed the change because he never travelled in that region to play golf. But I imagine that Peter Thomson, Eric Cremin, Kel Nagle, Frank Phillips, Ted Ball and a host of others would have seen the changes firsthand since they regularly played tournaments there. And the guy who undoubtedly saw more changes than most would have been Norman von Nida because he first started going to Asia even before the war in his never ending search for prize money.

Indirectly, Jack Harris would have felt the impact of these changes even within Australia because there was a steady stream of Asian visitors coming to play in local tournaments. Filipinos Larry Montes and Celestino Tugot were two regulars who Jack played against. As were Japanese players Pete Nakamura and Hideyo Sugimoto.

These days, prize money is only one of many income sources for the world's best golfers. The top performers often earn much more from their sponsorship deals than they do from their prize money. When Tiger Woods was reported a few years ago to have become the world's first sporting billionaire, the prize money he had earned at that stage was only about ten per cent of his total earnings. Almost every square inch of space on their shirt, cap and golf-bag is utilised for lucrative endorsement deals.

The upper echelon is also able to command appearance money when they play at events away from the US PGA Tour. For instance, Tiger Woods played in the 2009 Australian Masters at Kingston Heath in Melbourne. The night before the opening round my eldest son, Jonathan, and I, slept in the back of his car near Kingston Heath GC so that we could be at the course early the next morning. That was the year when all his personal indiscretions hit the headlines. On that occasion he received three million dollars appearance money, fifty per cent of which was paid by the taxpayers of Victoria.

It reminded me of Irishman George Best the former Manchester United football star who once told the world that he had 'spent most of his money on wild women and booze and the rest he just wasted.' For the record, Tiger did win the 2009 Australian Masters by two strokes and picked up the relatively paltry $250,000 first prize money to go with his three million dollars appearance money. Definitely no more sleeping in the back of cars for me! At least not unless Jack Nicklaus comes out of retirement!

Appearance money was paid to visiting overseas stars even going back to Gene Sarazen's days in the 1930s. Ampol also sponsored visits by groups of US stars throughout the 1950s. Jack Harris regularly got to play against people such as Tommy Bolt, Dutch Harrison, Ed Furgol, Marty Furgol, Jim Turnesa, Lloyd Mangrum, Dave Douglas and others. He was very competitive against all these players and indeed he beat many of them in tournament play.

These days appearance money is regularly and openly paid to the top stars to attract them to play in tournaments outside of the USA. Strictly speaking, it is not legal to pay appearance money on the US Tour. However, where there is a will there is a way! Instead of appearance money the stars are paid a big fee to participate in a Skins event or a Corporate Day immediately prior to the big tournament *et voilà*, all is sweet.

By contrast, most players in Jack Harris's era received very little sponsorship money. They may have received a small retainer from a golf club maker or golf ball manufacturer for playing with and promoting their products. However, I don't recall ever seeing anyone play with logos on their caps, shirts or golf bags. They may have also received free cigarettes but I doubt if any of the local players ever received tournament appearance money. The most they ever got would have been expense money when they played exhibition matches and gave golf clinics in provincial towns.

This all sounds to be very exciting times for modern golfers compared to golfers in Jack Harris's day, but is it really as good as it sounds? Have golfers really gone from paupers to princes? For the vast majority of professional golfers, their prospects have actually not improved that much since Jack Harris was playing. In fact, in many respects, their life has got even tougher. Most of them still have to earn their living by giving golf lessons or running pro shops.

There are estimated to be about 60 million people playing golf around the world. Maybe about 28 million of these play in the USA and about one million play in Australia.

This figure of 60 million could be quite low these days because although numbers in mature markets like USA, UK and Australia may be declining, emerging markets such as China are absolutely booming.

In the USA each year about 70 or 80 billion dollars is spent on golf. In Australia about three billion dollars is spent.

With over one million golfers in Australia and over three billion dollars now spent on golf, what a great legacy was left by the immediate post-war golfing pioneers like Jack Harris who did an enormous amount of work to promote the game.

According to an article in the *Sunday Herald* dated 19 October 1952, there were 400,000 golfers in Australia and they only spent about £1.3 million on golf sticks and balls in that year. Compare this to the Ernst & Young / Australian Golf Industry Council report in 2010 which mentioned that 1.18 million players had spent about 180 million dollars on golf sticks and balls in 2008. Even allowing for around 900% inflation this still looks like a fairly handy growth.

The only problem for Australia is that in 1952, most of the golf sticks and golf balls would have actually been made in Australia. These days more or less all golf balls and golf sticks are imported apart from a few small niche areas.

The US PGA Tour is still the world's most lucrative tour and week in week out, the players are playing for a total purse of around eight or nine million dollars with the winner taking well over one million dollars share.

The problem is that there are only about 230 players worldwide who have either full or partial PGA tour cards. So your chances of being one of those 230 players are very low indeed. From the 230 qualified golfers, generally only about 150-160 play each week. Apart from a few exceptions, in most tournaments, the playing field is cut after two rounds to the top sixty and all ties (top sixty only in US Open). So even for the ones who qualify and play, more than half do not receive any prize money at all but they still have to pay their caddies and their travel and accommodation expenses.

What all this means is that if you play golf and you have any aspirations to be a top golfer who at least makes the cut in PGA tournaments, you have about one chance in a million of being successful. Even if we narrow the competition down to golfers who manage to reach the status of being a professional golfer, the odds are still very low that you will ever be good enough to play on one of the five main tours (PGA, European, Japan, and PGA Tour of Australasia or Sunshine Tour). I don't know how many golfers successfully reach the status of being a professional but let's say it may be 0.5% of all golfers. Even then, I think 0.5% could well be too high. That would mean there are about 300,000 golf pros in the world. If there are 230 pro golfers qualified with tour cards each week playing in each of the five main tours that is a total of 1150. That would mean that even as a pro you only have about one chance in 261 of being good enough to even play on any of these tours and maybe one chance in 6000 of being a top ten player. These are not exactly great odds.

I suppose that *if* you do manage to secure a PGA tour card, you don't actually need to win a single event to enjoy a nice lifestyle.

For example, all Australians, even those who don't play golf, will know from watching TV, that both Adam Scott and Jason Day will have earned a nice living playing golf in 2013. And sure enough, they are ranked sixth and twelfth respectively on the 2013 PGA Money list with prize money of $4.89 million and $ 3.63 million. But what about the third ranked Australian golfer on the US PGA 2013 Money list? Maybe we start to think about other well-known household names in Australia such as Robert Allenby, Stuart Appleby, Geoff Ogilvy or Aaron Baddeley, all of them former Australian Open winners.

Actually the third best Australian performer in 2013 on the PGA Tour was Matt Jones who travels mostly under the radar as far as most average Australians are concerned. Although he didn't win a single event on the PGA tour or even one back here in Australia during 2013, he still managed to finish number forty-eight on the PGA Money list and to amass a tidy sum of $1.72 million from twenty-four events. I don't know if he made the cut in all twenty-four events, but assuming that he did, he averaged about $72,000 per event or $18,000 for each round of golf played on the tour.

Even if he spent $100,000 in the year for travel and accommodation and paid his caddie, he would still have a sizeable bank balance remaining.

Since I wrote the preceding paragraph on Matt Jones, he has since just recorded his first ever US PGA win on April 6, 2014 when he beat Matt Kuchar in a play-off at the Shell Houston Open by chipping in from forty-two yards over a bunker and in the process picked up a cool $1.2 million. This also qualified him for his first start in the 2014 US Masters Tournament which starts very soon. Go Matt!

Not only is it very tough to secure a PGA Tour card, it is just as tough to continue to play at the high level required week after week especially when not making the cuts. For example, at twenty-eight years of age, US golfer David Duval, in 1999, was number one golfer in the world for a short while. He still played eight events on the PGA Tour in 2013 at age forty-two, but only won $6200. Why would you bother? Maybe he is just marking time until he reaches fifty years of age when he can qualify to go on the Senior Tour?

It probably all boils down to a very rewarding pension plan which the PGA put into place in 1983. Arguably golf has the best pension plan of any professional sport. There are various elements to the scheme which are too complicated to try to explain here. But in a nutshell, providing the player makes a significant number of cuts, he can finish his career with a sizeable nest egg. The downside is that it is not so good if you don't make cuts. The upside is that you don't need to win a single tournament either. Even battlers who make enough cuts can find themselves with several million dollars in their account when they finally give it away. Provided that enough cuts are made, the nest egg keeps on growing. And it is pre-tax money which is compounding. As far as I understand it, when a player finishes on the regular tour and moves on to the Seniors Tour, the pension is just carried forward. It is probably only half as good as the pension which Australian politicians receive when they retire but that still means it is an extremely generous scheme.

Despite the extremely tough entry level requirements for any of the five main Tours, there are still many golfers around the world who just slug away for years on the so called Mini-Tours. Prize money at these events wouldn't even feed your cat after travel expenses. On the other hand, golfers who do eventually make it to one of the five main tours can and do often have long and fruitful careers. After the regular tours they can play in the senior tours once they have turned fifty years of age. As mentioned earlier, Peter Thomson did quite well on the Senior Tour and these days Peter Senior is also prolonging his career on the Champions Tour. In 2013 he was ranked thirteenth on the Senior Tour and earned $1.15 million prize money from twenty-five events. Even after taking out his caddie fees and travel expenses, he would still have made a nice sum.

As far as Jack Harris is concerned, it is easy to just say that he, along with many other golfers of his era, was simply born too early. But is that just wishful thinking? Would the likes of Jack Harris and Ossie Pickworth been able to perform on the world stage if their circumstances had been different? In my view the answer to this is a definite yes. During the era they played they would both have done well if they had chosen to be touring professionals rather than club based professionals.

As regards to how they would have fared in the modern era that is an entirely different proposition. These days the strength and depth of competition in all top tournaments is far greater than it was in the 1946-1970 period.

If we ignore the technology advances we have seen during the modern era, it is maybe safe to say that the best world players during Jack Harris's day would have been competitive against the best players today. However, the big difference is that today the sheer number of great players in any given tournament makes it exceedingly difficult to succeed.

When Jack Harris played, the winner of any of the big tournaments could usually be picked from just a handful of pre-tournament favourites. These days, in any PGA event or even in a major, any one of scores of great players can bob up and win.

Club professionals don't even get the opportunity these days to play against the world's best like they did in Jack Harris's day. However, the fact that Jack *did* have that opportunity and *did* perform well against the world's best of that era speaks for itself. Had he been a touring professional in the modern era the chances are that he would have done pretty well for himself.

One only has to have a cursory glance at the following list of world famous golfers and well-credentialed local stars who Jack Harris managed to beat or tied with to realise that he was an extremely talented golfer.

Ake Berquist	1959 Swedish Canada Cup player
Alan Brookes	South African winner of 1963 Singapore Open
Alan Murray	Australian PGA champion
Alan Waterson	Australian Amateur champion
Alex Murray	NZ Open winner
Alfonso Angelini	1959 Italian Canada Cup team
Andrew Shaw	seven-time winner of NZ PGA and NZ Open
Angel Miguel Gutierrez	Madrileño British Open player
Arnold Stickley	1960 British PGA Close champion
Arthur Gazzard	Qld Open and Qld PGA winner
Arthur Le Fevre	Australian Open winner
Barry Baker	Australian Amateur champion
Barry Franklin	South African 1968 German Open winner
Barry Warren	Australian Amateur champion
Bernard Hunt	Ryder Cup player
Bill Ackland-Horman	Australian Amateur champion
Bill Bolger	Australian Open winner
Bill Britten	Victorian PGA champion
Bill Clifford	Australian PGA winner
Bill Hector	1960 Martini Foursomes winner
Bill Holder	Australian PGA winner
Bill McPherson	WA Open winner
Bill Robertson	Australian PGA winner
Billy Dunk	five time Australian PGA champion
Bob Shearer	Australian Open winner
Bob Stanton	Australian Open runner-up
Bob Stevens	Australian Amateur champion
Bobby Cole	Dual South African Open winner
Bobby Locke	four times British Open winner
Brian Bamford	British PGA champion and Canada Cup player
Brian Boys	NZ World Cup player
Brian Henning	South African Hall of Famer

Brian Jones	Australian World Cup player
Brian Silk	NZ Amateur champion
Brian Waites	World Cup and Ryder Cup player
Brian Wilkes	South African winner of 1960 Italian Open
Bruce Crampton	Australian Open winner
Bruce Devlin	Australian Open winner
Carl Poulsen	Danish Canada Cup player
Cedric Amm	1966 South African Masters winner
Celestino Tugot	six time Philippines Open winner
Charles Booth	NSW PGA champion
Charlie Brown	Qld Open / QLD PGA winner
Charlie Snow	WA Open / PGA winner
Chen Ching-Pu	1959 Chinese Canada Cup player
Christy O'Connor	Played in ten Ryder Cup teams
Clive Clark	1965 Walker Cup player and third in 1967 British Open
Cobie Legrange	1964 Dunlop Masters and Wills Classic winner
Col Johnston	Dual Australian PGA winner
Dai Rees	three times runner-up in British Open and Ryder Cup player
Dave Thomas	Ryder Cup player
David Graham	US PGA and US Open winner
David Snell	British Matchplay Champion
Denis Hutchinson	French Open winner
Dick Carr	Queensland PGA / Open champion
Dick Chapman	US and British amateur champion
Dick Metz	US Open runner-up, 10 PGA tour wins including 17 top ten finishes in majors
Don Spence	NSW PGA winner
Donald Swaelens	German Open winner 1967
Doug Bachli	British amateur champion
Doug Katterns	Queensland PGA winner
Dudley Millensted	1967 Walker Cup player
Ed Oliver	runner-up in three majors plus fifteen PGA tour wins
Eddie Anderson	Queensland PGA champion

Enrique Orellana	twice winner of Chilean Open and Canada Cup player
Eric Alberts	WA Open / PGA winner
Eric Brown	Ryder cup player and twice runner-up in the British Open
Eric Cremin	Australian Open winner
Eric Lester	Penfold Swallow winner
Ernie Southerden	three time NZ PGA winner Cup player
Fernando Pina	1959 Portuguese Canada Cup player
Fidel de Luca	4 Argentine Opens and 5 Argentine PGA's, German Open, Canada Cup player
Flory Van Donck	twice runner-up in British Open 1956, 1959
Frank Buckler	NZ Canada Cup player
Frank Eyre	Australian Open winner
Frank Jowle	3rd behind Peter Thompson in 1954 British Open
Frank Phillips	two times Australian Open winner
Fred Boobyer	British Open player
Fred Popplewell	Australian Open winner
Fred Thompson	WA Open/ WA PGA winner
Freidrich and Herbert Becker	1959 German Canada Cup team
G Johnson	WA Open and WA PGA champion
George Bayer	Tied third in 1962 US PGA
George Bayer	four US PGA Tour events, runner-up 1950 US Masters
George Naismith	Australian Open winner
Gerard de Wit	five times Dutch Open runner-up
Glenn McCully	Victorian PGA winner
Graham Marsh	ten wins on European Tour, one PGA Tour win
Guy Wolstenholme	Triple Victorian Open winner
Harold Henning	twice tied third in British Open
Harry Berwick	Australian Amateur champion
Harry Bradshaw	Ryder Cup player and nine Irish PGAs
Harry Hattersley	Australian Amateur champion
Harry Karlsson	1959 Swedish Canada Cup player
Harry Kershaw	1959 NSW Open champion.
Harry Sinclair	Australian Amateur champion
Harry Weetman	long time Ryder Cup player

Haruyoshi Kobari	1959 Japanese Canada Cup player
Hedley Muscroft	British Matchplay semi-finalist
Henning Christensen	Danish Canada Cup player
Henrique Paulino	1959 Portuguese Canada Cup player
Hideyo Sugimoto	Japanese World Cup player
Horace Boorer	Victorian PGA winner
Hugh Boyle	World Cup and Ryder Cup player
Ian Stanley	1975 Martini International winner
Jack Brown	Qld Open / Qld PGA winner
Jack Hargreaves	1951 Ryder Cup team
Jack Newton	Australian Open winner and British Open runner-up
Jack Rayner	Australian Amateur champion
Jacky Bonvin	1959 Swiss Canada Cup team
Jerry Stolhand	Australian Seniors Champion
Jim Ferrier	1947 US PGA, 18 US PGA Tour wins
Jimmy Demaret	three times US Masters Winner plus 31 PGA tour wins
Jimmy Hitchcock	British Ryder Cup player
John Fallon	Ryder Cup player
John Hayes	runner-up behind Gary Player in 1965 South African Open
John Hayes	South African Australian Amateur champion
John Jacobs	Dutch Open champion and Ryder Cup player
John Kelly	NZ Canada cup player
John Klatt	Qld PGA winner
John Lister	NZ PGA winner and World Cup player
John Panton	Ryder Cup player with four top ten finishes in British Open
John Sharkey	British PGA Cup team vs USA
John Sullivan	Australian PGA winner
Joop Rühl	1959 Dutch Canada Cup player
Jose Gonzales	Mexican Canada Cup player
Juan Neri	1959 Mexican Canada Cup player
Justin Seward	WA Amateur champion
Keith Pix	WA Open winner
Kel Nagle	British Open winner and Australian Open winner
Kelly Rogers	WA Open champion

Kevin Donohoe	Australian Amateur champion
Kevin Hartley	Australian Amateur champion
Larry Harke	WA Amateur champion
Larry Montes	twelve times winner of Philippines Open
Leopoldo Ruiz	six times Argentinian PGA champion
Les Nichols	WA Open and WA PGA winner
Les Wilson	Australian PGA winner
Lionel Platts	Ryder Cup player
Lou Kelly	Australian Open winner
Luciano Calderon	1959 Chilean Canada Cup player
Mario Gonzales	Eight time Brazilian Open winner
Mark Tapper	1976 NSW PGA winner
Martin Roesink	three times winner of Twente Cup in Holland
Marty Furgol	five PGA tour wins and three top ten finishes in majors
Maurice Bembridge	Four times Ryder cup team
Max Faulkner	British Open winner
Michael Busk	British Open player from New Zealand
Miguel Sala	1959 Colombian Canada Cup team
Mike Cahill	1977 Australian PGA champion
Neil Coles	played in eight Ryder Cup teams
Norman Drew	Irish Ryder Cup and Canada Cup player
Norman von Nida	three times Australian Open winner
Ossie Pickworth	four times Australian Open winner
Ossie Walker	Queensland PGA champion
Otto Schoepfer	1959 Swiss Canada Cup team
Pablo Molina	1959 Colombian Canada Cup team
Peter Alliss	played in eight Ryder Cup teams
Peter Butler	Ryder Cup and World Cup player
Peter Croker	Australian PGA runner-up
Peter Harvey	1968 Queensland Open and 1970 Garden City Classic winner
Peter Heard	Australian Amateur champion
Peter Thomson	five times British Open winner
Peter Toogood	Australian Amateur champion
Pradana Ngarmprom	World Cup player
Ralph Moffitt	Ryder Cup player

From Paupers to Princes? 81

Ralph Peter Mills	British Ryder Cup player
Ramon Sota	won Spanish, French, Dutch, Portuguese and Italian Opens
Randall Hicks	Australian Amateur champion
Reg Jupp	Victorian PGA winner
Reg Want	Eight times winner of Queensland PGA, Qld Open winner
Robert De Vicenzo	1957 British Open winner
Ron Harris	Australian PGA runner-up
Ron Howell	runner-up Victorian PGA and Australian PGA
Ross Newdick	NZ PGA winner
Roy Draddy	WA PGA winner
Said Muossa	twenty-four times winner of Egyptian Open
Salim	1959 Indonesian Canada Cup player
Sam Richardson	Australian PGA winner
Sebastian Miguel	three time Spanish Open winner
Sewsunker Sewgolum	Triple Dutch Open winner
Sir Bob Charles	British Open winner
Sir Henry Cotton	Triple British Open winner
Sjamsudin	1959 Indonesian Canada Cup player
Stan Leonard	eight Canadian PGAs and three US PGA Tour wins
Stewart Ginn	Victorian PGA and Victorian Open winner
Syd Scott	Ryder Cup player
Ted Ball	Two time Wills Masters winner
Ted Naismith	Australian PGA winner
Ted Smith	dual Victorian PGA winner
Ted Taylor	WA Open winner
Terry Kendall	NZ PGA champion
Tim Woolbank	Queensland Open winner
Tim Woon	four times NZ amateur champion
Tom Crow	Australian Amateur champion
Tom Howard	Australian Open winner
Tom Linskey	1977 Australian Long Driving champion
Tommy Bolt	US Open winner plus fifteen PGA tour wins
Tony Limon	Australian amateur foursomes champion
Torakichi "Pete" Nakamura	1957 Canada Cup winner, triple Japan PGA champion

Trevor Wilkes	South African runner-up in 1956 French Open Cherif Said twice won Egyptian Open
Vic Allin	1959 Filipino Canada Cup player
Vic Bennetts	Australian PGA winner
Walter Godfrey	1972 Hong Kong Open winner
Walter Lees	Midland Professional champion
Willie Harvey	multiple SA PGA champion
Yoshimasha Fujii	Japanese Open winner
Yung Yo Shieh	1959 Chinese Canada cup player

Jack Harris played tournaments over such a long period which overlapped several generations of golfers. It is interesting to note that he beat the following groups of golfers. In each case the number refers to different golfers, bearing in mind that many of these winners also won an event on multiple occasions.

- 21   Australian Open champions
- 26   Australian PGA champions
- 52+ Canada Cup / World Cup players (including 10 winners of the Canada Cup)
- 7   British Open champions
- 8   British PGA champions
- 7   British PGA Close champions
- 25   British Ryder Cup players
- 3   American Ryder Cup players
- 13   British PGA Matchplay champions
- 3   British Amateur champions
- 2   US Open champions
- 2   US PGA champions
- 16   Dutch Open winners
- 16   German Open winners
- 14   French Open winners
- 1   US Amateur champion
- 27   Victorian PGA champions
- 16   Victorian Open champions
- 22   Australian Amateur champions
- 22   Victorian Amateur champions

21	NSW Open champions
22	NSW PGA champions
24	QLD Open champions
18	QLD PGA champions
15	Tasmanian Open champions
20	WA Open champions
14	WA PGA winners
11	South African Open champions
3	Japanese Open champions
1	Japanese PGA champion
12	NZ Open champions
15	NZ PGA champions
6	NZ amateur champions

Jack Harris also had the privilege of playing against 25 players who eventually found their way into the World Golf Hall of Fame. He beat almost half of them in tournament play and took rounds off nearly all the others in tournaments.

Perhaps readers have not heard of many of these players. However, just consider that collectively they won twenty major championships, over 120 PGA tour events, 30 Australian Opens, made over 100 Ryder Cup appearances and over 200 Canada Cup / World Cup appearances. This is the quality of player that Jack Harris often used to beat in tournament play.

Towards the end of his tournament career, Jack Harris also played a few times against Jack Nicklaus, Arnold Palmer and Gary Player and each time he was always in the mix. As far as I was able to ascertain, Jack never managed to beat any of the so-called Big Three in tournament play but he did sometimes outplay them all in some individual rounds within a tournament.

A big thrill for Jack would have been in a practice round just prior to the 1962 Wills Classic at the Australian GC. He played with Jack Nicklaus, Gary Player and Bruce Devlin. Jack Harris and Gary Player both shot six under par 66s. Jack Harris shot a fantastic six under par 30 on the front nine of this particular round. After the first round of the tournament proper Jack Harris was tied on 71 with Gary Player and one shot ahead of Nicklaus. When the tournament finished Jack Harris (296) was just six shots behind

Nicklaus (290) and eight shots behind Player (288). Nicklaus had arrived into Australia having just won his first major, the US Open. Gary Player was already a three times major winner. Not a bad effort by forty years old weekend golfer Jack Harris against the current US Open champion! For the record Bruce Devlin (281) won the Wills Classic that year.

The absolutely amazing aspect about the above list is that virtually all these golfers were battle hardened players with wide overseas touring experience or at least some overseas experience, whereas Jack Harris had none. And few if indeed any of them at all spent eight or ten hours a day, five days per week teaching golf like Jack Harris did with minimal time to practice. Couple that with lost war years and four years after the war working in a city indoor driving range in nets off rubber mats, and it is doubly amazing what Jack Harris managed to achieve.

Although working at an indoor golf school would not really help Jack's own personal golf game, I suppose it did have one big advantage: it was not exposed to the vagaries of the unpredictable Melbourne weather. Therefore, the income stream would have been more reliable and more predictable. This is not always the case in a golf course situation where golf lessons are often cancelled due to inclement weather.

Ossie Pickworth, who Jack had played against continuously for twelve years after they both came back from Borneo, did not make a great deal of money from the sport. This was despite the fact that he had won four Australian Opens, an Irish Open and more than 100 other Australian tournaments when he retired from golf in 1958 at the age of forty.

In fact in an article dated Feb 25, 1953 in *The West Australian* newspaper, Perth, it was reported that Ossie had just resigned from his club professional job at the Royal Melbourne GC. It went on to say that during his time at Royal Melbourne, Ossie had not been paid a retainer by the club and 'He would have had to survive on a mere pittance after paying overhead expenses had he been forced to depend on his business at the club for a livelihood. He only survived because he won prize money in tournaments, had a small retainer and expenses from a sporting goods firm and gave lessons outside of the club.'

Royal Melbourne was the most exclusive golf club in Victoria. One can only imagine that the majority of club professionals at smaller less prestigious clubs would also have been struggling, especially considering that most of them were nowhere near as successful as Ossie Pickworth at winning tournaments. Luckily for Ossie and his family, a financial solution came from a totally unexpected direction.

Jack vividly remembers one day when he was teaching at Keysborough GC, Ossie drove up to the club in a new car to tell Jack about his retirement. Ossie told Jack that he had won £10,000 on Tattslotto and that he was buying the Railway Hotel pub in Hawthorn and retiring from golf. Shortly after, there was a testimonial game for Ossie held at Rossdale GC. Ossie, Jack and Bob Brown all tied on seventy-two. Perhaps fittingly, Ossie was declared the winner on a count back! Ossie ran his pub for the next eleven years or so but sadly died in 1969 still shy of his fifty-second birthday.

After Ossie retired, Jack played on for about another eleven years until he also retired from tournament play in 1969 at age forty-seven. Just like Ossie, Jack Harris had not amassed a great fortune from his tournament days.

At this stage Jack went back to full time teaching and opened up his own indoor city golf school in Chapel Street, St Kilda with one of his former pupils, Trevor Hollingsworth.

While he was still running that school, in 1979, there was a senior golfer's event at Manly GC in Sydney sponsored by the Citizens Watch Company. Although he hadn't played any tournaments for the last ten years apart from a few local pro-am events, fifty-seven year old Jack Harris was tempted to pull his rusty clubs out of the garage and rub the mould off his golf bag. He played with Art Wall Jr in that event. Art had been the leading money winner on the US Tour in 1959 and had won the US Masters that year with one of the best finishes ever seen when he scored five birdies and a par on the last six holes to beat Cary Middlecoff. Arnold Palmer was third. A young nineteen year old chap called Jack Nicklaus made his Masters debut that year and missed the cut by one stroke.

For the record the Manly Citizens Watch event was won by Tommy Bolt on 214. Art Wall came in with 221 and Jack Harris had a 225. Sam Snead also played and scored 224. Sam was quite a bit older than Jack Harris but nevertheless he was still a formidable competitor. In 1979 Sam had still managed to make the cut on a regular PGA tour event at age sixty-seven, the oldest player ever to do so. Bobby Locke came home with 230. Peter Thomson who had just reached fifty years of age could have played in this tournament but chose not to. Maybe because he had bigger fish to fry on the US Senior Tour which was pretty close to kicking off.

It was during this tournament that Jack Harris first had the opportunity of meeting Kerry Packer and the Lavenders who he was introduced to by Norman von Nida. These were apparently a group of guys who shared Packer's love of gambling. No doubt they had pinched their name from the 1951 comedy film the *Lavender Hill Mob* which involved smuggling stolen gold out of England over to France in the guise of Eiffel Tower paperweights. There were about a couple of dozen men in the Lavenders group. They were all influential businessmen who were members of the Australian GC one of Australia's oldest golf clubs which had been founded in 1882. This group liked to play for very high stakes and they would bet against everyone else in the group on the result of each nine holes and the full round. Apparently vast amounts of money exchanged hands after each game. Jack Harris was very fond of a bet himself but this was one betting school he just could not afford to play in.

Jack Harris hung up his tournament playing boots again after the Citizens Watch but continued to teach in his city school until he got a call for help from Sorrento GC.

Chapter 8

Brotherly Love

One point which struck me when I was doing the research for this book was how many fathers and sons and how many brothers were involved in the golf pro business in Australia both before and after the Second World War.

When I lived in the UK, I remember a few father and son instances such as Percy and Peter Alliss or right at the very beginning Old Tom Morris and Young Tom Morris, but I can't recall many of them. Maybe it was the same in the UK and I just wasn't tuned in to it? In Australia however, fathers, sons and brothers in the golf pro business were certainly very common indeed in the bygone era. This family approach doesn't seem to be as prevalent today. At least I never heard of a Charlie Norman or a Tom Allenby or a Roger Ogilvy! A list of the family golfers who I came across is as follows:

Alan, Ron and Ray Smith
Alan, Stewart and Jim Maiden
Albert and Bill Robertson and father Jack
Albert and Fred Findlay
Alec and Dave Mercer
Alec and Duncan Denholm
Alec and Frank Kynnersley
Alf and Fred Findlay
Arthur and Ernest Le Fevre Bill
Arthur, Don and Harry Spence
Bert and Des Ferguson
Bill and Jack Clifford
Brian and Harry Huxtable
Brian, Murray and Jane Crafter
Cliff, George and Ted Naismith
Colin and Bob Campbell and nephew Bob Spencer

Colin and Ken Johnston
Dan, Jim and Don Cullen
David and Peter Johnston
Denis and EJ Denehey
Don and Alan Reiter
Don and Bill Walker
Doug and Len Katterns
Eric and Bill Wishart
Ern and Les Chaplin
Ernie, Geoff and Ernie Jr. Wood
Fred and Ted Bolger
Fred and Tom Popplewell
Fred Belle and son Graham Belle
Geoff and Ted Parslow
George, Bill and Henry Cussell
Harry Berwick and cousin Norman
Jack and Alec Harris
Jack and Les Rayner
Jack and Sid Coogan
John and Alf Toogood
Lenny, Horrie and Jack Boorer
Les and Neville Wilson
Martin and Brian Smith
Murray and Brian Crafter
Norman and Dudley von Nida
One-putt Charlie and Jack Brown
Ossie and Alan Pickworth
Peter and Tony Thomson
Ron and Jim Petterson
Sid, Tony and Charlie Cowling
Ted Cates and son Graeme
Tom and Charlie Booth
Tom and Peter Heard
Tom Howard and son Albert
Trevor, Ron and Phil Hollingsworth

There could well be many more I have missed.

Usually one member of the family was significantly better than the other. However, in a few cases, both names could often be seen on the same leader board, especially the Naismiths, the Toogoods, the Boorers, the Spences and the Bolgers.

Billy Bolger became famous when in 1934 he shattered the course record at Royal Sydney by seven shots in the Australian Open and beat the legendary US player, Gene Sarazen by three strokes.

Three years later in 1937, George Naismith also won the Australian Open at the Australian GC (Kensington). His brother Ted had three top five finishes in the Australian Open in the 1930s and another two in 1947 and 1949. He was another golfer possibly robbed by the war.

The Toogoods was a family of terrific amateur golfers from Tasmania. All of them could play great golf but Peter was the one who stood out with many excellent performances in the Australian Open in the early 1950s. In 1948, his father Alf had beaten Jack Harris by one stroke in the Australian Open. Ossie Pickworth won the Open that year in a play-off against Jim Ferrier.

Arthur and Don Spence were also perhaps two of the unlucky golfers who lost their peak opportunity to win an Australian Open during the 1939-1946 war years. Before the war they had both performed consistently well in the Australian Open, each having at least three top ten finishes in the late 1920s and early 1930s. Don finished third in 1934 and Arthur was fourth in 1930.

In the early days Jack Harris's brother Alec was club professional at Cheltenham GC but he did not persist with golf as a profession and changed career after a short stint.

Interestingly enough, when the first ever professional tournament was played at the Albert Park course in 1953, Jack Harris played against five of the above list in the same field. [5]

On that day Jack shot 65 and smashed the course record by ten shots. His nearest opponent, Martin Smith, former runner-up in the Australian Open, shot 72.

According to Ossie Pickworth, his brother Alan would have been a better player than him if he had continued to play golf. Alan played in the

---

5   Jack Boorer, Bill Clifford, Ted Naismith, Len Boorer and Bert Ferguson.

final of the 1946 NSW caddie championships having beaten sixteen years old Tony Rafty in the semi-final. Rafty had shot a sixty-eight off the back tee at Manly GC in an earlier round. Neither Rafty nor Alan Pickworth pursued a career in golf after that. Rafty went on to become a renowned Australian cartoonist and had been an official war artist during the Second World War. In fact he was in Kuching, Sarawak in September, 1945 when it was liberated from the Japanese by the Australian Armed Forces. This was not all that far away from Labuan Island, Borneo where Jack Harris had been stationed. In 1964 Tony Rafty did a famous cartoon of Arnold Palmer playing from the branches of a tree in the Wills Masters tournament at Victoria GC which featured three kookaburras laughing at Palmer.

Col Johnston was a legend. In 1958 he lost his right eye in an accident at work but that didn't stop him playing great golf. He won the Australian PGA at Oatlands GC in 1963 when he beat American Ron Howell three and two. The following year he successfully defended his title at Monash Country Club under a stroke play format. On this occasion he beat both Bruce Devlin and Peter Thomson. Earlier, in 1961, Col Johnston had tied fourteenth in the Australian Open at Victoria GC, eight strokes behind Jack Harris. Jack had finished in sixth place, two strokes behind Peter Thomson.

The Rayner brothers were champions from Queensland. Jack Rayner won the Australian Amateur Championship in 1955. Les had been a Queensland champion when he was only eighteen years old but sadly he was killed in a plane crash when he was just twenty.

The Coogan brothers were also Queensland champions. They also had won the Australian Amateur Foursomes title.

Geoff Parslow beat Jack Harris in the 1969 Victorian PGA and also went on to win a Victorian Open. His brother Ted was a very good amateur golfer who later made his mark as an international golf course designer.

Don Walker was killed in the Second World War. An annual memorial trophy was played at Heidelberg GC. Jack Harris won this trophy in 1952. Don's brother Bill had been a prisoner of war in Malaya.

Bill Wishart was once part of a foursomes team which beat Jim Ferrier and his partner in the 1937 Australian Amateur Foursomes final. His brother Eric was another top amateur who also played first grade football, baseball and cricket.

Tom Heard was an old Scottish golfer who died at the age of forty-seven while playing in the Dunlop Cup at La Perouse GC in 1939. He once shot seven consecutive threes at the Australian GC, Kensington which may still be a record even today. His son Peter was a leading amateur golfer who was just six strokes behind Jack Harris in the 1952 Australian Open Championship at Lake Karrinyup GC when Jack was fourth.

Denis Denehey a professional golfer who won the Tasmanian Open in 1939. His brother EJ was a good amateur golfer who held the Tasmanian Handicap title at one stage.

George and Bill Cussell were two former Irish golf professionals. George Cussell actually replaced Jack's earliest mentor, Ernie Wood, when he retired after a long spell at Kingston Heath GC. Right at the very end of his career Jack Harris played with George Cussell in the Victorian PGA Foursomes at Croydon GC. They finished second which wasn't bad considering they had a combined age of one hundred and eight! Jack and George shot an under par seventy in the first round but they ran out of puff in the afternoon with a seventy-seven. George's son Henry was appointed Yarra Yarra professional in 1980 to replace Geoff Parslow. He was only 20 years old at the time.

Neville Wilson was the twenty-first President of the Australian PGA and had been a PGA Member for 65 years. His brother Les won the ACT Open in 1962. Incidentally Jack Harris has been a PGA Member for 75 years.

Bert Ferguson won the Victorian PGA in 1933 and both brothers played in the 1936 semi-final of the same event.

Jack Robertson was the 1930 Australian PGA champion at Metropolitan GC.

Harry Berwick was the 1950 and 1956 Australian Amateur champion.

Dan Cullen won the 1937/1938 WA Opens, Jim won the 1936 WA Amateur title and Don was also a top WA amateur player. Doug Katerns and cousin Len were Queensland pros. Doug won the Queensland PGA in 1955.

Jack Harris played against both Fred and Graham Belle in the 1952 McWilliams Wines tournament. He finished in fourth position well ahead of both.

Albert and Fred Findlay were brothers of Alexander Hamburg Findlay who was prominent in early USA golf. They had all been born in Montrose, Scotland. Fred eventually went from Melbourne to the USA where he had a very good golf course design career.

Tom Howard won the Australian Open in 1923.

Charlie Booth was a NSW PGA winner.

Alan Maiden was an early Australian Pro. He and his two brothers were from Carnoustie. Jim and Stewart were golf pros in the USA. Stewart was an early mentor for the great Bobby Jones.

When Brian Huxtable was assistant pro at Riversdale, Harry won the State Boys Championship.

Ted Cates was a founding member of the Australian PGA in 1911. He died in 1941 which was the same year that his son Graeme played against Babe Didrikson Zaharias in an exhibition match at Ballarat GC.

Although there were lots of fathers, sons and brothers who played golf, there were not too many daughters and fathers who made it to high levels. Perhaps the most famous of one that did is Jane Crafter. Her father Brian was a very good golfer. Her uncle Murray, Brian's brother, was even better. And even her brother Neil was a good amateur player and later became a golf course architect. Jane won on the tough US LPGA tour and today is a celebrated TV commentator on that tour.

Despite all these examples of family golfers playing in Australian golf during that era, none of them could match the famous American Turnesa family. During the same period there were no less than seven Turnesa brothers playing top level golf. Six of them were professional golfers and one was a top amateur. Willie Turnesa won the US Amateur title in 1947. Jim Turnesa was the most successful. He won the US PGA Championship in 1952 having earlier lost to Sam Snead in the 1942 final. He was also third in the US Open in 1948. Mike and Joe Turnesa had twenty PGA tour wins between them and also three runner-up finishes in majors. Phil, Frank and Doug Turnesa all had successful club professional careers.

According to Jack Harris, the reason why so many fathers, sons and brothers had been involved in golf in that era was because unemployment in Australia was high and it was difficult to get a job. Like Jack Harris, many young men had left school at fourteen or fifteen years of age and did not have much formal education. Therefore, their prospects of finding a good job would have been fairly limited.

Jack had left school at a very early age to pursue what must have seemed like a tough and uncertain way to make a living. Even so, he was always very fortunate to have had the full support of both his parents. Not all young boys who chose that path were as lucky as Jack Harris in this regard. A 'not so lucky' young boy was David Graham. When David left school at a similar age and went to work for George Naismith at Riversdale GC in 1960, his father was very angry. He didn't talk to David for many years after that. Even after David had won his two majors I don't believe that there was ever a proper reconciliation, which is rather sad.

Chapter 9

Jack Harris the Teacher

Even though Jack Harris was a great tournament golfer, he was an even better golf teacher according to many people I have spoken to. He started teaching golf before the Second World War. By 1947, at age twenty-five, he was already building up a reputation as one of the most competent golf teachers in Melbourne. At ninety-one years of age he still dabbles in teaching golf in 2014. That means, if we exclude the actual war years, he has been teaching for at least seventy years. Eighty to ninety per cent or more of that time was actually spent teaching, so it is perhaps not surprising that he got pretty good at it. At his peak he was giving over one hundred golf lessons per week.

Probably no one in Australia has given as many golf lessons as Jack Harris has during his long life time. Brian Twite the golf professional at the Metropolitan GC would perhaps be a leading contender for having given the most lessons. However, he only started at Metropolitan in 1955 whereas Jack had already been teaching for sixteen years by that time.

Jack Harris has taught people with various levels of golfing ability. He instructed absolute beginners and low handicap club golfers. He coached good golfers who eventually reached professional status and even top level golf professionals who wanted to iron out some minor glitch in their swing. Naturally he mentored Bob Spencer who was with him in Hartley's sports store and later his assistant at Keysborough GC before having a very long and successful teaching career himself. The same can be said for Trevor Hollingsworth who is also a long-time teaching professional. Jack also tutored Tom Fielding for a short while in his St Kilda school. Tom currently runs his own Golf School on the Sunshine Coast in Queensland.

Colin Campbell and Jack Harris in 1939 at Long Island GC

A good young golfer Jack coached who achieved professional status was David Diaz. Jack taught David in his St Kilda Golf school. David won the Queensland PGA in 2003 at Emerald Lakes GC when he beat Aaaron Townsend in a first-hole play-off and also beat former double Australian Open winner Peter Senior into third place. He also won the Victorian Open in 2006, a feat Jack had earlier accomplished in 1960 and has made multiple appearances in the Australian Open, making the cut in most of them. In 2004 he also won the Border Open which Jack Harris had won in 1963. David Diaz had another claim to fame: in 2005 he qualified to play in the British Open.

As it happened, that year was the last British Open which the Golden Bear, Jack Nicklaus, ever played in. Originally the 2005 British Open had not been scheduled to be played at St Andrews but the R&A decided to change the course roster. This was a nice tribute to the world's best ever golfer and allowed him to say goodbye to the British fans at the Home of Golf. Jack Nicklaus was sixty-five years old at the time and he didn't quite make the cut finishing with 147 after round two. Nevertheless he did thrill the massive crowds by making a birdie on his final hole. As for David Diaz he didn't make the cut either. He finished just two shots behind Nicklaus on 149 and level with former US PGA winner Davis Love III, double major winner Angel Cabrera and British Open winner Stewart Cink but still ahead of fellow Australians Craig Parry and Marcus Fraser. Despite not making the cut at the 2005 Open, David did manage to become famous for another reason. Prior to the tournament he auctioned off on eBay the right to caddie for him at St Andrews during the tournament and had a great response. The privilege finally went to a London banker called Stephen Bridle who paid about twenty thousand dollars thereby paying for the trip for both David and his family.

It is far beyond me to try to explain exactly how Jack Harris teaches golf. It would need another book to do justice to that subject. However, I do know from listening in to some of his lessons that he places great emphasis on set-up position and on the initial takeaway part of the golf swing. I have heard him say many times that if the start of the takeaway is incorrect then the finish of the backswing will also be wrong, and from that position it is very difficult to execute a good down-swing.

The other talent which Jack seems to have is the ability to explain to a golfer who has a poor swing, just how he or she is feeling when they do that swing and then to tell them how they should be feeling when they do a proper swing. In other words he seems to be able to put himself into their shoes and he knows exactly how the swing feels to the golfer, even when they swing badly.

Trevor Hollingsworth, one of Jack's former pupils who did reach professional level and who is now a golf teacher himself, told me that Jack has the ability to mimic exactly any poor swing. So that he can repeat it and show his pupil precisely what it is they are doing wrong, not just tell them. I understand from Trevor that Jack would even practice these wrong moves in front of a mirror in order to feel just what the pupil was feeling. I don't know if all golf teachers do that. I would have thought, however, that for him to have switched backwards and forwards between thinking about what a bad swing feels like (and even demonstrating it) and then feeling what a good swing feels like, would not be good for his own golf game. However, his playing record was outstanding; therefore he must have been able to keep the two swing thoughts separate in his mind. He had the same modus operandi throughout the twenty-year period when he was both teaching and tournament playing. Obviously whatever he did had no great adverse effect on his game as shown by his excellent playing record.

This ability which Jack Harris had to mimic poor golf swings also gave him the skill to very quickly diagnose swing faults. Trevor Hollingsworth recalled the time when he and Jack were both watching Tiger Woods on TV during a tournament in the late 1990s. Tiger was trying to extricate himself from a poor position he had found himself in after a wayward drive and was playing a shot with a short iron. He was about one third the way through his back-swing when Jack suddenly exclaimed 'Oh, no!' As might be expected Trevor didn't know what he was talking about. However, all was soon revealed. The TV cameraman and the TV commentators initially had no idea where the ball had gone. But Jack knew in advance exactly where it had gone! 'He shanked it,' said Jack. 'Didn't you see it?' Eventually the TV cameraman located the ball and, sure enough, Tiger had hit a shank! Trevor was astounded. Jack had called a shank when Tiger was less than half-way through his back-swing!

Phil Hollingsworth, Trevor's brother, was also another of Jack Harris's pupils who became a professional golfer. Like Trevor, Phil also became a teaching professional and has done stints at Freeway Golf and Moorak GC amongst others. As will be explained later in the Wattle Park chapter, Phil Hollingsworth was to become a very important part in Jack Harris's life in an incident which occurred at Freeway Golf in 2005.

The other point worth mentioning is an observation I have made as regards the current 2013 golf swing versus the golf swing back in Jack Harris's playing days. In Jack's day there was much more hip turn and leg movement in the golf swing. I was looking at an approximately late-1970s David Graham swing on YouTube recently and even then he had an enormous amount of hip and leg movement. These days the hip turn seems to be very restricted.

As a seventy year old when I try to do a modern swing I find that my back starts to hurt after just a few holes. So I still allow everything to move just as it wants to with none of this business about trying to get a tight coil by coiling the top half of the body by resisting hip and leg turns. This may work for the pros but I would end up in hospital *tout suite*. I still hit my driver about 210 metres, when I get hold of it, so I am reasonably happy with that.

It could be argued that teaching thousands of ordinary golfers would not be very beneficial to keeping Jack in a razor sharp condition to play in big tournaments. However, the fact that he did play in many big tournaments and had great success must have had a very positive effect on the teaching side of his career. His consistent performances in all major Australian tournaments over a twenty five year period must have helped him to attract new pupils.

The fact that Jack had both great tournament and teaching success was also very beneficial to Keysborough GC. He was club professional there for most of the time he was playing in big tournaments. Many of the people who sought out his teaching services eventually became members at the Keysborough GC. Being virtually the first club professional at Keysborough GC when they moved from Albert Park to their current site, Jack Harris was very instrumental in the early development of what is now a very successful golf club.

Apart from the thousands of average Joe Hackers who Jack instructed, he has also helped to shape the golf swings of lots of more famous people. These included many well-known celebrities and top sports stars of that era.

One of the first students who turned up for lessons at his St Kilda Road golf school was the music conductor of the Melbourne Symphony Orchestra (MSO), a Japanese gentleman called Hiroyuki Iwaki. Iwaki-san had told Jack that some golf instructors in Melbourne had refused to teach him because of some residual ill feeling towards Japanese people which still existed at that time in Australia because of what had happened in the Second World War. Although Jack had first-hand experience of fighting the Japanese in Borneo, he bore no such malice, and he taught Hiroyuki Iwaki for several years. According to Jack, he was obviously a better music conductor than he was a golfer but it was certainly not for the lack of trying. Jack remembers that his pupil used to perspire profusely every time he had a golf lesson! Hiroyuki Iwaki served as Chief Conductor of the MSO from 1974-1997. In 1977 he was the first Japanese person to conduct the Vienna

Philharmonic. In 1995 the Australian Broadcasting Corporation named its Melbourne studio at Southbank the Iwaki Auditorium. Iwaki often offered to give Jack free tickets to his concerts but classical music was not Jack's cup of tea so he never took up the offers.

Although Jack didn't turn away Hiroyuki Iwaki from his golf school, there was one particular person who he did refuse to teach. That person was Herb Elliott, the runner, who had earlier won the gold medal for 1500 metres at the Rome Olympics in 1960. It was obviously way out of character for Jack to turn anyone away and I sniffed an interesting story. Unfortunately, Jack refused to elaborate.

The St Kilda Golf School in Chapel Street which Jack Harris operated bordered on the suburb of Balaclava. It is home to a big section of the Melbourne Jewish community and is just a few kilometres from the Melbourne CBD. The suburb was named after the Battle of Balaclava, which took place in 1854 during the Crimean War. This was very topical in March 2014 with what Comrade Putin was doing in that part of the world. Many of the streets in the Balaclava suburb are also named after famous people from that era. Raglan, Nightingale, Cardigan and Lucan are just a few of the streets which spring to mind.

Many of Jack's clients in those days were members of this Jewish community. Another of Jack's successful students who he coached for about 20 years was Jeff Gordon. Jeff was a single figure golfer who credited Jack with helping him to represent Australia in the 1985 Maccabiah Games in Israel. In fact, the first 18-hole golf course to ever open in Israel, where the Maccabiah Games are regularly hosted, was opened in 1961. It was the Caesarea GC which is located half-way between Haifa and Tel Aviv. This course was built as a memorial to philanthropist James de Rothschild. The course itself passes through ancient Roman ruins. When the course was officially opened, US golf legend Sam Snead and British Ryder Cup player Harry Weetman played an exhibition match there to mark the occasion. Jack Harris had great success playing against Harry in the 1950s and even had the great pleasure to play against Sam at the end of their careers.

The Cranbourne GC was founded in 1951 by Syd Kaufman and some of his Jewish friends. Additionally, Cranbourne GC's first club professional was none other than Jack Harris's old friend Ossie Pickworth who went there in 1954 after a spending several years at Royal Melbourne. Jack Harris himself played many times at Cranbourne and in fact it was the scene of one of his most memorable victories in the 1960 Victorian PGA Championship, his fourth win in that event.

Another famous person who was a regular customer for golf lessons at the Armadale Golf School was Dame Elisabeth Murdoch, mother of internationally famous media magnate, Rupert Murdoch, who used to get lessons for herself and for some of her grandchildren. Dame Elisabeth died at the age of 103 in 2012. She had spent her entire life helping people in need and supporting a myriad of worthy causes. She was born in 1909, so when she went to Jack for golf lessons she would already have been well into her sixties. She even got a golf buggy as a birthday present on her eightieth birthday! There was no report card from Jack on Dame Elisabeth's prowess as a golfer. Nevertheless, it is safe to assume that if her golf game was just a tiny fraction as good as everything else she did in her long and fruitful life, she would have potentially been a star golfer as well!

Thinking about Dame Elisabeth reminded me of one of Jack Harris's curious habits. Whenever Jack was introducing a lower ranked person to a higher ranked person or a junior person to a more senior person he always reversed the generally accepted introduction protocol. Trevor Hollingsworth always remembers the first day he met Dame Elisabeth in the St Kilda Golf School.

After one of Dame Elisabeth's regular golf lessons, Jack brought her across to where Trevor was teaching and said, 'Trevor Hollingsworth, I want you to meet Dame Elisabeth Murdoch.' Trevor was a little taken aback. He wondered why Jack had not said, 'Dame Elisabeth, I would like you to meet Trevor Hollingsworth.'

I don't think Jack was being mischievous when he did this. He treated everyone the same and it just never occurred to him that he should perhaps do it differently. In fact, he never changed. Only a few weeks ago in the Wattle Park pro shop during a meeting with AFL Hall of Fame Legend John Schultz exactly the same occurred. When he introduced the young club shop manager Jack said, 'Patrick Morgan I would like you to meet John Schultz.' I just chuckled to myself. Patrick, who is already well over six feet tall, visibly grew another six inches and John Schultz, who like Jack Harris is just a lovely man, never batted an eyelid.

In 1982, a young rookie US golfer called Payne Stewart came to Australia to play in series of tournaments culminating in the Australian Open at the Australian GC in Sydney NSW. One of the first events he played in was in Melbourne and on that occasion Payne had some minor glitch in his golf swing which he was concerned about so he visited Jack Harris in the St Kilda School to get Jack's thoughts about the problem. Jack quickly identified some minor issue associated with Payne's shoulder turn which had started to creep into his game and all was fixed up pretty efficiently. Payne left Melbourne to play in the $150,000 Resch's Coolangatta Tweeds Heads Classic in Queensland. He won that event by two strokes from a most unlikely runner-up, Kyi Hla Han, a golfer from Burma. This is the first time that I ever even heard of a golfer from Burma, or Myanmar as it is now called. On subsequent checking I found that Kyi Hla Han had in fact won ten times on the Asian Tour so he must have been a reasonably good golfer.

Payne went on from Coolangatta to play in the 1982 Australian Open at the Australian GC, Kensington, New South Wales. Bob Shearer was champion that year. Payne Stewart tied for second with Jack Nicklaus. All in all, a very successful first visit to Australia by Payne Stewart, no doubt helped in some small part by the timely coaching from Jack Harris. Payne Stewart went on to win eleven PGA tour events and three Majors before he died tragically in a Lear jet crash in 1999 in South Dakota. When some of the newspaper journalists got wind of the fact that Jack Harris had coached Payne Stewart while he was in Australia they were all clamouring for a story but Jack declined to give any interviews. No doubt he could have gained some mileage by advertising himself in this manner but the fact was that he really didn't want to be a coach to famous players. He got more job satisfaction from seeing the smile on the face of the average Joe Hacker after they had quickly learned how to get their worm burners into the air!

I doubt very much whether Jack Harris charged Payne Stewart for this consultation. According to Trevor Hollingsworth, Jack never charged any professional golfer who came to ask his advice.

From March 1983, the year our family emigrated from England to Australia, until December 1991, the prime minister of Australia was Mr Bob Hawke. I didn't know previously, but I learned from Jack Harris that the PM was a very keen golfer. It seems that Mr Hawke had a regular playing partner who he used to always manage to beat on the golf course. That is, until one day that playing partner (whose name Jack couldn't recall) came to Jack Harris for golf lessons. After only a few short lessons the tables were turned and the playing partner began to regularly beat the PM. From that point onwards it was a regular point of daily banter between Jack Harris and his business partner in the golf school, Trevor Hollingsworth. Every time Jack arrived at the school each morning he would ask Trevor, 'Have we had a call from Bob Hawke today?' They never did receive a call from the PM. No doubt the playing partner had kept his golf lessons a secret from the PM!

Perhaps the most remarkable golfer who Jack Harris helped in the 1960s was Eric Hailes. Eric used to regularly score between 95 and 100 for eighteen holes and could drive the ball 200 yards. He didn't have an official handicap. Nothing all that remarkable about that I can hear everyone saying. Well, actually it was remarkable because Eric was totally blind. He had lost his sight twenty years earlier when he served in the RAAF during the Second World War.

Eric worked as a piano tuner for Geoff Brash in one of Geoff's music stores in the city. He was a member at the Amstel GC where at one time a sixteen year old called Ian Stanley used to caddie for him. Ian later became a professional golfer and was a prolific winner on the Australian PGA Tour. Anyhow, Eric regularly came to the St Kilda Golf School for lessons accompanied by his faithful guide dog, Milla. Jack's eldest daughter, Marilyn, when she was a school girl, often used to have a job at the School teeing balls up for Eric to hit. Jack told me that when Eric was in the golf school and Marilyn walked in, Eric would immediately say 'hello Marilyn' even though he couldn't see her and even though she hadn't spoken. Eric had super sharp hearing and could recognise the sound of her footsteps!

Jack remembers at one time Geoff Brash paid for Eric to go over to the USA and play in a tournament for blind golfers. Eric was accompanied on that trip by Ray Wright who was the club pro at Cheltenham GC. Ray had broken Peter Thomson's course record at Amstel GC in the 1955 second qualifying round of the PGA State championship with a fantastic sixty-six. Apparently Eric didn't fare too well in the US tournament because he and Ray *played up* a bit the night before.

As mentioned previously, Jack had always been a keen supporter of the Footscray Football Club (now called the Western Bulldogs). In the 1950s and 1960s, now that he had achieved status as an elite sportsman himself, he frequently mingled with Bulldog football stars of that era and befriended many of them.

Naturally he was very happy to be present at the MCG when his team won their first and only premiership VFL flag in 1954 beating Melbourne 102-51 in the Grand Final.[6]

Several of this winning team regularly took golf lessons from Jack Harris, including Ted Whitten, Charlie Sutton and Jack Collins. Charlie Sutton was captain in the 1954 Grand Final and Jack Collins kicked seven goals in the final. Footscray did manage to play in another Grand Final in 1961 but they lost 51-94 to Hawthorn. They have not been in a Grand Final since.

When Keysborough GC rewarded Jack for his long service in 1960 by sponsoring him on a trip to play in Europe, several members of the Footscray Football Club were present at a special going away celebration night in St Kilda.

Jack taught other footballers of that period too. These included Des Tuddenham who played 182 games for Collingwood and sixty-nine games for Essendon and was inducted into the Hall of Fame in 2008.

Another was Graham Arthur who was captain of the first Hawthorn team to win a premiership in 1961. Graham played 232 games from 1955-1969 and was three times best and fairest. He was inducted into the Australian Football Hall of Fame in 1996, the same year John Schultz of Footscray was inducted. Graham had some involvement with Rothmans cigarettes and was instrumental in switching Jack away from the Turf brand over to Rothmans which he used to get supplied free of charge. I even heard a story that Rothman's had installed a cigarette dispensing machine free of charge into Jack's home but I don't know if that was true or not.

---

6   They had won several in the VFA prior to that.

There was no end to the list of AFL footballers who Jack Harris showed how to play the game of golf. Jack well remembers one day at Sorrento GC after he had just given a lesson to premiership player and coach, Tony Jewell. After the lesson Tony had decided to go out and play a few holes on the course. After a couple of minutes a very excited Tony came bounding back into the pro-shop to tell Jack that he had plonked his drive straight on to the green on the dog-leg first hole which was a par four! Of course, being his normal mischievous self, Jack insisted that they go out to the first tee because he wanted to see Tony do it again. The next drive fell about ten yards short of the ladies' tee and Tony was quickly brought back down to earth.

Having heard this story quite some time ago I did manage to use it to personal advantage on occasions. Many times at Wattle Park I would be practising putting with my driver on the practice putting green when Jack was passing by en route to the practice nets to hit a few iron shots. For some inexplicable reason when Jack was watching me I regularly managed to sink a ridiculous putt such as a sixty foot very fast downhiller or a long downhill putt with a three metre break. I can never do it on the course but it did happen regularly when Jack was there. Jack would immediately chirp up, 'Go on, do it again'. But I remembered the Tony Jewell story and I always refused to do the putt again so my reputation remained intact! I must admit that to make streaky putts like that when the King of Victorian golf was watching me did make me feel good. Amazingly, I always managed to do it with the very first ball.

One of Jack Harris's most frequent golf lesson clients was a man called Geoff Brash who was the CEO of a chain of 170 music store outlets across Australia. The business had been founded by Geoff's grandfather, a German immigrant, who started off selling pianos in 1862. Both Geoff and his wife Jenny were keen golfers. Apparently Jenny could play golf just about as well as Geoff. Jack remembers one time Geoff saying to him that if Jenny's handicap ever fell below his, he would stop playing golf!

Geoff was the captain and president of Sorrento GC which is in a beautiful setting down on the Mornington Peninsula. One day, while still running the St Kilda Golf School, Geoff called Jack and asked for help. Apparently the Sorrento GC in those days was struggling to get and retain new members, and Geoff wanted Jack to go down to Sorrento as club professional. Geoff Brash obviously knew about Jack's impeccable track record when he was club pro at Keysborough GC and of Jack's impressive tournament playing record. He knew that if anyone could attract new members and help build up the club it was Jack Harris. Jack took up the challenge and one only has to visit Sorrento GC today in 2013 to see what a thriving club it has become. Geoff Brash's judgment had been spot on and once again Jack Harris had managed to pull the rabbit out of the hat. Geoff passed away in 2010 at the age of eighty, but not before he had seen Sorrento GC grow into a great club.

Geoff Brash at the Armadale golf school farewell.

Two other well-known Melburnians Jack used to teach when he was at Sorrento GC were Vin Heffernan OAM and Ranald MacDonald. Vin Heffernan MP was Member of Parliament for Ivanhoe in the Victorian Parliament from 1985 to 1996. He was awarded the OAM in 1983 for services to youth. Ranald MacDonald is the grandson of Oswald Syme who had been in charge of *The Age* newspaper from 1942. John Fairfax Holdings later took over controlling interest of *The Age* in 1972 and full ownership in 1983. In those days, Ranald played with Japanese made Dai

Wa brand graphite shafted golf clubs. It was through one of his connections that Jack Harris started to play with Dai Wa clubs and also sold them in his pro shop when he was at Sorrento.

Anyone who has spent any time in the company of Jack Harris knows that he has a great sense of humour and is always up to some prank or other. One of the people Jack regularly taught during his long stay at Sorrento GC was a middle-aged spinster. He couldn't recall her name but maybe that is a good thing.

It was after one of her regular lessons that Jack got himself into a modicum of strife. That day the sun was shining and the lady in question had decided to spend some time after her lesson sitting on the balcony outside the pro-shop overlooking the eighteenth green. From there she could enjoy the beautiful setting of the Sorrento GC and also watch the men's four-balls finishing their morning rounds.

At one point Jack came out of the pro-shop to chat with her and she remarked how friendly the Sorrento men golfers were. In fact, as they finished their rounds every single golfer waved at her and shouted greetings. It wasn't until about an hour later when she came down from the balcony and saw a sign, which wasn't visible from the balcony, which read 'Man Wanted,' that she realised what had been happening. She was not amused and gave Jack some kind of a verballing! I'm not sure if she ever did return for lessons!

A concept I was keen to try to quantify about the teaching side of Jack Harris's golfing career was just how much a teaching pro was disadvantaged when he played against a full time touring pro in a big tournament. I was thinking about the fact that the touring pro obviously played in many more big tournaments in many different countries and thus was likely to be much tougher mentally than a teaching pro. Certainly the touring pro would also spend much more time practicing than a teaching pro: Jack Harris often had to try to sneak in a few practice holes after having spent eight or ten exhausting hours with his pupils. One would need a great deal of discipline to do that! If I had spent ten hours stood on my feet teaching I can guarantee that I would be too knackered to even think about going out to practice!

The typical view of several golf teachers I spoke with was that the touring pro had at least two to three strokes per round advantage. Bob Spencer the retired Keysborough GC professional thought it could be as much as ten strokes advantage over a four round tournament. This does not mean that a touring pro is inherently two to three strokes better than a teaching pro. Two players may actually be very close in terms of basic ability. However, if one focuses one hundred per cent on playing and the other focuses ninety-five per cent on teaching and only five per cent on playing, it's a no brainer which player will be best placed to perform in a tournament. If this assessment is even remotely accurate it means that Jack Harris's playing record was even more outstanding than I had initially thought.

If focusing entirely on practice and playing tournaments means that a touring pro can gain about ten shots per tournament over a club pro, I shudder to think what Jack Harris may have achieved if he had been competing on a level playing field.

Again it is all academic but let us just for fun compare performances in the particular Australian Opens in which both Peter Thomson (a touring professional) and Jack Harris (a club professional) played.

	Thomson	Harris
1948	299	306
1951	283	292
1952	286	286
1953	280	298
1957	289	295
1959	291	295
1961	281	283
1962	285	295
1964	294	304
1967	281	303

I decided to explore this further and analyse Jack Harris's playing record against the five players who were regarded at the time as being the best in Australia: Peter Thomson, Kel Nagle, Ossie Pickworth, Eric Cremin and Norman von Nida.

The results were as follows.

Opponent	Events Played	Rounds Played	Rounds/Events	Won	Lost	Tied	Stroke difference
Ossie Pickworth	176	388	2.20	39	126	11	-1.86
Kel Nagle	92	322	3.50	16	72	4	-1.65
Peter Thomson	91	318	3.49	15	72	4	-1.85
Eric Cremin	85	279	3.28	30	48	7	-0.68
Norman von Nida	46	172	3.74	18	26	3	-0.88

Jack's record vs opponents

The reason the rounds played per event against Ossie is lower than the other four players is because of differences in the event mix. The events played could be one round, two round, three round, four round or in the case of the Pelaco tournaments even five round purses.

Peter Thomson, Kel Nagle, Norman von Nida and to a lesser extent Eric Cremin, because they travelled extensively overseas, didn't play much against Jack Harris in one round purses, just the odd one or two.

Ossie Pickworth, on the other hand, didn't travel overseas so much. This is reflected in the overall number of times he played against Jack Harris. He also played in far more one round purses.

Jack's winning % against these five was 22.2% against Ossie, 17.4% against Kel, 16.5% against Peter, 35.3% against Eric and 39.1% against Norman. But they are skewed against Ossie because of the high number of one round purses played.

Anything could happen in these one round purses. Players generally didn't do any preparation at all for most of them. They would spend several hours teaching in the morning and then just rock up in the afternoon and play in the purse. Many players won one round purses who ordinarily wouldn't stand a chance in a properly prepared for four round event.

Having said this there are several conclusions to be drawn. Firstly, it tends to support Jack Harris's frequent comment to me that Ossie Pickworth was the best Australian player he ever played against. (Discounting the few times very late in his career when he played against young up and coming stars like David Graham, Graham Marsh, Bob Shearer etc.) Ossie's winning average stroke margin against Jack was only marginally better than either Peter's or Kel's. However, the important thing was that he achieved this without having had the enormous amount of international, battle hardening, playing experience which the others racked up. Although Ossie didn't travel anywhere near as much as Kel or Peter, he did travel much more than Jack. In the early 1950s he had two trips to Europe to play in the British Open and other UK tournaments. He also played in the first ever Canada Cup, partnering Peter Thomson. He also travelled much more than Jack throughout Australia. Jack did make one trip overseas at the end of his career but by this time Ossie had already been retired a couple of years from tournament golf.

Secondly, all these stroke margins are well below the mythical 2-3 strokes per round advantage which a touring professional has against a club based professional. But to also put them into perspective just consider that in 2016, in the Hyundai Tournament of Champions at Kapalua, there was a 33 stroke margin between the winner and the last player ie. An 8.25 stroke per round difference. More recently in the US Open championship at Oaklands, there was a 28 stroke margin between first and last ie. 7 strokes per round. Bearing in mind that qualifying requirements just to play in both these events are very tough. There are no duffers playing. No guys who are just making up the numbers. And these were only the results for the players who played all four rounds. The ones who didn't make the cut could conceivably have been even worse!

The difference in practice routine between a touring professional and a club based professional wasn't necessarily that one spent more or less time actually hitting golf balls. In Jack Harris's day few golfers spent hours and hours each day on a driving range a la Vijay Singh or Gary Player, hitting thousands of golf balls. The best insight into how the touring professionals approached things differently was given in an article which Arnold Palmer wrote in *The Age*, October 21, 1961. He wrote "For me the stimulating challenge of golf is to tackle different types of golf courses and plan how to conquer them". In other words, he didn't worry about how he was going to beat his fellow competitors but rather how he was going to beat the course.

Peter Thomson recognised this even long before he turned professional. According to *The Age*, September 15, 1949, when he played as an amateur in the Australian Open at The Australian GC, Kensington, Sydney from September 29 to October 1, he left Melbourne to go to Sydney on September 16 to prepare for the tournament. Ie. 13 days before it started. Ossie Pickworth, who was playing in the same event and was going for four Opens in a row, left Melbourne on September 19, 10 days early. In the same newspaper report Ossie said he planned to play at least 16 practice rounds on the Kensington course before the tournament started! Peter had gone even three days before Ossie so it is anyone's guess how many practice rounds he was planning to play. Compare this to what Jack Harris used to do. Maybe, and just maybe, one practice round if he was lucky on the course before it started. He just couldn't afford to be there one or two weeks early, mounting up expensive hotel bills and also losing teaching revenue from his club job at Keysborough. The inter-state hotel expense bill was a very big impediment in those days for most of the club golfers. In *The Argus*, 3 May, 1955 it was reported that only four Victorian golfers would contest the Australian Open at Gailes GC in Queensland that year. This was because expenses for the trip would be £150 which was equal to the first prize money in the tournament. Fifth place would only receive £25 and outside of the top 16 they would get nothing. Since most of them could earn £40 or £50 per week from teaching / trading at their club, this is what the majority elected to do.

Peter Thomson, however, did this kind of thorough preparation all through his career. An article in *The Age*, September 15, 1955 mentioned that when he played in the Speedo tournament at Bonnie Doon GC, he refused to play any practice round with any other competitor. Instead he played solo and hit four or five balls to every hole in a " Ben Hogan " style of preparation. No doubt he copied what Hogan did when he blitzed the field in the British Open at Carnoustie in 1953.

Peter was still doing it twenty years into his career when he played for the first prize of $55,000 in the Alcan International tournament at Royal Birkdale GC in 1968. In an article which Peter himself penned in *The Age*, 2 October 1968, he said he had arrived in Southport nine days early to get a jump on the competition and play a lot of practice rounds on the Birkdale course before the competition turned up. Unfortunately, on that occasion the plan backfired. It rained for one week solid and the water-logged course was closed prior to the tournament starting. So all he could do was twiddle his thumbs and practice on the carpet in his hotel room.

By comparison there were plenty of occasions when Jack Harris did no practice whatsoever. A good example of this was when he won the 1957 Victorian PGA Championship at Croydon GC. In an article in *The Age*, 4 May 1957, it mentioned that Jack had been so busy at Keysborough GC in the week leading up to the championship that, even the day before, he called his mate Harold Knights, a fellow professional at Southern GC, and told him of his intention to withdraw from the tournament. Harold kindly offered to help Jack with some club repairs etc and the pair of them worked all day into the early hours of the morning clearing up some of the back-log. Hardly an ideal preparation for an important championship! It didn't seem to affect Jack much though. He promptly played in the Victorian PGA the next day with zero practice and shot a tournament record 278 and in the process beat four times Australian Open winner, Ossie Pickworth, by twelve strokes! During my research I also found plenty of instances where Jack Harris had not entered tournaments / purses because he was just too busy at Keysborough.

I asked Jack Harris what he thought about this. He didn't think that he could have played two shots per round better if he had spent hours and hours practicing. It is something we will never know. But I still think that he would have done better than he actually did, if he had been able to focus more on practice and less on teaching.

Although Jack Harris didn't think that he would have had better tournament results if he had spent more time practising, his record actually shows the opposite. In late 1959 and early 1960, after he had made plans to have a belated crack at the British Open, he made a conscious decision to reduce his teaching hours. He cut them back from twelve hours to only eight hours per day, so that he could practice a bit more. Then, while he was over in Europe from mid-May to mid-August 1960, he obviously didn't do any teaching at all.

Even though his European trip wasn't super successful, he did play some good golf. When he arrived back in Australia, the three months of no teaching and more playing had a big impact on Jack's tournament play. Furthermore, the impact lasted even for a couple of years after he had already returned to his long-teaching-hours routine. Thus, although this did not put Jack into the touring pro category, it did give us a glimpse of what he could do when the playing field was levelled a bit.

During this two-year period, Jack won three consecutive Victorian PGAs even though he was past forty years of age. Additionally, he won a Victorian Open, had two thirds in the big money Coles tournament and had his best ever score in the 1961 Australian Open. His 283 at Victoria GC was only four shots behind Gary Player. It was also during this period when he used to eat Ryder Cup and Canada Cup players for breakfast. He beat every single British Ryder Cup player who ever set foot in Australia during the 1950s and early 1960s. He also beat the vast majority of Canada Cup players who came to Melbourne in 1959 including the two winners of the whole event.

There is no doubt in my mind that had he played on a level playing field against Pickworth, Thomson, Nagle, von Nida and Phillips when he was at his peak, he would have won even more often than he already did.

Another question which kept repeating itself in my mind was 'why did Jack Harris not write an instruction book on how to play golf many years ago when he was at the peak of his teaching career?' It would have been a best seller if he had done so. I got the answer to this question from Trevor Hollingsworth who had joined Jack in the early 1980s to assist teaching in the St Kilda Golf School. Trevor explained to me that in those days, he was trying to learn the teaching technique from Jack and to do this he would often replay hundreds of videos of what Jack used to say to individual clients during a lesson. Trevor was looking to try to identify a standard blurb or pattern to Jack's approach. To his surprise Trevor found that there was *no* standard approach. Virtually every video was different.

When he asked Jack about this, he was told that every swing is slightly different and no two golfers have exactly the same problem. It depends on their height and build, arm length, size of hands and fingers, flexibility, different muscle tone and a multitude of other factors. So basically, there is no one answer that fits all. As far as Jack Harris was concerned every single golf swing was individual and he taught that individual accordingly.

Therefore, to write a book which purported to suggest to readers that *this is the way everyone should play golf* would have gone against Jack Harris's basic teaching philosophy. In fact according to Trevor Hollingsworth, not only did Jack Harris never write a golf instruction book but during all the time they worked together, he never even read one either.

Chapter 10

Exhibition Matches

A large crowd watches Jack Harris on his way to his first big money tournament victory in the 1952 Adelaide Advertiser at Royal Adelaide GC

There had been exhibition matches in Australia before the Second World War like for instance the one at the Australian Golf Club in 1934 between US golfer Gene Sarazen and Australian star Joe Kirkwood. However, they appeared to have been more prevalent after the war.

When Babe Didrikson Zaharias visited Australia in 1939 she played many exhibition games. One was at Yarra Yarra GC which was mentioned earlier. Another interesting one was at Bendigo GC where she played against the Bendigo club professional, Viv Billings. This was a totally new experience for the Babe because it was played on sand scrape greens which she had never encountered previously. Despite this, she still managed to shoot 76 against Billings's 77 on the par 74 rated course.

Almost from the start of resuming his professional career after the war, Jack Harris regularly played in exhibition matches all over the state of Victoria. This was both to help promote the game in country areas such as Sale, Horsham, Maffra, Orbost or Ballarat and also to help raise funds for good causes. At many of the country clubs he also conducted regular clinics. Often Jack would be teamed up with a few other professionals who were all doing the same thing. Two of the regulars in these exhibition matches were Lenny Boorer, who Jack told me was a bit of a specialist at doing trick shots, and Jack's old nemesis, Ossie Pickworth.

The 1947 exhibition match at Yarra Yarra GC for the Royal Children's Hospital Good Friday Appeal when Jack played Arthur Spence and finally got found out by Grace as he came off the last green has already been mentioned earlier.

An early exhibition match after that which Jack was involved in was in 1949 at Box Hill GC. He partnered Ossie Pickworth in a match against Martin Smith (former runner-up in Australian Open) and Ted Naismith. Admission to the match was four shillings. The aim was to raise funds for the Red Cross.

In 1950, Jack Harris was one of several top golf pros amongst over one thousand players who played in the Returned Serviceman's League (RSL) tournament at Long Island. It was reported that Army walkie-talkies would transmit sports details to the players and the Royal Victorian Aero Club would carry out mock bombing raids. The Australian Governor General, Sir Dallas Brooks, also played in this event.

In 1951, Ossie Pickworth, Jack Harris, Colin Campbell and Ted Naismith played an eighteen holes match at Flinders Naval Depot. Proceeds from the match went to the Memorial Chapel Fund. Admittance was five shillings.

In 1952 Jack played with Ray Wright against Ossie Pickworth and Walter Scott in an exhibition at Portsea GC in front of a gallery of four hundred people in aid of Portsea Deaf and Dumb Children's Fund.

Jack shows the finer points of the golf swing to Governor General, Sir Dallas Brooks.

In 1953 Jack played in an exhibition match at Maffra GC with Ray Wright against Bert Clay and Fred Moorcroft. In that match Jack set a new course record of 66, completing the back nine in a sensational 29. Also in 1953 Ossie Pickworth and Des Ferguson played an archery golf match at Croydon GC to raise money for Lilydale Hospital.

Another was in 1955 at the Wattle Park GC. This one was between Jack Harris, Ossie Pickworth, John Crean and Jack Boorer and was held to raise funds for Burwood Boys Home.

At Medway GC in 1955, the Lions Club held a fundraiser where current VFL football stars caddied for professional golfers. John Coleman, former Essendon champion and later their coach caddied for Eric Cremin. Jack Collins and Charlie Sutton from the Footscray FC caddied for Ossie Pickworth and Jack Harris.

In 1956 the Carlton and United Brewery sponsored a £2500 series of eighteen matches between Peter Thomson and Ossie Pickworth called Operation Gratitude. All proceeds were given to the appeal for aged nurses and returned servicemen. Peter Thomson won the series 14-4.

In 1957, again at Box Hill GC, Jack Harris played with the current Australia and New Zealand ladies champion, Maxine Bishop, against Peter Thomson and former Australian Ladies champion, Janette Wellard to raise £150 towards the Box Hill Hospital Fund. Jack and Peter were each four under fours when the game ended. The match was squared.

In 1961, Jack played with Doug Bachli against Burtta Cheney and Joan Fisher in a charity game at Box Hill GC. The game was aimed at helping Alkira, Box Hill's centre for mentally handicapped children.

These kinds of events were typical of many which were held during that era. Jack Harris and many of his peers were very generous in giving their time as part of a way to help develop a further interest in golf.

When I first caddied for local mill owner Mr Hardaker and his doctor playing partner in England, golf was mostly a sport for rich men. But around that time social attitudes were already starting to change and public courses were springing up everywhere. Here, so-called blue collar guys could afford to play without having to fork out a big annual membership fee or even a big green fee. The change was probably speeded up by the early TV broadcasts. Sure, the quality of these public courses was not the same as Kingston Heath or Royal Melbourne, but at least anyone could play and get a first taste of what golf was all about. Old pros like Jack Harris played a big part in helping to bring the game of golf more to the attention of working class people. These days, people from all walks of life can and do enjoy a game of golf. They may never be able to afford or have the opportunity to play at Augusta National or St Andrews but at least they are out there enjoying the fresh air, the local wildlife and the three putts![7]

---

7   I like to think the latter are because the greens we play on are all different speeds. They have never even heard of a Stimpmeter never mind seen one at Wattle Park!

Chapter 11

Australian Open and Australian PGA

This chapter will undoubtedly be the most difficult one for me to write. It has been over fifty years since Jack Harris played in the Australian Open but even now just thinking about it stirs up all kinds of emotions for him. The fact that even though the Australian Open was not a big money event it was still the national tournament. It was once described by Jack Nicklaus as the unofficial fifth golfing major. It was and still is, the one every Australian golfer wants to have on his personal CV.

The record shows that Jack Harris played in the Australian Open sixteen times and made the cut in all but one. Out of sixteen starts he finished in the top twenty on thirteen occasions and in the top twelve on nine occasions. He had six top ten finishes. His best three finishes were two fourths and a sixth. There were five or six years during that period when Jack did not play in the Australian Open. It was usually when the event was outside Victoria and Jack could not justify being away from Keysborough or the travel expenses were prohibitive.

The only time Jack Harris didn't make the cut in the Australian Open was at the Gailes GC in 1955. From all accounts, that particular tournament was an absolute shambles. Early on in the tournament, tropical storms hit the course and several inches of rain fell in a very short period. The bunkers were full up to the brim with water. There were torrents of water streaming across the fairways and causing some players balls to be washed away and lost. Organisers were even building mud-bank levees in front of greens to stop them from being completely under water. All the players called for a suspension of play but the tournament officials steadfastly refused.

Jack Harris was one of the most unlucky ones. He played through the very eye of the storm and had no chance of making a decent score. Some players who had actually just made the cut withdrew from the tournament. Bobby Locke the eventual winner was more fortunate. He had already arrived at the eighteenth green before the peak of the storm passed through.

During the presentations at the end of the tournament, Norman von Nida, the runner-up, made a scathing attack on the event organisers. Apparently, his brother, Dudley von Nida, was a member of the Gailes GC at that time and took exception to the Von's attack. It seems that brotherly love was not high on the agenda that day.

Considering that Jack was essentially a club professional who had to teach and run a pro shop to make his living, this was an outstanding record. In fact when he competed in 1946 and 1948 Australian Opens he wasn't even based at a golf club. He was teaching for at least eight hours per day in an indoor city golf school, hitting off rubber mats with no bunkers or putting green to practice on. He made the cut in 1946 and was middle of the field. He did even better in 1948 when he came fourteenth. How he performed so well with that kind of preparation on top of several years lost at war is quite staggering.

For the ten years between 1951 and 1961 while Jack was at Keysborough, at least, in between teaching, he was able to practice on an actual golf course. Consequently, his results improved and he was consistently inside the top ten or just outside it for all of that period. He came fourth in consecutive years (1951, 1952) and both times had his chances to win but couldn't quite make it. In 1961, he posted his best ever score in an Australian Open when he came sixth on 283. When it is considered that the average winning score in the Australian Open for the preceding seventeen years had been 284, this was a magnificent effort for a weekend warrior. Unfortunately Jack had carded 74 in the first round and although he shot 209 for the last three rounds, same as Peter Thomson and four shots better than Gary Player, he fell just short in the end.

As previously mentioned, Jack Harris never ventured outside of Australia between 1949 and 1959. Therefore, he didn't have the same battle hardening experiences that almost all of his contemporaries had amassed. He really only played in three or four big events in Australia per year whereas most of the others were playing in big tournaments more or less every week over in the USA, Europe or in Asia as well as the Australian ones. This gave many of his contemporaries a massive advantage over Jack

Harris. Plus most of them were doing very little teaching, if any at all. Jack Harris, on the other hand was effectively a full time golf teacher and club professional who snuck off to play in a few tournaments whenever he got a chance.

It was not a question of Jack Harris not being good enough. If we look at the Australian Open winners between 1946 and 1962, by which time Jack had already turned forty years of age, we see the following list.

Ossie Pickworth	1946, 1947, 1948 and 1954
Eric Cremin	1949
Norman von Nida	1950, 1952 and 1953
Peter Thomson	1951
Bobby Locke	1955
Bruce Crampton	1956
Frank Phillips	1957 and 1961
Gary Player	1958 and 1962
Kel Nagle	1959
Bruce Devlin	1960

There is only ONE player on that list who Jack Harris never beat in tournament play. That player was Gary Player, who was much younger than Jack Harris and only came along as Jack was getting long in the tooth.

Even so, in 1961 when Jack was thirty-nine and Gary Player was only twenty-six, Jack shot 283 and Gary shot 279 at the Victoria GC in Melbourne – only four shots difference. In fact, in the 1957 Croydon Lawn Patrol tournament Jack Harris also shot 283 and on that occasion was only one shot behind both South African super-stars, Gary Player and Harold Henning.

Bear in mind also that Gary Player was well ahead of his time when it came to his fitness regime and his nutritional habits. Nowadays more or less every top PGA golfer spends many hours on gym work and is careful with his diet (maybe apart from John Daly?). But even in those days, Gary Player was already pumping iron and eating his special porridge! On the other hand, Jack was getting stuck into another packet of Rothmans special filters which played havoc with his health sooner rather than later.

The 1961 Australian Open at Victoria GC was perhaps the best tournament Jack Harris played which he didn't actually win. There was some phenomenal golf played by the leading players. Winner Frank Phillips shot 275 which at that time was the lowest ever score in Victoria for an Australian Open. The diminutive Billy Dunk, standing at five feet six inches tall and weighing just ten and a half stones, shot a 64 in round two which at that time was the lowest score ever recorded in an Australian Open. He did this playing with ladies grips because he had very small hands! Despite this great round Billy Dunk still finished seven strokes behind Jack Harris.

Thirty-nine year old Jack Harris only finished sixth on 283 but the only players ahead of him were very well credentialed indeed. Frank Phillips (1957 Australian Open winner), Kel Nagle (1960 British Open winner), Bruce Devlin (defending 1960 Australian Open winner), Gary Player (1961 reigning US Masters champion) and Peter Thomson (four times British Open winner). All these players were full-time touring professionals. It is simply mind-blowing that weekend golfer Jack Harris could mix it with these guys. And what is more he could do it when he was at the very end of his career and not even at his peak.

Every other single player on the above Australian Open winners list has been beaten in tournament play by Jack Harris and most of them on multiple occasions. We can even extend the list of Australian Open winners who Jack Harris has beaten in tournament play backwards in time and include three gentlemen who won it in the 1930s, Lou Kelly, Billy Bolger and George Naismith. But when Jack beat them he would have been about thirty and they would have all been well into their forties.

I remember the world famous English international golf commentator Peter Alliss once lamenting that neither he nor his father, Percy Alliss, had ever managed to win a British Open. This was despite the fact that they were both very accomplished players and clearly had the talent to win one. Peter himself had a long Ryder Cup history and had won many other big tournaments in England and on the European Continent. He once remarked somewhat sadly that 'it just never happened.' I think that the same can be said for Jack Harris. His fantastic talent was unquestionable.

He performed consistently in the top few Australian golfers over a twenty year period and on his day could beat anyone. But in the Australian Open despite often being in the thick of it, for Jack Harris 'it just never happened' either. Incidentally, Jack Harris actually beat both Peter Alliss and fellow Ryder Cup player Dai Rees when they played in the 1959 Coles £3000 tournament at Huntingdale GC in Melbourne.

In fact there have been lots of fantastic golfers for whom it just never happened in major tournaments even though they had superb playing records. Two that spring immediately to mind are the Scot, Colin Montgomerie who was runner-up five times in majors and Spaniard, Sergio Garcia who had four top three finishes in majors. However, unlike Jack Harris, they were both full time touring pros rather than Sunday club professional golfers. Closer to home, my mind also thinks about Billy Dunk. Billy was a fantastic Australian golfer for whom it never happened as far as the Australian Open was concerned even though, like Jack Harris, he had plenty of top ten finishes. Billy Dunk also won the Australian PGA Championship five times and broke over 80 course records. Perhaps the most famous golfer who never won his national Open title was Sam Snead. Even though he won the all-time world record 82 PGA tour events including seven majors and 47 top ten finishes in majors over a five-decade period, he never won a US Open championship. It just never happened for him either!

Even now, over fifty years later, Jack still gets down on himself when he thinks about the Australian Open. He thinks he should have won one and he has trouble shaking off the feeling inside that he somehow failed. In reality, anyone who looks unemotionally at Jack's record in the Australian Open and indeed at his overall golfing record, can only reach the conclusion that the word *failed* could not be further from the truth. The truth is that Jack Harris had an outstanding Australian Open record. And what is more, when it is looked at with the knowledge that he was essentially a teaching pro rather than a touring pro, who competed mostly in local Victorian events and whose preparation was always very restricted because of his teaching commitments, his Australian Open record is not just outstanding, it is bloody brilliant!

Winning golf tournaments at any level is a numbers game. Nobody, not even Tiger Woods or Jack Nicklaus, won every event they played in. Jack Nicklaus played seventeen or eighteen PGA tournaments after he turned pro before he even won his first one. Justin Rose who is about fourth or fifth in the world at the time of writing has only won about seven events on the European tour out of about 279 starts since he turned pro. This means that he has only won two or three per cent of events played. Adam Scott who is even more highly ranked in 2013 at second on the world ranking has just twenty-five professional wins in over 600 starts or approximately four per cent success rate. I don't suppose that anyone would describe either Justin or Adam as failures just because they have actually lost over ninety-five per cent of all the tournaments they have played in.

I must say that it seems to be a trait amongst old golfers that they seem to dwell a bit on the ones that got away rather than bask in the glory of the ones they won. Only a few weeks ago, Jack told me that he had recently received a phone call from Frank Phillips, a New South Wales golfer who he played against many times in the 1950s and early 1960s. Frank managed to win two Australian Opens in 1957 and again in 1961. Strangely enough on both of these occasions he beat Jack by the same eight stroke margin, Jack finishing eighth and sixth in these years. Anyway, Jack had not seen or even spoken with Frank for over forty years when he received this phone call out of the blue. By this time even Frank would be at least eighty years old. Well, in 1960 it had been just one of several occasions when Jack had been able to turn the tables on Frank when they played in the 1960 Victorian Open at the Metropolitan GC which Jack won at fourteen under the card. Bruce Crampton, Billy Dunk and Len Woodward had also been left trailing behind Jack. What was the reason for the phone call? Frank just wanted to know how the hell Jack had managed to beat him at Metropolitan GC in 1960! Frank must have been reminiscing after a few glasses of Glen Farklas. Maybe he should have asked about the 1961 Victorian Open as well? Jack only came in third that year but he still managed to beat Frank Phillips again as well as Bruce Devlin and Ossie Pickworth (two more Australian Open winners).

An interesting bit of trivia about Frank Phillips is that after he had finished his tournament playing days he followed in the steps of Jack

Harris's old mentor, Colin Campbell and worked on cruise ships. In the early 1980s he was a regular teaching professional on board P & O's *Oriana* cruise ship sailing around the South Pacific Islands calling in at Auckland, Suva, Nuku"alofa and Lautoka.

When it came to the Australian PGA Championship it was quite a different animal to the Australian Open. Although it had a proud history going back to 1905, the PGA didn't seem to command the same respect amongst the players in Jack Harris's day as the Australian Open.

Right from the start, apart from a two-year deviation, it had always been a match play format event. This didn't change until 1964 when it was switched to stroke play. By this time Jack Harris was already about forty-two years old.

During the period from 1946 to 1963 it was always match play. To qualify for the Australian PGA during that period, players had to be in the top sixteen professionals to finish in that year's Australian Open.

That often meant that a ragtag and bobtail field was ultimately assembled. There were two reasons for this. Firstly, if amateurs finished well in the Australian Open they were ineligible to play in the PGA. Secondly, often there were players who were amongst the top sixteen professionals to finish in the Australian Open but then elected not to compete in the Australian PGA. The 1960 Australian PGA Championship was a perfect example of this. That year ten out of the top thirteen in the Open were amateurs. The first three professionals to finish were Kel Nagle (tied 4th), John Sullivan (10th) and Jack Harris (tied 11th). However, although Harris and Nagle had qualified easily they decided not to contest the PGA. Only John Sullivan from the top three professionals went forward and was the eventual winner. There were at least seven of the sixteen players in the PGA that year who ordinarily would have no chance to be there.

Another similar situation arose in the 1946 Australian Open. Jack Harris had only been discharged from the Army a few weeks when he played in this event. Despite not having played golf for five or six years he still managed to tie 35th at Royal Sydney GC. Usually this would not have qualified him to play in the Australian PGA that year. However, there were over a dozen amateurs who finished ahead of Jack and they were ineligible. There were also several professionals who finished ahead of Jack but elected not to compete in the PGA which that year was held at Manly GC. The net result was that Jack Harris was actually elevated into a position where he did become qualified to play in the Australian PGA that year. Despite this "promotion" Jack chose not to play at Manly and returned home to Melbourne to get on with his teaching career where he could rely on a steadier income.

As far as Jack Harris was concerned, because he was a consistent performer in the Australian Open, he qualified to play in the Australian PGA virtually every year. The only years he didn't qualify were in the years when he chose not to enter the Australian Open (1947, 1949, 1950 and 1963). This was mostly if the Australian Open was being played outside of Victoria and he couldn't justify the time away from his pro shop business. There was only one time he missed qualifying in the PGA because he had missed the cut in the Australian Open and that was in the 1955 Gailes debacle described earlier in this chapter. In the 18 years from 1946 to 1963 Jack Harris qualified for the last 16 to play in the Australian PGA, thirteen times. However, on six of these occasions he chose not to enter the Australian PGA. This was usually if the event was to be played interstate and the cost/benefit analysis convinced Jack that it was not worth the effort. There were even several times when Jack was the third best qualifier, but he still decided to withdraw. Apart from what was likely to be a negative financial return, Jack also had to factor into the equation that the event was not seeded. So, he could easily meet the favourite in the first round. Add to this the fact that match play was not Jack's favourite format and it is easy to see why he didn't take the Australian PGA too seriously. Of course, because players knocked out in the run up to the final did not play off for the minor placings, it meant that any player losing in the first round finished tied ninth, any losing in the second round finished tied fifth and losing semi-finalists finished tied third. This meant that Jack Harris had seven top ten finishes in the Australian PGA when it was played in match play format.

Jack Harris was always much stronger in stroke play events. This was reflected in the fact that over the course of his career he registered tournament wins against 26 different Australian PGA winners ranging from Arthur Le Fevre (the 1921 winner) to Bob Shearer (the 1983 winner).

A few players in Jack's era did take the Australian PGA seriously. These included Kel Nagle who was a six-time winner and Billy Dunk who was a five-time winner. It hardly needs saying that Jack Harris beat both these players many times in stroke play tournaments.

On the other hand, Peter Thomson, who in many people's eyes was the best Australian player of that era, only won one Australian PGA title. And that win did not come during the match play era. It only came after the Australian PGA had switched over to a stroke play format. In fact, Peter's win came at Metropolitan GC in 1967 when he shot 282. This was the same score Jack Harris had shot at Metropolitan in the 1960 Victorian Open when he equalled Gene Sarazen's record. As a matter of interest, Jack Harris, who by 1967 was about 45 years old, also competed in the 1967 Australian PGA. He finished 11th on 294 and picked up three noteworthy scalps in David Graham, Bruce Devlin and Norman von Nida.

The switch from match play to stroke play came in 1964 when Jack Harris was already 42 years' old and already well past his prime. Despite this, Jack still bobbed up and played at least three Australian PGA events in the new era. I don't know what the qualifying criteria were under the new format but obviously the fields were much larger and much stronger than they had been under match play conditions.

Apart from the 1967 Metropolitan tournament he also played at Riversdale GC in 1965 with an identical result. This time he also finished 11th but shot 291, picking up nice wins against gun South Africans Cobie Le Grange and Cedric Amm as well as against Englishman Guy Wolstenholme. As far as I was able to ascertain, his last appearance in the Australian PGA was also at Metropolitan GC in 1968 when he was about 46 years old. Jack shot 76 in the first round and was three shots ahead of Peter Thomson / Japanese player Yasuda who each carded 79. After round two Jack was tied with Peter Thomson on 156, but both of them were well off the pace. Not really surprising because the big three of world golf (Jack Nicklaus, Arnold Palmer and Gary Player) were also in the field. At the end of the day even these world superstars were upstaged by Kel Nagle who was just shy of his 48th birthday. He romped away with the tournament. Nicklaus was second but well behind. Palmer tied 5th and Player tied 11th. Jack Harris missed the cut after round three but the much younger Peter

Thomson did improve and finished tied 22nd at twenty-three shots off the pace.

Anyhow Mr Harris, let us have no more of this *failure* business when you think back to your Australian Open days. You performed exceedingly well and should be extremely proud of your record in that event.

Chapter 12

King of Victoria

If Jack Harris ever felt disappointed that he never won an Australian Open championship, there is no way he could ever feel the same way about his playing record in the Victorian PGA, the Victorian Open, the Victorian Close and the Victorian PGA Foursomes. In his own back yard he was *the king*. Just have a look at the following magnificent record.

Six Victorian PGAs	1950, 1957, 1959, 1960, 1961, 1963
Eight Vic PGA r/ups	1949, 1954, 1955, 1956, 1958, 1965, 1968, 1969
Two Victorian PGA semi-finals	1948, 1953 (match play)
One Victorian Open	1960
Two Victorian Open thirds	1958, 1961
Three Victorian Close	1952, 1961, 1962
Three Victorian Close r/ups	1949, 1954, 1960
Three Victorian Close thirds	1948, 1953, 1965
Six Victorian PGA Foursomes	1946, 1949, 1950, 1958, 1959, 1960
Five Victorian Foursomes r/ups	1951, 1962, 1967, 1968, 1977
Two Victorian Foursomes thirds	1953, 1961
One West Victorian Open	1953
Five West Victorian Open r/ups	1951, 1954, 1955, 1956, 1957
One Victorian Open Provincial	1953
One Victorian Open Provincial r/up	1950
Three NE Victorian Open r/ups	1955, 1956, 1958
Two SW Victorian Opens	1956, 1962
Two SW Victorian r/ups	1959, 1961
One NSW/ Victorian Border Open	1963

I can't be sure that this list is complete or that there are no errors because Jack Harris never kept any detailed records and much of it was compiled from old newspaper reports. Nevertheless, it still serves its purpose to demonstrate what an awesome golfer Jack Harris was.

It is worth noting here that prior to 1956, the Victorian PGA had been a match play event. The problem, however, was that it was not seeded. Therefore, the two top favourites to win could be, and often were, drawn against each other in the first or at least one of the early rounds. Several times Jack Harris played Ossie Pickworth in an early round and lost narrowly with Ossie going on to win the event. Had this not happened, Jack would at least have been runner-up on even more occasions.

The Australian PGA event of the day was also a match play event and not one in which Jack Harris often competed. Nor was match play his favourite format. Jack Harris was too nice a golfer to get himself involved in all the mind games and antics which go on in match play. His forte was in stroke play and it was there where his remarkable consistency invariably shone through.

Jack only won one of his six Victorian PGAs when it was match play format. It was the other way around for Ossie Pickworth. He won four Victorian PGAs but three of these were in the match play days and only one when it moved to stroke play. Jack Harris and Ossie Pickworth held sway over the Victorian PGA between 1948 and 1962, whichever the format, winning it ten times between them. It reminds me of the Bobby Locke and Peter Thomson hold on the British Open in the 1950s. I don't believe either Jack or Ossie could have dreamt of this when they were in the jungles of Borneo only a few years earlier and wondering if they would ever even see another golf course let alone play on one.

From the moment the event changed to a four round stroke play format, Jack Harris came into his own because of his greater consistency. In the period from 1957 to 1963 he absolutely dominated the Victorian PGA championship winning it another five times. The only two other winners in that period were Peter Mills in 1958 and Kel Nagle in 1962. Jack's best win in the Victorian PGA was probably his last one in 1963 when he was forty-one years old. He shot an incredible 273 at the Long Island GC (nineteen under the card) and absolutely blitzed most of the field. Even five times

British Open winner Peter Thomson, still at the peak of his career, was twelve shots behind Jack and former Australian Open winner Eric Cremin was twenty-four shots adrift. His performance in the 1961 Vic PGA at Keysborough was no less impressive. On that occasion he shot sixteen under the card and left a big trail of champions in his wake including Frank Phillips, Billy Dunk, Kel Nagle, Alan Murray, Peter Thomson, Eric Cremin and Len Woodward. During this event, Peter Thomson asked permission from the organisers to pull out of the tournament after round three because he was suffering from hay fever.

JACK HARRIS, the new Victorian professional golf champion, hits off during his winning round against Ossie Pickworth at Kingston Heath on Saturday.

Jack Harris takes out his first Victorian PGA title at Kingston Heath in 1950, by beating his old nemesis Ossie Pickworth.

In the 1959 Pelaco tournament at Victoria GC Jack Harris played most of the match with heavily bandaged fingers after cutting them when opening a can of tuna fish at home. Peter Thomson won the Pelaco that year. Jack Harris still battled on to the finish well up the field in fifth place, level with Australian Open winner Frank Phillips and a stroke ahead of Ryder Cup stalwart Welshman Dai Rees. Certainly, Jack Harris could never be accused of being a prima donna.

Even after he was into his forties Jack still managed to come runner-up in the Victorian PGA three times. In 1965, when he was forty-three, he lost to Alan Murray; in 1968 he lost to Alan Heil and in 1969 he lost to Geoff Parslow. The match at Woodlands GC in 1965 was a very close affair. Jack shot 295 and only narrowly missed out to Murray on 293. The year before in 1964, Alan Murray had shot his best ever finish in the Australian Open at the Lakes GC in NSW when he finished fourth behind the great Jack Nicklaus. Jack Harris only lost the 1969 VIC PGA final against Geoff Parslow in a play-off. It is worth mentioning that Geoff Parslow the 1969 champion also went on to win a Victorian Open in 1977.

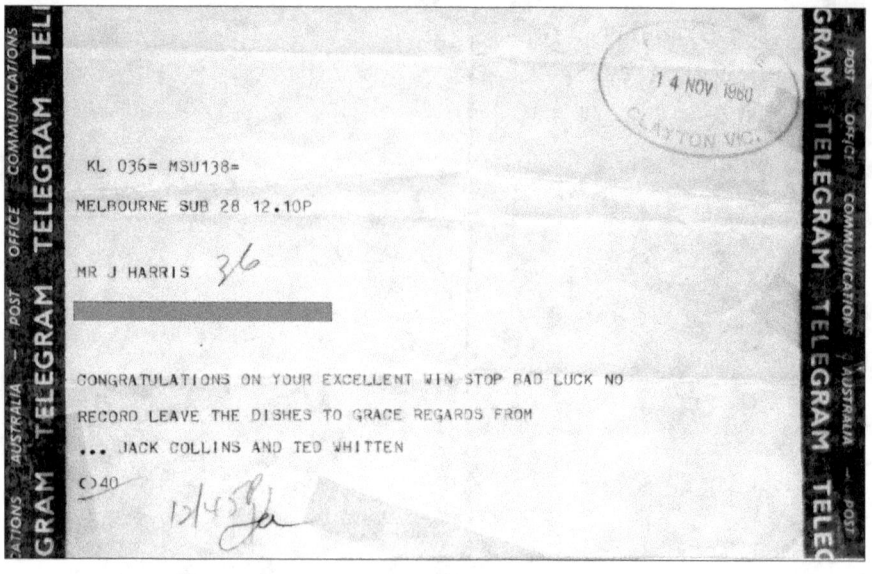

Ted Whitten and Jack Collins of the Footscray Football Club congratulate Jack on his fourth Victorian PGA win at Cranbourne in 1960.

There are only two players in history who have won three consecutive Victorian PGA Championships. You guessed it, the Boys from Borneo, Jack Harris (1959, 1960 and 1961) and Ossie Pickworth (1954, 1955 and 1956). When Jack won in 1960 at Cranbourne GC he received a nice congratulatory telegram from his good mates at the Footscray FC, VFL football legends Jack Collins and Ted Whitten.

To the best of my knowledge Jack Harris played in the Victorian PGA for 27 consecutive years between 1946 and 1972. He was only outside the top ten twice and these were the immediate two post war years, after he had just lost a crucial six years in his development because of the war. From 1948 to 1972 he had a twenty-five year stretch where he was NEVER outside the top ten! On no less than sixteen occasions he was in the top three.

No other Victorian player had this kind of record. It is true that these days the overall field in the Victorian PGA is much stronger than it was in Jack's day. However, at the pointy end of the tournament it was probably stronger in Jack's day. If Jack wanted to win a Vic PGA he invariably had to beat the current Australian Open champion and several former Australian Open champions to do it. And from the mid-1950s onwards he often had to beat both Australian Open and British Open champions (Peter Thomson and / or Kel Nagle) to do it. These days you rarely get an Australian Open champion playing in the Victorian PGA and you never get a British Open champion playing in it. His record in the Victorian PGA was legendary. No wonder the Victorian PGA Cup is now named after him!

The Victorian Open, however, was a more difficult event to win than the Victorian PGA. The first Victorian Open was held in 1957 when Jack Harris was already thirty-five years old. For some unexplained reason, Jack Harris did not play that year. However, from 1958 to 1970 Jack had a good run in this tournament too and played at least eleven times. He finished in the top ten on all but three occasions and these were all when he was way past forty years of age and getting towards the end of his playing career.

His win in the Victorian Open in 1960 was quite special. The year before Gary Player had won it at Yarra Yarra GC on 275. In 1960, the Victorian Open was held at the Metropolitan GC which arguably was a more difficult challenge than Yarra Yarra. Jack shot 282 which at the time equalled the 1936 course record which had been set by the legendary US

Champion Gene Sarazen. He won by four shots from Billy Dunk on 286, Alan Murray 287, Frank Phillips 290, Norman von Nida 293 and Bruce Crampton 297. When Peter Thomson won the Victorian Open in 1958 Jack came third but was only seven shots off the pace. Jack was third again in 1961 when Alan Murray won. Peter Thomson was runner-up that year but Jack still managed to beat Bruce Devlin the reigning Australian Open winner and former Australian Open winner Frank Phillips. Frank went on to win the Australian Open for a second time later that year.

The Victorian PGA Foursomes is another event where Jack Harris had great success and also showed exceptional longevity. His six wins and five runner-ups between 1946 and 1977 speak for themselves. However, it may have even been seven wins because in 1968 he tied first with Colin Campbell and just lost the sudden death play-off. The remarkable thing about this was that on that day Jack and Colin had a combined age of one hundred and ten years. They blitzed the first round with a fantastic sixty-seven. But this was back in the days when they always played two rounds in one day. They tired in the afternoon round and only managed a seventy-five. The same happened in 1977 when Jack played with George Cussell. On that occasion their combined age was about one hundred and eight. Again the first round was an excellent under par effort but almost inevitably the second round in one day proved too much and they finished runners-up.

Another event which Jack Harris regularly supported was the Victorian Close tournament. Actually this may have been the first tournament where Jack played against Peter Thomson. In 1949 the Victorian Close championship was played at the Yarra Yarra GC. After 36 holes Jack was leading by two strokes but in the last two rounds his putting let him down badly and he ended the tournament on 301 with Thomson on 293. Triple Australian Open champion, Ossie Pickworth (1946, 1947 and 1948) was tied fourth on 307.

The absolutely amazing feature about this tournament was that Jack Harris had very few opportunities to go anywhere near a golf course in those days. After coming home from the Second World War he had not been able to get a job at an actual golf club. In 1949 he had already spent three years teaching golf at a sporting goods shop in Melbourne city centre. In this environment he had almost no chance to practice putting on a proper putting green, no chance to practice bunker play, no chance to practice hitting over or around trees and could only practice hitting iron shots off rubber mats instead of grass.

JACK HARRIS (the winner) lining up a putt during the Penfold-Bromford Golf Purse at Kingston Heath yesterday.

GOLF PURSE WIN

Kingston Heath Lucky Course for Jack Harris

By Don Lawrence

Jack Harris won the 36-holes £200 Penfold-Bromford purse at Kingston Heath by three strokes yesterday and proved the Heath is his lucky course.

Jack Harris wins the Penfold-Bromford Golf purse in 1951

His very limited practice opportunity on an actual golf course definitely didn't help him in the 1949 Victorian Close. According to one of the reports I read about the final round, Jack was putting from six feet or less on sixteen of the eighteen greens but didn't make one single putt. Despite this severe practice handicap, in 1950, he won his first Victorian PGA title when he was still working out of the city golf shop.

Jack went on to win the Victorian Close three times and was runner-up another three times. In total he had fourteen top ten finishes in this event. He would most likely have recorded four wins in this event but for an incident which occurred in the 1958 Victorian Close at the Geelong GC. After the first round Jack was leading after a very solid 68. Unfortunately during that first round Jack had to report one of the players for an alleged rule violation. When the organizers declined to take any action Jack dramatically withdrew from the tournament even though he was the favourite to win.

Apart from his prowess in the Victorian PGA, the Victorian Open, the Victorian Close and the Victorian PGA Foursomes, Jack Harris also supported most of the tournaments around country Victoria. In the West Victorian Open, the Victorian Provincial Open, the North East Victorian Open, the South West Victorian Open and the NSW/VIC Border Open collectively he recorded five wins and came runner-up a further eleven times.

Another Victorian event which Jack regularly took part in was the Vicars Shield. This was an interstate competition between Victoria, New South Wales, Queensland, South Australia and Western Australia. It usually boiled down to a shoot-out between Victoria and NSW because most of the top Australian pros were domiciled in those two states. When Victoria won in 1951 it was the first time they had won since 1939. Jack Harris won his match against Kel Nagle two and one and his Victorian team-mates, Martin Smith and Ossie Pickworth, both beat their NSW opponents. Despite Peter Thomson going down three and two to Eric Cremin, Victoria still stormed home three games to one.

In 1952 Jack was a member of the Victorian team which retained the Vicars Shield at Lake Karrinyup in Western Australia. On that occasion he beat former Ryder Cup player, Jimmy Adams. Not long after this event Jimmy Adams returned to England and became the club professional at Royal-Mid-Surrey GC where Jack was able to catch up with him eight years later when he made a belated run at the British Open.

Apart from the various Victorian Championships, there were several occasions during the 1950s when groups of visiting international players came to Australia and played in the local tournaments both in Victoria and NSW. Gary Player, Harold Henning and Bobby Locke were regular visitors from South Africa. Dai Rees, Max Faulkner, Harry Weetman, Eric Brown, Dave Thomas, Jimmy Adams and Peter Alliss from England were also frequently seen.

In 1954, Ampol sponsored a group of top American golfers to play in a series of matches. The US group included Dutch Harrison, Tommy Bolt, Dave Douglas and Marty Furgol. Younger golfers may not be familiar with these names but suffice it to say that between them they won forty-six regular US PGA tour events and had thirty-two top ten finishes in MAJORS. So as a group they were definitely not mug golfers. But that meant nothing to our weekend warrior Jack Harris from Keysborough GC. He played against them all at both Yarra GC in Melbourne and at The Lakes GC in Sydney in 1954. On both occasions he beat Marty Furgol and US Open winner Tommy Bolt and was only a few shots adrift of Dutch Harrison. Apart from this he also racked up more good wins against the local Australian superstars, Peter Thomson, Norman von Nida, Eric Cremin and Frank Phillips.

Ampol had sponsored big golf tournaments in Australia from about 1946 and continued until about 1957. It will not come as any surprise to learn that six out of the first eight Ampol events held were won by Jack's old mate Ossie Pickworth. In 1957, at the Australian GC, Kensington, the Americans were not present but Gary Player and Harold Henning were here from South Africa and there was also a strong contingent from the UK in Dave Thomas, Peter Alliss and Eric Brown. Gary Player won that year and Jack Harris finished ten strokes back in eleventh place tied with Bruce Crampton. Jack was five shots behind Peter Thomson and three behind Kel Nagle but well ahead of Frank Phillips, Norman von Nida and Billy Dunk as well as seeing off Ryder Cup players Eric Brown and Peter Alliss. Eric Brown had actually been third in the British Open in 1957 and he was third again in 1958. Another highlight for Jack Harris was in the 1957 Ampol at The Australian Club, Kensington. He shot the lowest score of all the players in the field in the final round when he came home with a four under par 68.

For Jack Harris, his performances in the Ampol tournaments were very similar to his Australian Open performances in terms of consistency. Jack never won an Ampol but for the eight Ampol tournaments I was able to find that Jack had played in, he was only outside of the top ten on one occasion. His results were eighth, tenth, eighth, third, sixth, fourth, third and eleventh, averaging seventh position.

The 1956 Ampol tournament at Yarra Yarra GC was a very memorable milestone for one of the world's golfing greats. This was the first big money tournament ever won by twenty-one-year-old South African Gary Player. After he picked up the £5000 first prize money for this event he went straight back to South Africa and married his long time sweetheart Vivienne and a very long and successful career was set in motion. Gary Player played exceptionally well in that tournament and thoroughly deserved to win with a total score of 280. American Bo Wininger, who at that stage had three PGA tour wins under his belt and later had a few top ten finishes in majors, was second with 286. Jack Harris tied third on 288 with Belgian champion Flory Van Donck and four times Australian Open winner Ossie Pickworth.

Ampol did not just support men's golf in Australia. They also helped to promote ladies golf as well. In 1953 they sponsored a team of American ladies to visit Australia which included Marlene and Alice Bauer, Peggy Kirk and Jackie Pung. The Bauer sisters were a couple of glamour girls, Peggy Kirk was a renowned putter and Jackie Pung at the time was the 1952 US Women's Amateur Champion. Jackie was quite a character. She was a 235 pound (fifteen-stone) lady from Honolulu in Hawaii who could drive a golf ball 300 yards.

The four ladies played a series of exhibition matches around Australia in 1953. One of these matches, a mixed foursomes, was played at Victoria GC and was watched by over 2000 people. Peter Thomson partnered Jackie Pung and they defeated Denis Denehey and Marlene Bauer three and two. Ossie Pickworth partnered Peggy Kirk. They beat Jack Harris and Alice Bauer three and two. Jack Harris didn't win this particular match but at least he got to play with one of the Golden Girls of American golf. In hindsight this may have made it difficult for him to concentrate on the match!

Ron Hollingsworth, Ossie Pickworth, Jack Harris at 1960 Victorian Open which Jack Harris won in convincing fashion.

Jackie Pung turned professional shortly after visiting Australia. A few years later, she won the 1957 US Ladies Open Championship but signed an incorrect scorecard and was duly disqualified. She had signed for the correct total score but a hole was incorrectly marked. The fans and members at the Winged Foot Golf Club, Mamaroneck, New York where the event was held, felt sorry for Jackie. So sorry that they held a collection and later gave her $3000 which was almost twice as much as the prize money that year for the US LPGA Open!

Just as a matter of interest, Winged Foot is where Australian golfer Geoff Ogilvy won his US Open title in 2006. It is a very tough golf course. Geoff's winning score that year was five over par after runner-up Phil Mickleson had double bogeyed the seventy-second hole.

Chapter 13

British Open, Here We Come!

In 1960, when Jack Harris was thirty-eight years old, he had been the club professional at Keysborough GC for ten years. He had earlier applied to the club in December 1959 for three months leave of absence so that he could go to the British Open. As a reward for his loyal service the club decided to sponsor Jack on a trip to England, France, Holland and Germany. The plan was to play a few minor tournaments and also to try to qualify for the British Open at St Andrews. The various tournaments he played were arranged prior to leaving Australia in conjunction with the Australian PGA.

It was Jack's one and only trip overseas other than his war days in Borneo. He went on the trip by himself. Grace stayed home and looked after Marilyn and Christine, who were only eight and five years old respectively at that time. Before he left Melbourne he was given a nice letter signed by Henry Bolte, the Premier of Victoria. He travelled to England by air on BOAC airline. In those days it was a very long trip with frequent touchdowns for re-fuelling. Jack remembers not being very enamoured with the West Bengal city of Calcutta![8] He was away for about three months and it seemed like an eternity to Jack. Before that, he had never been away from Grace for more than a few days when he had been playing golf interstate.

Just prior to Jack leaving for England, a sportsman's farewell dinner was held for him at a city hotel in St Kilda. Many of Jack's friends from the Footscray football club were in attendance. These included Ted Whitten, John Schultz, Jack Collins and Jim Miller. Ted Whitten had been their captain in the 1954 Grand Final win. Jack Collins had kicked seven goals in that famous win and was a Coleman Medal winner. Jim Miller was the Footscray Football club vice president. The President of the Sportsman's

---

8   He would probably be even less impressed today even though it has a new name, Kolkata.

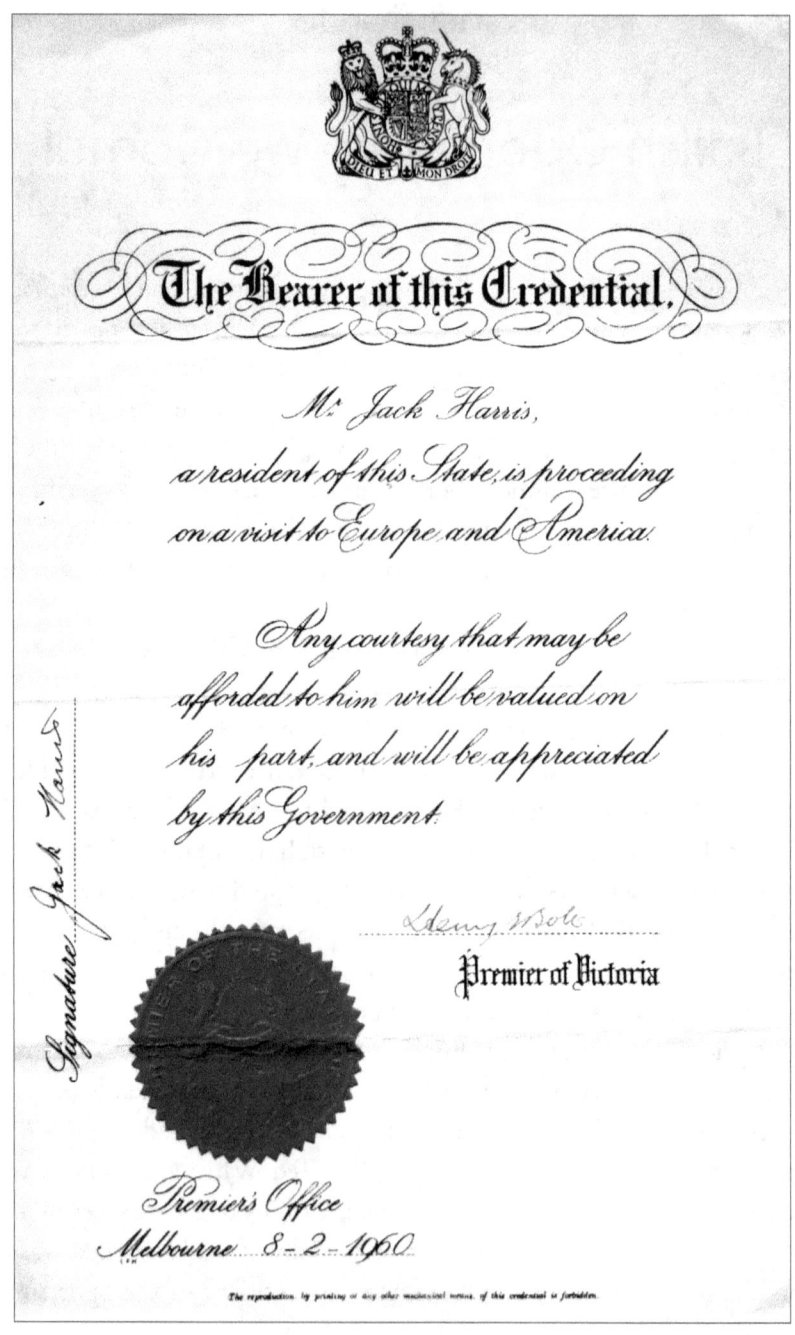

Jack Harris is given a letter from Henry Bolte, Premier of Victoria to take with him on his trip to Europe in the event that he required consular assistance.

Association, Walter Lindrum MBE OBE, was also there. During the dinner, Jack, who was and still is a very keen Bulldog supporter, was presented with Ted Whitten's famous number three football jumper. I don't know if this jumper was the one Ted Whitten wore in the 1954 Grand Final which they won. In any case, a number of years later, Jack unselfishly gave the jumper away to a neighbour's young son who had been ill. Marilyn nearly crucified her dad when she found out!

Walter Lindrum was the legend of all legends. He won the World Professional Billiards Championship in 1933 and held it until he retired undefeated in 1950. He had 57 world records and more than 800 breaks of 1000 including the world record break of 4137. Jack was still in Europe when Walter died suddenly on 30 July, 1960 while on holidays in Burleigh Heads. The doctors didn't know whether it was from a heart attack or from food poisoning after eating a dodgy meat pie. He was given a State Funeral. In 1981 he was honoured when Australia Post issued a postage stamp with a caricature of him drawn by famous artist Tony Rafty. He had previously been made a Member of the Order of the British Empire in 1951 and an Officer of the Order in 1958.

I don't know if Walter ever played golf but his nephew Horace, who was also a very successful professional snooker and billiards player, certainly did. But from one story I read in *The Referee* dated 26 October, 1937 Horace was not particularly good at putting. One time he was playing with a friend at the Woollahra GC in Sydney. He had already taken four putts on one green and was still quite a long way from the hole when someone chirped 'Silence on the stroke, please. Let the gentleman finish his break!'

John Schultz was only twenty-one when thirty-eight year old Jack Harris made his tilt at the British Open in 1960. Later that year he won the 1960 Brownlow Medal and in 1961 he was an All-Australian. He went on to play eleven years for the Footscray FC, won their Best and Fairest five times and also served for many years on the football league tribunal. Due to John Schultz's outstanding fairness on the football field, he was often referred to by the press as 'Gentleman John.' If there had ever been such an award as Best and Fairest in the game of golf, Jack Harris would have won it every year. As it was the journalists of the day often referred to Jack Harris as 'Gentleman Jack.' Whatever their individual accomplishments, I am sure that both John Schultz and Jack Harris must be extremely proud. These kinds of accolades, from both their peers and the sports writers of the day, don't come easy. They have to be earned!

John Schultz (1960 Brownlow Medal winner), Ted Whitten (AFL Legend), Jack Collins (Footscray FC star goal scorer), Walter Lindrum (World Billiards Champion) and Jim Miller (Footscray FC) present Jack Harris with Ted Whitten's famous number three Footscray football jumper.

Although Jack was still playing very well here in Australia at that time, it would have been a daunting task to travel 12,000 miles across the world, away from his family, to play on courses he wasn't familiar with.

Before I retired I had travelled to more than a hundred different countries. I still remember the trepidation I felt when I made my very first overseas trip. That was only a very short trip across the North Sea to Scandinavia in 1973 to give a lecture at the fiftieth anniversary of the Norwegian Rubber Society in the Telemark Mountains where the war film *Heroes of Telemark* was made.

You worry about losing your passport, misplacing your tickets or having your travellers cheques nicked. Maybe your luggage will not turn up on the carousel at your final destination. You sweat about missing your next plane connection or the airline losing your golf clubs. What to do if the hotel has lost your booking and a million other things. To say nothing about a fear of flying which I had in the early days. I did eventually get confidence that the aircraft wasn't going to fall out of the sky every time the pitch noise of the engines changed! Once you have done it a few times you are on autopilot but for the first time it can certainly be a bit stressful. The fact that you are not going on a holiday and people are expecting you to give a good performance, as well as the high expectations you may place on yourself, can all add to the stress.

At least most of Jack's trip was in the UK where they more or less spoke the same language. That is until he arrived in Scotland where he may have been somewhat flummoxed by a barrage of *hoots mon* and *och aye the noo*.

It would also have been a bit more of a challenge when he went over to Continental Europe, having to cope with several language changes in Holland, France and Germany. It would have been especially difficult for him in France because the French generally don't like to assist English speakers. I don't know how adventurous Jack was when it came to sampling all the different kinds of food he came across during his trip. I do recall that in the early days when cheap package tours from the UK to Spain and Portugal started to become popular, many English holiday makers would be dismayed when they got to Spain and found out that they couldn't find warm beer or a fish and chip shop. They had to survive on *tapas* and *vino tinto* until they worked out that the Spanish word for beer is *cerveza*! Maybe Jack really liked the frog's legs and snails in Paris and his steak swimming in half a litre of blood?

In addition to all the above-mentioned factors, I don't suppose that Jack would have had any strategy worked out for coping with jet lag which can wreak havoc with your biorhythms for quite a while after a long flight. Effect of biorhythms on sports performance was probably never even considered in those days.

The first port of call once Jack arrived into Europe was England. In those days Jack was playing with Penfold brand golf balls and the Penfold Company gave him plenty of assistance in transporting him from hotel to the golf courses where he was playing. Likewise, Rothmans cigarette company were also keeping Jack supplied with plenty of freebie cancer sticks and they also helped him with local transport arrangements.

It has to be said that smoking was very fashionable amongst golfers during that era. Jack Harris was certainly not the only golfer smoking. Jack's old mate Ossie Pickworth was a smoker and both Jack Nicklaus and Arnold Palmer were both regular smokers at one point. Arnold Palmer even appeared in cigarette adverts for the Liggett and Myer Tobacco Co (L & M brand). Before them, both Bobby Jones and Ben Hogan were also regular smokers. Apparently Jack Nicklaus at least stopped smoking on the golf course after he saw himself in a TV recording of the 1962 US Open when he beat Arnold Palmer in a play-off. He thought the image of him making the winning putt with a cigarette dangling from his lips was not a good one to promote for the young people in the USA.

This all transpired before *Smoking and Health: Report of the Advisory Committee to the Surgeon General* hit the world headlines in January 1964. However, it was not until January 1971 that advertising cigarettes on TV and radio in the USA was finally banned. Nevertheless, sponsorship of sporting events by tobacco companies continued for many years after that.

These days, smoking by golfers during tournaments is not as prevalent as it was back in Jack Harris's day. However, despite the overwhelming evidence of the adverse effects on health, some modern day professional golfers can still be seen indulging in this curious habit. Irishman Darren Clarke, Spaniard Miguel Angel Jimenez and Argentinian Angel Cabrera are all players who I have seen enjoying a quiet puff. I don't know if they all still smoke or whether they have now seen the light. Certainly smoking on golf courses seems to be much less common these days. I have played with hundreds of different players at Wattle Park GC and I can only think of one guy who regularly smokes when he is playing.

When Jack first arrived in London he renewed contact with an old foe called Jimmy Adams. Jimmy had played some golf in Australia in the early 1950s after leaving the Wentworth GC. He was a canny old Scot, who Jack had managed to beat quite a few times in Australia but who was maybe about ten years older than Jack. Jimmy had won the Lakes Open in Sydney in 1952, an event which Jack also played in. In his heyday Jimmy had played in five Ryder Cup sides and had been runner-up twice in the British Open.

Jimmy had gone back to England in 1952 and taken up the position of head professional at the Royal Mid-Surrey GC in Richmond. He replaced Max Faulkner there who had won a British Open and who Jack had also beaten in Australia. Before Max, the Royal Mid-Surrey GC had an even more famous son as professional, Henry Cotton, who had won three British Opens. In fact it was during his win at Royal St Georges in 1934 that Henry shot a then record round of 65. This prompted the Dunlop Company to launch their *Dunlop 65* brand of golf ball which can still found being used on golf courses in 2013. In later years, the club secretary at the Royal Mid-Surrey GC was former top English amateur player Michael Lunt (as far as I know no relation to yours truly). Michael retired from Royal Mid-Surrey GC in 1998. Later he became club captain at the Royal and Ancient GC of St. Andrews in 2006 and he was still in that position when he passed away in 2007.

No other club in the world merited the *Royal* status more than Royal Mid-Surrey. There had been royal connections associated with that piece of land going back to the days of Henry V in the 1400s who built a monastery there. George III had grazed his sheep on that land in the 1700s and even Queen Elizabeth the first died in a palace which stood where the links are now. The old club house was destroyed in a fire in 2001. Prince Andrew, Duke of York, himself a keen golfer, opened the current swanky new clubhouse in 2003, thus maintaining the longstanding royal connection.

Anyhow, Jimmy Adams had arranged for Jack to have a social round of golf at Royal Mid-Surrey GC in a fourball with himself and two of the clubs prominent members. These were Gubby Allen, Chairman and later President of the MCC Cricket Committee, and club captain, Lieutenant Colonel HL Hollis. Gubby Allen, later to become Sir Gubby Allen, was actually born in NSW, Australia but went to England when he was very young. He first came to the attention of Australians as early as 1932 in the infamous Bodyline Ashes Cricket Series. Afterwards, he spoke out strongly against the tactics employed by England in that series and as a result, the MCC passed a new law which 'prohibited the bowler targeting the batsman's body.' How things change over the years!

The result of the fourball which Jack played at Royal Mid-Surrey GC is not known. However, after the game the club captain offered to drive

Jack back to his hotel in the centre of London. On the way, they made a detour to his home to have a few drinks. When they arrived, they found that the good lady of the house had already started on the Uncle Joe's (Tio Pepe's) while the boys had been playing golf and was by this time a tad tipsy. When Jack was introduced as 'Jack Harris from Melbourne, Australia', she must have only heard the 'Melbourne, Australia' part because thereafter she insisted on calling him Frank.

It turned out that she was a big tennis fan and she had mixed Jack up with another Melburnian, tennis legend Frank Sedgman. Frank had enjoyed most of his success in the late 1940s and early 1950s but in 1960 he was still very much part of the Australian Davis Cup team. The fact that Frank Sedgman was about five feet eleven inches tall and Jack was only five feet seven inches didn't seem to bother her. It didn't bother Jack either. He still has a little laugh about it. In those days Jack did look a bit like Frank, dark haired, clean cut and good looking. They are also mostly dark haired and good looking from Tio Pepe Land, just like the golf wizard from Las Asturias, the late great Severiano, so maybe she can be forgiven! The strange coincidence was that Frank Sedgman did actually have an indirect connection with golf. According to what Jack told me, Frank had married the daughter of Arthur Spence. Jack had worked for Arthur in 1939 as assistant pro at Yarra Yarra GC and had caddied for him the same year in the Australian Open Championship. Small world!

While still in the South of England Jack also took the opportunity to look up Max Faulkner, the British Ryder Cup and former British Open winner. Jack had played with and against Max in many tournaments in Australia during the 1950s and had beaten him on multiple occasions. At this stage in his career, Max owned a small nine holes golf course with his father, at Selsey near Chichester in West Sussex. Max was also playing a few weeks later in the same tournaments which Jack was entered for. They played a few practice holes together at Selsey GC.

While he was in the London area Jack also practiced quite a bit with UK professional Fred Boobyer who was the club pro at the Highgate GC. This club was situated in North London near to Hampstead Heath and was the closest eighteen holes course to Central London where Jack was staying. Fred had originally come from the Bristol area. He helped Jack quite a bit during this visit. He also played in most of the warm up tournaments which Jack played in and actually qualified for the British Open that year finishing twenty-eighth, fourteen shots behind Kel Nagle.

After the friendlies at Royal Mid-Surrey, Highgate and Selsey, Jack travelled to Solihull in the West Midlands to play in the Penfold-Swallow tournament. This is a town about ten miles south east of Birmingham. It was a big tournament with £4000 total purse money and a £1000 first prize. This was almost as much as the British Open that year which came in at £1250. Copt Heath had been designed in 1907 by the legendary Harry Vardon who is maybe even more famous for the way he gripped the golf club. The Penfold-Swallow tournament had been going since 1932 when Percy Alliss won the inaugural event. Other notable past winners of this tournament include Jimmy Adams, Dai Rees, Max Faulkner, Peter Alliss and Norman von Nida. Notable also because Jack Harris had previously beaten all these players many times.

There was a strong field of 250 entrants and it was played over two courses. All players played both courses and then the field was cut. There was a second cut after the third round and only 66 players qualified for the final round. The two courses played were Olton GC and Copt Heath GC. Some highly ranked players including triple Dutch Open winner Sewsunker Sewgolum missed the half-way cut. Ryder cup captain Dai Rees and Ryder Cup player Harry Bradshaw missed the cut after round three. This was undoubtedly the strongest overall field that Jack Harris ever played in. There were at least 20 Ryder Cup and former Ryder Cup players taking part and Jack beat fourteen of them. He also finished ahead of triple British Open winner Henry Cotton and former British Open winner Max Faulkner. The 1961 British PGA champion Brian Bamford could not keep pace with Jack. Nor could Arnold Stickley the British Close champion and the 1961 Spanish Canada Cup player, Ramon Sota. Jack finished on 279 tied eleventh with Norman Drew, another Ryder Cup player, which was a fabulous effort on his first and only overseas campaign.

After Solihull Jack went south again to play in the Daks tournament at Wentworth GC. This course is located in Surrey, south west of London and not far from Windsor Castle. It is not far from Heathrow airport and close to Sunningdale GC. Wentworth is in the middle of a very posh, upmarket housing estate where only the very wealthy can afford to live. Many of the top modern golfers used to live there including Retief Goosen, Ernie Els and Colin Montgomerie may still live there for all I know. These days there are at least three eighteen-hole golf courses there.

It was a very dry English summer in 1960 and the fairways at Wentworth were rock hard. The ball was bouncing everywhere and was just about impossible to stop. Jack did not make the cut in that event and nor did South Australian golfer Murray Crafter.

Following the debacle in Wentworth, Jack went north again to play in the Yorkshire Evening News tournament at Moortown GC in Leeds. With a £1750 total purse this was a smaller tournament than the Penfold-Swallow but still had a quality field. First prize was £500. This tournament had been established in 1925. Australian Norman von Nida had won the event twice in past years. In 1947 he tied with Henry Cotton and in 1951 he tied with Dai Rees. The 1960 tournament was also destined to be an Australian win. But it was Peter Thomson and not Jack Harris who went home with the bikkies. Jack had a very good start. After the first round he was joint leader on 69 tied with Ryder Cup player Bernard Hunt and Spanish player Angel Miguel. He had one-putted eight greens to be a surprise leader. Jack told me that this was down to very accurate approach chips rather than great putting. Peter Thomson was on 70 and Ryder Cup player Neil Coles was on 71. Jack was one of the twenty-seven players who made the cut. He finished tied 16th on 288 with Ryder Cup player Ralph Peter Mills. There was a whole string of well credentialled players behind Jack including Ramon Sota (Severiano Ballesteros's uncle), Sebastian Miguel, Argentinian Open winner Leopoldo Ruiz and John Player Trophy winner Ross Whitehead. Peter Thomson collected the £500 first prize.

A story Jack told me about this event made me wonder if he had fallen for the old three card trick. In those days they played eighteen holes in the morning and eighteen holes in the afternoon. During the break he had lunch with Max Faulkner who he had played with in the morning session. Over lunch Max had complimented Jack on his putting during the morning round and had made the seemingly innocuous comment that 'Jack putted just like Ossie Pickworth'.

Whether this was just a chance remark or a more deliberate ruse by Max to get into Jack's mind we will never know (along the lines of do you breather in or breathe out when you are swinging?) Whatever the case it had an immediate effect on Jack as soon as he started the afternoon round. He came to make his first short putt and all he could think about was how does Ossie Pickworth putt? Jack proceeded to putt like a dog for the remainder of that round.

It may have been in the same event where Jack had seen where a fellow competitor's ball had crossed fairways and had come to rest in some thick scrub not far away from where Jack had been standing while waiting to play his next shot. Being the good sportsman that he is Jack waited for the player to come along and then told him exactly where his ball was hiding. However, another player who saw this act of chivalry gave Jack a bollocking for seemingly helping a competitor who he was ostensibly out there to beat. Welcome to the dog eat dog atmosphere of international golf! These were perfect examples of the battle hardening experiences I was talking about earlier.

From Yorkshire, Jack did a U-turn back to the London area to play in the £3000 Bowmaker purse at Sunningdale GC in Berkshire. This was only a two-round tournament and Jack shot 143 to finish 30th. He was just three strokes behind Kel Nagle who finished 18th on 140. Just over two weeks later Nagle went on to win the Centenary Open Championship at St Andrews. Peter Thomson collected the £350 first prize at Sunningdale, Bernard Hunt was second and Harry Weetman / Peter Butler tied third.

It was getting close to the time when Jack had to confront the main reason for his UK visit, to try and qualify for the British Open which that year was played on the Old Course at the Royal and Ancient GC of St Andrews in Scotland. That year it was the hundredth anniversary of the tournament's founding in 1860. Needless to say, it had not been played a hundred times because of the two World Wars .It was in fact the 89th Open Championship.

Jack was playing quite well by this time. He had got over the jet lag, had blown the cobwebs off and the benefit of extra practice or playing and not having to teach all day was starting to show. He was very confident that he would at least qualify for the main event. However, he may have been over confident. On the day he was allowed to play a practice round on the actual qualifying course, some English club golfers who had earlier that year visited Keysborough GC in Melbourne on a holiday and who had rented clubs from Jack, contacted Jack and told him that they were going to play the iconic Carnoustie golf course just a few miles up the coast from St Andrews. They bet Jack fifty pounds that he couldn't beat par on that course which was renowned at the time for having the toughest three finishing holes in golf. Being quite fond of a bet, Jack couldn't resist the offer and he passed up his opportunity to practice on the actual qualifying course. He duly won the fifty pounds bet by shooting under par at Carnoustie.

However, when it came to playing his qualifying round the next day, this diversion proved to be a disaster for him. Although he hit the ball well all day and drove long and straight he kept on finding those pesky little pot bunkers. These are a well-known feature at St Andrews but Jack Harris didn't know the course well enough to avoid them. Having played St Andrews several times in company trade days I know just how difficult they are. There is no chance at all to get any distance from them. Net result was that despite hitting the ball well, Jack failed to qualify by a few strokes and his British Open campaign was over before it even started.

For the record, an Australian golfer did win the British Open that year but it wasn't Peter Thomson who already had won it four times by then. It was the great Kel Nagle who came in with 278, just in front of Arnold Palmer on 279. Harold Henning was fourth on 282 and Peter Thomson tied ninth with Dai Rees and Harry Weetman on 286 just behind Gary Player on 284. Naturally, Jack was very disappointed with his one and only British Open campaign. Of the top eleven players in the 1960 British Open, Jack had beaten at least five of them in recent tournaments back in Australia including multiple wins over the actual winner, Kel Nagle.

Every player who played the British Open in those days had to get through two qualifying rounds. There were no exempt players. That didn't come until a few years later. So, for any player to win a British Open meant that he had to play six rounds of golf and more if there was a tie.

In 1960, maybe because it was the Centenary Open, there was a record field of 410 entries which had to play the qualifying rounds. Each player played 18 holes on the Old Course and 18 holes on the New course. The qualifiers were played on 4-5 July 1960. To get so many players through two courses in one day was quite a logistical exercise. Included in the 410 entries were 95 players from overseas, 70 Scottish entries and 81 amateurs. They went out in three-ball groups at eight-minute intervals, starting at 8 am and with the last group going out at 5.40 pm. Luckily in a Scottish summer they often have good daylight until 10 pm at night or even later. As it turned out, the first day's play did not end until 9.55 pm which was just under 14 hours play. The total purse for the 1960 British Open was £7000. The winner received £1250, runner-up £900 and third £700. This reduced in blocks down to £40 for the last player who played all four rounds.

Only 23 players out of the 410 entrants managed to shoot under 70 on the first day, eleven on the Old course and twelve on the New course. The New course was 6612 yards long and the Old Course was 6936 yards. Gary Player and Arnold Palmer both shot 67 and pre-tournament favourite, Peter Thomson, was well placed on 69. Gary Player was the defending champion having won at Muirfield one year earlier. Jack Harris played the New course first and had a disappointing 77. Lack of course knowledge cost him dearly.

The second qualifying round was played on a very rainy day with a strong east wind. When play ended at 9.40 pm it was bucketing down with rain. There were only 102 players who scored 148 or better. But the final field was limited to 100 players. So, twenty-eight players on a score of 148 were cut leaving only 74 players to play in the tournament proper. Unfortunately, Australian Murray Crafter was one of the unlucky ones just missing out on 148. Gary Player was the lowest qualifier shooting 135. Gary was the defending champion having won his first major at Muirfield in 1959. On this occasion, at the home of golf, Player decided to wear his famous pants which had one black leg and one white leg to make some kind of statement about apartheid. Peter Thomson on 141 was seventh best qualifier tied with evergreen 1932 British Open winner 58 years old Gene Sarazen.

Kel Nagle, the eventual winner of the 1960 Open, just scraped in at 145. I couldn't find Jack's final non-qualifying score but it would have been 150+.

Twenty-two of the 74 qualifiers were overseas players but only four were Americans. And of those four Americans only ONE had a realistic chance to win the Open: Arnold Palmer. The other three included the previously mentioned Gene Sarazen, Bill Johnson and Jack Isaacs. The great Sam Snead had originally entered the tournament but scratched before it started. Interesting to note that four times British Open winner Bobby Locke also scratched before the start. In total, the entry field of 410 was whittled down to just under 400 through pre-tournament scratchings.

Gene Sarazen shot 83 in the first round proper and withdrew from the tournament. Jack Isaacs missed the cut after two rounds and Bill Johnson finished 27th in the Open. Although he wasn't an Arnold Palmer, Bill Johnson went to Paris one week later and came runner-up tied with Leopoldo Ruiz behind winner Robert de Vicenzo in the French Open at St Cloud. This was the same Leopoldo who Jack Harris had creamed four weeks earlier in the Penfold-Swallow tournament! In fact, of the 74 qualifiers, Jack Harris had played against at least 35 of them during the past year and beaten 29 in tournament play.

After round two the field was cut to 47 players which included just two Americans, Palmer and Johnson. The cut point for the final two rounds was 149. Jack Isaacs had missed the cut by five shots and Bill Johnson just made the cut with 149. Arnold Palmer was tied on 141 with Peter Thomson after round two but he pulled his finger out after that and in the end finished runner-up, losing by one stroke.

This was Arnie's first attempt at the British Open. He came back in 1961 and 1962 and won it both years. After that he was a regular at the British Open for the next 35 years. His last appearance was in 1995 when he would have been at least 65. He missed the cut on that occasion.

1960 was a significant turning point in the history of the British Open. Thereafter, American golfers started to steadily trickle back to play in subsequent British Opens and this gradually built up to the American invasion which we see today.

Because the 1960 Centenary Open was a unique occasion, there was a special dinner laid on in the St Andrews R&A clubhouse on the Saturday night before the qualifying rounds started. At this dinner, twelve former Open champions were given 'the freedom of the Old course' from the

Town Council of St Andrews. These players included Willie Auchterlonie (1893), George Duncan (1920), Jock Hutchison (1921), Arthur Havers (1923), Gene Sarazen (1932), Henry Cotton (1934,37,48), Alfred Padgham (1936), Dick Burton (1939), Fred Daly (1947), Max Faulkner (1951), Peter Thomson (1954,55,56,58) and Gary Player (1959). Between them this bunch won seventeen Opens but only three of them were won at St Andrews. Henry Cotton won three Opens but none at St Andrews. Peter Thomson won five Opens but only one at St Andrews. Harry Vardon, Gene Sarazen and Walter Hagen won eleven Opens between them but also none at St Andrews. During the dinner it was mentioned that the first Open played in 1860 at Prestwick Links was a three-round tournament played on a 12-hole course. Thus 36 holes in total. Only eight professionals played. The event was planned to find a successor for the great Allan Robertson who had been the unbeaten champion of Scotland for many years. Allan had died in 1859. The organisers decided to throw the competition "open" to any players from Scottish or English clubs. The truth is that it was really a misnomer to call the 1860 tournament "open" because no amateurs were allowed to enter, only professionals. Of the eight professionals who entered, seven came from Scottish clubs. The other came from Blackheath in England. Scot Willie Park Sr won with rounds of 55, 59 and 60 (174 for 36 holes) when he beat fellow Scot Old Tom Morris. But Old Tom got his revenge in 1861 when Willie Park Sr was runner-up. The prize in those days was a Championship belt and not the Claret Jug they have today. The tournament only became fully "open" in 1861 when both amateurs and professionals could play. The first year that prize money was offered in the Open was 1863 when the grand sum of ten pounds was up for grabs.

At nearly forty years of age, this was Jack's first ever trip outside of Australia to play golf. The only other times he had been overseas was in Borneo during the war or when he went to Tasmania but that hardly counts! Everything about overseas travel would have been a big learning curve for him. Everything about playing golf in England, Scotland, Holland, France and Germany was a first time experience for Jack.

Something which Jack told me about his British Open trip did rather surprise me. There were several other Australian golfers playing in the UK and on the Continent that year and they all played the same warm up tournaments that Jack played and the same tournaments after the British Open. They played in at least eight of the same tournaments during that trip. Not once at any time did any of these fellow Australian golfers ever take the trouble to give Jack any assistance even though some of them were by that time very old hands at the touring game. Maybe they didn't want to help a fellow competitor because they were hell-bent on winning themselves and that is somewhat understandable. I suppose there is no such characteristic as being nice to each other in international golf.

None of this worried Jack Harris. He was a big boy and could take care of himself. However, if the shoe had been on the other foot it would have definitely been different. I can say unequivocally that Jack Harris would have been falling over himself to help a fellow Aussie or even a fellow pommy competitor if he could. As it was he did receive a lot of help from Jimmy Adams, a former Ryder Cup player who had played for a while in Australia and also from Fred Boobyer, a less well known British club pro. It takes all kinds I suppose? What a pity the other boy from Borneo, Ossie Pickworth, had not been there on the same trip. Unfortunately he had retired from competitive golf about two years earlier.

Before I conclude the story of the British Open I will permit myself the opportunity to reminisce a little about my own experiences of playing on British Open courses. I worked in Manchester between 1975 and 1983 as a technical salesman. One of our best customers was a large chemical company called BP Chemicals which manufactured polyethylene in Grangemouth, Scotland. For most of that period, once a year, we used to invite a group of BP employees for a day's golfing followed by a big dinner in the evening. This was usually at our favourite watering hole, the Houstoun House hotel, just outside Edinburgh. Each year we always chose a different Championship course to play on. Over the years we played on most of them. My three favourites however, were St Andrews, Muirfield and Carnoustie. Just the long history, the large double greens and the pesky little pot bunkers at St Andrews leave a lasting memory. One time we played St Andrews just a few weeks before the Open Championship was to be played there and they made us even tee up on the fairways so that we didn't dig the course up too badly. Even though it was just a friendly I can still remember vividly how I botched up the seventeenth hole! I was never good enough to try to cut the corner and fly one close to the hotel so I always had to go the long way around. Nevertheless I did manage to get on to the very front edge of the green in three so I was still fairly happy. The pin that day was up the slope and near to the edge of the road-hole-bunker. The very same bunker where Japanese golfer, Tsuneyuki 'Tommy' Nakajima had blown up in the 1978 Open which resulted in the bunker being known as the *Sands of Nakajima* thereafter. He was playing with Tom Weiskopf at the time and was tied for the lead before the disaster struck.

Anyhow, even though I was on the putting surface I didn't have a direct line to the flag so I elected to play safe and putt to the centre of the green and leave myself a long second putt. Problem was I didn't hit the putt hard enough and I was horrified to see my ball take a vicious left turn straight into the infamous road hole bunker where I took about six shots to get out and promptly proceeded to record a double figure hole! Even worse than Nakajima had done when he putted into the bunker and ended up with a nine. Talk about feeling stupid!

A few weeks later, I was sat in the pub back in Manchester with some mates watching the British Open on TV. A Scottish professional golfer called Brian Barnes had put his second shot on to the green at the seventeenth in exactly the same position where I had been. Brian was no slouch. He played in six consecutive Ryder Cups and most notably, during the 1975 Ryder Cup played at Laurel Valley GC, Ligonier, Pennsylvania, he beat Jack Nicklaus twice in one day in singles matches. Anyhow, he had also elected to putt and make the same shot I had been trying to do. Imagine my delight when he made the very same mistake which both I and Tommy Nakajima had made and the bunker enticed his ball just as though it was a big magnet. I didn't feel so bad after all and just about fell off the bar-stool laughing. Unlike me however, Brian did manage to extricate himself with his next shot and at least carded a semi-respectable bogey.

Another memory from those days was to witness a young purchasing manager from BP shoot a hole-in-one at Glen Eagles during his first ever round of golf. It can't get much better than that! Easy game golf! Maybe I should add that the hole-in-one was a topped tee shot which bounced three times before the ladies tee! It then rolled all along the ground downhill and into the hole going at about two hundred miles an hour after hitting the flag pole dead centre! No pictures on the card though, just a beautiful number one.

Even though Jack Harris's British Open adventure was over that wasn't the end of his golf in Europe on that trip. He still had three more tournaments to play: the French Open, the Dutch Open and the German Open. By this time Jack was getting very homesick. He was missing Grace and the girls terribly. Nevertheless, he soldiered on and caught the overnight car ferry across the North Sea. Jack can't remember where he caught the car ferry from or which Continental port he arrived at. However, he does remember getting off the ferry and taking a train ride to Paris.

The French Open golf championship in 1960 was played at the St Cloud GC which is located on the Buzeneval estate and is a place steeped in history. The estate was founded by Bozon V, the Duke of Burgundy in the year 870 AD. Later the whole domain was owned by Napoleon Bonaparte's ex-wife, Josephine of 'Not tonight, Josephine' fame.

The St Cloud GC website mentions that during the 1924 Paris Olympics the golf event was played there. However, this seems to be at odds with other sources where I read that golf was only played as an event at two Olympics games, 1900 in Paris and 1904 in St Louis, USA. Both of which were back in the days of Baron Pierre de Cubertin. In 1900 it was apparently played at the Compiegne GC and not St Cloud. The good news is that golf will be back as a sport in the 2016 Olympics in Rio de Janeiro, Brazil.

In any case, St Cloud is a golf course with a glorious past and many famous people apart from Jack Harris have played there. King Edward VIII, who later became the Duke of Windsor, was a regular patron there after he had abdicated the British throne in 1936 and run off with American divorcee, Mrs Wallace Simpson, to live in Paris. The story has it that every time he went there to play golf, the course was closed to all other patrons apart from the Duke's own party.

King Leopold of Belgium, Dwight Eisenhower, Billy Graham, Francois Mitterand, Gina Lollobrigida, Sean Connery and Arnold Swhartzenegger have all belted the little white pill around St Cloud.[9] In 1960 the great Argentinian golfer, Robert De Vicenzo won the French Open. Another Argentinian, Leopoldo Ruiz, tied second with US golfer Bill Johnston.

---

9   Pronounced in French as *San Cloo* which rhymes with loo.

Jack Harris did make the cut and tied 24th on 294 with Mexican golfer José Gonzales. In the final round Jack played with fellow Australian Murray Crafter and saw him shoot a superb new course record 63 which catapulted him into fourth place on 280. The exiled Duke of Windsor was a spectator at St Cloud on the last day.

From Paris, they drove across the border into Holland and made their way to Eindhoven which is where the Dutch Open was to be played. Eindhoven GC itself was also a very interesting place. It had been built in 1930 at the instigation of a gentleman called Dr Philips. He was the brother of Gerard Philips who had founded the giant Philips Electrical Company in 1891 which in 2012 was still the largest manufacturer in the world of lighting products employing 122,000 people worldwide. In many ways Eindhoven GC was similar to the heath and heather courses found in Surrey, England where Jack had been earlier on the trip. The clubhouse at Eindhoven GC had a thatched roof and was very quaint and picturesque. Jack did not play his best golf but he still made the cut and finished tied 14th with South African Bobby Verwey on 300. After the event, Jack remembers that the Philips Company invited all the players to a sumptuous banquet. However, by this time, living out of a suitcase and eating fancy foreign food was starting to get to him and he looked forward to some of Grace's simple home-style cooking and enjoying an ice cold Victoria Bitter.

The King of Victoria, Jack Harris, was not the only 'royalty' visiting Eindhoven in 1960. Later that year King Bhumibol and Queen Sirikit of Thailand also went there. When King Bhumibol died in October 2016 he had reigned Thailand for just over 70 years.

The real story from the 1960 Dutch Open however, was created by the eventual winner, a gentleman by the name of Sewsunker Sewgolum. Nicknamed Papwa, this guy played with a very unusual, self-taught golf grip, right handed but with left hand below the right hand on the club. He had in fact also won the Dutch Open the year before when it was in The Hague, so he had successfully defended his title. There is nothing unusual about that. Plenty of people successfully defend titles. However, Papwa was very special and had an almost unbelievable fairy-tale story of how he ever got to be there in the first place. Just like Jack Harris, in 1960 he had also been in the UK to try to qualify for the British Open and had also played in the *Yorkshire Evening News* tournament at Moortown. He finished fifth on 281 behind Peter Thomson on 268 and ahead of Jack Harris who finished tied sixteenth on 288.

Only three years before this Dutch Open, this guy was *discovered* as a twenty-seven year old caddie at the Beachwood Country Club in Durban, South Africa. At the time, he had been caddying for a German industrialist called Graham Wulff. Wulff is not exactly a household name but the product he invented certainly is. He was the man responsible for bringing the ladies skin care product Oil of Olay (also Oil of Ulay and Oil of Ulan) to the world. Papwa had apparently taught himself to play golf on the beach by hitting golf balls with a piece of a tree branch roughly carved into the shape of a golf club.

Graham Wulff immediately recognized the great golfing skill of his caddie and wanted to assist him to use this skill to its full potential. However, it wasn't as easy as this. The problem was that this was South Africa and the year was 1957. Papwa was a black South African of Indian origin who was also very poor and illiterate. Because of the apartheid laws in South Africa at that time, he could not play there in tournaments against white people. Wulff applied for him to be able to play in Australia but the Australian Government of the day refused. A breakthrough for Graham Wulff and Papwa came in 1959 however, when their entry into the British Open at Muirfield was accepted. Papwa couldn't write so he had to be coached by Wulff to be able to sign his name on the entry form. Wulff was very wealthy and had his own private aircraft. He flew Papwa to the UK to participate in the British Open in 1959 where he qualified for the Championship proper but didn't make the cut for the final two rounds. On the way back, an even bigger breakthrough came. Papwa took part in the 1959 Dutch Open in The Hague and lo and behold he won it.

After that the British PGA realised that he wouldn't be allowed to compete on the regular South African circuit so they accepted his membership to the British PGA and this allowed him to play in European and UK tournaments from 1960 onwards.

He competed for a number of years on the UK circuit with some success including several more successful visits to the British Open. In 1963 he finished thirteenth on 290 ahead of the current reigning Open Champion

Arnold Palmer who came twenty-sixth on 294. He won his third Dutch Open again at Eindhoven in 1964, and was also second in 1967.

In 1963 there was a bit of a breakthrough inside South Africa and Papwa was allowed to play with white people in the Natal Open in which he promptly won beating Harold Henning into second place. He got away with that one without ramifications but when he played in the Natal Open again in 1965 and beat the national hero and Grand Slam champion Gary Player, it was a different outcome. From people I have spoken to who played against Gary Player, I understand that he was a very fierce competitor who just hated to lose. It must have been quite a shock to lose to a non-white player during the height of the terrible apartheid system.

This victory was apparently seen as some kind of threat to the apartheid authorities. They later banned Papwa from playing on the South African circuit and also revoked his passport. This meant that he could not play overseas either apart from on one or two odd occasions when they must have relented and given him a special dispensation. Thus the fairy-tale international golfing career of Sewsunker 'Papwa' Sewgolum came to an abrupt end. I do not know if Gary Player ever spoke up against what happened to Papwa at that time. I did read however, that in a book, *Grand Slam Golf*, Gary Player wrote about a year after the 1965 Natal Open, that he made a statement apparently in support of apartheid. In later years, however, I also read that Nelson Mandela himself wrote a glowing tribute summarising all the great work Gary Player had done over the years to help breakdown the apartheid system.

Papwa was the son of a very poor Natal sugar cane worker. Through his prowess on the golf course he was also an important catalyst in helping to change the oppressive apartheid system. He won his first Natal Open in 1963. On this occasion he received his trophy stood outside the clubhouse in the pouring rain while Harold Henning and all the other white players were keeping dry inside. Photos of this presentation were sent all around the world and whether he wanted it or not, his face became perhaps the most recognised face of the ugly apartheid system. This subsequently culminated in the South African sporting boycotts of the time. The boycott and anti-apartheid demonstrations continued for quite some time after the 1965 Natal Open.

I was pleased to learn that long after Papwa's untimely demise at the age of only forty-eight, he posthumously received various honours in South Africa such as Hall of Fame status and a golf course named after him. I also heard that a film was being made about his life story but I don't know if it has been released yet. I can't wait to see that.

It's been fifty-four years since Jack Harris played in the same tournaments as Papwa. However, as soon as I mentioned his name, Jack immediately and without any prompting, told me about the unorthodox golf grip which Papwa employed. According to Jack Harris it was because of this cack-handed grip that Papwa generally hit the ball with a very low trajectory. Not worm burners like mine but much lower than most pros of the day were hitting. Jack Harris and Papwa both played in the 1960 Dutch Open at Eindhoven GC and in the *Yorkshire Evening News* at Moortown GC the same year but Jack couldn't remember exactly where they had played in the same group. He also has a vague memory of actually playing with him at Victoria GC in Melbourne sometime after that but I have so far not been able to find any information about that game. Nor can I find any evidence of Papwa ever playing at all anywhere in Australia.

The last leg of this first and last visit to Europe by Jack Harris was the German Open in Cologne. . The tournament was won by Peter Thomson who collected the 3000 Deutsche Marks first prize. It was played at the Refrath Golf and Country Club in Cologne. Jack's memory of this course was that it was cut in the middle of a large mature forest and almost every hole was a dog-leg. It was the end of a long trip and again Jack didn't play his best golf. But he still made the cut and tied 21st with Italian star Alfonso Angelini on 306. There were 140 starters but only 50 made the final cut. This course had the reputation of being the most difficult in Germany.

The big adventure was now at an end. The journey home, just like the outward leg, was a long, slow grind back in the big white bird but was otherwise uneventful. When I say *big* white bird, this really should be qualified. Melbourne Airport in those days was where Essendon airport is today. The current Tullamarine airport site was not around until 1970. So in 1960, the *big* white bird Jack arrived back into Essendon on was as likely as not, only a relatively *little* white bird. Most international flights from Australia in 1960 departed from Sydney Airport because Essendon could not handle the bigger aircraft. Even when the Beatles came to Melbourne in 1964 they had to wave at the thousands of screaming girls from the viewing platform at Essendon's main terminal building. There was no such crowd of screaming girls to welcome Jack Harris home, only three very important people he was dying to see: Grace, Christine and Marilyn.

Chapter 14

Caddies

It would be remiss of me, if at some stage in this book, I did not say something about caddies.

Firstly, because in Jack Harris's day and even before his day, lots of professional golfers came from the caddie ranks. Indeed Jack Harris himself was one of them. Jack had caddied at Kingston Heath GC for Dr Elliot True in the early 1930s. If the good doctor had not given Jack Harris a set of second-hand golf clubs, I may not be writing this book today. And I am sure that the same happened everywhere. The remarkable story of South African Sewsunker Sewgolum and Graham Wulff in the last chapter is perfect testimony to this. Even lots of non-professional golfers like me got their first taste of golf by caddying as school kids just to earn some extra pocket money.

Secondly, there were no TV cameras all over the place during those days. This meant that the caddies could have quite an influence on the outcome of the match. I am talking influence other than spotting golf balls, advising club selection, reading putt lines or advising yardages. This was because there was a lot of side betting which used to go on between the caddies. Balls could mysteriously disappear when they didn't look as though they should be lost. Or balls could suddenly magically appear when they looked as if they had definitely been lost.

There was a notorious case in the very early days where a caddie had a false sole built on to the bottom of his golf boot which had a trap door mechanism. This allowed him to just stand on the ball which was then just *lost*, trapped inside his false shoe sole. By doing this not only did he *help* the guy he was caddying for to win the match and himself to win the bet but after the game he also could sell the stolen golf ball to some other unsuspecting player. Golf balls were handmade in those days and were relatively expensive to buy.

To be sure, cheating in golf in the early days was not restricted to the caddies. Before TV cameras with zoom in lenses came on the scene which can just about read the logo on golf ball from a hundred yards away, it must have been fairly widespread. Jack Harris recounted several incidents which he saw over the years. One of these incidents probably even cost him a Victorian Close championship when he took a stance against it and withdrew from the tournament.

Even as late as the early 1980s, I personally witnessed a very dubious incident at Huntingdale GC with a caddie in the Australian Masters. I had been following a top contender around the course but could not get close enough to see him hit off from the tee because the crowds were too big. So I decided to wait part way down the fairway near to where most of the drives were landing. On one particular hole, and I don't remember which, he hit an almighty slice and it was miles away from where all the ball spotters were standing but not too far away from where I was waiting. I clearly saw the ball disappear into a very thick large clump of scrub. I decided not to say anything about where I had seen the ball go in and just waited around to observe what happened. To my absolute amazement, in no time at all, the caddie announced that he had found the ball. Not only that, but it just happened to be in the only small cleared area amongst the thick trees with even a clear shot to the green. There was no way in the world that the ball could have found its way to where it was eventually played from, not unless it had miraculously pinballed off about seventeen trees! The player made the green with the second shot and walked off smiling with a par. I was in two minds whether to go and find the original ball and have it mounted on a plinth for my mantelpiece but I quickly decided against it because I wanted to watch the rest of the golf. Not only that but I may have been in grave danger from a few tiger snakes because where the ball was reminded me of the Brazilian jungle.

In the days before Jack Harris started to play, golfers often used to have two caddies, one to carry their clubs and the other to go ahead of the player and act as a ball spotter. He was called the fore caddie. Most golf courses employed a caddie master and there was a grading system for caddies, a kind of caddie apprenticeship. Nowadays, following the introduction of the ride-on buggy and the pull buggy, caddies have just about totally disappeared from the average golf club, at least in the USA, Europe and Australia. They can definitely still be found in some of the Asian countries and maybe in South Africa where labour is still plentiful and much cheaper and also at a few of the more exclusive golf clubs in the USA and Europe.

Jack Harris started caddying when he was about eleven or twelve years old. There was in fact a *Rules and Discipline of Caddies* booklet published by St Andrews GC as early as 1864. This stated that no boy under the age of eleven was to be allowed to caddie. After a young boy had eventually been admitted to the caddie ranks one of the stipulated requirements was that he must attend Sunday school! I must remember to ask Jack if he abided by that particular rule!

Jack told me that when he started caddying at Kingston Heath in the early 1930s, there were 15 or 20 caddies permanently at the club and a caddy master in control of them. It would have been the same at all the other top clubs in Melbourne. I recently checked up at some of the more exclusive golf clubs in Melbourne, namely Royal Melbourne, Kingston Heath, Metropolitan and Victoria Golf Clubs. The only one where you can still hire a caddie is Royal Melbourne. Even there you cannot just roll up and hire one. You must book the caddie well in advance so that they can bring one in for you. It will cost you A$100 per round for a caddie which is payable at the pro shop. This presumably means that they take a cut and the caddie doesn't get the full $100. The $100 is exclusive of any tip you decide you may wish to give. All this is far cry from what was happening even towards the end of Jack Harris's playing days. Even in 1962, Ray Wright the club professional at Woodlands GC had forty-three A Grade caddies on his register and sixteen B Grade boys.

In the USA today maybe only five per cent of golf clubs employ caddies. Augusta National Golf Club in Georgia is still one of them, all dressed in their familiar white jump suits. But there again, Augusta National GC is a VERY exclusive golf club. If you wanted to play there, hiring a caddie would be the least of your problems. Most ordinary golfers would give their right arm just to have an opportunity to play there!

Currently, there is a Professional Caddies Association (PCA) in the USA and even a PCA Worldwide Caddie Hall of Fame. The PCA offers a Caddie Apprenticeship Programme and a Graduate Programme.

Despite this, one has to think that employment opportunities for caddies have to be somewhat limited. Only very wealthy people and the professional golfers playing on the PGA tour and maybe the other main tours can afford to employ a caddie.

However, if you are lucky enough to get a job caddying for any of the 230 PGA players who have a tour card, especially one who makes the cut on a regular basis, then it can be a rewarding job. I read somewhere that PGA caddies get a basic salary plus a percentage of the winnings. That percentage is obviously negotiable, but apparently it can be something like five per cent if they make the cut, seven per cent if they make the top ten and up to ten per cent if they win the tournament. If this is accurate, it means that even someone caddying for a lesser known PGA player can make a decent living. Consider Australian player Matt Jones who was forty-eighth on the 2013 PGA money list with US$1.72 million. Matt was third Australian on the 2013 PGA list. Even his caddie could perhaps pickup $86,000 plus a basic salary. At the other end of the scale, if you are Steve Williams who is now on Adam Scott's bag and was previously employed for quite a number of years by Tiger Woods, then the sky is the limit. I understand that at one stage Steve Williams was reputed to be the highest paid sportsperson in New Zealand and may still be for all I know. . In fact, in 2014 the top ten paid caddies on the PGA tour earned US$8.75 million between them, ranging from $625,000 to $1,570.000.

Even back in Jack Harris's day there was apparently an un-written law that if a player won a big tournament then his caddie would get ten per cent of the prize money. Thus when Alan Murray won the £500 first prize in the 1961 Victorian Open at Commonwealth GC, he gave his caddie, John Wright from Frankston, £50 plus his daily rounds payment. Defending champion Jack Harris only came third in that tournament, two shots behind British Open winner Peter Thomson but still ahead of super-stars Kel Nagle, Bruce Devlin, Frank Phillips, Ossie Pickworth and Billy Dunk. No doubt it was still a good day for Jack's caddie.

Some caddies became quite famous. One of them was a Greek-born gentleman by the name of Angelo Argea who was caddie for Jack Nicklaus during a big part of Jack's career. Angelo was an inaugural inductee into the Caddie Hall of fame in 1999. Another famous caddie was Carl Jackson, who did fifty or more Masters Tournaments and at least thirty-five of them carrying for Ben Crenshaw. And who can forget the bubbly Swedish lady, Fanny Sunneson, who for most of her career caddied for Nick Faldo (Sir Nick as we should now call him). I do believe that Fanny is also now in the PCA worldwide Hall of Fame.

Some caddies even became quite infamous. In 2001, at the age of forty-three, Ian Woosnam was making a comeback in the British Open at Royal Lytham and St Annes GC. He was going well until the final round when he discovered after a few holes that he had fifteen clubs in his bag. Caddie Miles Byrne had not checked them properly and Woosie got a two stroke penalty which knocked him from runner-up position into a tied for third with five other players. David Duval won his only ever major that year.

Another classic was David Graham's caddie in the 1979 US PGA which David won at Oaklands GC. When David asked for a yardage after his wayward tee shot on the final hole, the caddie told him to figure it out for himself! I hope David docked his pay for that little tantrum. How David ever resisted from stuffing his three-iron right up the guy's backside remains a mystery to this very day.

The importance of getting a good caddie at important tournaments could never be downplayed. When Peter Thomson won his first British Open at Royal Birkdale GC in 1954 he managed to acquire the services of a gentleman called Timmy Timms. No, definitely not Herbert Khaury, aka 'Tiny Tim', who thrilled us all with his high falsetto/vibrato voice when he sang Tiptoe Through the Tulips. Timmy had been an ex-Guardsman and an ex-professional footballer. He had caddied the previous year at Carnoustie for American superstar, Ben Hogan, who easily won the British Open on his one and only appearance in that event.

In 1954, lady luck smiled on Peter Thomson from all directions. Firstly, he had the previous year's winning caddie in his corner. Secondly, and more importantly, reigning and defending champion Ben Hogan decided that the British Open was a tinpot event. And it is not difficult to see why. When he won in 1953 he received £525 (US$1400). This compared to the US$4000 he also received in 1953 for winning the US Masters. Just like Sam Snead had done after his win in 1946 when he received £150 for winning, he didn't go back to defend his title. Had he done so he would probably have cleaned up again. He had won all three majors he played in during 1953 and had already been runner-up in the US Masters in 1954. In 1953 Ben Hogan became the only man in history to win the US Masters, the US Open and the British Open in the same year. Not even Tiger Woods or Jack Nicklaus managed to do that. Probably the only reason which prevented him from also being the only man in history to complete a calendar Grand Slam was the fact that he didn't play in the US PGA that year. Unfortunately, the British Open was held from 8 – 10 July and the US PGA from 1-7 July. He elected to play in the Open with a $7000 total purse instead of the US PGA with a $20,700 total purse and far less travelling expenses if he had stayed home to play the PGA!

According to *The Age*, 9 July 1954, Timms and Thomson did not get on well together at the start. Apparently, Thomson would not listen to club advice from Timms and this cost him strokes in the early rounds. Timms was quite eccentric in both dress and mannerisms. One of the strange things he did was to clean golf balls by sticking them in his gob! In the end it all worked out OK. Thomson won the 1954 British Open and Timms won his second in a row. Thomson won again in 1955 and 1956. Not sure if Timms was still with him on the bag at that time.

The caddie I always felt most sorry for was the fifteen year old Scot, Neil Ballingall, who caddied for Tommy Nakajima in the 1978 British Open at St Andrews. Nakajima had just got through the qualifying rounds after a play-off at Lundin GC when Ballingall landed the job of caddying for him even though he had never caddied for anyone in his life. After two rounds Tommy had shot 141 and even after he had just played his second shot on to the seventeenth green at the notorious Road Hole in the third round, he was still tied for the overall tournament lead. However that was when disaster struck. Having been on the green of the par four in two shots, he proceeded to shoot a quintuple bogey (nine) which not unexpectedly ruined his chances.

The problem was that even if Ballingall had been an experienced caddie it may not have made any difference because neither he nor Tommy spoke each other's language. All the way round the course any communication between them had to be done more or less in sign language. So even if Neil had been experienced enough to advise Tommy to play a different third shot to the putt he eventually played into the bunker, he may not have actually been able to get his message across. In the event he could only watch in absolute horror at the nightmare which unfolded.

At the end of the day it wasn't altogether a bad experience for Neil Ballingall. Before the final four rounds started he didn't think Tommy Nakajima would stand any chance at all in the tournament. As it turned out, even after the shambles at the seventeenth, Tommy still managed a respectable seventeenth placing. Ballingall still went home with a £160 pay packet for a few days' work which in those days for him was what he normally earned in a full month. Jack Nicklaus won his third and last British Open that year by two strokes from Raymond Floyd and Ben Crenshaw who tied for second place. (Yet another American whitewash)

Some golfers don't always have long and fruitful relationships with their caddies. In 2011, an article written by Peter Stone in the *Sydney Morning Herald* mentioned that Australian golfer, Robert Allenby had already changed his caddie at least thirty times during the twenty years or so he had been a touring professional. Another three years have passed since then and Robert has not performed especially well on the tour during that time. So no doubt a few more caddies have bitten the dust since then.

The record for the shortest ever relationship between a player and his caddie may well be owned by the Wattle Park GC teaching professional, Trevor Hollingsworth. He was playing in the Victorian PGA event at Albert Park GC in the late 1980s and had decided that his lovely wife Josie could caddie for him.

On the first tee Trevor hooked the ball very badly into the trees, at which point Josie proceeded to chastise Trevor for not taking her advice on club selection. Trevor spun around and told Josie that he didn't require any advice from her about club selection and that she was only there as a *bag puller*.

Josie hails from the island of Mauritius in the Indian Ocean and her native language is French. Maybe something was lost in the translation but all hell let loose. Josie tore off her caddie's bib, told Trevor that he could pull his own bloody trolley and stormed off. Josie's caddying career had lasted less than one hole! In fact only one stroke! Trevor never did find out what he had said wrong but they kissed and made up afterwards and are still happily married over twenty-five years later.

Girl caddies had actually first made their appearance in Australia about forty years before Josie Hollingsworth ventured out at Albert Park GC. In fact it was 1947 when schoolgirls on holiday were first allowed on to the links at Blackheath GC in the picturesque Blue Mountains to earn some extra pocket-money. However, girls humping bags around were not considered to be very lady-like and they didn't get many customers. The caddie profession had always been male dominated. Even today, despite the great success of Miss Sunneson, one doesn't find too many *Fannies* on Australian golf courses. (If you will pardon the expression!)

John Harris caddies for son Jack in professional purse won by Jack in 1949 at Victoria GC.

Robert Coates from Highett was a young man who used to caddie as a teenager for Jack Harris and Colin Campbell in the 1947-1950 period. This was back in the Manchester Unity golf school days and it was a good source of some extra pocket money for Robert. He recalled that life for the professional golfer in those days wasn't all that easy. For one thing, they were often treated pretty badly by the snootier clubs. Sometimes they would travel to three or four different courses before they could find one which would allow them to have a practice round there. Apart from this, the professionals were not even allowed into the club houses. Of course, Robert did not caddie for Jack in big tournaments. It was only in practice rounds.

In the early days, while Jack was working in the city golf school environment, it was his dad John who usually carried his bag in order to keep down their costs.

For most of his later tournament-playing career, Jack had the same bag man. He was a groundsman at the Metropolitan GC and later at the Keysborough GC where Jack was club professional. His name was Norm Kingshott, who according to Jack was 'a decent chap and a very good caddie, albeit a bit of a rough diamond.' Ever since he had become a groundsman at Metropolitan GC, Norm Kingshott had dreamed about walking on to the eighteenth green at Metropolitan on the final day, caddying for the winner of the Victorian Open. In 1960, Norm's dream came true when Jack Harris won the championship and in the process shot 282. This equalled the 1936 record for the Metropolitan course set by the legendary US Champion Gene Sarazen in the Australian Open. Jack also beat a few other very handy golfers that day including Billy Dunk 286, Alan Murray 287, Frank Phillips 290, Norman von Nida 293 and Bruce Crampton 297, just to name a few!

The last player to win the Victorian Open when it was played at Metropolitan was Greg Norman in 1984. He pipped Jack's score by one stroke to shoot 281 but it has to be said that the layout of the course had been changed by that time so it was not a strict comparison. Gary Player had won the Victorian Open in 1959 at Yarra Yarra GC.

While Norm Kingshott was a regular caddie for Jack Harris, his old mate Ossie Pickworth also had a long-time caddie. His name was Doug Ferguson. Ossie used to refer to Doug as his "baby-sitter". Doug was a pretty good sportsman in his own right. He had represented Victoria in swimming and he had also played Australian Rules football for North Melbourne. Sadly, Doug passed away after a long illness in 1957, only one year before Ossie retired from tournament golf.

According to the *Referee*, (Sydney, NSW) 7 November 1935, Ossie Pickworth's 19-year-old brother Allan Pickworth won the NSW Caddie championship in 1935. According to golfing sources Allan was arguably a better golfer than Ossie at that stage. However, he elected to remain an amateur golfer and follow in his father's footsteps as a stone mason.

I wonder when caddies in the PGA events will be allowed to pull a buggy around the course like the rest of us instead of humping a big heavy bag around day after day. I have read about all the reasons why this is currently not permitted but none of these reasons seem to me to be in any way convincing. It is true that the buggy tyres can flatten down the grass temporarily. However, the temporary flattening by buggy tyres is nowhere near as severe as the grass trampling done by hordes of spectators in many of the big tournaments. This can be very severe when the weather is wet. Personally I cannot see a problem with using a buggy providing they are kept off the putting surface.

I often think that the crowds are actually a very big advantage to professional golfers. Many times when the pros hit the ball off the fairway into what should be the rough they often find themselves in a half decent lie because the grass has been trampled flat by the crowd. Also many times a player hits a wayward shot which is prevented from going even deeper into the rough because it hits someone in the crowd. Often the ball is stopped dead by the crowd or sometimes even bounces back on to the fairway.

The truth is that the massive golf bags which the touring pros have are quite heavy even when empty. Once they are filled with fourteen clubs, an umbrella, wet weather gear, spare balls and tees, drinks and food, replacement gloves and towels, they are much heavier. I am surprised that Work Safe has not jumped on this as a Health and Safety issue. I wonder if caddies ever suffer from Repetitive Strain Injury (RSI)? Tennis players get tennis elbow. I wonder if caddies get caddies' shoulder.

In the old days the caddie's lot when it came to humping stuff around was even worse than it is today. The use of golf bags to put the clubs in was only introduced during the 1880s. Prior to that the caddie just tucked the clubs under his arm or slung them over his shoulder. That maybe wasn't too bad because the number of clubs used by the early golfers was quite low. The great amateur golfer, Francis Ouimet, won the 1913 US Open Championship using only seven clubs. However, from 1913 to 1938 conditions got steadily worse for caddies. At that stage there was no limit to how many golf clubs a golfer could use in a tournament and over this period the number of golf clubs and hence the weight the caddie had to carry around gradually increased. In 1934, the British Amateur Championship at Prestwick GC was won by US golfer Lawson Little who had an amazing thirty-one clubs in his bag! He retained the title in 1935 at Royal Lytham and St Annes GC.

Jack Harris, Norm Kingshott and Bob Spencer. On their way to winning the 1959 Victorian Foursomes

Obviously the situation was getting out of hand so in the 1938 the USGA brought in a new rule limiting the number of golf clubs permitted to fourteen. The R&A followed suit in 1939 and caddies around the world breathed a collective sigh of relief. Lawson Little turned pro in 1936 and won the US Open in 1940. He would have been down to fourteen clubs by then which just goes to show that he didn't really need thirty-one clubs to win tournaments. Even quite a time after the rule had changed, Jack Harris once remembers Jim Ferrier playing in a practice game in Melbourne with a massive golf bag which had a normal set of irons plus a set of *half* irons. So for example there were two, three, four and five irons and also two point five, three point five, four point five irons. As for me, I am down to only ONE club so it would obviously be a dream job caddying for me!

We may continue to see caddies in the PGA tour and other main tours for a long time yet. Also caddies will continue to be used by wealthy people as shown by the success of the Ponte Vedra Beach based Caddie Master Company. This company offer a premier caddie management service for the more up-market golf clubs with over two thousand caddies on their books. But for the average Joe Hacker and the average golf club, they have long since disappeared. The opportunity for someone like Jack Harris to progress from caddie right through to professional golfer or for my grandchildren to earn some pocket money has gone. It is just a thing of past, at least as far as Australia is concerned. Maybe if we go to live in Thailand, Cambodia, Myanmar or Vietnam it could still be done?

Chapter 15

When Is a Rule Not a Rule?

When is a rule not a rule? The answer to that question is when the USGA and the R&A governing bodies decide to withdraw the rule from the Rule Book. This is exactly what they did in 1952 with a quirky little rule known as the Stymie Rule. The change was actually approved by the USGA in August 1951 and agreed to by the R&A in September that year. The abolition of the stymie finally came into effect on January 1, 1952. Perhaps no rule in the history of the game had ever divided the golfing community as did the stymie rule. Even when this rule was finally withdrawn there were still plenty of golfers who wanted it to be retained.

This rule was in place for about the first fifteen years of Jack Harris's career, and indeed had been in place for many years before Jack was even born. Therefore it is maybe worth having a brief look at the rule and what effect it may have had on matches. There is evidence that the R&A GC in St Andrews, Scotland, had been deliberating the stymie rule even as long ago as the late 1700s so it had been around for a very long time indeed.

I don't pretend to know all the ins and outs of the stymie rule but in simple layman's terms it seemed to me to be akin to being snookered at the game of snooker or pool. I personally never had any personal experience playing with this rule. By the time I played my first game of golf in 1959 the rule had already been dead and buried for six or seven years but I do remember many old-timers of the day telling me about it.

In golf apparently this rule was only invoked when playing a singles match-play format. It didn't apply to stroke-play. The situation arose when both the player's and his opponent's ball were on the putting surface. If the opponent's ball was on a direct line between the hole and the player's ball, thus effectively blocking his path, then the player was said to be stymied. This was because the opponent was able under the rule to leave his ball where it was and was not obliged to lift and mark it. This could only happen if the gap between the two balls was six inches or less. In the old days they even had a red line exactly six inches long marked on the bottom of scorecards. This was called a Stymie Gauge and was there to avoid any disputes when checking if the gap was six inches or less.

This meant that the player had more or less two options. He could try to bend his putt around the other ball or he could try to chip over the top of it. If he actually hit his opponent's ball there was no penalty like there is in stroke-play. The player then had to make his next putt from wherever his ball had stopped whereas his opponent had a choice. If his ball had finished nearer to the hole he could elect to putt from there. Conversely, if it had been knocked further away from the hole, he could elect to play his ball from the original spot. When the player accidentally knocked his opponent's ball into the hole then it was deemed that the opponent had holed out with his previous shot.

The laying of stymies and the getting out of stymies would have been something of an art form with the best match play exponents of the day. Obviously, the trick when playing to this rule would be to make sure if at all possible that you pitched or chipped your ball closer to the pin than your opponent in the first place. However, one can imagine that for the very skilful player it could even be an advantage to leave his second shot on the fringe rather than on the green a long way from the pin. I suppose a player would be most annoyed when he played a shot and stymied himself! Or herself!

In a 1936 match between Mrs Robinson the Royal Sydney champion and Mrs Slack, the latter player had been leading for most of the match until she unfortunately stymied herself on the seventeenth which resulted in her losing the match. That was a bit slack! *Coo coo ca choo, Mrs Robinson*! In professional matches, the consequences of a stymie could be very significant.

In the 1927 *News of the World* £1040 tournament held at Tadworth in Surrey, George Duncan lost the match on the second extra hole after he had been stymied by Charles Whitcombe. Legends of the game Harry Vardon, James Braid and Ted Ray were also playing in that tournament.

There has been some very creative ways over the years to get out of a stymie situation. Arthur Gazzard, the former Queensland Open champion, did one such shot when he beat One-putt Charlie Brown in a Dunlop Cup semi-final just before the last war. Playing at Yeerongpilly GC in Queensland, Arthur was dead stymied when Charlie's ball stopped on the lip of the cup. However he played his own putt hard with some top spin which knocked Charlie's ball six feet away from the cup and allowed his own ball to follow through and go into the cup. Charlie still halved the hole because under the rules he was able to replace his ball back near the lip of the cup. But the incident unnerved Charlie and Arthur ended up winning the match. I also read that Kel Nagle had played exactly the same shot in 1949 at the eighth hole at Royal Perth in the Australian PGA Championships when playing against Alf Toogood.

One of the best ever players of stymie shots was the Australian golfer Joe Kirkwood. Joe had a whole bag full of trick shots and went around the world doing exhibition matches in the 1920s and 1930s often with US golfer Walter Hagen. He could bend the ball around his opponent's ball, and he could chip or pitch over it to hole out. He could even chip where his ball bounced before his opponent's ball and then hopped over it on the next bounce and into the hole.

Another great stymie player was the American golfer Joe Ezar. Jack remembers Joe Ezar very well from the days when Joe toured Australia with Paul Runyan and Leo Diegel. This was back in the 1930s when Jack was still at the caddying stage or very early days with Colin Campbell. According to Jack, Joe Ezar was very much a showman. He was also the king of golfing hustlers and regularly performed a perfect cashectomy on the locals wherever he went.

A very significant match was won by virtue of a stymie in the British amateur Championship of 1930. In the penultimate round Bobby Jones stymied Cyril Tolley on the first extra hole to get through to the final which he won easily seven and six against Roger Wethered. This was one of Bobby Jones's Grand Slam victories in 1930. He was the first man in history to achieve the Grand Slam and retired immediately afterwards.

In the pre-war years, it was quite common to have Pro Golf Challenge matches. On one occasion in 1941, the brother of Jack Harris's old school friend Paddy Smith, Martin Smith, had issued a challenge to play Norman von Nida in a thirty-six hole match in a winner take all situation. The members at the Northern GC had raised £100 to match the £100 put up by the Von. The match was very tight and was watched by about two thousand five hundred people. Martin was one down as they reached the seventeenth green but he managed to stymie the Von. However with Martin's ball ten inches from the hole, von Nida managed to chip over from two feet into the hole and score a dramatic two and one win to pocket the £200. It would be difficult to imagine two golfers as different in appearance as Martin Smith and von Nida. von Nida was fairly short in stature and of slender build. On the other hand, Martin Smith was an imposing giant of a man standing over six feet and weighing around eighteen stone. Talk about Little and Large!

I can imagine that the stymie shot was not all that loved by green keepers because if lofted clubs were used to get out of a stymie the putting surface could easily be damaged. Bobby Locke was renowned as a great putter and he used to play all his putts with a slightly closed putter face so that all his putts hooked a bit. I wonder if he developed this style of putting from his experience of getting out of stymies.

For a long time prior to 1952 there had always been a lobby of golfers trying to persuade the governing bodies to abolish the stymie rule but the R&A had steadfastly refused to budge . However, in 1934 they did partially relent. At the behest of the Bendigo GC in Victoria, Australia, they changed the rule and decided that the stymie rule on sand scrape 'greens' be abolished. This was done because the damage caused to the sand scrape when trying to execute an escape from a stymie was causing havoc and infuriating the members. Actually this was not the first abolition of the stymie rule. In 1931, the German Golf Association had already totally abolished the stymie in all competitions for that year because they had argued that it robs the skilful player and assists the less skilful player. But this did not have any impact worldwide at that stage because Germany only had a handful of golf clubs in those days and were not really in any position to influence the major governing bodies.

As far as Jack Harris was concerned, match-play was never his favourite format. His strength on the golf course was his great consistency and he generally did much better at stroke-play for this reason. He wasn't a flashy player who went for hero shots which looked great if they came off. Nevertheless he did play quite a lot of match-play games, so I did ask him if he could recall any interesting incidents which had arisen when he had played under the stymie rule. He told me that in actual fact it was quite rare to be stymied. It did happen to him on a few occasions but it was never at a crucial point in the match and he never won or lost a match because of a stymie situation. He told me that he personally never deliberately tried to lay stymies when he played match play but he knew that some golfers did try to do this. Nor was any of his practice (the little practice that he did) ever devoted to the laying of or the getting out of stymies.

Jack Harris's old mate Ossie Pickworth once mentioned in a newspaper article he wrote in the *Sunday Herald* in March, 1949 that he also never deliberately tried to play for stymies. In fact he even went on to say that he thought stymies were mostly fluke shots. Having said that, Ossie then described a truly remarkable, once in a lifetime, stymie experience which had happened to him in early October, 1948.

The great Jim Ferrier had just arrived in Melbourne from the USA to prepare for the Australian Open later that month. Jim had won the US PGA Championship in 1947 and was winning US PGA Tour events all over the place. As part of his preparation he had challenged Ossie to a series of match-play challenge matches. During a game at Huntingdale GC, Jim Ferrier laid seven consecutive stymies on Ossie and each time it resulted in a lost hole for Ossie. Even though Ossie managed to dead stymie Jim on one hole it didn't help him. Ferrier won the match ten and eight.

As if it wasn't bad enough to lose by such a crushing margin, Ossie reported that Ferrier was even more intimidating than just his skill at laying stymies. Throughout the round at Huntingdale, Ossie mentioned that Ferrier had been bombing his drives 300 to 320 yards whereas his own drives were only averaging about 240 yards.

A lesser man may have been seriously scarred by such a heavy defeat with the 1948 Australian Open at Kingston Heath only about two weeks away. But Ossie had won the Australian Open in 1946 and 1947. He was the defending champion and was going for three in a row. There was no way the boy from Borneo was going to drop his pants. Besides which the Australian Open was a stroke-play event so there was no chance of Ferrier pulling seven consecutive stymies out of his backside again because stymies could only happen in match-play events.

The other amazing thing about the 1948 Australian Open championship, and a not so well-known fact, was that BOTH Ossie Pickworth AND Jim Ferrier were going for three in a row when they met at Kingston Heath. Before World War II, and before he had emigrated to the USA, Jim Ferrier had won the 1938 and 1939 Opens playing as an amateur. The tournament was not played between 1940 and 1945 and Jim did not contest the 1946 and 1947 tournaments which Ossie won. Jim Ferrier played in the Australian Open more times as an amateur than he did as a professional. In the 1930s, apart from winning it twice, he also came runner-up three times and had three other top ten finishes.

History shows us that Ossie Pickworth won the 1948 Australian Open at Kingston Heath GC when he beat Jim Ferrier in an eighteen-hole play-off after the first-ever tie in the Australian Open. In doing so he became, and to this day remains, the only man in history to win three consecutive Australian Opens.[11] No doubt his once in a lifetime stymie experience against Ferrier two weeks earlier had been a big motivating factor for him. Whatever the case I am sure that revenge was never sweeter.

---

11   In 1947 Ossie had also set another Australian record when he became the first Australian golfer to win both the Australian Open and the Australian PGA events in the same year.

Chapter 16

Characters of the Game and the John McEnroe of Golf

In the time I have been watching and reading about golf, there have been quite a few golfers who stood out from the crowd. They were characters who brought something to the game apart from their exceptional golfing abilities.

In the very earliest years that I became interested in the game, there was Arnold Palmer (nicknamed 'The King') who played golf in a truly swashbuckling way. He didn't know what it was to play safe. He just went for everything and the crowd, dubbed Arnie's Army, just loved it.

Soon after that there was the jovial Mexican, Lee Trevino, who more or less laughed and joked his way around the course. When people saw his extremely unusual, very wide open stance they also wanted to laugh but not for long when they saw that he hit the ball straight down the middle nearly every time.

As far as charisma was concerned there has never been anyone who came even close to the young man from Pedrena in Las Asturias on the northern coast of Spain. This is not far from the Basque cities of Bilbao and San Sebastian and not a million miles away from where they run the bulls at Pamplona, the capital of Navarre, in the Rioja wine region of Spain. The popularity of golf worldwide certainly got a big shot in the arm when Severiano Ballesteros burst on to the scene in the mid-1970s. Incidentally, his first professional win was in 1976 at the Dutch Open. A feat he shared in common with the little master, Sewsunker Sewgolum.

In later years there was a guy called Payne Stewart who dressed a bit like a clown in very colourful clothes. When you dress like that you had better be able to play and play he could, to the tune of three majors and eleven PGA titles. As mentioned earlier, tuition he received in 1982 from none other than Jack Harris, golf teacher, may have played some small part in Payne's success.

Then coming right up to date we cannot omit John Daly from any list of characters. He had a grip it and rip it approach to golf and life in general. This coupled with a golf swing which had to be seen to be believed, always attracted a crowd wherever he played. John won two majors including one at the home of golf, St Andrews, in 1995, when he beat Constantino Rocca in a play-off. Unfortunately his life off the course sometimes attracted more media attention than his on-course endeavours.

If we now go back in time to the era when Jack Harris played, it seems more difficult to name many real characters of the game. When I asked Jack Harris about this he agreed. Golf seemed to be a serious business in those days even though prize money was very low. Maybe it was because it was the period immediately after the Second World War and life everywhere was still a big challenge for most people. Having said this, there was one undeniably colourful character in Australian golf during that era. His name was Norman von Nida. From the hundreds of newspaper match reports I have read, I could devote a whole book just to describe the antics of the Von. I think the best way to describe it is to say that what John McEnroe was to tennis, Norman von Nida was to golf. They were two guys at the pinnacle of their sport, yet they certainly knew how to infuriate both the officials and their opponents.

It seems that everyone who ever played with von Nida has a story to tell. He had fights with opponents, with starters, with official photographers, with organisers and with people in the crowd. In fact with anyone at all he could pick a fight with. He used to complain about slow play, fast play, screeching cockatoos and the equipment other players were using. Besides this he was continually chuntering and swearing to himself if things were going wrong. And then there was the golf club throwing. Never mind about shouting fore if you had hit a big slice. Just get ready to duck if Norman's mashie or putter were about to be launched.

Jack Harris remembers the very first time he played with von Nida was at a tournament in Adelaide. von Nida had heard the starter calling earlier groups to the tee and just calling out their surnames. So before he and Jack were due to be called up, he went to the starter and insisted that he be called up as Mr von Nida. The starter was an old experienced guy who had seen it all before and who wasn't one bit phased by the Vons's approach. When it was time to call up Norman and Jack, the starter calmly announced 'Messrs von Nida and Harris to the first tee please', thus neatly defusing the situation. I asked Jack about this and if it upset his concentration in anyway. He said it didn't. Jack told me that von Nida had told him that he used to play these games as a way to fire himself up to play his best and that he needed to attract a crowd around him to do that. But from all accounts many of his actions were clearly aimed at putting his opponents off or getting under their skin. Obviously gamesmanship, or legalised cheating as I like to call it, was present in golf just as much as in other sports. As far as the public has been concerned however, golf has always appeared to maintain a good image as far as sportsmanship is concerned. There are literally dozens of instances of where golfers call penalties on themselves for a ball they saw move at address which no one else saw.

Jack said that he personally was never affected by anything von Nida did or said during a game and he played with him many times (and beat him many times). But there again Jack Harris was from all accounts a true gentleman both on and off the golf course. Everyone enjoyed playing with him, whereas Norman von Nida often provoked very bad reactions in some golfers.

In 1952 Ampol brought out a group of American golfers to play in a series of matches. During a match at Yarra Yarra GC there was one American, Ed 'Porky' Oliver (three times runner-up in major championships), who threatened to walk off in the middle of a match rather than continue to play with von Nida who was niggling him throughout the game. The problems appeared to start after the ninth and tenth holes both of which von Nida had three putted. Unfortunately, as often happened, his behaviour was rewarded because he got into the mind of Oliver and finished up halving the match and then winning the play-off.

His approach to golf was not restricted to matches in Australia either. He was just the same when he played overseas. I recall that when he played in English tournaments he had a certain notoriety and event organisers never knew when the next incident was coming. One time in a 1948 PGA event in the USA he had been playing with a big Texan called Henry Ransom.

The Von had been niggling Henry the whole game. In the bar, after the game was over, von Nida wanted to carry on the discussion. Finally Henry got a bit tired of this Aussie guy annoying him, so he just turned around and floored him with a bunch of fives. For his indiscretion Henry was banned from playing for a while. Just like often happens in AFL football the person who retaliates is always penalised but the one who commits the original infringement usually gets away scot- free. *C'est la vie!*

Despite all von Nida's aggressive behaviour on the golf course, according to Jack Harris, most of his Australian peers at least seemed to get on with him OK and more than that, most of them even liked him. Jack Harris only ever had nice words to say about Norman von Nida throughout our many discussions.

Often when Norman von Nida was in Melbourne he would call Jack Harris and arrange to visit Keysborough GC and have a practice round with him. But when the Von turned up, Jack would usually invite a couple of regular Keysborough high handicap club members to play with them. This used to infuriate von Nida. That bloody Jack Harris will play with anyone he used to say.

Certainly a golfer didn't need to be as belligerent as Norman von Nida to get under the skin of other players. A good example of this was a story I heard of a young up-and-coming NSW pro. This guy found himself drawn in the first round of a tournament played at Royal Sydney GC in the early 1970s against an older well established super-star of Australian golf. The young pro had not played with the super-star before and in fact had never even met him. So on the first tee he introduced himself in a courteous manner only to be somewhat taken aback by the very off-hand response he got. There was no 'pleased to meet you' or 'have a good round' or any of the normal pleasantries you might say to someone you haven't met before. The only response to the young pro was 'you look for your ball sonny and I'll look for mine.' These kinds of incidents, even forty years, later remain vivid in the memory bank. I am sure that the super-star didn't win a new friend for life on that particular day!

Another golfer of that era who seemed to have a lot of appeal to golf aficionados was Jack Harris's old mate Ossie Pickworth. When he was on a roll in a match, which was quite often, he could frequently be seen blowing kisses to the crowd to liven them up a bit. One time he was even given a reprimand by the event organisers for cheering, along with the large crowd, when an opponent missed an important putt late in the game. But anything Ossie did was pretty tame compared to some of the von Nida shenanigans.

Since we are talking about characters in golf, it would be remiss of me if I didn't mention Jack's early mentor and subsequent partner in several ventures, the late Colin Campbell. He was the original Mr Golf of Victoria. Whatever was happening around golf Colin was always involved. Whether it was a golf school on the roof of a city skyscraper, golf segments on TV in the early days of *World of Sport* or getting punters to hit golf balls off the back of cruise ships while swanning around the South Pacific Islands, Colin was into it. Or even serious stuff like designing the original Dunes golf course on the Mornington Peninsula back in the days when it was called Limestone Valley GC. Colin did it all, as well as teaching Jack Harris how to be a top class golfer!

As for Jack Harris, I never read one single negative comment about his behaviour on or off the golf course in all the hundreds of newspaper reports I have scrutinised during the research for this book. Nor have I heard one single bad word about him in all the discussions I have had. Jack Harris was in fact the very antithesis of all the above mentioned characters. He never drew attention to himself either on or off the golf course. In fact, journalists frequently referred him to as 'Gentleman Jack' – just like that other quite well known Gentleman Jack from Ohio who managed to sneak away with eighteen majors before he retired.

Jack did witness one or two amusing incidents on occasions when he was playing golf interstate. He recalled one time he was staying in a Queensland hotel with a few other travelling golfers. Some of them were having a quiet nightcap at the hotel bar when a colleague was seen sheepishly trying to sneak past them dressed only in his underpants. Apparently the rest of his clothes had been flung out of a bedroom window by an irate young lady and he was *en route* to the front of the hotel to retrieve them. Obviously there must have been 'tigers' in the ranks of professional golfers even in the 1950s!

Chapter 17

Best Ever World Golfers

Whenever any group of golfers get together over a coffee or a few beers after a game, the conversation often drifts around to 'who was the best golfer ever?' And as might be expected, opinions are always divided between the Tiger Woods camp and the Jack Nicklaus camp. Generally the older golfers in the group like me vote for Jack Nicklaus. Meanwhile, younger golfers who were brought up in the Tiger era vote for him.

Both groups can point to a large array of statistics which support their view, such as Jack has won four more majors or Tiger reached certain milestones at a younger age than Jack.

At the end of the day it is always difficult to compare sportsmen across different eras, because so many factors change. However, it is precisely because of many of these changes why I personally think that Jack Nicklaus was and still is, simply the best.

Yes, Jack Nicklaus has to date won more majors and his consistency in majors is better than Tiger's. Jack won eighteen majors versus fourteen to date for Tiger and his overall average finishing position in majors is significantly better than Tiger's. Both players have had five year droughts during which time they didn't win a major, but Jack's drought occurred between the age of forty-one to forty-five whereas Tiger's has occurred between the age of thirty-four to thirty-eight and still continues at the time of writing (February 2014). But even these statistics are not why I think Jack Nicklaus was the best and Jack Harris agrees with me.

I think that what really sorts out the men from the boys is not the size of their toys: it is the equipment they used. Jack Nicklaus played all his regular PGA golf with old technology equipment, old style golf balls and old style golf clubs.

Let us consider the golf balls first. In Jack Nicklaus's day, all the golf balls were made by winding a stretched natural rubber thread around a small hollow rubber ball which had been filled with a barium sulphate paste. Barium sulphate has a high specific gravity (4.5) and this gave weight to the golf ball. Once the appropriate amount of thread had been wound around this little ball, a final cover, made from balata (gutta percha), was moulded-on. Midway through Jack's regular tour career the covers had been replaced by ionomer resin which gave a dramatic improvement in cut resistance.

The big problem for the golf ball manufacturer in those days was to try to ensure that the small barium sulphate ball stayed in the very centre of the ball during the winding process. This wasn't always easy to do and often the finished product would have a slight built-in bias because the inner ball was not dead centre. In other words, although the final weight of the golf ball was fairly consistent at 1.62 ounces (45.93 grams), this weight was not always evenly distributed across the ball. Then there was the quality of the natural rubber which was used. Most natural rubber in Jack's day came from the Malaysian rubber plantations. (These days most of the rubber plantations in Malaysia have been replaced by palm oil plantations) Natural rubber is made by a coagulation process of latex which comes from the rubber tree (*Hevea Brasiliensis*). The quality varies quite a bit from tree to tree. And one never knew if the plantation workers had peed in the latex before it was coagulated. (Sometimes it used to smell as though they had!) The Malaysian rubber producers did eventually introduce an improved quality grading system (SMR grades, Standard Malaysian Rubber) but still quite a bit of variation remained. This would manifest itself in modulus and rebound resilience variation of the final natural rubber thread which in turn could change slightly the way the balls performed on the golf course.

Thus Jack Nicklaus always played with golf balls that wouldn't necessarily always run true on a putting green and which wouldn't always perform the same on the long shots either. Even the moulding process for the final balata cover was much less sophisticated in those days than it is in today's high- tech balls. By comparison the balls which Tiger has always played with never had the natural rubber winding in the centre and never suffered from the built-in bias problem. In addition, all the raw materials used in modern golf ball manufacture are synthetic materials and are considerably more consistent in quality that natural rubber ever was. The quality of the final golf ball is further enhanced these days because everything is computer controlled and human error is mostly eradicated.

Eventually the boffins in the laboratory at companies such as Goodyear did learn how to make a synthetic version of polyisoprene which was still a crystallising polymer. This gave the polymer high gum strength which meant that it didn't need reinforcing with fillers such as silica or carbon black to obtain high tensile strength. Overall the quality was much more consistent than natural rubber. Synthetic polyisoprene was sometimes used in golf ball manufacture during the wound thread days and would have improved quality significantly. But the built-in bias problem would still have been an issue.

Since at the elite level of golf the difference between winning and losing often comes down to putting, it is easy to see that Tiger and his peers have a big advantage. Tiger plays with golf balls that are very consistent from batch to batch. Every time he pulls out a new ball he can always expect that it will perform exactly like the last one he pulled out. And all his competitors are in the same boat.

Jack Nicklaus did not have this advantage. There was much more variation in those days which Jack Nicklaus had to overcome and this variability could vary from player to player in a tournament even if they were playing with the same brand of golf ball. We are not talking about massive variation. But when golf often comes down to a game of millimetres, even a very small variation in the ball can make a significant difference to the outcome.

It is highly likely that Jack Nicklaus was unaware of this variation when he played because I doubt whether the golf ball makers would highlight it to the players. The players would just look at a missed putt and think they had misread the line of the putt when in reality the ball may also have been making a significant contribution to the deviation.

Another difference which Jack Nicklaus had to contend with which Tiger never had to bother about was to decide whether to play with the American big ball (1.68 inch diameter) or the British small ball (1.62 inch diameter).

In the USA the 1.68 in. ball had been the norm since 1932 whereas in England the 1.62 in. ball had been the norm since 1920. Both balls were the same weight 1.62 ounces. Until 1974 when the R&A standardised on the bigger ball, players in the British Open had the choice of using either size ball. The fact was that the smaller ball gave better driving distance and better control in windy conditions. So Jack Nicklaus and the other Americans who travelled to England in the 1950s and 1960s to play in the British Open were in a dilemma. They had to decide whether to play the bigger ball they were most familiar with and sacrifice both distance and control to UK players. Alternatively they could play the small ball which they were not used to playing with and this would affect the distance they hit any particular club. In fact the R&A did not completely ban the small ball totally until 1990, so for UK club players still had a choice as to which ball they would use.

The other point I always used to wonder about when the change was made to the big ball, was, what effect did that really have on putting? The size of the hole on the green never changed. It was kept at 4.25 inches outside diameter. This meant that when changing from the small ball to the big ball, the available area left around the ball as it entered the hole was about one point three per cent smaller. Assuming of course that I have done the sums properly! I always suspected that the big ball would be slightly more prone to Mick Jaggers (lip-outs) than the small ball. It is nearly fifty years since I studied physics and I have forgotten most of it by now. No doubt some fourteen year old school boy can do the calculation and tell us whether my suspicion makes sense or not.

Since we have been talking a lot about putting, let us mention another big advantage which Tiger has always had in this section of the game. For about two thirds of the time Jack Nicklaus played on the regular tour there was no Stimpmeter used to check the speed of the greens. This equipment only came into regular use in 1978 even though it was first designed in 1935. For most of Jack's career he had to overcome more variable speed greens. The Stimpmeter technique used today is not a perfect science but it is definitely a big improvement over what Jack Nicklaus had to cope with. At least I assume that it makes an improvement otherwise they wouldn't have continued to use it.

Science and technology has made monumental strides since Jack Nicklaus's playing days. Putting has not only been made more consistent because of the Stimpmeter. For sure the technology used by the curators to maintain the greens in tip top condition through improved moisture and chemical balance control has also developed out of sight. Even the mowing equipment used to cut the grass is extremely sophisticated these days and undoubtedly will give much more uniform putting surfaces that the ones Jack Nicklaus had to cope with.

So Jack Nicklaus had to cope with golf balls which didn't always run true, which didn't always fly through the air consistently and also had to play on different speed greens. And yet when Jack Nicklaus needed to make a crucial putt he often found a way to make it.

Then we come to the golf clubs and there have been massive changes here too. The irons have changed quite a bit although the changes are maybe less apparent to the layman's eye than the changes in the woods, especially driver design.

Probably the biggest impact was the change in the driver. The transition was made from club heads made out of hard persimmon wood to clubs made out of metal, usually titanium. This also allowed the size of the club head to increase without radically changing the weight and balance. So when the old persimmon driver is put side by side with the modern 460 cc. titanium head driver they are like chalk and cheese.

Apart from the different construction materials used on the drivers and the fairway wood club heads there has also been enormous change in the club shaft technology. Modern computer controlled production techniques for making the carbon fibre composite golf shafts is light years away from where it used to be. As could be anticipated, all these changes resulted in increased driving distance. This in itself didn't necessarily help the golfer because wherever possible the event organisers responded by making the holes longer. As far as I am concerned though, the real benefit in the new driver technology, came not from the fact that it made the drives longer, but because it generally gave much better control over the direction of the drive.

In the old days with the persimmon clubs I was absolutely terrified of using my driver. I knew that if I mishit the old driver, it was very unforgiving and the ball went just about anywhere. These days my trusty old Tailormade Burner is my favourite club. Most times I hit the fairway with it and when I do miss the fairway I am generally only in the first cut and virtually always have some kind of a shot. Jack Nicklaus would have played with persimmon drivers for his entire career when he was on the regular tour. Persimmon woods dominated until the late 1980s so I am guessing that Tiger has mostly played with modern titanium drivers.

Just as a matter of interest the average driving distance in the 1963 US Open was 245 yards. Into the breeze it was 228 yards and with the breeze it was 263 yards. This figure had only increased to an average of 257 yards by 1980. This compares in modern times with an average of about 290 yards. So despite the perception that the modern tour players knock the ball a mile, the truth is that they are on average only forty-five yards further than they hit the ball in 1963. Another way to look at this is to look at the rate of improvement per year over any given period. Between 1960 and 1980 the extra length gained was approximately 0.70 yards per year. Whereas from 1980 to 2014 the extra length gained is about 0.97 yards per year. So the gain over a twenty year period with persimmon technology was only about 0.27 yards per year less than what has been seen with the modern titanium technology.

When it came to driving a golf ball, Jack Nicklaus was an absolute freak. Even though the average in the 1980 US Open was only 257 yards, Nicklaus was averaging 275 yards throughout the 1968 season with old technology balls and clubs. Only ten players averaged better than that on the 1995 PGA Tour using modern balls and clubs!

What surprised me about this is the swing speed comparison between the two eras. According to an article in a 1972 edition of *Golf Digest* a swing speed comparison between Jack Nicklaus, Arnold Palmer and Gary Player was carried out using 33 mm. movie frames. This measured the total time elapsed from starting the back-swing to impacting the ball. Palmer was the quickest at 1.36 seconds, Player was 1.60 seconds and Nicklaus was slowest on 1.96 seconds.

This seemed strange because Jack Nicklaus always hit the ball further than Player and Palmer. What the article didn't mention however, was the difference in the speed between the back-swing and the forward-swing. Although Nicklaus's overall swing time was slower, I think that his club must have actually been travelling faster at the moment of impact. This suggests to me that maybe his forward-swing was up to four times quicker than his back-swing. Most modern day swings are completed in 1-1.2 seconds with the forward-swing being about three times faster than the back-swing. In other words perhaps Jack Nicklaus had a different swing tempo to modern day golfers?

In 1954 there was a driving competition at Royal Perth GC when some of the US players were in attendance and the prize money for the longest drive was twenty pounds. The wind on that day was a cross wind. Results were as follows:

1	Dutch Harrison (USA)	273 yards
2	Tommy Bolt (USA)	259
3	Kel Nagle	256
4	Dave Douglas (USA)	252
5	Marty Furgol (USA)	250
6	Norman von Nida	245
7	Jim McInnes	235
8	Ossie Pickworth	230

It is interesting to note that all the US players were generally hitting way longer than most of the Australian players, apart from Kel Nagle who was keeping up with them. Jack Harris generally used to outdrive Ossie Pickworth so he would most likely have been in the 240-250 yard range.

The US Open figures would almost certainly have been with the 1.68 inch ball. The Royal Perth figures could have been either size ball and may well have been a mixture. It was not recorded which ball they used but presumably all the players knew that the small ball travelled further and so very likely they all chose to hit the small ball since it was just a long driving competition.

Although most of the talk about distance between golf eras is usually about driving distance, it is also interesting to look at distance with irons. I was reading an article recently about the 1949 Victorian Closed Championship at Yarra Yarra GC when in his first ever appearance as a professional, Peter Thomson beat Jack Harris into second place to take the title. During that match, according to newspaper reports, Peter had apparently played a 130 yard shot out of a bunker on to the ninth green using a six iron. That sounded like a lot of club to me for such a short distance so I decided to do some investigating.

The most famous iron shot in history was possibly the one iron shot which Ben Hogan played at Merion in the 1950 US Open to square the match and take him into a play-off which he won. In 1949, the same year that Peter Thomson and Jack Harris were playing at Yarra Yarra, Ben Hogan had been badly injured in a car accident. The 1950 US Open was his first big tournament after the accident and he was still suffering with severe pain. Ben hit the seventy-second green with the one iron from 213 yards. These days the top professionals would be using a six or seven iron under calm conditions for this distance. That (six iron) is the same club Peter Thomson was playing from 130 yards which suggests to me that maybe distance improvement with irons could be at least as good or maybe even more than distance improvement with drivers. In the same Merion 1950 US Open, George Fazio at one point played a four iron to a green from 170 yards. Presumably this comes down mostly to improved golf club shaft technology.

Another big change since Jack Nicklaus's day has been the proliferation of wedges now available. In his day there was generally only a pitching wedge and a sand wedge. Nowadays, in addition to these two clubs, the modern players can also add one or two gap wedges and also a lob wedge if they wish. The fourteen club rule still applies so if they have extra wedges they need to leave some other club out of the bag.

The various wedges available now can be summarised as follows:

Pitching wedge	(44-50 degrees)
Gap wedge	(46-54 degrees)
Sand wedge	(54-58 degrees)
Lob wedge	(60-65 degrees)

This development in wedges means that finesse shots around the green are easier to make than previously. Tiger certainly had a big equipment advantage in this area.

The other change which happened in Jack Nicklaus's era was golf club modification by club professionals. They used to tailor make clubs to suit by changing the loft or the lie angle or offsetting the club head. They generally did this by eye, in a very crude and unscientific manner. Although many of the club pros would pride themselves on this skill, in reality there must have been a lot of variation introduced by this process. Club modification, these days, is done in a much more precise manner by using advanced computer programmes and camera techniques.

In one respect, I think that it is harder today than it was in Jack Harris's day. At least it can be much more confusing and many golfers suffer from the well-known golfing disease, paralysis by analysis. There are a million different gurus all telling us that their way is the *only* way to play golf. The golf club makers tell us we should be paying attention to shaft weight, shaft flex, shaft length, tip flex, loft setting and lie angle. Not to mention face angle, grip diameter, head size, swing speed, ball speed off the club face, flight pattern and maybe many others that I have forgotten. Absolutely everyone should definitely have a swing speed radar device and a swing tip computerised analyser which plugs into his mobile phone. Bugger me! They will be telling us how tight our underpants should be next! Then after we have done all that we have to choose between six million different brands of golf ball, every one telling us that theirs' is the best. After we have navigated our way through all that bullshit (or just gone with whatever the slick sales guy told us), we definitely can't play golf properly unless we buy one of those new-fangled GPS devices for measuring the distance from ball to green. Why would we bother? The average golfer hardly ever hits the same distance twice with any given club during a round of golf.

When I talk with Jack Harris about all these developments he just chuckles. He never used to pace out yardages when he played. He just looked at his ball, looked at where the green was, guessed at a club and plonked it to the middle of the green just by *feel*. He still regularly came in with scores in the 270s and 280s back in the days when the par for many of the top courses was seventy-four and that was with old technology clubs and balls.

In Jack's day he played with balls like Dunlop 65, Slazenger 51 and Penfold Ace which were all popular balls in that era. Although the first two brands are still available today no top golfer would play with them because they are too *hard*, opting instead for balls such as Titleist Pro V1s or Bridgestone B330s. These are so-called *soft* balls which allow them to get the extraordinary amount of back spin on the ball and supposedly much better control.

The point about there being more variation in the golf balls, more variation in green speed, choice whether to use 1.62 or 1.68 size ball and more difficult to control the driver in Jack Nicklaus's era, is that I think that these factors would sometimes work against the top players. That is to say, all these things would have an *equalising effect* which tended to bring the better players back to the field. The same happens when the weather is inclement. As soon as the players struggle to keep their grips dry it becomes a lottery. Consider what happened in the 2011 British Open at Royal St Georges GC when forty-four year old Darren Clarke won it in very bad weather. Clarke shot minus five when more favoured players like Adam Scott and Rory McIlroy tied on twenty-fifth with plus seven. Clarke was probably outside the top one hundred in the betting list when the tournament started but the *equaliser effect* kicked in and he triumphed on the day even though he has done nothing since.

I believe that the fact that Jack Nicklaus was able to cope with all these old technology *equalising effects* and still build such a fantastic playing record, cements his place as the world's best ever golfer. Despite the fact overall that Tiger has a similar number of wins from just under half the number of starts, Jacks performance in majors is significantly better than Tigers both from number of wins and from a consistency view point.

Another *equalising effect* which Jack Nicklaus had to cope with in his early days which Tiger Woods never encountered is what I like to call the *Arnie's Army* effect. Jack Nicklaus burst on to the scene in the early 1960s. At that time Arnold Palmer was already in full flight and was a big crowd favourite because of his ebullient nature. Many times when Palmer hit an errant shot which looked as if it would disappear into oblivion, the ball was stopped by the crowd. Indeed on some occasions the ball even miraculously bounced back into the fairway. However, if Jack Nicklaus hit a bad shot the crowd would always *part* and allow the ball to continue into the jungle. I never heard Nicklaus ever complain about this but he must have known that it was happening.

This opinion is held in January 2014. However, I am well aware that Jack Nicklaus ended his playing career many years ago, whereas if Tiger Woods keeps healthy and maintains his motivation he can conceivably still be playing majors in another twenty years' time. So in theory at least, Tiger still has plenty of time to claim the number one best ever spot. History tells us however that he would need to get a wriggle on. Out of 423 majors played to date only thirty-seven have been won by players forty years or older. Only eight have been won by players older than forty-three. No player has won more than one major after the age of forty. Jack Nicklaus himself leads the tally of majors won by oldies. He won two when he was forty and his last when he was forty-six. Tiger is now thirty-eight, so he will definitely need to get moving. Not impossible, but something that gets even more difficult with every passing year.

One advantage which is in Tiger's favour is the life expectancy factor. When Julius Boros was born in 1920, his life expectancy at birth was just over fifty-three years. So when he became the oldest ever major winner in 1968 at the age of forty-eight, he was getting pretty close to the theoretical D-Day. When Jack Nicklaus was born in 1940 his life expectancy at birth was about sixty-one, so when he won his last Masters in 1986 he was about seventy-five per cent way through his average allotment. In 2014 at age seventy-four he is still batting on and hopefully for many more years to come. When Tiger Woods was born his life expectancy at birth was about sixty-nine years. So if, like Jack Nicklaus, he managed to win a major at seventy-five per cent through his theoretical life expectancy, then it could be when he is fifty-one or fifty-two years old.

I hope I am still around to see the conclusion of this great Nicklaus versus Woods supremacy battle. But it may go on for another at least another twelve years or more, so I have to pray that my genes will take me there.

The life expectancy factor during Jack Harris's era was not insignificant. Quite a number of the golfers Jack played against died young. Consider Ted Ball (56), Ossie Pickworth (51), Martin Smith (54), Eric Cremin (60), Sam Walsh (56), Norm Berwick (42), Harry Williams (46), Laurie

Duffy (49)). Jim Petterson (45), Terry Kendall (55), Sewsunker Sewgolum (49), Fergus McMahon (43), Fred Bolger (56), Bert Yancey (56), Lloyd Mangrum (59), Ed "Porky" Oliver (46), Willie Harvey (54), Alf Chitty (53) and Guy Wolstenholme (53).

At this stage I would like to add a rider to my thoughts on who was the best ever golfer. Although I have gone for Jack Nicklaus, I have to conclude that if he had played longer, I suspect that I may have been voting for Bobby Jones. Jones played in an era where there were some fantastic golfers. In the 1920s Walter Hagen and Gene Sarazen between them won eighteen majors which is the same total as Jack Nicklaus. However, the US Masters tournament had not even been started at that stage. Now here's the rub. Neither Walter Hagen nor Gene Sarazen, as great as they were, managed to win a single major tournament when Bobby Jones was playing in the same competition as them. Jones was a full-time lawyer who only played golf part-time. He retired from competition golf when he was only twenty-eight years old. Had he continued to play, the chances are, he would be wearing the *best ever* crown today.

Chapter 18

Best Ever Australian Golfers

Although this book is about Jack Harris, one of Australia's greatest post-war golfers, I was keen to see how he fit into the overall picture. I needed to identify the best Australian golfers of the 1946 – 1971 period and the best ever Australian male golfers. I suspect that this is a meaningless exercise but nevertheless still a fun thing to do.

In the early part of this period Ossie Pickworth was the shining star with his still unbeaten record of three consecutive Australian Opens. However, more or less at the same time, in the USA, Jim Ferrier was having fabulous success on the tough American golf circuit. He became Australia's first-ever major winner in 1947 and also racked up an impressive tally of PGA tour wins.

In the middle part of the period Peter Thomson chalked up five British Open wins and many other big tournament victories.

Kel Nagle started winning from the end of the war but after he had won the 1960 British Open, when almost forty years old, he became a full-time touring player and his career took off like wild fire.

Players such as Norman von Nida, Frank Phillips, Billy Dunk, Eric Cremin and Jack Harris were also having a degree of success.

Based on most major wins alone it seemed like a no brainer. Peter Thomson with his five British Open wins was well ahead of the pack. However, during my extensive research, I read many articles which suggested that the British Open was not a very strong tournament in that period. Also, that in those days it was never referred to as a PGA tour event. I decided that these criticisms needed further investigation.

After a very close inspection of the results from that period, and of the golfers who competed, I had to agree with the reports. The Open fields in those days were comprised mostly of ageing British professionals with only a sprinkling of overseas players and very few Americans. Generally, the Americans who did turn up to play were mostly low ranked players or amateurs. On the rare occasion that a top American played he usually won.

Sam Snead played in 1946 and won. However, his prize money was only $600 and he lost money on the trip despite winning. By comparison, the 1946 US Open, US PGA and US Masters paid the winners $1833, $3500 and $2500 respectively. Also consider that travel expenses in the USA would be far less than having to cross the Atlantic to play in the British Open. Sam didn't return until 1962 by which time he was fifty years old.

Ben Hogan, the world's best golfer in the 1950s, played at Carnoustie in 1953 and won. He didn't defend his title the following year and in fact never played in the Open again.

The reason there were virtually no Americans playing is very clear. If you subtract trans-Atlantic travel expenses from the $600 Sam Snead was paid he was already in negative territory. If we just consider prize money alone he would earn between four and six times as much by winning an American major. However, if differences in travel expenses are also considered then this multiple would be much higher. In fact, even if he had made just a $20 profit instead of a loss, he would be at least 100 times better off staying in America to play. And he wouldn't need to play in US majors. Any old PGA tour event would pay more than the British Open in those days.

When we look today at the list of British Open winners, five wins looks to be phenomenal. Problem is that we are looking at it through the prism of what a massive event the modern day British Open has grown into. The reality is that for at least 15 years after WW2 it was not a strong tournament. In those years the field consisted of 70+% of ageing British professionals and 30% of amateurs and overseas players, with very few Americans playing each year. When I say "ageing" I am talking about an average age in the thirty-five to forty range! Yes, the British Open had close to one hundred years of history by then but during that period it just did not attract the best players in the world.

When we look at the five British Opens which Peter Thomson won we see that there were eight players who finished as runners-up across the five events. The average age of these eight runners-up was approximately thirty-eight. Five of the eight were in the forty-one to forty-four years old range. None of these eight runners-up were Americans. Fifty per cent were ageing

British Pros averaging forty-one / forty-two -years old, one was a forty-four years old Belgian pro, one was a thirty-seven-year-old South African, Bobby Locke, who had played his best golf in the USA in the late 1940s, and there were just two British players who were under thirty.

To be fair, we must note that in 1954 there were six Americans who qualified to play in the Open and five of them made the cut. Peter Thomson recorded an impressive win over fifty-five years old Al Watrous who had been born in the nineteenth century. He also disposed of fifty-two years old Gene Sarazen, forty-six years old Toney Penna who missed the cut, forty-four years old Jimmy Demaret and forty-two years old Jim Turnesa. By and large, these five Americans performed admirably considering that their combined age was 239 years! On the other hand, a whole posse of British Ryder Cup players, playing on home turf and with the big advantage of playing with their normal 1.62-inch diameter balls, didn't fair quite so well. Six of them qualified but missed the half-way cut. Three others didn't even get through the qualifying rounds.

In 1955 five Americans qualified for the Open and all of them made the cut. The most impressive was the legendary forty-three years old Byron Nelson. Byron had retired from tournament golf almost ten years earlier after he had created the still unbeaten record for most number of PGA wins in one season. After he had sand-papered the rust from his clubs he still managed to finish tied thirty-second. Two (40%) of the five Americans who played that year were amateurs. Two were quite good scalps to take. Forty-one years old Johnny Bulla and thirty-seven years old Ed Furgol both had good careers on the PGA Tour.

In 1956 only four Americans qualified. Two of these missed the cut. One was the evergreen fifty-four years old Gene Sarazen and the other was Peter Burke. Peter who? The two US players who made the cut were Mike Souchak and Frank Stranahan. It was the first time Souchak had played in the Open. He was not familiar with the British links courses plus he had the small ball / big ball dilemma to cope with. This was the only time he played in the Open apart from a token visit in 1976 when he was forty-nine years old. Stranahan however was an old timer. He had won the US Amateur twice and prior to 1956 had played the Open seven times as an amateur. He turned pro in his early thirties and by 1956 had won once on the PGA Tour.

In 1958 the Americans went walk-about. Only one American qualified for the Open. Yes, you guessed it. Fifty-six years old Gene Sarazen who made the cut and tied sixteenth. Not really a bad effort for a man whose life expectancy at birth was just about 50 years!

In 1965, which is often held up as being the best of all Peter Thomson's Open wins, the Americans turned up in droves. Out of the total field of 130 players, nine Americans qualified. Five of these missed the cut. The most notable of the cut-missers was fifty-three years old Sam Snead who had won the Open on his first outing in 1946 and who had tied sixth in 1962 when he was fifty-years old. Of the four who did make the cut, three were very good players. Ie. Jack Nicklaus, Arnold Palmer and Tony Lema. On this occasion Jack and Arnie had an off-day and never troubled the scorers. Tony Lema had won the Open at St Andrews in 1964. He was the in-form US player coming into the tournament and gave a very good account of himself. The fourth American to make the cut was twenty-six years old Terry Dill. Terry had the distinction of playing on the US Tour from 1962 to 1989 without ever recording a single win! However, all was not lost. In 1992 he finally broke through for a win on the Seniors Tour when he beat none other than Australian Bruce Crampton by one stroke. Apart from the good Americans, the current US Open champion, Gary Player, was also in the field. However, he pulled out with a neck injury part way through the tournament. His US Open win that year was very special because it gave Gary Player a career Grand Slam of all four majors. Gary achieved this Grand Slam before Jack Nicklaus got any of his. But of course, Jack did it at a younger age.

Although a few good Americans turned up for the 1965 Open, the vast majority of Americans who would have been exempt to play didn't bother making the trip. The exempt US players who could have played included the last ten US Open winners, the top thirty plus ties on the 1965 US PGA money winners list, the US Seniors champion and the last five US Amateur champions. i.e. forty-six players. But only nine Americans arrived to play and four of these were not on any of the exempt lists. So, let's not get hoodwinked into believing that the Americans "were back" in 1965. About

80% of the top thirty 1965 PGA money winners stayed away and 70% of the last ten US Open winners also stayed away.

The other thing which was significant about the 1965 open was that the organisers were still playing about with the way players were able to qualify for the tournament. For the first four of Thomson's Open wins in the 1950s, every single player had to play two qualifying rounds. There were no exemptions. Problem with this format was that very large numbers of amateur players and "no-hopers" played in the qualifying rounds. E.g. In the 1960 Centenary Open, which Kel Nagle won, there were 415 initial entries. Even after a few late scratchings the field was still above 400 players. Only 74 (about 18%) of this lot finally qualified for the tournament proper and only 47 (about 11%) of these made the cut and played the last two rounds. The first year it started to change was 1963 when forty-four players were exempted, including six Americans.

In 1965 the final Open field had 130 players. There were forty-nine players with exemptions and eighty-one players who had to play qualifying rounds at either Hillside GC or Southport & Ainsdale GC. However, included in the forty-nine exempt places were the last five British Amateur champions, the last five US Amateur champions, the entire 1964 GB & Ireland Walker Cup team (all amateurs) and the current Senior Champions from both GB and the USA. i.e. over 12% of the total field or a whopping 33% of the exempt list. Which meant that about one third of the exemptions were given to guys with little chance. Add to this the possibility that amateur players could also maybe get through the Hillside and Southport qualifiers. These days the percentage of amateurs in an Open field is just a tiny fraction of what it was in 1965.

We may say that the British Open golf championship, particularly in the 1950s, was most remarkable for who didn't play rather than who did play. Let's for instance take the list of players who had topped the annual US PGA money winners list in the 1950s. For that decade there were nine individual winners because Julius Boros had topped the list twice. The list included Art Wall Jr, Arnold Palmer, Dick Mayer, Ted Kroll, Julius Boros, Bob Toski, Lew Worsham, Lloyd Mangrum and Sam Snead. Wall, Mayer, Kroll, Toski and Worsham never played in the Open. Julius Boros never played in the Open when at his peak in the 1950s. He did make a token visit in 1966 when he was already forty-six years old. Lloyd Mangrum only ever played once in the Open in 1953 when he was thirty-nine years old. Sam Snead played five times in the Open but this was over a thirty-nine year period (1937-1976). He won the Open in 1946 when he was thirty-four years old but didn't play at all in the 1950s. His last three visits were all after he was fifty-years old and his last visit in 1976 when he was sixty-four years old.

Let's also look at the major winners in the 1950s. We know that Peter Thomson and Bobby Locke dominated the British Open from 1950 – 1960 with seven Opens between them. Englishman Max Faulkner won in 1951, American Ben Hogan in 1953, South African Gary Player in 1959 and Australian Kel Nagle in 1960. But what about the thirty-three US majors in that period? Well for a start every single one of those thirty-three majors was won by an American. Five players had multiple wins. This meant that there were twenty-one different US players who shared the thirty-three majors between them. Sixteen (over 76%) of these US major winners never played in the British Open during the 1950s.

The remaining five only ever played once in the British Open. Three of these five were already well into their forties when they made the token visit to the Open. One of these golden oldies was Ben Hogan who won at Carnoustie in 1953 when he was almost forty-one years old. According to newspaper reports Ben didn't like anything about his trip. He didn't like links courses, he didn't like the hotel where he stayed and of course he probably didn't like having to cope with the ball change dilemma. Despite all these negatives and struggling with influenza on the final day plus the lifelong after-effects of a serious car crash he had in 1949, he still beat all his rivals (including Peter Thomson) with consummate ease. Peter Thomson did play in six US Masters and four US Opens during the 1950s. He never competed in the US PGA. In the ten events played he was disqualified once and missed the cut once. Across the other eight his average placing was nineteenth. In other words, he didn't set the world on fire, but he didn't disgrace himself either. In the 1960s he played twice more in the US Masters for a tied nineteenth and one missed cut and once in the US Open for another missed cut.

Bobby Locke by comparison, had a much superior record in US majors to Peter Thomson. He was much older than Thomson, so his appearances spread across the late 1940s and the early 1950s. He played in twelve events and made the cut twelve times. This included four US Masters where his average place was fourteenth. Seven US Opens where his average across six of them was about fifth. He made the cut in the seventh but then withdrew. One US PGA where he tied thirty-third.

Apart from the US major winners who voted with concrete feet and stayed home instead of tackling the British Open, there were also lots of US players in that era who never won a major but who did win multiple PGA tour events and never competed in the British Open either. This book is not long enough to include all these by name. But suffice it to say that all of them won more regular PGA tour events in America than Peter Thomson.

In summary, a grand total of 25 Americans played across the five Opens which Peter Thomson won. i.e. an average of five per Open. One third of these missed the cut. If we compare this with the last five Opens (2014-2018), we find that about 260 Americans played for an average of 52 per Open. And these days the quality of the Americans who play is far higher than the ones playing in the 1950s. Today, every US player who plays is capable of shooting in the low sixties and often does. If Tiger Woods or Jordan Spieth or one of the high-profile Americans doesn't win, then one of the lesser known Americans often bobs up and wins. Zach Johnson, Todd Hamilton, Ben Curtis, Stewart Cink, David Duval, Justin Leonard, Tom Lehman and John Daly all spring to mind.

In a modern day British Open it is a totally different situation. The 70 / 30 still applies but in reverse. There would be 70% of overseas players and 30% British professionals. The average age of these British pros would be thirty to thirty-five. Furthermore, there would be at least ten times more Americans in the field than in those earlier days but far fewer amateurs playing.

In September 2018, The Walt Disney Company Australia will take over the sponsorship of the AFL stadium at Docklands. I couldn't help thinking that Walt had missed a trick in the 1950s when he could probably have bought the rights to the British Open for a song. The Michael Mouse Cup would have been a perfect fit in those days. Alas, there WAS a tide in the affairs of men.

The truth is that in the 1950s, despite all the long history and tradition, it was far easier to win a British Open than it was to win a regular PGA tournament – never mind a US Open, US PGA or a US Masters. Peter Thomson himself demonstrated this quite well. In the time he won five British Opens he was able to win just one regular PGA event in America, the Texas Open. And it wasn't for the lack of trying. Although he never played full-time in the USA he did make frequent forays there throughout the 1950s and into the 1960s.

If we look at Peter Thomson's official PGA profile, we see that he played 112 events. By subtracting his thirty British Open appearances we can deduce that he played in 82 events in the USA. Therefore, he won one in every six in the British Open and one in eighty-two in PGA events in America. It seems that he found it fourteen times easier to win in Britain than in America. If we compare this with his sometime British Open nemesis, Bobby Locke, we can see that the South African didn't have the same difficulties. Bobby won about one in seven of the British Opens he played in (four from twenty-nine), about one in five of the PGA events in America (eleven from fifty-nine) and he also won what may have been his only Australian Open appearance in 1955. In just over a two-year period Locke was in the top three thirty times out of fifty-nine events. We should also bear in mind that when Bobby Locke won these eleven PGA tour events in America he was playing at a time when some absolute legends were around and at their peak. These included Sam Snead, Ben Hogan, Byron Nelson, Lloyd Mangrum, Jimmy Demaret, Cary Middlecoff, Dutch Harrison, Jim Ferrier and Tommy Bolt. These nine alone won 356 PGA tour events including thirty majors. Clearly, at his peak, Locke was a much more complete player than Thomson. Particularly when we take into account that he lost what may have been his six most prime years as a bomber pilot in WW2. Locke would have had a far better record than he actually achieved if the USGA had not banned him. They trumped up some charge about him not adhering to playing commitments when the true reason was that the US players were just getting pissed off because he was winning everything. A few years later they removed the ban, but Bobby gave them the two-finger salute and never went back to play full time on the tour. He just made visits in the early fifties to play in a few majors.

Peter Thomson's relative lack of success in America in the 1950s was not because he played badly. Quite the reverse. He played well and many of the scores he shot would have given him a podium finish in either British or Australian tournaments. The trouble was that in the USA he was a little fish playing in a big pond. I don't think he relished shooting a score like 275 only to find himself tied in twelfth place. In 2018 things haven't changed in the USA. The John Deere Classic just concluded this weekend. Australian Matt Jones performed exceptionally well when he shot 269 which was fifteen under the card but also found himself tied in twelfth place!

The myth is often bandied about that the reason for his (Peter Thomson's) lack of success in the USA was because he didn't like the courses and preferred the English courses. However, this is very questionable. He may indeed have enjoyed playing in English conditions. However, if we also look at how he performed against the Americans in his own back yard, back in Australia, it reveals an interesting picture.

The so-called Big Three, Arnold Palmer, Jack Nicklaus and Gary Player, regularly played here in the 1960s and 1970s. Gary Player had in fact been playing in Australia from the mid-1950s. Between the three of them these three players won thirteen Australian Opens and three seconds. Peter Thomson won three Australian Opens, but he never won one if any of the big three were competing! This tournament was always played on golf courses where Peter Thomson knew every blade of grass. As an amateur he had played pennant on most of them and as a professional he had played all of them many times. He certainly could not complain that he didn't like the courses or that they didn't suit his style of play. In this regard he had a massive advantage of local knowledge over the big three, but he still couldn't cut the mustard.

When he was in his own back yard he didn't just need to worry about the top Americans either. The American super-star, Ben Hogan, never came to play in Australia in the 1950s. However, in 1952 and again in 1954, American teams did play some tournaments here. Four American golfers came each year. They were not the players at the very top of American golf, but they were players who had won several PGA tour events, played

Ryder Cup and also won the odd major. Most of them were near the end of their careers. These golfers included Lloyd Mangrum, Jimmy Demaret, Jim Turnesa, Ed Oliver, Dutch Harrison, Tommy Bolt, Dave Douglas and Marty Furgol. They played in Ampol tournaments and some others including Adelaide Advertisers. In the majority of these tournaments, played on Thomson's own turf, these second-string Americans were able to give Thomson a golfing lesson. They did this even though it was clear from the newspaper reports of the matches that the Americans were not taking the tours too seriously. They were all being paid handsome appearance money by Ampol. Apart from personal pride it didn't matter to them whether they won or not. It was just a nice holiday break for them.

It is true that Peter Thomson / Kel Nagle did beat an American team into second place in the 1959 Canada Cup which was played at the Royal Melbourne GC. However, even this doesn't sound so impressive when we learn that forty-seven years old Sam Snead was on the American team. To be fair to Sam, I should point out that he was the third best individual performer in the tournament and did shoot the lowest round of the whole event (65). It was his partner, Cary Middlecoff, who let him down! Despite being long in the tooth Sam Snead wasn't done after the 1959 tournament. Playing with either Arnold Palmer or Jimmy Demaret he won the next three Canada Cups in a row. It would have been sweet revenge for him indeed in 1961 in Puerto Rico when he teamed up with Jimmy Demaret. Their combined age was over 100 years but they still creamed Peter Thomson and Kel Nagle by a whopping twelve strokes over four rounds. Peter Thomson played in eleven Canada / World Cups between 1953 and 1969 mostly with Kel Nagle as his partner. These events were played in ten different countries during that period. Thomson / Nagle won the Cup twice in the eleven years. The Americans had six wins from the same years. Plus another four wins in the 1953 – 1969 period for the years where Peter Thomson didn't play. i.e. ten wins in a sixteen-year period for the Americans. This was another perfect indication of just how dominant the Americans were in that era. And that dominance was wherever they played and not just in the USA.

When we look at how Peter Thomson performed in the USA versus his performances in Australia and in the UK, we must also consider the part played by different ball sizes. In Australia and in the UK at that time he would almost certainly have been playing the small 1.62-inch diameter ball. This small ball travelled about fifty yards further than the larger 1.68-inch American ball. It was also much easier to control in very windy conditions such as those frequently encountered when playing the British seaside links courses which generally didn't have any trees on them. However, when he played in America he didn't have the option to play the small size ball. Under USGA rules he would be compelled to play the larger size ball which had been the only ball allowed in US tournaments since 1932. Thus, he would lose distance, suffer less control in the wind and would not be as familiar with the distances he could hit with each club. These days top sportsmen talk about "one-per-centers" as being important to their success. Well, I suspect that losing fifty yards and having less control in the wind would be far more than one per cent and could easily be five per cent or more.

He didn't have this problem in the UK. The small size ball was not banned in the British Open until 1974. American players going over to the UK in the 1950s and 1960s had the option to play either the small or large ball. Most of them chose to play the small ball even though that meant that they lost out on yardage familiarity.

Jack Harris told me about the first time he realised how much difference the big ball changed the game and also just how good Jack Nicklaus was. It was in the early 1960s and at that stage Jack Harris had never seen let alone played with a big ball. He was playing at the Wills Classic in Sydney and he was in the same group as Jack Nicklaus. Nicklaus's reputation as a big hitter was already legendary and Jack Harris was expecting to see big things. Jack Harris as usual was playing with a small ball. Early in the match they had played into a strong wind and Jack Harris had noticed that all his own drives were about the same length as Nicklaus's drives. So, he was thinking to himself ...what is all this bull dust about Jack Nicklaus being a long driver? He hadn't realised at that stage that Nicklaus was playing with a big ball. It was only when they came to holes which played down wind that the penny dropped. Nicklaus started booming his big ball drives about 70 or 80 yards past Jack Harris's small ball drives! At one hole which was a par four with a very long carry over a lake, Jack was flabbergasted when Nicklaus drove the green. He was hitting the big ball further than Jack could hit the small ball! If Jack Harris had been also playing the large ball he would have been 120 yards behind Nicklaus!

Before I reached my conclusion about the British Open, however, I had to satisfy myself that it would have made a difference if the Americans had been at the British Open in larger numbers during the 1950s. I know that Snead and Hogan won in Britain, but they were absolute superstars. How would good American golfers below them perform? I therefore checked out the Ryder Cup results from 1947 to 1965. When the cream of American golf played the cream of British golf. I discovered that America had won ninety per cent of the time.

Ryder Cup Results:			
Year	USA	GB	Venue
1947	**11**	1	USA
1949	**7**	5	UK
1951	**9.5**	2.5	USA
1953	**6.5**	5.5	UK
1955	**8**	4	USA
1957	4.5	**7.5**	UK
1959	**8.5**	3.5	USA
1961	**14.5**	9.5	UK
1963	**23**	9	USA
1965	**19.5**	12.5	UK
	9 wins	1 wins	

When played in the USA the GB team was usually trounced. The matches were a bit closer when the GB team had home advantage and the added advantage of playing with the small size ball which was unfamiliar to the USA team. No matter where the match was played the British players usually received a pummelling from their American cousins. Not only could the best golfers in England / Ireland / Scotland / Wales at that time not do well in the Ryder Cup but when they played in other events in the USA from time to time they couldn't win any of those either. Peter Thomson was not the only multiple British Open winner who struggled to win there. Englishman Henry Cotton who was a three-time British Open winner couldn't win in America either.

In fact, throughout the 1950s, when very few Americans played in the British Open, the same happened in reverse. Very few non-Americans played in the US majors either or even on the regular US Tour even though the prize money in the USA was orders of magnitude higher than in Europe or Australia. Only one or two had any real success, like Jim Ferrier and Bobby Locke, and they did it by basing themselves in the USA. Towards the end of the decade Gary Player came on the scene and he made a big impact. It couldn't have been for financial reasons why most of them chose not to play in America because the potential rewards were much higher in the USA than in any other country. Besides which, unlike Australia and the UK where the prize money didn't go far down the playing list, the number of players who received some kind of recompense in the USA went much deeper. It could have only been that most of them didn't think they could win in America where the talent pool was considerably more formidable than anywhere else.

For me this was a good indication that the Americans would have had a big impact on the British Open if they had chosen to compete.

Incidentally, a plethora of British Ryder Cup players regularly played tournaments in Australia during the 1950s and 1960s including in 1959 when the Canada Cup was held in Melbourne. Jack Harris, who would have been ranked fifth or sixth in Australia at that time, had great success against every single one of those Ryder Cup players. Bear in mind that these were the top British players of the day and even a club-based teaching professional like Jack Harris, who had no overseas experience whatsoever, had no trouble kicking their backsides.

Prior to WW2 the Americans had totally dominated the British Open. From 1920 to 1933, when Jack Harris was sailing up and down Port Philip Bay on the Weeroona paddle steamer, US player Walter Hagen ruled the roost with four British Opens and two other top three finishes. He was aided and abetted by other legends such as Bobby Jones, Gene Sarazen, MacDonald Smith, Tommy Armour, Jim Barnes, Jock Hutchinson, Al Watrous, Leo Diegel, Horton Smith and a host of others. This bunch of golfers could really play. Between them they had 250 US PGA tour wins and thirty-nine majors. That is truly awesome! It has to be noted that Smith and Armour were Scots who had emigrated to the USA and become US citizens and Barnes was an Englishman from Cornwall who also emigrated to the US, lived the rest of his life there but never became a citizen. Jim Barnes is only one of three Britons in history to win three DIFFERENT majors, the other two being Rory McIlroy and the Silver Scot, Tommy Armour.

On many occasions throughout this decade Americans filled all top three places in the British Open. In 1929 eight out of the top ten were Americans. When the Americans were at the British Open in force they won it more often than not.

British Opens Performance Results	
1920-1933	Very strong US presence USA won 79% of the Opens
1934-1959	Americans mostly absent USA won only 10% of the Opens
1960-1970	Americans started to trickle back USA won over 45% of the Opens
1971-2013	Strong American presence USA won 56% of the Opens

The percentage wins by country in the British Open from 1920 to 2013 has been as follows:

USA	47.7%
England	15.9%
South Africa	11.36%
Australia	10.22%

Scotland	3.4%
Spain	3.4%
Northern Ireland	2.27%
Ireland	2.27%
Argentina	1.13%
Zimbabwe	1.13%
New Zealand	1.13%

It is perhaps ironical that it was a British player who first started off all the American domination at the British Open. Not only that, but it was a guy who had been born in St Andrews, Scotland. He was born in 1884 and later emigrated to the USA where he became a naturalized citizen. His name was Jock Hutchinson. He was the first American to win the British Open in 1921. Walter Hagen was the first American born man to win it.

One must feel sorry for Australian Joe Kirkwood who played outstandingly well in this tournament in the 1920s without a win. In any other era he may have had several.

The US dominance has not only been in the British Opens. It extends to all majors. Since 1950 the Americans have won 177 majors out of the 254 majors played! A whopping 68.7% of all majors!

Apart from studying the British Open and Ryder Cup results over the period I also consulted the Ainsworth Sports Top 136 (1950-1959) and Top 142 (1960-1969). These lists told an interesting story and highlighted the dramatic rise of Kel Nagle late in his career.

Let's now return to who was the best Australian golfer of the 1946-1971 era, bearing in mind that we are not necessarily looking for who won most tournaments or who won most money.

Considering all the previously discussed points I finalised my top three as follows:

1. Jim Ferrier

2. Kel Nagle

3. Peter Thomson

Jim Ferrier with 18 PGA tour wins, including Australia's first ever major win, was light years ahead of both Thomson and Nagle.

Notwithstanding that Peter Thomson (1988) and Kel Nagle (2007) are both inductees into the World Golf hall of Fame and Jim Ferrier is not in that club. (very big oversight!)

I personally would only rate each of Thomson's Open wins as being equivalent to one PGA tour win. However, even if we are very generous and rate each Open to be worth two or three PGA tour wins, it would still fall well short of Ferrier. Ferrier's major win is to me much more valuable than any of Thomson's Open wins because it was achieved on the much tougher American tour.

I am well aware that these days all the Thomson Open wins are classified in the statistics as PGA Tour wins. It was not a PGA tour event in the 1950s / 1960s when these Opens were won. The British Open has only been an official event on the PGA Tour since 1995. All the wins before 1995 have been retroactively classified as PGA Tour wins. The PGA Tour brand was only established in 1975 after the tour players had split from club-based professionals in the Professional Golfers Association of America in 1968 in order to get a bigger slice of the cake. So, the 1995 re-classification was in fact a "retro-retro". Nice one Cyril!

Having firmly cemented Jim Ferrier at the top of the pile, there obviously needs to be more explanation as to why I think Kel Nagle edges Peter Thomson into third place. Especially since Thomson had five Open wins during the period in question plus one win in America, whereas Nagle only won one Open and once in America.

The main reason for my choice was because on the Australasian Tour Nagle outshone Thomson by 61 wins to 33. If that happened today, we would just say...so what? The PGA Tour and the European Tour are both much stronger that the Australasian Tour. These days the world stars just don't turn up in big numbers to play in Australasian events because the prize money is too small. The odd one or two top players who play here are enticed to come by large appearance money incentives but that is all.

However, back in the Thomson / Nagle days it was a different story. The big three, Palmer, Nicklaus and Player, came to Australia year after year throughout the 1960s and 1970s. Player had even been coming since the mid-1950s. Gary Player's seven Australian Open wins ranged from 1958 – 1974 spanning sixteen years. Jack Nicklaus's six wins spanned fourteen years from 1964 to 1978. Jack even came runner-up in 1982 making an eighteen-year span. The Australian Open in those days was such a strong tournament that Jack Nicklaus himself often used to refer to it as "the fifth major".

And appearance by world stars was not limited to the big three. Big names such as Lee Trevino, Billy Casper, Gene Littler, Tony Jacklin, Bob Charles, Jay Herbert, Roberto de Vicenzo and heaps of British Ryder Cup players also came. And they did not just come to play in the Australian Open. They often would also play in the Australian PGA, Wills Classic, Wills Masters, Coles and even the Victorian Open.

I suspect that golf fields in Australia were stronger than the fields in England...certainly in the 1950s and early 1960s.

The important factor for me was Nagle's lost war years and the fact that his full-time touring career only started after he had won the Centenary British Open in 1960 forcing Arnold Palmer into second place. He was almost forty years old in 1960 but some of the wins he had between 1960 and 1970 were astounding.

E.g. In 1968 when Nagle was about 47/48 years old, he shot 20 under par at Metropolitan GC in the Australian PGA to beat Jack Nicklaus by six strokes. By this time Jack Nicklaus was already a seven times major winner including all four majors. He also had fifteen other top ten finishes in majors by 1968.

E.g. In 1966 Nagle shot 278 at Victoria GC to beat British Open winner Roberto de Vicenzo by two strokes in the Wills Masters.

E.g. In 1967 Nagle beat US Open/ British Open winner Tony Jacklin by four strokes at Yarra Yarra GC to win the Victorian Open.

He was even runner-up in the Australian PGA in 1975 at age fifty-five.

If we take the Australian Open / Australian PGA as a package we see that Nagle had seven wins and seven seconds. Thomson had five wins and six seconds. A similar pattern emerged looking at the NZ Open / NZ PGA as a package. Although Thomson had been plundering easy pickings against ageing NZ pros since 1950 he couldn't match Nagle's overall performance. This was despite the fact that Nagle was nine years older, had lost nearly six years at war and didn't start going to New Zealand regularly until 1957 when he was thirty-seven years old. In New Zealand Nagle still amassed fourteen NZ Open / NZ PGA wins against ten by Thomson.

Later in their careers both these players won the British Senior Championship too. But Thomson only won one and Nagle won three.

The Nagle story could go on and on. Needless to say that his twenty-eight more Tour of Australasia wins in very strong fields convinced me that he was THE man!

I must confess that arriving at this conclusion did surprise me. Before I started to do extensive research, I would have ranked Peter Thomson as numero uno without any hesitation.

I must also confess that Jack Harris didn't agree with my assessment. Long before I started writing this book, he told me that the best Australian golfer he ever played against was Ossie Pickworth. Jack didn't play very often against Ferrier since he mostly played in the USA, at least after WW2. But he did often play against Peter Thomson and Kel Nagle. So, his observation is very interesting.

After these top three it is much more difficult to rank the golfers of the 1946 – 1971 period. Names like Ossie Pickworth, Norman von Nida, Frank Phillips, Eric Cremin, Jack Harris, Billy Dunk, Len Woodward, Bruce Devlin, Bruce Crampton, Alan Murray, Ted Ball would all have a shout. Bruce Crampton and Bruce Devlin may have had the best ultimate record but much of it could have been later.

One feature which stands out from the extended list is that there is only ONE player who did not have extensive overseas experience: Jack Harris[12].

But who were the best ever Australian golfers of all time?

For a start, as of the end of February 2014, only ten Australians have won a major.

Peter Thomson	(five British Opens)
Greg Norman	(two British Opens)
David Graham	(one USPGA, one US Open)

---

12 There were plenty of Australian teaching club professionals who had no overseas tour experience, but none who could equal Jack Harris's playing record.

Kel Nagle	(one British Open)
Adam Scott	(one US Masters)
Jim Ferrier	(one US PGA)
Geoff Ogilvy	(one US Open)
Steve Elkington	(one US PGA)
Wayne Grady	(one US PGA)
Jason Day	(one US PGA)
Ian Baker-Finch	(one British Open)

All but the last three also won one or more Australian Opens.

Since I firmly believe that the US PGA Tour is still the world's toughest I have arrived at this final list considering just PGA tour wins and major wins. The list has changed quite a bit from the one in the original book. Firstly, it changed markedly after the meteoric rise of Jason Day since the original book was written in 2014. He has gone from two PGA tour wins to twelve including one major during the 2015-2018 period. Secondly, because I am now only looking at PGA wins, Stuart Appleby and Joe Kirkwood come into play. On reflection I may also have overvalued David Graham's two different major wins. [13]

As for Peter Thomson's Open wins, I have rated them as each being equivalent to one PGA tour win even though they were not PGA tour events back in the day.

Taking all the above-mentioned things into consideration my top ten best ever Australian golfers as of end June 2018 is as follows.

1. Greg Norman (20/2)
2. Jim Ferrier (18/1)
3. Adam Scott (13/1)
4. Jason Day (12/1)
5. David Graham (8/2)
6. Bruce Crampton (14/0)

---

[13] Since writing the book I have been very pleased to see that in October, 2014 David Graham was chosen by the selection committee to enter the World Golf Hall of Fame in 2015. At the same time my favourite lady golfer, Dame Laura Davies, will be similarly honoured

7. Joe Kirkwood (13/0)
8. Steve Elkington (10/1)
9. Geoff Ogilvy (8/1)
10. Stuart Appleby (9/0)

Scott, Day, Ogilvy and Appleby are still playing in America and could still add to their tallies. But Jason Day is only thirty and still playing well so he is the most likely to add more wins.

Because of the changed ranking system used, Peter Thomson and Kel Nagle have both dropped off the list. I am sure that this will raise lots of eyebrows. However, winning lots of Hong Kong Opens, Indian Opens, New Zealand Opens etc is nowhere near the same as winning in the very tough American environment.

It is obvious from the above that I am talking about best-ever male golfers. Had I included the ladies, Karrie Webb would easily top the list. In March 2014 she notched up her forty-first win on the LPGA Tour and equalled Babe Didrikson Zaharias's record.

Although Peter Thomson only had one American win on the regular tour he did win eleven Senior PGA Tour events in just about one year between 1984/1985. Many people have highlighted this to me and said that this proves that he was great in America as well as in Britain.

Well wins are wins and undoubtedly eleven wins in one year is obviously an outstanding achievement which cannot be denied.

Having said that, I did ask myself the question...why could he win in 1984 when he couldn't do it earlier in the 1950s? Had he just aged better than most of the other oldies? Had the Americans changed their courses so that they played more like British courses or was there another reason? Well it is true that one of the former super-stars, Arnold Palmer, who was the same age as Thomson, was also playing on the Senior Tour. In his case it had been well documented that by this time he suffered with a bad back. However, he was just one golfer. So, what about the others he came up against? It didn't take me long to find out what had happened. It turns out that in 1984 eighty-five per cent of the golfers who had been winning all the majors in the 1950s and early sixties, were either too old to be effective when the Senior Tour started, or they had not yet reached fifty and didn't qualify to play on this tour. Jimmy Demaret was 74, Jim Turnesa was 72, Chick Harbert was 69, Tommy Bolt was 68, Ed Furgol was 67, Walter Burkemo was 66, Roberto de Vicenzo was 61, Kel Nagle was 64, Art Wall Jr was 61, Jack Fleck was 63, Cary Middlecoff was 63, Doug Ford was 62, Dick Mayer was 60, Sam Snead was 72, Ben Hogan was 72, Bobby Locke was 67 but had a serious car accident when he was 42 and was never the same golfer again. Jack Nicklaus was still only 44 and had to wait another six years before he could play Seniors. Lee Trevino was 45 and still had five years to wait. Bob Charles was 48 and still had another two years to wait. Gary Player qualified for the Senior Tour about one month before Thomson decided to cut and run. Bruce Crampton was another who only qualified for the Seniors Tour just as Thomson was leaving. As it was, Nicklaus, Player, Trevino, Charles and Crampton between them eventually won 101 Senior Tour events once they got cracking. If we included Palmer with his bad back, it goes to 111. God knows how many Hogan, Snead et al would have won if they had been a few years younger. Of the eleven players who came runner-up to Peter Thomson in the senior events he won, seven of them (64%) had never won a major on the regular tour. However, the other four were indeed star players. These included Arnold Palmer (with his bad back), Billy Casper a three times major winner, Gene Littler a double major winner and Don January who won one major. So, although his senior campaign was very timely, it did also appear that he had improved with age.

Sadly, there was no place on the list for Jack Harris, nor for his old sparring pal Ossie Pickworth even though they both ranked well in their own era. Nevertheless, they both had the satisfaction of knowing that on their day they could beat anyone. And they often did!

Ossie Pickworth was once asked by a journalist what he thought about Jack Harris's game. This was just after a close match which Ossie had managed to win. Ossie had replied, " if Jack Harris ever finds out just how good he is , he will beat all of us". Maybe it was a touch of graciousness coming out or some Borneo mateship rearing its head. Either way, Ossie Pickworth clearly had a lot of respect for Jack Harris and vice versa. Ossie made this comment as early as 1948, not long after he had just become the only player in history to win three consecutive Australian Opens.

Before concluding this chapter, I would like to indulge myself and select just one golf tournament I read about which I would like to have been at. I could have picked any number of famous Tiger Woods or Jack Nicklaus tournaments. Maybe David Graham's Merion win or Jack Harris's Victorian PGA win in 1963 at Long Island when he demolished Peter Thomson. In the end it came down to a choice of just two. Maurice Flitcroft's tilt at the British Open qualifier in 1976 or Papwa Sewgolum's humiliation of Gary Player in the 1965 Natal Open. In the end there was no contest. The little master from Durban with the idiosyncratic grip won my vote hands down.

Chapter 19

Amateurs and Professionals

As mentioned in an earlier chapter, Jack Harris was born in 1922 and came up through the caddie ranks to become a professional golfer. Another Australian golfer born in the same year was Douglas Bachli, the son of a publican, who also developed into a very skilful golfer. In Douglas's case however, he chose not to become a professional golfer, and he maintained his amateur status throughout his career. He won his first Australian Amateur Championship in 1948 when he beat a young amateur Peter Thomson. In 1954 he was the first Australian to win the British Amateur Championship: at Muirfield. This was the same year that Peter Thomson won his first British Open at Royal Birkdale GC. No other Australian amateur golfer won the British Amateur again until Bryden MacPherson won in 2011 at Hillside Golf CC which is adjacent to Royal Birkdale near Southport. Douglas Bachli also represented Australia in winning the Eisenhower Cup at St Andrews in 1958. He was awarded the MBE in 1996 (Member of the Order of the British Empire) and was a Life Member of Victoria Golf Club.

Although Douglas was an amateur he regularly played in the Australian Open and therefore played against Jack Harris many times. In 1951 Douglas was eighth in the Australian Open at Metropolitan and Jack Harris was fourth. At Lake Karrinyup in 1952 Douglas was twelfth and Jack Harris again was fourth. In 1957 at Kingston Heath, Jack and Douglas tied in eighth place. It was this kind of consistent performance by Douglas Bachli in the Australian Open which made me have a closer at the role which other highly skilful amateur golfers had played in Australian golf over the ages.

Professionals Jack Harris and Colin Campbell, get ready to do battle with leading amateur golfers, Bill Edgar and Doug Bachli

I found that in the early 1900s through to about 1931, the Australian Open golf had been very much dominated by amateur golfers. At first it was an Englishman, the Hon. Michael Scott who dominated in a field mostly comprising of amateur golfers. He won the first ever Australian Open in 1904. It was common in those days for the first three positions in the Australian Open to be filled by amateur golfers.

Then between 1912 and 1931 one man, Ivo Whitton, virtually made the Australian Open his own. He won it five times and also had four top ten finishes. This was despite the fact that the Australian Open was not played from 1914 to 1919 because of the First World War. Just like Douglas Bachli, Ivo Whitton never turned professional and maintained his amateur status throughout his long career. From what Jack Harris could recall it was Ivo Whitton who had been instrumental in persuading the great Ossie Pickworth to move from Manly GC in NSW to Royal Melbourne GC in the late 1940s. Ivo Whitton was only eighteen years old when he won his first Australian Open in 1912. But for the war he may have added considerably to his five Opens.

After Ivo Whitton, throughout the 1930s in the run up to the Second World War, the outstanding amateur performers were Jim Ferrier and Harry Williams. In a seven year period from 1933 to 1939 Ferrier had two wins, two seconds, one seventh and two tenths in the Australian Open. He then turned pro and went to play in the USA with great success including the first ever win by an Australian in a major. After the war he played in the Australian Open again as a professional and lost the final in a play-off to Ossie Pickworth. Before the war they had both started off playing golf at Manly GC in NSW. Jim was older than Ossie and in the early days at Manly he had apparently lorded it over Ossie. So Ossie's win in the 1948 Australian Open was a bit of payback time. It was a great win for Ossie too because at that time Ferrier was in the middle of a fantastic purple patch in his career on the US PGA tour. He had won the US PGA Championship in 1947 and was also winning plenty of regular US PGA Tour events as well.

Jim Ferrier hailed from Sydney but in the early to mid-1930s he had some very stiff opposition from a young Victorian amateur called Harry Williams. Harry Llewellyn Carlington Williams, to give him his full moniker, was the son of a wealthy manufacturer. He was a left-hander who beat Jim Ferrier in six of their seven encounters having won both the Victorian and Australian Amateur Championships in 1931 at the tender age of sixteen.

Harry Williams was a super talented golfer. When he was only twenty-one years old he played in the 1936 Australian Open at Metropolitan GC and finished runner-up to Gene Sarazen. The American legend set a new course record that day (282) and Harry Williams was just four shots behind. No other golfer managed to shoot a score of 282 at Metropolitan again until 1960 when Jack Harris equalled that score when he won the Victorian Open.

Harry played in the Australian Open again in 1939 at Royal Melbourne but this time Jim Ferrier beat him. Ferrier turned professional shortly afterwards and went to play with great success on the US PGA Tour. Williams, however, turned down several lucrative offers to join the professional ranks before drifting out of golf soon after that as booze and gambling took over. He died tragically destitute in 1961 in a double suicide with his mother in a tiny apartment in East Kew.

Jack Harris never played against Harry Williams but as a young fifteen years old assistant to Colin Campbell he did see him play in an exhibition match against Walter Hagen during one of Hagen's regular visits to Australia during the 1930s with Joe Kirkwood. Jack also remembers that Harry Williams regularly used to come to see him play during the 1950s at golf courses all around Melbourne.

During the period from 1900 to 1950 the number of amateur golfers playing in the Australian Open steadily declined and the number of professional golfers steadily increased. This trend has continued right up to the present day. In fact since Jim Ferrier's win as an amateur in 1939 there have only been two amateur golfers who have won the Australian Open: Bruce Devlin (1960) and Aaron Baddeley (1999). Both these outstanding golfers turned professional soon after these wins and both had very successful US PGA tour careers.

I couldn't really find an explanation as to why it happened, but 1960 appeared to be a glory year for amateur golfers in the Australian Open. At Lake Karrinyup GC in Western Australia the trend away from amateurs was briefly reversed. That year the first three positions were filled by amateurs. Bruce Devlin won. Ted Ball and Tom Crow came second and third. Apart these three there were five other amateur golfers in the top ten. The others were Eric Routley, Phil Billings, Douglas Bachli, Kevin Donohoe and Bob Stevens. Kel Nagle, who had won the British Open earlier that year at St Andrews, came fourth. John Sullivan was the second placed professional in tenth place. Since none of the amateurs could receive any of the prize money Jack Harris picked up third place prize money by coming eleventh tied with two more amateurs: John Hood and Kevin Hartley. Kevin Hartley went on to have a terrific amateur golf career including winning ten Riversdale Cups between 1958 and 1978 and the Australian Amateur title in 1958. In fact most of the amateur golfers mentioned above won either the Australian Amateur Championship or the Victorian Amateur Championship or both during their careers.

There was and still is a strict set of rules issued by the USGA and the R&A which govern what skilful amateurs can and can't do when they play in tournaments where prize money is involved. Not only can they not receive any prize money but they cannot accept any money if they give any teaching lessons either. However, if there is a prize such as car on offer for a successful hole in one they can accept that and they can also accept a small money voucher to spend in the pro shop.

The 1960 Australian Open at Lake Karrinyup was one of the first tournaments Jack Harris played after he had returned from his 1960 British Open campaign. Grace also travelled over to Perth on that particular trip. Jack recalls that they visited a stable somewhere in the Perth area where Norman von Nida kept some of his race horses. In that tournament Jack beat Norman von Nida by one stroke. He also beat an outstanding amateur, Tasmanian Peter Toogood, by three strokes. South African Harold Henning and the 1961 Australian Open winner Frank Phillips were four strokes back. Jack recalls that the Von was complaining bitterly nearly all the match because the cockatoos on the Lake Karrinyup course were screeching incessantly and disturbing his concentration. Jack also recalled another incident in a practice round before the Open started where they had some young kids caddying for them. Apparently Von had been putting badly and finally after yet another missed putt he tossed his putter away into some bushes. The young boy who was caddying for Von thought that he had thrown it away because he didn't want it so he didn't retrieve it. Von arrived at the next hole only to discover that there was no putter in his bag!

I must say that many of the images I have seen of Norman von Nida with his little beret perched on his head in a jaunty manner, remind me of Sir Bernard Law Montgomery. First Viscount Montgomery of Alamein was a famous British General in the Second World War. He eventually became a Field Marshal. I don't know if Monty played golf though. I wonder if that is where the saying *the Full Monty* came from.

The above mentioned Peter Toogood was from a family of outstanding amateur golfers in Tasmania. He won the Tasmanian Open eight times. In 1956 the first three places in the Tasmanian Open were, first Peter Toogood, second Alf Toogood (his dad) and third John Toogood (his brother). This has to be some kind of a golfing record? Peter Toogood was awarded the MBE in 1981 and John Toogood was awarded the OAM in 2010. Peter Toogood had earlier taken third place in the 1952 Australian Open when he beat both Jack Harris and Peter Thomson by one stroke when they tied fourth on 286. Peter Toogood was also a member of the winning Eisenhower Cup team in 1958 along with Douglas Bachli. In 1954 Jack Harris played against Peter, Alf and John Toogood in the Riverside and Tasmanian Tyre Service tournament in Launceston. Jack finished one stroke behind Peter Thomson but beat all the Toogood family and also beat Australian Open winners Eric Cremin and Frank Phillips.

Jack Harris played against all these outstanding amateur golfers many times. He also often played against another legend of Australian Amateur golf, Bill Edgar, who had won the Victorian Amateur Championship three times in 1927, 1938 and 1951. I read somewhere that Bill had played to scratch or better for almost a forty year period. Incredible! As early as 1947 twenty-five year old Jack Harris played in a fourball with Colin Campbell against Bill Edgar and Fred Morecroft in a pro versus amateur exhibition match at Sale GC to raise money for the Knibbs Appeal. They raised eighty-five pounds for the cause. Jack and Colin won the match but Bill Edgar shot the lowest score of the day with a fine 69. Jack Harris came in with 71.

Another little interesting story I heard from Jack Harris, which involved a very good amateur golfer, came from the short time he spent just before the outbreak of the Second World War at Yarra Yarra GC as assistant to Arthur Spence. Jack was a junior assistant pro there and one of his daily jobs was to clean members' golf clubs after they had played a round. These were golf clubs which the members just left in storage at the club until they next played. Jack has very clear memories of a bag of very old hickory shafted clubs kept in the storage racks there which belonged to Willie L Hope the 1933 Australian Amateur champion. According to Jack more or less every club in the bag was from a different golf club maker. WL Hope was a member at Yarra Yarra GC and had only arrived in Australia from England about one year earlier when he beat AW Jackson six and five in the final. He had apparently learned all his golf in Scotland. Later that year he also won the Yuill Gold Cup at Mornington GC and in the process beat two other very good amateurs: Mick Ryan the reigning Australian Open Champion by four strokes and the legend Ivo Whitton.

I am sure that if time and space permitted I could have also found great stories about several other outstanding amateur Australian golfers. Names like Harry Williams (five times Victorian Amateur winner), Harry Berwick (double Australian Amateur winner), Eric Routley (six times Victorian Amateur winner), Kevin Hartley (Australian Amateur champion), Phil Billings / Kevin Donohoe (Eisenhower Cup team members), Tom Crow (Australian amateur champion), Bob Brown (Victorian Amateur champion) and Laurie Duffy (eleventh in 1935 Australian Open) were standing out. Suffice it to say that there is obviously a great legacy for Australian golf left by all these very talented amateur players.

Throughout Jack Harris's playing days there was always an annual tournament between the Victorian professionals and the Victorian amateurs. It was generally a very keenly contested affair and quite often the amateurs won the day. On reflection it is perhaps not surprising that the amateurs sometimes won. It was very obvious from all the research that I did that the amateurs had far more opportunities than the professionals to play in a competitive situation. They played every week in pennant competitions. They played in all the amateur championships both at a state and national level and they also played in many of the competitions which the professionals played in.

Apart from these competitions, the best four amateurs also had a chance to play on the world stage in the Eisenhower Trophy which is a biennial world amateur team championship. Over the years, the Australian amateurs have done exceedingly well in this event. They won the very first Eisenhower Trophy held at St Andrews in 1958 when a team consisting of Douglas Bachli, Bruce Devlin, Bob Stevens and Peter Toogood beat a US team. They also won again in 1966 in Mexico City when Harry Berwick, Phil Billings, Kevin Donohoe and Kevin Hartley got the job done against another US team. In more recent times they won in 1996 and over the years have also been runners-up three times.

On the other hand, the professionals could not play in the amateur tournaments and sometimes they went several weeks without any form of purse to play unless they travelled interstate. In reality it should certainly have been easier for the amateurs to maintain their games in razor-sharp condition compared to the professionals.

Most of the amateur golfers mentioned so far who Jack Harris played with and against never turned professional. However, for all those great amateur golfers out there it is worth remembering that it is never too late to turn professional.

The classic case of a late starter was an American golfer called Jay Sigel. Although he had a fantastic amateur career winning both the US and British Amateur Championships he didn't actually turn professional until 1993 when he was fifty years old. He then played on the US Seniors' (Champions) Tour and proceeded to win eight tour events over the next twenty years or so which netted him over nine million dollars. Of course you cannot just decide to play on this tour. As with the regular PGA tour there is a very tough qualifying school to get through first. But if you are good enough it can be done.

All the amateur golfers I have mentioned so far have been men. However, I should at least mention one remarkable Victorian lady amateur golfer. Her name was Burtta Cheney MBE. Just like Jack Harris, Burtta was associated with Victorian and Australian golf until well into her nineties. Jack Harris played with her many times in Exhibition matches and in Jack's words 'she was simply the best.' Her complete list of achievements is far too long to list here. However she won an Australian Championship, was Huntingdale ladies champion eighteen times, played for the Victorian State team fifteen times and the Australian National team six times. She was also awarded an MBE and was an inaugural inductee into the Victorian Golfing Hall of Fame in 2011: the same year as Jack Harris. Burtta's father was an entrepreneur who had made his fortune in the automobile industry and the name still lives on in the Patterson Cheney Company. Sadly Burtta passed away in 2012 aged ninety-five. As with many of the stories in this book all roads lead to Wattle Park GC.

One of our regular merry band of Wednesday golfers at Wattle Park called Ian is friends with Burtta Cheney's nephew, David, in his Rotary Club. After Burtta had left us, David was looking for a good home for a set of Burtta's golf clubs. The net result is that one of Wattle Park's regulars is now the proud owner of a set of famous Burtta Cheney golf clubs.

Ian actually told us a funny story about one time Burtta gave a talk to their Rotary club. Burtta was apparently using a hand held microphone to deliver the speech but for a while there was a loud crackling noise coming out of the speakers which was tending to spoil the talk. That was until nephew David realised that the microphone had a wire dangling down from it which was just about touching Burtta's knees. Problem solved. The metal knee replacements which Burtta had in both knees were causing the static interference!

The connection between Burtta Cheney and Wattle Park GC doesn't even end there. Burtta was very much involved in the development of junior golf and in May, 1967 she was instrumental in organising a junior clinic at Wattle Park GC. How appropriate that almost fifty years later, another great advocate of junior golf, ninety-one years old PGA Life Member Jack Harris, is back at Wattle Park. When teaching pro Trevor Hollingsworth holds his regular junior golf clinics there, Jack Harris can often be seen casting his experienced eye over the young golfers' swings. Another twist to this story is that Burtta was also good friends with the aforementioned star amateur player Doug Bachli. The two were from all reports a formidable combination in the mixed foursomes. They played in lots of tournaments together and won virtually all of them.

Although they were not Australian, and as far as I know they never played in Australia, I feel that I should also say something about the two most famous amateur players of all time, American players, Robert Tyre *Bobby* Jones Jr and Francis De Sales Ouimet. By the time Jack Harris started his apprenticeship with Colin Campbell in 1937, Bobby Jones had already been retired from competitive golf for about seven years. He retired at only twenty-eight years of age in 1930 after having won thirteen majors including the first ever grand slam, all four majors of the day in the same year. Absolutely amazing bearing in mind that Jones's main profession was as a lawyer. He only played golf part time.

Francis Ouimet is widely regarded as the Father of Amateur golf in the USA. He won the US Open in 1913 and played in his last tournament, the British Amateur Championship in 1950, the same year that Jack Harris won his very first Victorian PGA Championship. Shortly after in 1951, Francis became the first ever non-Briton to be elected Captain of the Royal and Ancient GC of St Andrews. A film called *The Greatest Game Ever*

Played was released in 2005 about Ouimet's exploits in the 1913 US Open against Harry Vardon the British legend.

When Doug Bachli won his British Amateur Championship at the home of The Honourable Company of Edinburgh Golfers (Muirfield) in 1954, he beat a long hitting American golfer called Bill Campbell 2 and 1. The same year a first ever Australian Captain of the R&A was elected. He was Viscount Bruce of Melbourne, who over twenty-five years earlier, when Jack Harris was just a young boy, had been Australia's eighth prime minister. Almost another sixty years passed before a second Australian, Sandy Dawson, was honoured by being elected Captain of the R&A for the 2013-2014 year. Dawson was born in 1943, the same year as me. At the time he was elected he was President of Royal Sydney GC.

It is maybe interesting to note at this point that the Royal and Ancient Golf Club of St Andrews has always had a 'men only' membership policy and that is still the case in April, 2014. However, I understand that in September, 2014 they will vote on the motion to admit female members. It has been a 'men only' establishment since it was founded two hundred and sixty years ago in 1754 so if I was a lady golfer hoping to become a member I would not be holding my breath. (I hope I am wrong!) [14]

---

14 In September 2014 the unthinkable happened. The Royal and Ancient Golf Club of St Andrews finally became a mixed-member club when 85% of the members who voted were in favour of allowing women to join their club. Not before time is what I say!

Chapter 20

Sorrento and the Non-Playing Years

In 1972, fifty-year-old Jack Harris played his last regular Australian Tour tournament, the Victorian PGA Championship, when he finished sixth behind John Davis. Seven years later, in 1979, he did play in a Citizens Watch Seniors tournament at Manly GC in Sydney when he finished one stroke behind the legendary Sam Snead. Apart from this he has spent the last forty-five years of his career as a golf teacher.

From 1967 to 1983, he ran his golf school in Chapel Street, St Kilda. Around that time he was more or less head hunted by the late Geoff Brash to become the club professional at Sorrento Golf Club. At sixty-one years of age Jack was very hesitant to make this move. The St Kilda golf school was going very well and Sorrento GC at that time was nowhere near the thriving club which it is today. However, Geoff's wife Jenny finally convinced Jack to accept the challenge and he found a way to keep the St Kilda School running as well by going into partnership with one of his former pupils, PGA professional Trevor Hollingsworth.

At the start, Jack spent part of his time at Sorrento and part of his time in St Kilda. However, as time went on it was clear that to help build up the membership he would need to spend more and more time at Sorrento. He had done the same many years earlier with his seventeen years spent at Keysborough GC. Eventually the St Kilda School had to close and Jack stayed at Sorrento until he retired at age seventy-four in 1996. By this time he had helped to lay a strong foundation for Sorrento GC to re-build and grow into the flourishing club it is today. I understand that he had been the longest serving golf professional at Sorrento GC in their one hundred years history.

The Harris and Hollingsworth Golf School in Chapel Street, St Kilda in the early 1980s

When they were running the St Kilda golf shop and school together Trevor Hollingsworth recalled an occasion when he decided to do an annual stock-take on all the items in the shop. It took him two full days to count every golf ball, every golf-shoe spike and every tee as well as all the golf clubs, bags and golf buggies. At the end of the second day he tallied everything up and arrived at a grand total of fifty thousand dollars for the stock value. The next morning when Jack arrived at the shop Trevor asked him to have a guess at the value of their stock. Jack just strolled around the shop for about two minutes then declared that 'about fifty thousand dollars should cover it.' Jack may not have had an MBA Degree but he was still on the ball.

Recently I was privileged to see a limited edition copy of a coffee table sized book which had been presented to Jack Harris by Sorrento GC and which gave a detailed account of the Sorrento GC history. It was very clear from comments made in that book that Jack Harris was much loved at Sorrento GC just as he had been earlier at Keysborough GC. This was also reflected in the fact that Jack Harris was made an Honorary Member at both Keysborough and Sorrento Golf Clubs.

Sorrento and the Non-Playing Years

Left: Jack Harris, Trevor Hollingsworth and Phil Hollingsworth outside St. Kilda Golf School in 1980s

Right: Jack presents his trophy to Mrs Jill Nankivell of Sorrento GC after their annual tournament in March 2014 with Yarra Bend GC Ladies

Towards the end of his days at Sorrento Jack was involved in arranging a series of Pro-Am events in which he himself played along with a few other retired professional golfers. It was just prior to such an event that he happened to mention to a few lady golfers from the Yarra Bend GC that he was going down to Sorrento to play in such a day and he suggested that they may want to also go down and join in. When he arrived at Sorrento on the morning of the tournament he was amazed to see women everywhere. About eighty ladies had turned up! He had only expected about three or four! Anyhow, the net result of that particular day was that it turned into a very popular annual event. Over the years, the professional golfer participation in the event dwindled because many of the old golfers either died off or became too old to play.

However, the ladies were not to be deterred and every year the Sorrento ladies and the Yarra Bend ladies still get together and play for the Jack Harris Trophy. And what a magnificent trophy it is! It is actually a trophy which Jack Harris won for an event in the early 1950s when he beat his old mate Ossie Pickworth. Jack had donated the trophy which was later modified for this event. As usual Jack was on hand to present the trophy to the winning team when they last did battle on Monday, 31 March, 2014 at Sorrento GC.

For one of the first Pro-Am events which Jack arranged at Sorrento he managed to persuade quite a few of his old professional buddies to support the event. Even guys like Dan Cullen and Dave Mercer came down from Sydney. Jack also played in the event. However, Trevor Hollingsworth, who was helping Jack to organise the tournament, recalls that Jack pulled out of the tournament after about fourteen holes under the pretext that he needed to check some of the post-tournament arrangements. Trevor couldn't really understand this because they had plenty of helpers and everything was under control. It was only later when Trevor had a peep at Jack's card that he realised what Jack had done. The tournament was won with a score of two or three over par. When Jack pulled out he had been two under the card which wasn't too bad for a guy who was already in his seventies! Obviously he would have been too embarrassed to win his own tournament.

Most people at seventy-four years of age would smell the roses or swan around the world on a cruise ship, but not Jack Harris. After he retired from Sorrento in 1996 he started up another golf store and golf school in

Armadale fairly close to where he now lives. He ran this school for several more years. In 2001 he was made a Life Member of the PGA of Australia. But when he sadly lost Grace in 2002, he didn't have the heart to keep the school going and the Armadale facility closed. Much of the teaching equipment from Armadale was sold off to Jeff Boyle, a former Australian tour player who now runs his Boyle Golf Shed in Airport West and also gives golf lessons there.

Jack Harris at the Armadale golf centre

Needless to say, without Grace, Jack was not likely to jump on any cruise ship real soon. So at eighty years of age, to keep his mind occupied, he did what he had already been doing for the past seventy years or so. He looked up Trevor Hollingsworth's brother Phil, who at that time was the teaching professional at the Freeway public golf course in Camberwell. Then for a couple of days each week he dabbled in assisting Phil with his golf lessons. It was during one of these dabbling sessions about nine years ago on 24 June 2005 that Jack suffered a severe cardiac arrest. Luckily Phil Hollingsworth was close at hand and knew what to do. The paramedics were quickly summoned and responded brilliantly. In the meantime Phil had managed to resuscitate Jack and had saved his life. After that there followed a few years of rehabilitation with Jack chasing the nurses around the hospital and slowly but surely he was up and running again. Jack never forgot the extra bonus years he had been granted thanks to Phil's quick action. Every year after that on 24 June, Phil has had a telephone call from Jack. Jack regards this day as his *second birthday* and he wants to celebrate it with the man who made it possible.

Anyone would think that a close call like this would be enough to make Jack finally call it a day and sit by the poolside all day drinking pina coladas. However, it wasn't too long before he was back at his old tricks again. By the time Jack had recovered, Phil Hollingsworth had already left Freeway Golf and moved to Moorak GC. Not to be deterred, Jack looked up Trevor Hollingsworth again who by this time was the teaching professional at the Wattle Park GC.

Several years later, at age ninety-one, Jack still rolls up to Wattle Park GC a couple of times per week and is again dabbling in golf lessons. More about this in the final chapter but meantime it would be remiss of me if I didn't mention that in 2011 the Victorian PGA decided to start up a Hall of Fame (HOF). The inaugural night was held at the world famous Melbourne Cricket Ground (MCG) and six golfers were given the honour of being the inaugural inductees.

These included Peter Thomson AO, CBE (five times British Open winner), Bob Shearer (Australian Open winner), Doug Bachli MBE (British Amateur Champion), JACK HARRIS (six time Victorian PGA winner), Burtta Cheney MBE (Australian Ladies Amateur Champion) and Ivo Whitton (five times Australian Open Champion).

At the same time this HOF honour was being bestowed on Jack, it was announced that from that day forth the Victorian PGA Championship trophy would be re-named as the Jack Harris Cup. I had the great pleasure recently of accompanying Jack to the 2014 Victorian PGA event held at the Jack Nicklaus designed Heritage GC in Wonga Park and see him present the Cup to the eventual winner, Gareth Paddison from New Zealand.

In late 2013 I also had the pleasure of attending an event at the Woodlands GC along with Jack and long serving former Metropolitan

GC pro Brian Twite. They were both there to present an award to Margie Masters who had been the first Australian lady golfer to play and win on the US LPGA tour in the 1960s. Margie paved the way for later champions like Jan Stephenson, Jane Crafter and in more modern times, Karrie Webb. Margie Masters has since also been inducted into the Victorian PGA HOF. Jack Harris actually recalled an occasion in 1961 when he played against Margaret Masters in the Sir Dallas Brooks Mixed Foursomes at Metropolitan GC. Jack was partnered with Mrs B. Dunn and Margaret was playing with Don Lawrence the renowned sports writer from *The Age*. Mrs Dunn and Jack romped away with the goodies after a resounding 7 and 6 match-play victory.

Jack presents the *Jack Harris Cup* to New Zealand player Gareth Paddison at the 2014 Victorian PGA Championship held at the Jack Nicklaus designed Heritage GC in Wonga Park.

Without writing a whole book about golf teaching, I feel as if I can hardly do justice to Jack Harris's long career. From the time he became an assistant golf professional at Patterson River GC in 1937 to his Wattle Park GC dabbling days in 2014, he has spent at least fifty of those years just teaching.

Ignore the lost war years and that means he spent maybe an additional twenty-two years doing a combination of teaching and tournament playing. So in reality he was a professional golf teacher who just happened to dabble in tournament play rather than the other way around. Bear in mind also that he left school at age fourteen. He didn't attend Melbourne Grammar, Scotch College, Carey Grammar, Xavier College or any of the other prestigious Melbourne schools. He didn't have a Master's degree in business to help him cope with all the things he did and he never had a manager. He just had to rely on his experiences from the School of Life! I am still amazed at the tournament record he was able to achieve!

Before I complete this chapter, I feel compelled to say something about why Jack Harris has to some extent flown under the radar and has mostly remained in the shadow of some of his contemporaries. It is true that other golfers had better playing records than Jack Harris because they travelled extensively overseas and played in many more tournaments. They were more battle hardened and were able to win more big tournaments. Had Jack Harris done the same amount of overseas travelling and focused entirely on tournament golf as the others did, he would almost certainly have had similar success. As I have mentioned earlier, golf is just a numbers game.

Knowing that you have the ability to beat anyone as Jack Harris had demonstrated many times, it all boils down to persistence, more practice, self-belief and racking up the number of tournaments played. I call it the *Amway* principle where established distributors in their multi-level marketing organisation, to boost the commission they earn, are constantly contacting anyone they know to persuade them to become distributors too. This is also a numbers game. They know from years of experience that if they make enough phone calls, they will eventually sign up more distributors.

If you are a golfer with great ability, just play enough tournaments and eventually you are going to win some. That is the nature of the game of golf.

Bruce Crampton was a perfect example of this persistence philosophy. After Bruce had won the Australian Open at Royal Sydney in 1956 just before his twenty-first birthday, he went to play in America. Like Peter Thomson before him, initially he found it very tough to win on the regular US PGA Tour. However Bruce Crampton persisted and on his *eightieth* attempt, five years later, he finally won his first PGA Tour event, the 1961

Milwaukee Open. He went on to win thirteen more PGA events and twenty events on the Champions Tour including four times runner-up in a major. The Amway Principle strikes again!

Having said that, I also believe that a big part of the reason why Jack Harris is not as well-known as the others can partly be put down to the nature of the man himself. Jack Harris is a very quiet, shy and humble man who just hates talking about himself and who has always shunned the limelight. During our many hours of interviews on the preparation of this book, getting Jack to talk about what he had done was often like pulling hens' teeth. He was always very happy to tell me stories about how great Ossie Pickworth was. More than fifty years later he is still in awe of the famous shot he saw Jack Nicklaus play at the old sixteenth hole at the Lakes GC when Nicklaus drove the green with a 300 yards plus double water carry shot. But details of Jack Harris's own remarkable playing exploits were hardly ever forthcoming and I had to rely on old newspaper reports to find them.

I even heard one old contact of Jack's tell me that he even suspected sometimes that Jack deliberately played for second or third because he just dreaded the idea of having to make an acceptance speech. In fact several people have made the same comment to me. It is difficult for me to believe that this story was true but the fact that someone would even consider this as a possibility speaks volumes about the kind of quiet shy man Jack Harris was and still is.

It is true that many of the top sports stars, or for that matter, many people at the pinnacle of whatever it is they are doing, tend to have big egos. Many also have a tendency to be arrogant or are often condescending towards us lesser mortals. But they don't necessarily have to be like that. In the golfing world I don't recall Jack Nicklaus or Tom Watson ever showing those kinds of traits. I have never once heard Jack Nicklaus boast about what he did. But there again there was only ever *one* Jack Nicklaus!

For some time now I have been someone who likes to study body language and I always think that you can tell a lot about a golfer's personality just by the way that they walk and their general mannerisms on the golf course even, if they do not say anything. I never saw Jack Nicklaus swagger around the golf course thinking that he was the greatest. He really *was* the greatest, so he didn't need to swagger!

My profound admiration for Jack Nicklaus was formed long before he won all his eighteen majors. It was formed way back in 1969 when he had only won eight of them.

It was during the 1969 Ryder Cup at Royal Birkdale in Southport where I first saw what kind of man Jack Nicklaus was. This was the first Ryder Cup which Jack Nicklaus ever participated in. The match had been very fiercely fought and during the contest there had been several bitter exchanges of bad sportsmanship from several members of both teams. The match was all square as the last two players, Jack Nicklaus and Tony Jacklin, arrived at the eighteenth green. Nicklaus made his putt and that left Jacklin with a knee knocking two foot putt to half his match with Nicklaus and record the first ever tie in Ryder Cup history. As he approached his putt, Tony Jacklin must have had knees of jelly and must have been thinking that he needed a change of underwear. But without any hesitation and in a supreme moment of fantastic sportsmanship, Jack Nicklaus bent down and picked up Jacklin's marker thereby conceding the putt. The Ryder Cup was tied at 16-16. This gesture was all the more amazing when it will be recalled that Jacklin had beaten Nicklaus 3 and 2 in the morning's singles matches and this would have been a chance for Nicklaus to square the ledger if Jacklin had missed.

Reflecting on this moment, it made me wonder whether this kind of gesture could have happened in Australian golf during the 1947-1969 era. If it ever did happen I am absolutely sure that it would have been Jack Harris picking up the marker!

Chapter 21

Knights and Dames... and Other Baubles

In March 2014, Tony Abbott the current prime minister of Australia decided to re-introduce the appointment of Knights and Dames for pre-eminent Australians. Good timing, Tony! I think that *Sir* Jack Harris has quite a nice ring to it!

All jokes aside, the fact is that golfing knights are quite a rare species. As far as I can discover there have only been three professional golfers in history that have had this honour bestowed on them and none of these was an Australian. (Although one was an Antipodean from across the ditch)

The first was Englishman Sir Henry Cotton MBE who was made a Knight Bachelor in 1988. He actually died in December 1987 so he really didn't get much chance to bask in the glory of his knighthood.

The second was the famous Kiwi lefthander, Sir Bob Charles ONZ, KNZM, CBE who became a Sir in 1999. Sir Bob was actually the first left hander to ever win a major when he won the British Open in 1963.

And last but not least was Sir Nick Faldo MBE who arose as Sir Nick in 2009. Most Australians would not have very fond memories of Sir Nick because he was the one who dashed the hopes of Greg Norman in the 1996 US Masters. Starting the last round six shots behind, Faldo went on to win by five shots after an incredible eleven shot turnaround. Even though I find the term very distasteful, I was very proud to be called a *pommy bastard* on that particular day. I did genuinely feel very sorry for Greg though.

The nearest I ever got to Sir Nick was way back in the late 1970s when he was just plain mister Faldo. My wife Kathleen and I were staying in the Hotel Majestic on Paseo de Gracia in Barcelona just off Plaza Catalunya. It was just across the road from the renowned Catalan architect Antoni Gaudí designed house, La Predrera, and quite near to Las Ramblas.

Anyhow, I recognized Nick Faldo and also an Irish Ryder Cup golfer called Eamonn Darcy in the foyer as we were checking out. So being a perfect English gentleman I sent Kathleen across to get Nick's autograph. Nick very kindly obliged but the only item I could find for him to write on was a book I had just bought on how to solve the Rubik's Cube. He signed on the inside cover and it still sits somewhere on my bookshelf. I never did learn how to solve the Rubik's Cube. Those Hungarians are just too clever! Isn't that true, Mr Fehervari?

Jack Harris never played against Sir Nick because Nick was only born around the time Jack was playing his best golf. However, Jack did manage to play a few times against Sir Henry and Sir Bob, albeit they had not yet been knighted.

Jack's first encounter with Bob Charles was probably in the 1956 Ampol at Yarra Yarra. Bob was only twenty years old and still learning his trade. Jack was pretty much at his peak. It was no contest. Bob missed the cut and Jack finished tied third behind Gary Player in what was Australia's richest ever golf tournament up to that date. Over the next few years they met again several times in various Melbourne tournaments and Bob usually had the upper hand. But even when they met in the Australian Open at The Lakes GC in 1964, when Jack was forty-two years old and well past his prime, Jack was still competitive. Jack finished 28th on 304 and Bob came 11th on 296. Jack Nicklaus won that year on 287.

When Jack had his one and only tournament against Henry Cotton it was in the Penfold-Swallow at Copt Heath GC in England in 1960. Jack was approaching 38 years old and Henry was about 52 years old. On that occasion Jack finished well up the field (11th) with 279 and was comfortably ahead of Henry who shot 283. In his younger days Henry had won three British Opens. He had remained competitive for most of the 1950s and even finished top ten in the British Open in 1956, 57 and 58.

Apart from the three above-mentioned professional golfers, there has been at least one amateur golfer who was knighted. Having received an OBE in 1971, Michael Bonallack was made a Knight Bachelor in 1998. He was later inducted into the World Golf Hall of Fame in 2000. Sir Michael won the British Amateur Championship five times and was also playing captain at St Andrews in 1971 when Britain beat America in the Walker Cup for only the second time.

We do not want the ladies to feel left out of all these goodies. So in June 2014, my favourite lady golfer, Laura Davies, was made a Dame Commander of the Order of the British Empire (DBE) in the Queen's Birthday honours list. Dame Laura has won four major championships in her long career plus eight other top three finishes in majors.

It is clear that not everyone in golf can hope to become a Knight Bachelor. The only night hood most of them can hope for is one to keep their ears warm in bed on a cold night. However, the less prestigious honour awards are a bit more accessible to the golfing fraternity. Examples of the honours which Australian golfers have received in the past are seen in the following list.

Peter Thomson	AO,CBE, MBE (Officer of the Order of Australia, Commander of the Most Excellent Order of the British Empire, Member of thE Most excellent Order of the British Empire)
Brian Twite	OAM, (Medal of the Order of Australia)
Greg Norman	AO, (Officer of the Order of Australia)
John Toogood	OAM, (Medal of the Order of Australia)
Peter Toogood	MBE, AM (Member of the Most Excellent Order of the British Empire)
Karrie Webb	AM, (Member of the Order of Australia)
David Graham	AM, (Member of the Order of Australia)
Len Nettlefold	CBE (Commander of the Most excellent Order of the British Empire)
Lindy Goggin	AM, (Member of the Order of Australia)
Douglas Bachli	MBE, (Member of the Most Excellent Order of the British Empire)
Burtta Cheney	MBE (Member of the Most Excellent Order of the British Empire)
Graham Marsh	MBE (Member of the Most Excellent Order of the British Empire)

Billy McWilliam	OAM (Medal of the Order of Australia)
Norman von Nida	OAM (Medal of the Order of Australia)
Kel Nagle	OAM (Medal of the Order of Australia)
Bruce Devlin	OAM (Medal of the Order of Australia)
Charlie Earp	OAM (Medal of the Order of Australia)
Frank Phillips	OAM (Medal of the Order of Australia)

This is not meant to be a complete list. It is just a sample to give an idea of the range of honours which have been dished out in the past.

Two great Australian golfers who appear not to have been recognised are Jim Ferrier and Ossie Pickworth. Jim Ferrier actually became an American citizen in 1944 so maybe that would have ruled him out. However, the omission of Ossie Pickworth is more puzzling. The only man in history to win three consecutive Australian Opens surely must have deserved more recognition.

Not everyone who is nominated for an award in the Honours list will automatically accept the award. It was reported that in 1993, the British champion Ryder Cup golfer Peter Alliss who after his playing days became an internationally renowned golfing commentator, and a very humorous one at that, did actually turn down an appointment as Officer of the Order of the British Empire (OBE) for services to golf. Maybe he was disappointed because he felt that he should have at least been made a Sir Peter or even Lord Alliss.

Or maybe he just thought, 'What British Empire?' Sir Winston had to agree to let it all go around the time of the Second World War otherwise the Yanks wouldn't have come in and saved the world. The biggest chunk was India which went back to the Indians in 1947 and after that it all just trickled away until the final remnant, Hong Kong, went back to the Chinese in 1997. Bloody hell, even Scotland wants independence now! There would be no British Open Golf tournament then, at least when it is played in Scotland. The *British* part would have to be dropped. Even now the official name of the British Open is simply The Open Championship, so I guess nothing much would really change as far as golf is concerned. Actually, the Kingdom of Scotland existed quite happily for about nine hundred years as a sovereign state before they became part of Great Britain in 1707, so they have already been there and done that!

To be fair to Peter Alliss, I did actually read later that he had apparently turned it down because he felt that only people who had done some act of bravery should be recognised in this way. He thought people who were just doing their job didn't fall into this category. So much for all my conjectures!

The reality is that Peter Alliss is only one of a very long list of people from all walks of life who has declined to accept one of these honours. In 2003 an incomplete secret list of three hundred people who have refused to accept knighthoods and other awards was leaked to the *Sunday Times*. This list had been compiled by the Cabinet Offices Ceremonial Branch.

I couldn't find another golfer on the list that had refused an honour but Peter wasn't the only sportsperson to refuse one. In fact even as long ago as 1934 Australian test cricketer Bill Woodfull was said to have turned down a knighthood. Bill had been offered one for his cricketing prowess but he felt that his contribution as a teacher of mathematics and Headmaster at Melbourne High school had been more valuable. Almost thirty years later in 1963 he was eventually given an OBE for services to education. Two years later, he died while playing golf at Tweed Heads.

For me the strange part about this story was that in 1934, Bill must only have been teaching for a fairly short time. Less than fifteen years if you exclude his cricketing commitments for both Australia and in the Sheffield Shield. If that is the case then to receive a knighthood at that time for services to education would have been somewhat hopeful. Just consider that Jack Harris has been teaching golf for about seventy-five years without so much as a guided tour around Buck House.

The superstar and record-holder when it came to refusing honours wasn't a sportsman however. It was the famous artist from Stretford near Manchester, Laurence Stephen Lowry. He politely refused to accept honours on six different occasions including a knighthood! Match-stick men and match-stick cats and dogs were all he needed!

And for all the head bangers out there, just imagine this: we have Sir Elton John, Sir Tom Jones, Sir Cliff Richard, Sir Mick Jagger and Sir Paul McCartney. But we don't have Sir David Bowie because he politely turned it down!

The concept of knighthoods goes back hundreds of years in English history. Knight Bachelor is actually the oldest form of knighthood and dates back to King Henry III in the thirteenth century. Despite this it is the lowest ranking of all the various knighthoods. It is the only knighthood which doesn't emanate from the six orders of chivalry. Nevertheless a Knight Bachelor is still knighted by the reigning monarch.

Interestingly enough, there is no equivalent to Knight Bachelor when it comes to honours for ladies. In this case the lowest ranking available is Dame Commander (DBE) which does come from an order of chivalry (The Order of the British Empire). This is in fact the equivalent of a Knight Commander (KBE) for men. All this means that Dame Laura Davies is technically ranked higher in the pecking order than Sir Henry, Sir Nick, Sir Bob and Sir Michael. So put that in your pipe and smoke it!

Where does all that leave Jack Harris? At ninety-one years of age he has done as much for Australian golf at the grass roots level as any other living Australian golfer and more than most. Trouble is, he always did it in his own quiet way. He never made a song and dance about it and generally shied away from any publicity. Maybe his time is running out, so I had better give him my own award. Jack Harris, MHGOWP (Most Honourable Golfer of Wattle Park) and King of Victoria!

I had not long written this particular piece about Knights and Dames and also the chapter on *Amateurs and Professionals* when, shortly afterwards I was playing golf one afternoon at Wattle Park. By chance I met up with two young guys, Jackson and Michael, who told me that they had just wagged off a few lectures at the nearby Deakin University campus to play a few holes of golf. I think they may have even sneaked over the fence without paying but don't quote me! Little jockeys!

As is my wont, I told them about this great old golfer who plays at Wattle Park called Jack Harris. This prompted Jackson, to tell me that his grandfather had been a good golfer and had won the British Amateur Championship. He was amazed when I told him that his grandfather must have been the above mentioned Doug Bachli MBE who won the British Amateur title in 1954 at Muirfield. He was even more amazed when I told him that I was writing a book about Jack Harris and there is already something in the book about his grandfather's achievements and also a nice photo of Douglas Bachli with Jack Harris, Bill Edgar and Colin Campbell. Coincidences don't come any better than that. I never played golf with the late Doug Bachli but I can now say that I did play golf with his grandson. I can also report that Jackson seemed to be a chip off the old block. He had a very smooth shoulder turn and played with nice rhythm too. Yet again, all roads lead to Wattle Park!

Chapter 22

Wattle Park Days

In March 1955 there was an exhibition match held at the very modest short little nine holes public golf course at Wattle Park in Melbourne's east. The match involved Ossie Pickworth, the only man in history to win three consecutive Australian Open titles (1946, 1947 and 1948) and his partner John Crean, the pro at Wattle Park. They played against Jack Harris, Victorian Open winner and six times Victorian PGA winner and his partner Jack Boorer another top Victorian professional of the day. The match had been arranged to raise funds for the local Burwood Boys' Home but also to bring attention to the Wattle Park course. This kind of event was just one of many exhibition matches which golfing pros of that era did to promote the game of golf throughout the state of Victoria. It would be totally unheard of today for golfing giants of their stature to play a match at such a humble little municipal course as Wattle Park.

However, this in fact was not the first time it had happened at Wattle Park. On 6 October 1937 when The Melbourne Tramways Board officially opened Wattle Park GC to the public, they also held an exhibition match to mark the event. On that occasion, the 1937 Australian Open golf champion, George Naismith, who was the club professional at the nearby Riversdale golf club, played against his brother, the Victorian PGA champion, Ted Naismith. At the same time Clem Enderby was appointed the first club professional of Wattle Park GC. Before he joined Wattle Park GC, Clem Enderby had been teaching at Hartley's sports store in Flinders Street where a half-hour lesson in 1933 cost two shillings and six pence.

Even before the Wattle Park course officially opened in 1937, the Wattle Park club had been active as early as 1935 and was one of only five founding member clubs of what was initially called the Public Golf Links Association of Victoria, changing their name later that year to what is still known today as the Victoria Golf League (VGL). The 137-acre park had been officially opened in March 1917 by the then Governor, Sir Arthur Stanley. And even as early as 1924 it had been proposed by the Tramways chairman that part of the park be used as a nine-hole public golf course. At that time, the Victorian golf champion, Arthur Le Fevre, was taken to inspect the land and gave his opinion that it would indeed be suitable for use as a golf course.

But this is not the end of Wattle Park's glory days. In 1959 there was a young thirteen years old chap working a part time weekend job in the Wattle Park pro shop. He also played for the Wattle Park pennant team. That same year he won a junior tournament at Wattle Park against eighty other school boys playing as a left hander. The next year as a fourteen year old, he left school and took up a job as assistant to the Riversdale GC professional, George Naismith, who quickly switched him over to playing right handed. In 1962 at age sixteen, he turned professional. At twenty-three he was playing on the US tour where he went on to win eight PGA tour events and two majors. He also had sixteen top ten finishes in majors and won a heap of other tournaments across the globe.

His name was Anthony David Graham. David was never regarded as a long hitter. However, he was once reported as saying that playing the short narrow tree-lined fairways at Wattle Park with the small upturned saucer like greens is where he learned about the importance of accuracy and course management when it came to scoring. Even today, many of the low handicap golfers who sometimes play Wattle Park often don't score as well as they expect to do on this very short golf course.

Not many years later, in 1973, a young man called Ross Baker also started off his career at Wattle Park GC as assistant to professional John Creen. He stayed there two years before finishing off his traineeship at Commonwealth GC. These days Ross can be found at the Barnbougle GC (Lost Farm) in Bridport, Tasmania. Besides being a very keen golf historian, Ross also runs a business which involves handcrafting traditional wooden golf clubs and forged irons. There are actually two golf courses at Barnbougle and according to the March 2014 edition of *Golf Digest* both courses are ranked in the first six on the Top 100 Australian golf courses list.

In 2014 Wattle Park is still a thriving little public golf course which attracts both beginners and more established players alike. There are actually three distinct clubs operating at the course: Wattle Park Men's Club, Wattle Park Ladies' Club and Wattle Valley Ladies' Club. Trevor Hollingsworth is the teaching professional who looks after the needs of all three clubs as well as the needs of any visitors. He also regularly conducts junior clinics, especially during school holidays.

It is perhaps fitting therefore, that more than fifty years later, Jack Harris, at the age of ninety-one, has turned full circle and is back spending the twilight of his stellar golfing career at Wattle Park. His was a career which encompassed over thirty years as a club pro most of which was spent at two very prestigious clubs, Keysborough and Sorrento. A career which saw Jack Harris give many thousands of golf lessons both to total hackers like myself and to many famous celebrities of the day. Even to superstars like the American golfer Payne Stewart who tragically died prematurely in a plane crash in South Dakota late 1999 en route to Dallas, Texas. A career which saw Jack Harris have incredible success playing in all the major Victorian and Australian golf tournaments even though his time to practice and prepare for such tournaments was very limited because of extensive club pro and teaching commitments.

I have observed on many occasions that whenever Jack Harris visits any golf club in Victoria he is received like golfing royalty. Yet, he chooses to shun any limelight and prefers to melt into the relative anonymity of Wattle Park. So why does a man who is an Australian PGA Life Member, a Victorian Hall of Fame Legend and a man who has trodden the fairways of all Australia's top golf courses with icons of the game such as Jack Nicklaus and Arnold Palmer, choose to spend his last days at Wattle Park?

The answer to this question is very simple: Jack Harris is just a very humble unassuming man who loves the game of golf. He visits Wattle Park every Wednesday and Saturday mornings. He is not there in any official capacity. He visits to offer some support to one of his former pupils, Trevor Hollingsworth, who is the current teaching professional at the course. Every week you can find Jack clearing away empty coffee cups and washing them up in the kitchen or giving free golfing tips to anyone who wants to improve their game.

He also still likes to spend time in the practice nets each day hitting shots with his trusty five iron. He may not have the strength now which he had when he was playing world class golf but his posture when addressing a golf ball is still perfect and his swing is still silky smooth and he still wears a hole in the net where every ball hits the same spot! Jack is happy to talk about golf with anyone and everyone: he just loves being at or around a golf course and being around golfers, no matter how proficient they may be at playing the game. His quiet words of encouragement and profound insight into the game of golf are greatly appreciated by regulars in the Wattle Park pro shop.

Despite being such an insignificant little public course, Wattle Park still has a good share of golfing characters. Jack often sits in the coffee shop overlooking the first tee and gets great amusement at watching some of the antics which go on.

It may be someone having ten air shots before hitting a beauty which is still ten yards short of the ladies tee. Or it may be a young buck that slams a mighty drive only to see it hook violently on to the cricket ground next door. It may even be yours truly starting out to play the full round with just one club in the bag, my driver. I usually score in the thirty-two to thirty-six range on our par thirty-two nine holes course, Thus, I have reached a stage in my golfing life where I have taken all confusion out of the game and simplified it to the point of where it is impossible to simplify further. In other words I am in golfing heaven. I employ the KISS principle: Keep it Simple Stupid! Jack Harris is horrified at the way I play and he tells me so just about every time we meet.

However, The Lunt Bunt always gives Jack a good laugh! He never ceases to be amazed that someone like me who has the wrong grip, the wrong posture, the wrong takeaway, a non-existent wrist cock or follow through, can ever manage to get the ball off the tee. Rhythm, I keep on telling him. Get the rhythm of the swing right and it can mask many of the other faults, at least for the average Joe Hacker.

Some other advice which an old codger gave me over sixty years ago has always kept me in good stead. He told me, 'try to make sure laddie that when you duff the ball it goes straight. A one hundred and fifty yard duff shot which goes straight down the fairway is usually better than a two hundred and fifty yards shot which ends up under a bush!' Not sure that Jack believes me. There again, why should he believe me? As a golf teacher I would no doubt make a good opera singer!

Most days of the week, we all have the pleasure of watching the Italian maestro, Tony Radatti. Tony has a split grip when he holds the club and always bounces the club two or three times on his right shoulder during his back swing before hitting one straight down the middle. Not exactly silky smooth but it works for him which is all that matters. Tony didn't even start to play golf until he retired at age sixty-five. He has since improved maybe more than anyone else playing at Wattle Park. And when he gets on a putting streak even Bobby Locke would need to watch out! He could perhaps be the only man in history to have more holes in one than Art Wall Jr by the time he calls it a day! Then there is Tony's old mate Doug Tingay who also took up golf after he retired. Doug had been a welder during his working life and he often fixes our golf trolleys for us when parts start to fall off them.

The Dominator, aka Domenic Coniglio (or Mr Rabbit, as he is sometimes known), is yet another of the regulars who only took up golf after he retired. He can often be found in the practice nets with Jack Harris showing him how to improve his swing. Dom sometimes gets a bit frustrated. He has had great success at another sport, pistol shooting, and he wants to master golf in just one season.

Wednesday mornings is usually when we sit down for coffee with a retired barrister called David and his golfing partners Klaus, John and Ian. I often wondered if he really meant *barista*! Two skinny lattes, please!

Actually we regularly solve all the current world problems, and David always manages to sound very intelligent so I think on reflection that he really had been a barrister! He must also be OK at golf too because he always seems to have won their four-ball. However, like all barristers, when it comes down to who is going to buy lunch he always seems to have left his wallet at home! As for John, his playing partner, I think that he must have a bladder problem because he always buys a small bottle of orange juice after the game but only ever drinks half of it and leaves the rest of it for the cleaning lady.

On weekends, we would often see a young couple called Kari and Penny pushing their baby son around the golf course with them in a push chair while they both enjoyed a game of golf together. Most of the time baby James would just sleep all the way around the course. However, by the time he was about three years old he didn't want to sleep any more. He already had his own set of short golf clubs and was hitting balls on the practice ground, and was hitting them better than some of the grownups! As for James's dad, Kari, I am quite sure that he has a fetish about sand buckets! Every time you see him on the course he always has at least half a dozen sand buckets dangling from his golf trolley. He just can't bear to see a big divot mark which someone has left and not filled in. So he has appointed himself as the chief divot mark repairman of Wattle Park! Good on yer, Kari!

We also had Lawrence (or Mister 103) who recently shot through and went to live somewhere on the New South Wales or Queensland coast to go surfing every day. He used to think I called him Mister 103 because that was his score. Actually Mister 103 was derived from the radioactive chemical Lawrencium which is number 103 on the Periodic Table. This reminded me of my old college days and was named after Ernest Lawrence who had invented the Cyclotron at the University of California for accelerating nuclear particles. Lawrence was the master of the reverse pivot but he still managed to hit the ball a lot further than me.

Saturday morning is, however, when the real characters come out to play. We have Graeme Clark, an accountant. He is so tight that I think he is playing with the same ball he first found at Wattle Park in 1953! Then there is Don Brookes, a lawyer, who used to play VFL football with South Melbourne before they became known as the Sydney Swans. Don still has the strength of a VFL player and if he ever gets his swing right he will need to change golf courses because Wattle Park will not be long enough for him. The real super star of our group is Billy Peers. At least he is part of a super star sporting family. His wife Elizabeth played for Australia at tennis and was the club champion at the famous Kooyong Tennis club for about twenty five straight years. Both his son John and daughter Sally are following in mum's footsteps. After playing college tennis in the USA, son John is currently featuring in doubles at all the major tennis tournaments around the world playing with Jamie Murray, brother of Wimbledon champion Andy Murray. When he is not off swanning around the world playing major tennis tournaments John can often be found having a quiet game of golf at Wattle Park with his dad. He is pretty good at golf as well as tennis!

And last but not least of our regular group is fellow Rotarian Warren Fricke, a retired pharmacist who made squillions out of selling little blue pills to old men with erection problems. Warren tells us that he was also a pretty good sub-district cricketer. He has been giving this old Pom some curry recently since fast bowler Mitchell Johnson has suddenly found a bit of form and has the English cricket team jumping up and down all over the place with his fearsome bumpers. However, he doesn't like me reminding him of the days when Jimmy Laker, English off spinner, took nineteen wickets for ninety runs at the Old Trafford Ground in Manchester in 1956 against Australia. What's more Jimmy still holds the Ashes series record with forty-six wickets at an average of about nine each. Eat your heart out, Shane Warne! A young Australian leg spinner called Richie Benaud was bowling in the same match and was tonked all around the ground finishing up with two wickets for one hundred and twenty three runs. As far as golf is concerned, however, Warren certainly still has some adjustments to make. He still wants to hit a golf shot as if he was executing a David Gower off drive at cricket.

Most days we see George and Lillian who often walk down to Wattle Park baby-sitting their daughter's little dog, Pearl. They are just two of the regulars who appreciate that Wattle Park GC serves up the best cappuccino in the area, not to mention Richard Chelotti's homemade carrot cake. Yummy!

In our regular group, we have developed a lot of our own golfing terms when we go around the course. For instance when we are on the green and a putt just misses and shaves the hole, we call that a Brazilian. We only call it that when men are in the group. Care is required if there are any ladies around! Then again if we are on the green and a putt hits the hole but lips out, we call that a Mick Jagger (all lips). And then there are my own idiosyncratic worm burning shots with my driver from any distance were very quickly referred to by Don Brookes as the 'Lunt Bunt.' Wattle Park is only a very short par sixty-four course so I can often score less than my age off the stick. When anyone scores a sixty-nine we always call that dinner for two. I can't remember where that one comes from, ha! Apart from these we get the usual profanities which can often be heard on any golf course when a shot goes wrong, but best not repeat them here! Thank goodness we don't have too many Norman von Nidas playing on our course!

For a long time, the routine golfing day of all these old farts used to be brightened up by the frequent appearance of Florence, a very sexy young French lady who regularly used to arrive at the course in a very short miniskirt to play and also have golf lessons. Sadly, Florence left us a few months ago to join the nearby more swanky up-market Riversdale Golf Club so we don't have the pleasure of seeing her quite so often these days. Most golfing aficionados will probably recall that Riversdale GC is where golfing legends Peter Thomson and David Graham spent time in their early years with head professional George Naismith. Actually we have two French-speaking ladies who regularly visit our course. Trevor Hollingsworth's beautiful wife Josie is from the island of Mauritius in the Indian Ocean. Josie would definitely qualify as being the prankster of Wattle Park. I certainly need to keep an eye on my golf shoes when Josie is around!

Wattle Park may be just a very humble public course but we still get some very interesting visitors coming to play. One day I found myself playing with the Manufacturing Director of Ford China. I don't recall his name (The chances are I couldn't spell it anyway!), but I do remember that he had a set of golf clubs which I would have needed to mortgage my house for if I wanted to buy them.

Recently, I played a round with a guy who played clarinet in the Melbourne Symphony Orchestra. He told me that he had played in an ensemble at Dame Elisabeth Murdoch's hundredth birthday celebration. He was amazed when I rattled off the history about Hiroyuki Iwaki, the late chief conductor of the MSO, because Hiroyuki had given him his first job at the MSO.

Naturally, none of this affects Jack Harris. He just derives great pleasure in talking with all these characters and is always offering encouragement for them to improve their games and to continue to enjoy the game of golf no matter what their individual abilities may be. Jack Harris also has a mischievous sense of humour. Whenever I am sitting with him having a coffee waiting for my regular playing partners to arrive, as soon as they turn up, he pipes up in a loud voice so that everyone can hear, 'hey look, the victims are here.' Actually, if truth be known it is usually me who most often has to pay for the drinks after the game!

The last verse of a very famous poem penned by Rudyard Kipling over one hundred years ago goes something like this:

If you can talk with crowds and keep your virtue,
Or walk with kings nor lose the common touch,
If neither foes nor loving friends can hurt you,
If all men count with you but none too much,
If you can fill the unforgiving minute with
sixty seconds worth of distance run,
Yours is the earth and everything that's in it,
And which is more, you'll be a man my son.

Jack Harris has lived and continues to live the sentiments expressed in this poem throughout his long life.

He is equally at home in the company of golfing nobodies like myself as he was playing golf with the best golfer the world has ever seen, Jack Nicklaus, or with Sir Gubby Allen former chairman of the English cricket selectors or with former Governor of Victoria, General Sir Reginald Alexander Brooks CGMG, KCB, KCVO, DSO, KStJ.

No one has filled the unforgiving minute better than Jack Harris did and continues to do. I know that Jack Harris will just hate me for saying this because he is an overwhelmingly modest man, but I am going to say it anyway: I salute you, sir! You are a superstar man who just happened to be a superstar golfer. Jack, I hope that you have enjoyed reading this book as much as I have enjoyed writing it.

Patrick Morgan, (Wattle Park Manager), Jack Harris, David Lunt and Trevor Hollingsworth (Wattle Park teaching professional) in March 2014.

Jack Harris and John Schultz talk about the good old days.

Afterword

I began to write the Jack Harris story full of excitement but not without a tinge of apprehension. Never having written a book before or even an article for a newspaper, I didn't know whether or not I could string two words together or for that matter, even if I could, whether it would just sound like a babbling rant. Hopefully, despite my very limited vocabulary, I have managed to cobble something together which doesn't send the half a dozen or so people who are likely to read it to sleep before they even get through the first chapter!

Writing this book has been a journey and a huge learning curve for me. All my shortcomings were exposed very early on in the piece. Even though I attended a Grammar School in the UK, my English language skills, especially when it comes to the fine detail of punctuation, have never been a strong point. My computer skills are at an even earlier stage of development, so in this area I needed to rely very heavily on the expertise of number one son, Jonathan. I should explain that I use the description number one son only because he is my eldest son and not for any other reason. I wouldn't want to upset his younger brother, Richard. I love them both dearly – their two sisters also!

My main objective when I began writing was to document for posterity all the many achievements of Jack Harris. From his humble beginnings at the caddie ranks of Kingston Heath GC to become one of the greatest Australian golfers of the post war era and also a most respected golf teacher. It had been very obvious to me soon after meeting Jack Harris that there was no way he would ever write his own story because he is disarmingly averse to talking about himself. Since I felt strongly that someone ought to do it, I had concluded that it may as well be me.

Going through all the old history of Jack Harris's life and through all the old golfing records was fascinating, albeit at times somewhat laborious. However, the fact that I did have a long standing love of playing golf and of watching the great players, whether it be on TV or at major tournaments, did make the task easier for me. What I didn't expect, however, was the degree to which I became almost obsessed by the process. It was not unusual for me to start writing straight after breakfast and still be writing at ten o'clock at night with very little to eat in between apart from frequent cups of coffee to keep me alert. If golfers can get swallowed up by the desire to actually play golf then it seems that the same can happen to people who write about golf! Before I knew it the book was growin' like Topsy.

The other discovery I made is that being a professional golfer is even more difficult than I ever imagined. Learning to hit a golf ball on the sweet spot with the club face at right angles to the chosen target line is a difficult enough task in itself for the vast majority of would-be golfers. In reality, most of the time, it is beyond the capabilities of most of them no matter how many golf lessons they take or how many hours of practice they put in or how many instruction books they read or instruction videos they watch. But that is only an entry point for a professional golfer.

Jack Harris has lived a very long and fruitful life. I finished the first draft of this book a few months ago and since then I have fine-tuned it more times than I care to remember. Even now I continue to unearth new facts almost daily which I had not known previously about Jack or about the era in which he played. But sooner or later I knew that I would need to draw a line under what I had done so far and call it a day.

At the end of the day, Jack Harris can hold his head up high. He can look the world in the eye and he can look at himself in the mirror and know that whatever he did, he did with great distinction, great honour, great integrity and even greater humility. In the words of the famous Frank Sinatra song, he can also say, 'I did it my way.'

The Final Chapter

It was 12.02 pm on Friday 22 August, 2014 and I had just driven off over the ravine at the fifth tee at Wattle Park GC. Strangely enough I had hit what for me was quite a good drive. It was straight down the middle and well over two hundred metres. As I walked towards the ball the thought had crossed my mind that Jack Harris would have been proud of me. It was just a few seconds after that thought when the mobile phone in my pocket started to emit a series of pips to alert me to the fact that a text message had just been received. It was a message I had been expecting but one I definitely didn't want to read. Two or three minutes passed before I summoned up the courage to read it. It was from Jack's daughter Marilyn and read 'Dad passed away peacefully this morning.'

Jack had fallen at home on Saturday 9 August just a few hours after a meeting at Wattle Park with one of his Footscray football heroes, John Schultz. The result of the fall was a broken hip. A few days later, he had a total hip replacement at the Epworth Hospital in Richmond. Unfortunately there were some post-operation complications and Jack was not strong enough to handle them. It was certainly not for the lack of trying. I visited him in the Epworth a few days after his operation and he was already sat up in a chair at the side of his bed and was joking with all the nurses! I knew about the complications and had been expecting the unwanted news but that didn't ease the absolute emptiness I felt when I read the message. I hadn't experienced that same feeling since my own father, also called Jack, had died from lung cancer in December 1973 at the young age of fifty-three when I was only thirty years old.

I remembered reading earlier that morning on the Australian PGA Twitter page a message congratulating Peter Thomson on reaching his eighty-fifth birthday. I couldn't help thinking how ironical that was.

I had only known Jack Harris for about eight years since he first started to regularly visit Wattle Park after he had recovered from his cardiac arrest in 2005. However, over the past couple of years I had spent many hours a week drinking coffee with him and chatting about all the things he had done during his long life. If someone at Wattle Park hadn't told me that he had been a champion golfer I would never have known. It is not something that Jack himself would voluntarily ever tell anyone. Despite only knowing Jack for a relatively short time I felt as though I knew him as well as anyone.

He told me how much he loved and missed his dear wife Grace. I knew how he loved to make regular visits to see his youngest daughter Christine and her family in Tasmania and he often brought in photographs to show me of his grandchildren and great grandchildren. I knew that on the very day he had his fall he had brought pamphlets to show me of a trip which oldest daughter Marilyn was planning to take him to Darwin. They were to re-visit the places where Jack had served during the early part of the Second World War before he was sent up to Labuan Island, Borneo. And of course, through all the research I did for this book, I knew perhaps better than anyone, just how unique and special he had been as a golfer.

Jack himself generally played down his tournament playing success. He regarded his main contribution to golf was as a golf teacher and there is no doubt that as a teacher he touched the lives of thousands of Australian golfers and had a massive impact in this area. However, after twelve months of trawling through the golfing records of Australian golf during the 1946 to 1970 period, I came to the conclusion that Jack Harris was a far better tournament player than he ever gave himself credit for. The only players who had better playing records than Jack during that time were either full time touring professionals or were club based professionals who somehow still managed to tour extensively overseas.

The big names in golf during that period were Jim Ferrier, Peter Thomson, Kel Nagle, Norman von Nida, Frank Phillips, Ossie Pickworth, Eric Cremin and towards the end, Bruce Crampton and Bruce Devlin. Jack Harris had comprehensive wins over every single one of those players and in most cases many times. I really do believe that when Ossie Pickworth once said 'if Jack Harris ever finds out just how good he is he will be better than all of us,' he probably meant it.

This book was virtually completed when Jack was still with us even though it still hadn't been published. Jack had received various copies of the manuscript to read throughout the process. Even though he didn't necessarily agree with everything I have written, there were not too many things he asked me to change. He gave me almost total freedom to express my own personal opinions and my own interpretations of what had happened in Australian golf during his era. For this reason, apart from the dedication, I have not gone through the book and changed the parts which refer to Jack still being with us.

This really is *the final chapter*. It is Saturday morning 23 August, 2014 and I am just about to depart home for Wattle Park to meet my regular playing partners. But Jack won't be there to laugh at me and 'the victims' as we each make our pathetic attempts to drive the green on the two hundred metre par-three first hole.

We said our final goodbyes to Jack Harris in the Boyd Chapel at Springvale Cemetery on 2 September, 2014. The two Borneo boys were now back together again. Ossie Pickworth had also been laid to rest there forty-five years earlier in September, 1969 when he was just short of his fifty-second birthday.

Wattle Park is never going to be the same again. Rest in peace, dear friend.

Postscript

It is important for me to clearly state at the conclusion of this book, that any ideas or opinions expressed about the interpretation of various events which occurred during the period covered, are entirely those of the writer and do not necessarily concur with any views held by Jack Harris.

At a very early age, it was drummed into me by my first English teacher, the much loved Terry Land at Colne Grammar School, that one should never automatically believe everything that one sees written in a newspaper or a book. And this applies even more so in today's environment with the internet. I should therefore caution readers of this book in a like manner.

Most of the detailed information about old golf tournaments was obtained from hundreds of old newspaper reports dating back fifty, sixty, seventy or even eighty years. When crosschecking data, inconsistencies between different newspaper reports on the same tournament were very common. Inevitably there will be errors and omissions in the facts presented which I must accept responsibility for. Hopefully, any such errors will not cause major distortion and will not seriously detract from the main theme of the book.

Acknowledgments

The first person I must thank for making this book possible is Jack Harris. He sat patiently for many hours, drinking coffee and being bombarded with questions. Despite his ninety-one years, Jack was able to recall an amazing amount of detail for events which occurred sometimes over eighty years ago. He could even remember crucial shots in some of the tournaments he played. Jack also gave me total access to his scrap book from where many of the photos came.

The second person I must thank is Englishman Sir Timothy Berners-Lee who invented the World Wide Web (w.w.w.) late 1989 or early 1990 when he was working at the CERN nuclear research laboratory. Without this fantastic tool, the task of trawling through hundreds of old newspaper articles would have been far too daunting and the book would in all probability not have happened.

The third person I must thank is my eldest son Jonathan, also a fellow *NAGA*. He shared my passion and enthusiasm for getting out the Jack Harris story and has been an integral part of the whole process. Was it not for his untiring support, marketing expertise and relentless attention to detail, I would still be floundering about somewhere near the starting point. Thanks mate!

I am also indebted to following people who have made significant contributions. Libby Margo for all her advice on writing styles and expert editing skills. Luisa Laino for all invaluable guidance through the publishing stages. Jessica Dimasi from JD Creative Designs for the cover and marketing material. Sylvie and the team from BookPOD, for final typesetting.

After that there is a host of people who have assisted me in all manner of ways. In no particular order, these include Bob and Lyn Spencer who very kindly gave me access to their scrap books and photo albums from where several illustrations and photos in the book emanate. Bob also gave me a very good first hand insight of how Jack used to operate in his Keysborough days. He was also able to confirm and reinforce impressions I had formed about Jack after talking with other people as well as recounting lots of funny stories some of which are included in the book. Josephine Lunt, Audrey Cunningham, Jenny Simon, Susanna Lunt and Marilyn Rouhard who frequently read the manuscript and offered ideas for improvement and corrections.

Trevor and Phil Hollingsworth, two of Jack's proteges who attained professional status and who were Jack's partners in the St Kilda Golf School were a constant source of stories and information.

My good friend John Nunn who kindly sent me lots of advice from his home in Coolum on how to set about getting the book published. John has had two of his own books published so he was well placed to give me guidance in this area. Wendy Woods, who sent me some historical information on the Wattle Park Ladies' club. My thanks should also go to Jeff Gordon who provided all the photos from the Armadale Golf School and to my good friend and golfing buddy, Don Brookes, who read the final script and provided background legal advice.

I am also indebted to John Schultz the Footscray Football Club legend who won the Brownlow Medal in 1960, the same year Jack Harris went to the British Open. John had attended the Sportsmans' Dinner when Ted Whitten presented Jack with his famous number three jumper and luckily, still had a good quality photograph from that night which he kindly gave me access to. John also very generously contributed the foreword to this book for which I am extremely grateful.

Likewise I should acknowledge two golfing websites. Firstly, the About.Golf.com website which provides full results on previous British Open Championships. And secondly, the AinsworthSports.Com website which gives golf rankings for different periods and the Mark McCormack world golf Rankings which can be found on Wikipedia. Indeed much of the historical data, especially on the pre-war days and the Second World War days was also obtained in this manner. I am conscious of the fact that Wikipedia data is not always super accurate so apologies in advance for any errors.

As I have stated elsewhere a great deal of the information discussed in this book was garnered from old newspaper reports on golf matches played throughout Australia and Tasmania dating back to the 1930s, 40s, 50s and

60s. Some of the newspapers such as the *Melbourne Argus* which ceased circulation in 1957 are no longer in circulation. I suspect that many of the journalists who wrote the articles have long since retired and many of them may no longer be with us. However, I am indebted to these reports because without them there would not be much of a story since mostly we are talking about events which occurred mostly between fifty and sixty years ago and there was little chance that Jack Harris could remember details of all his matches going back that far. I would like therefore to acknowledge and thank Jack Dillon (*Herald*), Don Lawrence (*Herald/Age*), Peter Thomson (*Melbourne Argus*), Alan Trengove (*Melbourne Argus*), Frank Besemeres (*Adelaide Mail*), Dave Andersen (*Melbourne Argus*), Keith Brown (*Brisbane Courier Mail*), Brian Feely (*Sun*), Tom Richards (*Sydney Morning Herald*), Bill Moorhead (*Melbourne Argus*), Les Ryan (*Sydney Sun Herald*), Bill Fleming (*Melbourne Argus*), Max Ward (*Melbourne Argus*), Barrie Bretland (*Sun*) also John Dean and Jack Dunn.

I must acknowledge the PGA of Australia for providing me with various photographs of Jack. Also the Golf Victoria and Australia PGA websites where detailed results of previous Victorian PGA, Victorian Open and Australian Open Championships are freely available. Thanks also to Woodlands Golf Club for providing details of all Jack Harris's wins in the Woodlands Open Championship and also to Peter Swan at the Yarra Yarra GC for confirming Jack's playing record at that great club.

Finally, the last person I must thank, and definitely the most important, is my loving wife Kathleen. Without her endless support, great patience and at times much needed encouragement, this project would have been even more challenging.

References

The Argus, 8 December 1936
Jack Harris (Kingston Heath) won the Under 15s Victorian Caddie Championship at Riversdale GC. He collected the grand prize of two shillings and sixpence and also won the VLGU Cup.

The Age, 30 November 1937
Playing off a handicap of 20, fourteen years old Jack Harris (net 145) won the 36 holes Handicap Event at the Assistants Championship at Long Island GC. He beat P Barber in the play-off. At the 415 yard sixth hole Jack was on the green in two and sank a 25 foot for a birdie. He won the grand sum of £2 and a cup donated by Hartley's Sports Store.

The Argus, 3 December 1938
Playing out of Long Island GC, sixteen-years-old Jack Harris / B Lazer (163) tied 8th in the Victorian Assistant Professional's championship at Kew GC. Jack Beazley (149) won, J Green (154) was second and J Dunn / Alec Kynnersley (155) tied third. Other scores included Charlie Newman (160), Len Bottrell / Jack's brother Alec Harris (161) and Alec Orr (165).

The Age, 3 December 1938
Jack Harris (143) won the 36-hole Handicap Event at Kew GC playing off a very generous handicap of 10. He successfully defended the title he had won in 1937 even though his handicap had halved from the previous year. Jack won the magnificent prize of £2-2/- and a cup donated by Leviathan Sports Store. J Green (144 off 5) was second and J Dunn (147 off 4) third.

The Argus, 18 September 1940
17 years old Jack Harris (168) was 24th in the £100 Major-General H W Grimwade purse at Peninsula GC. Martin Smith / Sam Walsh (147) were joint winners and collected £37 and £41 respectively. Colin Campbell (149) was third for £11. Other scores included George Naismith (153),

Arthur Le Fevre / Reg Jupp / Don walker (157), John Creen (158), Keith Clark / Arthur Spence (159), Ernie Wood (160) and Bill Iles (169).

The Argus, 4 April 1941

Jack Harris / Ernie Wood, Don Walker / H Gillespie and John Young / M Ingeigneri (2 up) tied third in the Yarra Yarra GC four-ball event, George Naismith / T Levy (4 up) won and Arthur Spence / H Kaufman (3 up) were second. Also played Colin Campbell / M Ahern (square).

The Argus, 6 May 1941

Eighteen years old Jack Harris / Sam Walsh (157) tied 10th in the Dunlop Cup at Metropolitan GC. Top three were Martin Smith (146), Ted Naismith (147) and George Naismith (150). Other scores included Bill Clifford / Ernie Wood / Don Walker (151), Arthur Spence / Reg Jupp (153) and Graham Cates / Alec Orr (159).

The Argus, 13 May 1941

Eighteen years-old Jack Harris / 1937 Australian Open champion George Naismith / Arthur Spence / former Victorian PGA winner Reg Jupp (81) tied 9th in the Kingswood GC purse. Jack Bahen (77) won and 1939 Australian Open runner-up Martin Smith / Alwyn Whykes / Colin Campbell / Bill Smith (78) tied second. Other scores included Ted Naismith / Bob Jamieson (79) and Jack's older brother Alec Harris (80).

The Argus, 10 June 1941

Jack Harris / Alwyn Whykes (167) tied 7th in the £50 PGA Handicap Purse at Kingston Heath GC. Graham Cates (158) won the £20 first prize. Martin Smith / Bill Smith (160) tied second and shared £15. Other scores included Ernie Wood (164), Ted Naismith / Jock Whillans (166), George Naismith (168), Don Walker / Bill Clifford / Jack Beazley (169), Arthur Spence (170), Ted Nelms (172), Bill Fowler / Harry Jones / John Young (174), John Creen (175) and Alec Harris (176). This was one of the few times where Jack and his brother Alec played in the same event. Jack played off a handicap of two and Alec played off three.

The Argus, 15 October 1941

Jack Harris (156) was 8th in the £100 Major-General H W Grimwade purse at Peninsula GC. Martin Smith (144) won, Ernie Wood (147) second and

Ted Naismith (148) third. Also played Reg Jupp (151), Colin Campbell (153), George Naismith (154), Bill Fowler / Arthur Le Fevre / Arthur Spence (158), Walter Spicer (163), Jack's brother, Alec Harris (170) and Jock Whillans (174).

Frankston Standard, 14 November 1941
Jack Harris / Hartley Mitchell won the Legacy Club's Gymkhana at Huntingdale GC Four-ball event with 9 up.

The Argus, 23 August 1946
A rusty Jack Harris (352), only recently de-mobbed from the Army, was 23rd in £300 purse at Huntingdale GC. Ted Naismith (314) won £100 first prize, Ossie Pickworth (322) second received £50 and Martin Smith (330) got £30. Also played Eric Cremin / George Naismith (331) for £21 each, Bert Ferguson (332) for £14, Bill Clifford / Horrie Boorer (334) for £7 each, Viv Billings / Bill Fowler (336) for £4 each, Ted Nelms / Jack Beazley / Sam Walsh / Bill Smith (340), Colin Campbell / Len Boorer / Arthur Spence (341), Ernie Wood (349) and Graham Cates (351).

Adelaide Advertiser, 28 September 1946
Twenty-three years old Jack Harris / Dan Cullen / Fred Bolger / Ted Naismith / Graham Cates / Sid Cowling (72) tied 4th in the Royal Sydney GC £100 purse. Ossie Pickworth / Albert Cecil Howard (70) were joint winners and Ernest Chaplin (71) was third. Other scores included former Australian Open winners Billy Bolger / Lou Kelly (74), Sam Richardson / Kel Nagle / Eric Cremin (75), Reg Want (76), Jim McInnes / Harry Sinclair (77), Len Boorer (78) and Martin Smith / Dick Carr / Bill Fowler / former Australian Open winner Tom Howard (79). Only the first four places received any prize money. This was probably Jack's first cheque after he returned from the war.

Sydney Morning Herald, 2 October 1946
Jack Harris (159) was 15th after two qualifying rounds for the **Australian Open championship** played 18-holes at The Australian GC and 18-holes at The Lakes GC. Peter Heard (147) was first, Horace Henry Alfred 'Ossie' Pickworth (148) was second and Eric Cremin (149) was third. Other scores included Alan Waterson (152), Sam Richardson (153), Billy Bolger (155),

Dan Cullen (156), Martin Smith (158), Reg Want / Horrie Boorer (160), Kel Nagle / George Naismith (161), Ron Harris (168) and Stan McGeorge (171). Behind Stan were 24 other players down to 183.

Sydney Morning Herald, 7 October 1946
After being placed 15th from 123 entrants after two 18-hole qualifying rounds played at The Lakes / Australian GCs, Jack Harris tied 35th with Dick Payne / A Thomson / Bob Brown (309) in the **Australian Open championship** at Royal Sydney GC. Jack had only been de-mobbed from the Army just a few months earlier. Ossie Pickworth (289) won his first Australian Open and the £100 first prize. He also got his name for the first of four times on the Stonehaven Cup. Alan Waterson (291) was second and Martin Smith / Harry Hattersley (293) tied third. Martin Smith had been joint runner-up with Norman von Nida to Jim Ferrier in the last Open played before the war in 1939. Who knows what he may have done if the war had not intervened. Other scores included Peter Heard (297), Keppel Enderby (298), Kel Nagle / Eric Cremin / former Australian Open champions Lou Kelly / Bill Bolger (298), Alf Toogood / Doug Bachli (299), Ted Naismith (300), Bill Higgins (301), Denis Denehey / Bill Edgar / former Australian Open champion Fred Popplewell (303), Reg Want / Colin de Groot (306), Keith Pix / Norm Berwick (307), Viv Billings / former Australian Open winner Mick Ryan (310), Sid Cowling / Dick Carr (311), Graham Cates / Eric Alberts (313), Hartley Mitchell / Charlie Snow (314), EJ "Ted" Smith USA (315), Jim Petterson (318) and Willie Harvey (326). Because there were a lot of amateurs playing in this event, Jack still finished 16th professional and qualified for the Australian PGA ...but did not play. After the first two rounds of the Australian Open the field was cut to include scores of 158 or better. Sixty-four players made the cut. Arthur Gazzard the former Queensland Open and Queensland PGA winner was one of those who missed the cut.

Adelaide Advertiser, 21 October 1946
Jack Harris (158) was 12th in the £250 **Adelaide Advertiser** tournament at Kooyonga GC. Eric Cremin (146) won the £75 first prize. Ted Naismith (151) was second for £45 and Ossie Pickworth / Martin Smith / Jim Mills / Bill Robertson (152) tied third and shared £90. Other scores included Fred

Thompson (153), Bill Smith (155), Willie Harvey (156), Colin Campbell (157), George Naismith (159), Gordon Westthorpe (162), Bruce Auld (163), George Jordon (164) and Cliff Naismith (167). Prize money only went down to the first nine finishers.

The Age, 4 November 1946
Jack Harris / Bert Ferguson / Horrie Boorer (306) tied 5th in the £190 purse at Patterson River GC. Martin Smith / Eric Cremin (293) won and Bill Smith (303) was third. Other scores included Jack Beazley (305), Ted Naismith (307), Colin Campbell (308), Bill Clifford (309). Jack Boorer / George Jordan (311), George Naismith (312), Ron Harris (313), Alwyn Whykes (316), Bud Russell / Bob Jamieson / Viv Billings (319) and Ted Nelms (321). Assistant professional Jack Harris received a special prize for the best afternoon round (70) which included a front nine of only 33... easily the best nine of the tournament.

The Age, 6 November 1946
Jack Harris (155) was second in the 100 Guineas purse at Kingswood GC and picked up 25 Guineas. Eric Cremin (151) won 50 Guineas and Jack Beazley (157) was third for 15 Guineas. Other scores include Ted Naismith (10 Guineas) / Bill Edgar (158), Jack Boorer (159), Martin Smith / Bill Higgins (160), George Naismith / Des Ferguson / George Jordan (162) and Alwyn Whykes / Graham Cates / Bert Ferguson (163). Only the first four finishers collected any prize money.

The Age, 11 November 1946
Jack Harris (311) was 8th in the **Victorian PGA championship** at Victoria GC. Eric Cremin / Norman von Nida (289) tied first and Martin Smith (295) was third. Other scores included Bill Clifford (297), Colin Campbell (301), Denis Denehey (309), Alec Kynnersley (310), Jack Boorer (312), Ted Naismith (314), Ernie Wood / Horrie Boorer / H Jones (316), Viv Billings (317), Jack Beazley / Graham Cates / A Griffin (319), Alwyn Whykes (321), D Young (324) and Sam Walsh / Ron Harris (328). Eric Cremin won the play-off.

The Argus, 6 December 1946
Jack Harris / Colin Campbell (152) won the **Victorian PGA foursomes championship** at Victoria GC. Denis Denehey / Bill Smith (156) were second and Horrie Boorer / Dick Holding (159) third. Other scores included Ron Harris / Graham Cates (160), Martin Smith / Bill Clifford and Bill Fowler / Ted Nelms (161), Ernie Wood / Arthur Spence (162), Jack Boorer / Sam Walsh (163) and George Jordon / Alec Kynnersley (164) and George Naismith / Ted Naismith (166).

The Argus, 5 April 1947
Jack Harris / Colin Campbell, Jim Petterson / Martin Smith and Sam Richardson / Eric Cremin (73) tied third in the ACT Four ball championship. Les Chaplin / Dick Carr (71) won and Colin de Groot / Billy McWilliam (72) were second.

The Sun, 7 April 1947
Jack Harris (151) was 11th in the £125 ACT Open championship at Royal Canberra GC. Colin Campbell (138) won, Eric Cremin (141) was second and Martin Smith / Dick Carr (144) tied third. Other scores included Bob Brown (145), Fred Bolger / Bill Higgins / Sam Richardson (146), Tom Tanner (147) and Keppel Enderby (148).

The Sun, 7 April 1947
Jack Harris was 25th in the 54 holes purse at Royal Canberra GC. Eric Cremin won, Colin Campbell was second and Martin Smith third. Jack still finished ahead of Dan Cullen, Kel Nagle and Viv Billings.

Sydney Morning Herald, 21 April 1947
Jack Harris / Bill Holder (312) tied 12th in **the £1000 Ampol tournament** at The Australian GC, Kensington. Ossie Pickworth (294) won the £250 first prize. Bill Bolger (295) was second and Eric Cremin (296) third. Other scores included NZ player Alex Murray / Reg Want (305), Fred Bolger / Viv Billings (308), Martin Smith / Billy McWilliams (309), Denis Denehey / Colin Campbell (310), Lou Kelly / Dan Cullen / Sam Richardson (313), Eddie Anderson / Jim Petersen / Albert Howard (315), Alf Toogood / Sid Cowling / A Thomson (316), Len Boorer / Dick Carr / Charlie Booth / NZ player Alf Guy, W McKenzie (318), Keith Clark (319), Les Chaplin

/ G Kay (320), George Naismith / Jack Beazley (321), Bill Clifford (322), Colin de Groot / Jim McInnes (324), Arnold Victorsen (329), Bill English (330), Bill Smith (331) and Jack Harvey (332). Former Australian Open winners Frank "Happy" Eyre and Fred Popplewell were further down the field.

The Argus, 10 May 1947
Jack Harris / Bert Ferguson / Bill Fowler (159) tied 11th in purse at Victoria GC.
Ted Naismith (145) won, Bill Clifford (147) was second and Ossie Pickworth (150) was third.
Also played Martin Smith (153), Jack Boorer (155) and George Naismith / Bill Smith / Sam Walsh (158).

The Age, 17 May 1947
Jack Harris / Colin Campbell (317) tied 8th in the Dunlop Cup at Commonwealth GC. Ossie Pickworth (294) won on ten under par. Ted Naismith (298) was second and Len Boorer (307) third. Other scores included Jack Boorer / Martin Smith (309), Arthur Spence / Sam Walsh (316) and Ron Harris (319).

The Sun (Sydney), 2 June 1947
Jack Harris (157) was 17th in the £50 purse at Brisbane GC. Ossie Pickworth (140) won and Reg Want / Dick Carr (146) were runners-up. Other scores included Eric Cremin (148), Kel Nagle (150), Martin Smith (151), Len Boorer / Bill Holder (152), Ossie Walker / Jim McInnes (153), Sid Cowling / Ted Naismith / Bill Bolger / Doug Katterns (154), Eddie Andersen (155), Harry Sinclair (158), Bill Fowler (159), Arthur Gazzard (161), Arthur Spence (163), Alex Gemmel (169) and Len Katterns (176).

The Age, 25 July 1947
Twenty-four-year-old Jack Harris (305) was second in the £200 purse and Spalding Bowl at Kingston Heath GC and collected £40. Ossie Pickworth (296) won the £70 first prize and Ted Naismith (307) was third for £25. Other scores included Martin Smith (310), George Naismith (311), Ernie Wood / Bill Clifford (314), Arthur Spence (317), Graham Cates / Jack Beazley / Len Boorer (318), Des Ferguson (319), Sam Walsh / Colin

Campbell / Ron Harris (320), Horrie Boorer (322), Bob Jamieson (326), Jack Boorer (329) and Bud Russell (330).

The Age, 26 September 1947
Jack Harris (153) was 8th in the £50 purse at Amstel GC. Eric Cremin (143) won and Ossie Pickworth / Denis Denehey / Jack Beazley (150) tied second. Other scores included Len Boorer (151), George Naismith / Bill Smith (152) and Viv Billings / Colin Campbell / Graham Cates / Bill Fowler / Sam Walsh / Jack Boorer / Bill Robertson (155).

The Age, 27 September 1947
Jack Harris (159) was 27th in the **Victorian PGA championship** at Riversdale GC. This was the only year between 1946 and 1972 when Jack didn't get through the qualifiers. The PGA were experimenting with the format of this event in the immediate post war years. This was a stroke play event BUT for some reason the field was cut to only 19 players after the first two rounds and Jack missed out by a few strokes. In the subsequent 25 years, till he played his last Victoria PGA at the age of fifty, he never again missed the cut and was never outside the top ten in this event.
The format wasn't the only thing the PGA experimented with in 1947. It was also the first year that the players were numbered. I.e. Caddies wore a numbered armband which corresponded to each player's number given in the souvenir programme.

The Age 18 October 1947
Jack Harris (320) was 13th in the **£200 Slazenger purse** at Yarra Yarra GC. Ossie Pickworth (301) won, Martin Smith (307) was second and Ted Naismith / Colin Campbell (311) tied third. Other scores included Len Boorer / Sam Walsh (314), Bill Clifford (316), Viv Billings (318) and Arthur Spence (319). The course par was 74.

The Argus, 22 October 1947
Jack Harris / Colin Campbell (165) were 9th in the **Victorian PGA Foursomes** at Woodlands GC. Martin Smith / Bill Clifford (156) won, Ernie Wood / Arthur Spence (157) were second and Jack Boorer / Sam Walsh (160) tied third with Len Boorer / Bill Robertson. Ossie Pickworth / Alec Orr (161) and Ted/George Naismith (163) also played.

The Age, 28 October 1947
Jack Harris / Bill Fowler / Viv Billings (136) tied 7th in the 36-hole £100 Silver Jubilee purse at Woodend GC. Colin Campbell (131) won, Ted Naismith (133) was second and Bill Clifford / Ossie Pickworth (134) third. Other scores included Martin Smith / Len Boorer (135). Horrie Boorer's 63 in the morning was the best round of the day but he faded in the afternoon and finished behind Jack Harris who shot 66 in the second round.

The Age, 6 November 1947
Jack Harris (157) was 4th in the Kingswood purse. Ossie Pickworth (154) won, Martin Smith (155) was second and Len Boorer (156) third. Other scores included Bill Clifford (158), Bill Higgins (161), Eric Wishart (163) and Laurie Duffy (169).

The Argus, 15 January 1948
Jack Harris / Sam Walsh / Martin Smith / George Naismith (2 down) tied 6th in a pro-am at Kingswood GC. Denis Denehey with a great 7 up won and Ossie Pickworth / Ted Naismith (1up) tied second. O Campbell / Horrie Boorer were 1 down.

The Age, 13 April 1948
Jack Harris / Dick Destree (300) tied 5th in the **£500 Adelaide Advertiser** purse at Royal Adelaide GC. Jack won £40. Ossie Pickworth (287) won the £150 first prize. Eric Cremin (289) was second for £100 and Kel Nagle (291) received £75 for third. Other scores included Bill Bolger (299) £50, Mick Kelly (301) £30, Ron Harris (302) £25 and Denis Denehey / Norm Berwick / Fred Thompson (303) £10 each. Other scores included George Jordon / Viv Billings / Len Boorer (310), Len Nettlefold (311), Dick Foot (312), Bill Shephard (316), Gordon Westthorpe (319) and Harry Thredgold (333).

Sydney Morning Herald, 19 April 1948
Jack Harris (317) was 15th in the **£1000 Ampol** tournament at Huntingdale GC. Ossie Pickworth (300) won the £250 first prize. Reg Want (302) was second and Eric Cremin (303) third. Other scores included Kel Nagle (305), Martin Smith (307), Colin Campbell (308), Denis Denehey (309),

Bill Holder (310), Ted Naismith (311), Jack Beazley (312), Lou Kelly (313), Fred Bolger / Ernie Wood (314), Sam Richardson / Len Boorer (318), Dick Carr (320), Graham Cates (324), Bill Fowler (325), Bill Robertson / Billy McWilliam / Fred Thompson (327), Sam Walsh (328), Ted Nelms / Alwyn Whykes / Norm Berwick (329), Bob Jamieson (330), Cliff Naismith (341), Walter Spicer (342), Charlie Newman (344), Bill Smith (350) and Norm Taylor (351). The par for the course was 77. Jack played with Ossie in the final round and both shot 77. However, if they had been playing match-play Jack would have won that round because he won more holes.

The Age, 20 April 1948
Jack Harris (146) was 4th in the £100 Wally Frazer purse at Victoria GC. Ossie Pickworth (142) won, Eric Cremin (143) was second and Martin Smith (145) third. Also played Colin de Groot (147), Colin Campbell (149) and Fred Thompson (150). Jack Harris shot the best round of the tournament when he had a 70 in the final round on the par 75 rated course.

The Age, 26 April 1948
Jack Harris (3 up) won **the Yarra Yarra Open** scratch 36-hole bogey event and collected £30 prize money. Ted Naismith / RP Barber (1 up) tied second. Naismith took home the £10 second prize money because Barber was an amateur. Other scores included Ernie Wood (square) and Jack Beazley (1 down).

The Age, 26 July 1948
Jack Harris / Bill Edgar (306) tied third in the **Victorian Close championship** at Huntingdale GC. Ossie Pickworth (293) won and Doug Bachli (305) was second. Other scores included Martin Smith (309), amateur Peter Thomson (310) and Barry West / Hartley Mitchell / Bill Clifford (313). Huntingdale was a par 77 rated course in those days.

The Argus, 19 August 1948
Jack Harris / Colin Campbell and Bill English / Alwyn Whykes (157) tied 4th in the **Victorian PGA foursomes championship** at Northern GC. Len Boorer / Bill Robertson (153) won, Martin smith / Bill Clifford (154) were second and Ossie Pickworth / Alec Orr (156) were third. Other scores

included Bill Smith / Viv Billings (158), George Jordon / Alec Kynnersley (159) and George Naismith / Ron Harris (160).

The Argus, 10 September 1948
Jack Harris / Colin Campbell (155) tied 7th in the £200 Spalding Bowl at Yarra Yarra GC. Ossie Pickworth (151) won the £80 first prize and Len Boorer / Martin Smith (152) tied second. Other scores included Ted Naismith (153), Viv Billings / Jack Boorer (154), Ted Nelms (156), Bill Clifford (157) and George Naismith / Ray Wright (158). Down the field were Ernie Wood, Horrie Boorer, Bill Fowler, Bill Robertson, Alec Orr, George Jordan, Graham Cates, Dick Holding, Alwyn Whykes, Alec Kynnersley, Ron Harris, Bill English, Allan Ellis, Bud Russell, Jack Beazley, Bert Ferguson, John Creen, Bill Smith, Bob Jamieson, Norm Taylor, Sam Walsh and Arthur Spence.

The Argus, 15 September 1948
Jack Harris / Ron Harris / Bill Robertson (154) tied third in the £200 Slazenger purse at Woodlands GC. Martin Smith / Ossie Pickworth (149) were joint winners. Also played Jack and Len Boorer (155), Ray Wright (156), Colin Campbell (157), Ted Naismith / Horrie Boorer / Bill English (158) and Bill Fowler / Bill Clifford (160).

The Age, 2 October 1948
Jack Harris / Colin Campbell / Graham Cates / Jack Boorer (96) tied second in a purse at Amstel GC. It was played over 24 holes because 6 holes were under re-construction. Martin Smith (93) was the winner.

The Age, 15 October, 1948
After beating South Australia by 5-0, Victoria were runners-up to NSW in the **Vicars Shield** at Kingston Heath GC. Eric Cremin beat reigning Australian Open champion Ossie Pickworth (4 & 3). Former Australian Open champion Bill Bolger lost to Martin Smith (5 & 4). Bill Holder beat Ted Naismith (6 & 5). Kel Nagle beat Bill Clifford (4 & 3). Former Australian Open champion Lou Kelly beat Jack Harris (3 & 2).

Sydney Morning Herald, 25 October 1948
Jack Harris (306) was 15th in the **Australian Open championship** at Kingston Heath GC. Former Australian Open winners Ossie Pickworth /

Jim Ferrier played the first ever tie in this event. Ossie won the 18-hole play-off to become the only man in history to win three consecutive Australian Opens. Jack Harris shot a final round 73 which was the same as Ferrier. Reg Want (296) was third. Other scores included Eric Cremin (298), Peter Thomson (299), Martin Smith / Alan Waterson (300), Kel Nagle / NZ player Bob Glading (302), Denis Denehey (303), Bob Brown (304), Bill Holder / Alf Toogood / J Prendergast (305), Sam Walsh (307), Hartley Mitchell / former Australian Open winner Mick Ryan / Graham Cates (308), Eric Routley (309), Bob Stevens (310), Ron Harris / Bill Higgins (311), Len Boorer / Bill English (312), John Hood / former Australian Open winners Lou Kelly / George Naismith (313) and Sid Cowling / former Australian Open winner Billy Bolger / NZ player Tim Woon (314). Behind Tim Woon was the NZ Amateur champion Brian Silk. Only the leading 60 players qualified to play the last 36 holes. Eric Alberts the former WA Open winner missed the cut.

The Age, 2 November 1948

Jack Harris (145) took home first prize money in the Croydon GC Open when he came runner-up to nineteen-year-old amateur Peter Thomson (142) who shot 4 under the card to Jack's 1 under. Martin Smith / Ted Naismith (146) tied third. Other scores included Bert Ferguson / Bill Robertson (148), Len Boorer (149) and Colin Campbell (152).

The Argus, 13 November 1948

Jack Harris / Martin Smith tied third in the **Victorian PGA championship** at Commonwealth GC. Jack lost 2 and 1 to Ossie Pickworth in the semi-final. From tee to green Jack generally outplayed Ossie but too many missed short putts ruined his chances. Ossie went on to win the tournament easily beating Trawden born Sam Walsh in the final.

The Age, 29 November 1948

Jack Harris / Eric Cremin (304) tied 8th in **£1000 Ampol** tournament at The Lakes GC. Jack collected £35 prize money. Ossie Pickworth (293) won and received £250 plus £100 share of £380 gate money. Kel Nagle (298) was second for £125 / £44 and Reg Want (300) was third for £100 / £38. Other scores included Norman von Nida / Billy McWilliam (301) for £70 / £27 each, Billy Bolger / Bill Holder (302), Eddie Anderson (308),

Denis Denehey / Fred Bolger / Sid Cowling (310), Sam Richardson (313), Bill Clifford (314), Norm Berwick (315), Lou Kelly (316), Jim Moran (317), Dan Cullen / Arthur East (319), Ted Naismith (320), Jack Brown (321), Dick Carr (322), Martin Smith (323) and Colin de Groot (325). After de Groot in no special order came Alan Myers, Tom Gorman, Fred Popplewell, Les Chaplin, Colin Campbell and A Thomson.

Sydney Morning Herald, 15 March 1949
Jack Harris / Doug Bachli / Bill Higgins (151) tied 6th in the Victoria GC Open Scratch. With the big advantage of playing on his home course Peter Thomson (142) won. Hartley Mitchell (147) was second and Martin Smith (148) was third. Other scores included Laurie Duffy (149), Ted Naismith (150), Ossie Pickworth / Len Boorer / John Hood / Ron Harris / Colin Campbell (152), Harry Papworth (153) and Ray Wright / Jack Boorer (154). Jack Harris still picked up some prize money as the third professional to finish.

The Sunday Herald, 3 April 1949
Jack Harris / Bill Edgar / Dick Carr (310) tied 31st in the **£2500 McWilliams Wines** tournament at The Australian GC, Sydney. Norman von Nida (281) won and collected the £600 first prize. Ossie Pickworth (287) was second and Peter Thomson (289) third. Other scores included Eric Cremin (291), Denis Denehey / Bill Holder (294), Larry Montes (296), Filipino Celestino Tugot (298), Keppel Enderby (299), Kel Nagle / Ted Naismith (300), Len Boorer (301), Peter Heard (303), Reg Want / Mick Kelly / Billy McWilliam / Harry Hattersley / Sam Richardson (304), Alf Toogood (305), Colin de Groot / Eric Routley (306), Fred Bolger / Viv Billings (307), NZ player Bob Glading / Bill Bolger / Eddie Anderson (308), Sid Cowling (309), Keith Pix (311), Ron Menzies (312), George Naismith / Doug Bachli / Norm Berwick (313), Jack Boorer / Ossie Walker (314), Bruce Auld / Jack Barkell (315), Jim McInnes (316), Les Chaplin (319), Bob Jennings (321), Jim Mills (322), Bill Smith (323), Harry Sinclair (327), Kevin Kirby (333) and Harry Rowan (342). Former NSW PGA champion Don Spence also played but didn't trouble the scorers.

Sunday Herald, 10 April 1949

Jack Harris (300) was 5th in the **£500 Advertiser** tournament at Kooyonga GC. Norman von Nida (284) won, Eric Cremin (288) was second and Kel Nagle (292) was third. Other scores included amateur Peter Thomson (296), Jim Mills (301), Denis Denehey (302), triple Australian Open winner Ossie Pickworth (303), Fred Thompson (306), Ted Naismith / Norm Berwick (307), Dick Destree / Bob Stevens (308), Bill Ackland-Horman (309), Bill Shephard (310), Billy McWilliam (312), Sam Walsh / Colin Campbell (313), Willie Harvey (315), Bill Clifford / George Jordan (320), Bill English / Murray Crafter (321), Bud Russell (323), Alwyn Whykes (327) and Cliff Naismith (333).

The Argus, 30 April 1949

Jack Harris (71) won the £50 purse at Victoria GC on five under par. His round included three three-putts! Ted Naismith (73) was second and Ossie Pickworth / Bill Robertson (74) tied third. Other scores included Jack Beazley / Horrie Boorer (75), Des Ferguson / Martin Smith (76), George Naismith / Bill Smith / Bob Jamieson (77) and Ted Nelms / Ray Wright (78).

The Age, 10 June 1949

Jack Harris (153) tied 11th with Bill Clifford and John Creen in the first £100 Don Walker Memorial purse at Heidelberg GC. Bill Smith (148) won, Ossie Pickworth (149) was second and Ted Naismith / Len Boorer / Martin Smith (150) tied third. Other scores included Jack Boorer / Colin Campbell / Bert Ferguson (151) and Bill Robertson (152). Behind them came Horrie Boorer, Ted Nelms, Graham Cates, Bud Russell, George Naismith, Bob Jamieson, Harry Jones, Alec Orr and Bill Walker. (Don's brother). Don was killed during the Battle of Britain.

The Age, 2 August 1949

Jack Harris (301) was second in the **Victorian Close championship** at Yarra Yarra GC. Peter Thomson (293) won and Hartley Mitchell (304) was third. Other scores included Ossie Pickworth / Bill Richardson (307), Bob Brown / Eric Routley (308), Colin Campbell (311), Bert Ferguson (312), Barry West / Jack Boorer / Ted Naismith (313), Len Boorer / Bob Bull (315) and John Hood (316).

The Age, 11 August 1949

Jack Harris (157) was 5th in the Dunlop Cup at Metropolitan GC and won £10. Ossie Pickworth (149) won and collected £72. Colin Campbell (153) was second and took home £32. Ted Naismith (154) was third for £20. Other scores included Bert Ferguson (155) for £15, Martin Smith / Jack Boorer (158), Horrie Boorer (159), Ray Wright (160), Bill Clifford (161), Bill Smith (163), Alec Kynnersley (164) and Bill Fowler / Viv Billings / Ron Harris / Len Boorer (165).

The Age, 29 August 1949

Jack Harris tied third in the RSL tournament at Victoria GC. He lost to Bill Robertson in the match-play semi-final.

The Argus, 31 August 1949

Jack Harris / Colin Campbell (151) won the **Victorian PGA foursomes championship** at Long Island GC. Dick Holding / George Jordon, Martin Smith / Bill Clifford and Ted Naismith / Cliff Naismith (156) all tied second. Other scores included E Clement / Bill Smith (157), Des Ferguson / Bert Ferguson, Ossie Pickworth / Alec Orr and Bill Fowler / Jack Beazley (158), Ernie Wood / Arthur Spence (159), Horrie Boorer / Harold Knights (163) and Graham Cates / Lindsay Newlands (164).

The Age, 5 September 1949

Jack Harris captained Frankston RSL team when they beat Northcote in the RSL Grand Final.

The Age, 15 September 1949

Jack Harris (151) was third in the £200 Slazenger purse at Kingston Heath GC. Ossie Pickworth (147) won and Jack Beazley (148) was second. Other scores included Martin Smith / Ted Naismith / Bill Clifford (152), Len Boorer (154), Ray Wright (156), Bert Ferguson (158) and Colin Campbell / Graham Cates / Ernie Wood (160).

The Argus, 21 October 1949

Jack Harris / Alec Kynnersley / Horrie Boorer (158) tied 9th in the 36-hole Stableford event £200 purse at Metropolitan GC. Bill Clifford (146) won with six under par on the par 76 course. Ossie Pickworth (150) was second and Jack Boorer (153) third. Other scores included Viv Billings /

Jack Beazley / Harold Knights (154), Ted Naismith / Martin Smith (156), Bill Fowler / John Creen (160), Ray Wright / Cliff Naismith (161), Colin Campbell / Bill Smith / Alwyn Whykes (162) and Bert / Des Ferguson (163).

The Age, 22 November 1949
Jack Harris was runner-up in the **£150 Victorian PGA championship** at Yarra Yarra GC. Eric Cremin won the final 5 & 4. Cremin received £50 and Harris received £30. Jack's long game was far superior to Eric's but his putting was poor. In the final round Jack missed three putts one yard from the hole and several others under 10 feet. On the other hand, anything less than 10 feet on the day was just about a gimmie for Eric. Very difficult to practice putting on rubber mats when you are teaching all day in a city department sports store like Jack was at the time!

The Age, 29 November 1949
Jack Harris / Dan Cullen / Martin Smith / Bob Jamieson (302) tied 10th in the **Ampol £1000** at Woodlands GC. Ossie Pickworth (277) won the £250 first prize, Eric Cremin (287) was second for £125 and Reg Want (294) was third for £100. Other scores included Jack Boorer / Colin de Groot (298), Ted Naismith / Bill Bolger / Kel Nagle (300), Sid Cowling (301), Viv Billings (303), Len Boorer / Jim Moran (304), Bill Holder (305), Doug Katterns / Ray Wright (306), Alf Toogood (308), Allan Ellis / Bert Ferguson / Graham Cates / Horrie Boorer (312), Norm Berwick (314), Alec Kynnersley / John Creen (316), Bill Smith (318), Harold Knights (319) and Alwyn Whykes (323). Pickworth / Cremin / Jamieson all shot a new course record 67 in the last round.

The Age, 15 December 1949
Jack Harris (150) was fourth in the £200 Chesterfield purse at Commonwealth GC. Ossie Pickworth (144) won, Viv Billings (146) was second and Len Boorer (149) third. Other scores included Horrie Boorer (151), Jack Boorer (152), Bill Clifford / Ted Naismith (153), Allan Ellis / Bill Robertson / Bob Jamieson / Colin Campbell (154), Martin Smith (155), Bill Fowler (156), Des Ferguson (158), Ray Wright / Alec Kynnersley (159), and Bill Smith / George Naismith (160).

The Age, 22 December 1949
Jack Harris / Bill Clifford / Viv Billings (145) tied 5th in Riversdale GC purse. Colin Campbell (140) won on six under par and Ossie Pickworth / Bill Robertson (142) tied second. Other scores included Ted Naismith (144), Bill Smith / Len Boorer (150), Martin Smith (151), Alec Kynnersley / Bert Ferguson / George Naismith (152), Ernie Wood / Ray Wright / Bud Russell / Jack Boorer (153), Bill Fowler / Alwyn Whykes (154), Horrie Boorer (155), George Jordon (156), Ted Nelms / Cliff Naismith (157), Stan McGeorge / John Creen (158). Ernie Wood Jr (160), John Young (164) and W Walker (165).

The Argus, 2 March 1950
Jack Harris / Bob Jamieson (150) tied 8th in the Findlay Cup and £50 purse at Croydon GC. Ted Naismith (143) won this event for the seventh time. Alec Kynnersley / Bill Robertson (146) tied second. Other scores included Viv Billings / Jack Boorer (148), Len Boorer / Colin Campbell (149), Des Ferguson (152), George Naismith (154), Bill Smith (156), John Creen (157), Bill Fowler (158), Ted Nelms (162), Stan McGeorge / Cliff Naismith (163) and Horrie Boorer (187).

The Age, 8 March 1950
Jack Harris (148) on four under par won the £200 purse and Spalding Bowl at Commonwealth GC. Len Boorer (149) was second and Ted Naismith / Martin Smith (150) tied third. Other scores included Denis Denehey (151), Bill Robertson / Viv Billings / Harold Knights (152), Ossie Pickworth (153), Jack Boorer / Ray Wright / Bill Clifford (155), Colin Campbell (156), Bob Jamieson / Alec Kynnersley (157), Bill Smith (158) and Ernie Wood Sr / George Naismith (159). Jack had married Grace only four days before this tournament. The £67 first prize Jack won came in very useful!.

The Age, 15 March 1950
Jack Harris / Denis Denehey (151) tied 5th in the Victoria GC Open scratch. Amateur Charlie Feltham (146) won with a course record 68 in the final round. Martin Smith / Dick Payne / Jack Boorer (150) tied second. Other scores included Len Boorer / L Baxter (152), Doug Bachli / Ted Naismith / Ron Harris / John Greenhill (153), Alec Kynnersley /

Tel Thomas (154), Colin Campbell / Viv Billings (155), Bill Smith / Bill Fowler (156) and Ray Wright / Hartley Mitchell / George Jordon (157). Feltham and Payne were amateurs so Jack shared third prize money.

Sydney Morning Herald, 26 March 1950
Jack Harris / D Davies (315) tied 40th in the **£2500 McWilliams Wines** tournament at The Australian GC, Kensington. They won £15 each. Eric Cremin (283) won with 1 under par and collected £600. Welshman Ryder Cup player Dai Rees (285) was second for £300. Ossie Pickworth (288) was third for £200. Other scores included Norman von Nida (289) for £150, Kel Nagle (295) for £100, Norm Berwick / Harry Berwick (297), Alex Murray (298), Jim Moran / Bill Holder (299) for £90, Doug Bachli (300), Bill Bolger / Colin de Groot (301), Harry Hattersley (303), Peter Heard (304), Reg Want / Martin Smith (306) for £30, Billy McWilliam / Doug Katterns / Lou Kelly / Ted Naismith / Sam Richardson (307), Alan Myers (309), Bill Clifford / NZ player Bob Glading (310), Mick Kelly / Eddie Anderson (311), Jim McInnes / Sid Cowling (312), Murray Crafter / Bob Jennings (314), Ernie Chaplin / Colin Campbell (316), Tom Booth / Jack Boorer (317), John Kelly (318), Bill Robertson (320), Dick Carr (321), Keith Angus Clark (322) and Neville Wilson (323). There was a total field of 142 players. Some of the also-rans included Dan Cullen, Bert Auld, Arthur Gazzard, Bob Jamieson, Harold Knights, Jim Pettersen, Fred Popplewell, Ted Nelms, Charlie Brown, Alec Mercer, Ernie Wood Jr, Les Chaplin, Frank Eyre, Fred Bolger and Ted Bolger. Keith Clark was the son of Australian Open legend, Carnegie Clark.

The Age, 4 April 1950
Jack Harris / Jim Moran (304) tied 10th in the **£500 Advertiser** tournament at Royal Adelaide GC. Eric Cremin (284) won, Ryder Cup player Dai Rees (285) was second and Ossie Pickworth (286) third. Other scores included Kel Nagle (291) Ted Naismith (292), Bob Stevens (297), Dick Destree (298), Bill Clifford (301) and Bill Harvey (302).

The Age, 11 April 1950
Jack Harris / Colin Campbell (1 down) tied 5th in 36 holes Pro-am at Yarra Yarra GC. Tel Thomas (3 up) won and Hartley Mitchell / Len Boorer (1 up) were tied second.

The Age, 19 July 1950
Jack Harris (152) on level par was 3rd in the £200 Penfold-Bromford purse at Commonwealth GC. Ted Naismith (150) won and Jack Boorer (151) was second. Jack's four under par 72 in the afternoon was the best round of the day. It could have been even better had he three-putted from 15 feet on the 16th hole for a bogey five. Other scores included Bill Clifford (154), George Naismith / Martin Smith (156), Bill Robertson (158), Alec Kynnersley / Bill Fowler (159), Colin Campbell / Jack Boorer (160) and Bill Smith / Harold Knights (161).

The Age, 5 August 1950
Jack Harris / Bill Smith (152) tied second in the £200 Slazenger tournament at Victoria GC. After a disastrous 79 in the first round, Jack opened with five birdies in the outward nine in the second round and proceeded to shoot the lowest round of anyone in the tournament. George Naismith (151) won. Other scores included Len Boorer (153), Ted Naismith / Jack Boorer (154), Viv Billings / Martin Smith (156), Bill Clifford / Colin Campbell / Cliff Naismith (157), Ray Wright / Bill Robertson (158), Bob Jamieson (159) and Graham Cates / Bud Russell / Horrie Boorer (160).

The Age, 11 August 1950
Jack Harris (151) was 5th in the Don Walker memorial purse at Heidelberg GC. Ted Naismith (143) won, Martin Smith (147) was second and Len Boorer (149) third. Other scores included Viv Billings (150), Ray Wright (153), Bill Clifford / Bill Fowler / Colin Campbell / Bob Jamieson (155), Alwyn Whykes / Denis Denehey (157), Cliff Naismith (158), George Naismith / Ted Nelms / John Creen / Des Ferguson (159) and Horrie Boorer / D Young (160).

The Age, 31 August 1950
Jack Harris / Ted Naismith (305) tied 7th in the £500 Silver King tournament at Long Island GC. Ossie Pickworth (289) won, Eric Cremin (294) was second and Kel Nagle (295) third. Other scores included Alan Murray (299), Martin Smith (302), Colin Campbell (304), Norm Berwick / Bill Clifford (308), Jack Beazley / Billy McWilliam (313), Doug Katterns (314), Len Boorer (315), Viv Billings (317), Horrie Boorer / Des Ferguson / Denis Denehey / Jim Moran (319) and Bill Smith (320).

The Age, 13 September 1950

Jack Harris / Jack Boorer / Bob Jamieson (157) tied 11th in the Dunlop Cup at Yarra Yarra GC. Ossie Pickworth (138) won, Martin Smith (150) was second and Bert Ferguson / Alec Kynnersley (152) tied third. Other scores included Len Boorer / Viv Billings (153), Colin Campbell / Ted Naismith (154), Bill Fowler (155), Denis Denehey (156), Bill Clifford / Des Ferguson (158), George Naismith / Arthur Spence / John Creen (160), Horrie Boorer / George Jordon / Alec Orr (162), Ron Harris (163), Harold Knights / Ray Wright (164), A Swabey (165), Bud Russell (166), Cliff Naismith / Alwyn Whykes (167), Ted Nelms / Bill Smith (169) and Don Ebsworth (170).

The Argus, 29 September 1950

Jack Harris (70) won the £50 purse at Amstel GC on three under par which was a new course record. First prize was £25. Ossie Pickworth (71) was second and Ted Naismith / Colin Campbell (73) tied third. Other scores included George Naismith (75), Bill Smith / Jack Beazley / Bob Jamieson (76), Alec Orr / Ray Wright (77), John Creen / Ron Harris (78), Jack Boorer / Viv Billings (79) and Harold Knights / Martin Smith (80).

The Argus, 2 October 1950

Jack Harris (148) on level par was second in the RSL State championship at Long Island GC. Ossie Pickworth (143) won on five under.

The Age, 7 October 1950

Jack Harris / Bob Jamieson (74) tied 6th in the £50 purse at Torquay GC. Bud Russell (72) won and Colin Campbell / John Creen / Ray Wright / Allan Ellis (73) tied second.

The Argus, 16 October 1950

Jack Harris / Jack Boorer / Bill Richardson (308) tied 9th in the **Victorian Close championship** at Metropolitan GC. Ossie Pickworth (291) won on 13 under par. Laurie Duffy (297) was second and Martin Smith (298) third. Other scores included Eric Wishart (302), Bill Higgins / Bob Brown (303), Denis Denehey / Ted Naismith (305), Alec Kynnersley / Viv Billings (309), Eric Routley / Horrie Boorer (310), Ray Wright (313), Hartley Mitchell (315) and Bill Smith / Barry West (315).

The Age, 19 October 1950
Jack Harris / Ron Harris (105) tied in first place in a 30-hole £50 purse at Woodend GC. Three holes were not played because of water-logged conditions. Jack and Ron were not related. Ron had been a POW during WWII and had played some of his best golf before the war. Ted Nelms (107) was third. Other scores include Martin Smith / Ted Naismith / Colin Campbell (109) and Jack Boorer (110). Also played were Graham Cates, Harry Jones, Bill Fowler, Denis Denehey, Bill Smith, Horrie Boorer, Ernie Wood, Arthur Le Fevre, George Jordan and Bob Jamieson.

The Age, 23 October 1950
Jack Harris / Martin Smith (150) tied 4th in the £150 purse at Waverley GC. Viv Billings (142) won his first purse for 12 years. Denis Denehey (146) was second and Ossie Pickworth (147) third. Other scores included Ted Naismith / Colin Campbell (152), Jack Boorer / Ernie Wood Jr (154) and Bill Smith (155).

The Age, 31 October 1950
Jack Harris / Martin Smith (141) tied 2nd **in Victorian Provincial** tournament at Ballarat GC. Ted Naismith (140) won. Jack Harris shot a 3 under par 68 to equal the course record in the first round. Other scores included Max Nunn (143), Len Boorer (144), Bert Auld / Jack Boorer (147) and Denis Denehey / Graham Cates (148). Jack dropped three shots over the last five holes and lost his chance to win.

The Age, 3 November 1950
Jack Harris and Colin Campbell (154) won their third **Victorian Professional Foursomes** title at Long Island GC after beating Ossie Pickworth and Alec Orr in a play-off. In a nine-hole play-off Harris's team shot a two under par 35 to Ossie's score of 40. This was the first ever play-off in the 25-year history of the event. Bill Smith and Jack Boorer (156) were third. Other scores included Ted Naismith and John Young / Len Boorer and Viv Billings (159). Jack Beazley and Bill Fowler / John Creen and Alec Kynnersley (160) also played.

The Argus, 4 December 1950

Jack Harris beat Ossie Pickworth on the 37th hole in the **Victorian PGA championship** at Kingston Heath GC. Jack had beaten Denis Denehey in the semi-final. This was the first of six wins in this event for Jack but the only one he ever won under match-play format.

The Argus, 21 February 1951

Jack Harris / Denis Denehey (152) tied third in the £200 Chesterfield purse at Victoria GC. Ossie Pickworth (137) won and Len Boorer (151) was second. This was a great performance by Ossie on a day when wind gusts reached 50 mph. Other scores included Alec Kynnersley (153), Ray Wright / Bob Jamieson (155), Jack Boorer / George Naismith / Martin Smith (156), Viv Billings (157), Alwyn Whykes (160), Bill Clifford (162) and Bill Swabey (165).

The Age, 2 March 1951

Jack Harris / Bill Smith (158) tied 9th in the £200 Spalding purse at Kingswood GC. Ossie Pickworth (144) won and collected the £70 first prize. Ted Naismith (148) was second and Jack Boorer (153) was third. Other scores included Len Boorer / Bob Jamieson / Colin Campbell / Horrie Boorer (156) George Naismith (157), Bill Swabey (159) and Jack Beazley / Denis Denehey (160).

The Age, 13 March 1951

Jack Harris / Keith Pix / NZ player Ernie Southerden (302) tied 12th in the **£2500 McWilliams Wines tournament** at the Australian GC, Kensington. Norman von Nida (289) won the £600 first prize. Ossie Pickworth (291) was second for £300 and Eric Cremin (294) third for £200. Other scores included Martin Smith (296)-£150, Alan Murray / Peter Heard / Kel Nagle (297) -£110, Dan Cullen / Filipino Larry Montes (299) -£90, Bill Bolger / NZ player Bob Glading (301), Lou Kelly / Ryder Cup player Dai Rees (303), Norm Berwick (304), Jack Brown (305), Doug Bachli / Ryder Cup player Max Faulkner (305), Bill Holder (306), Fred Bolger / Tony Thomson (307), Sam Richardson (308), Bill Clifford (309), Len Boorer / Harry Berwick (310), Jim Moran / Reg Want / Murray Crafter (311) and NZ player Andrew Shaw / Colin de Groot (313). A few months later Max Faulkner won the 1951 British Open Championship at

Royal Portrush GC, Northern Ireland. Some of the also-rans included Eric Alberts, Eddie Anderson, Bruce Auld, Bill Duval, Chris Porter, Frank Eyre, Bob Jamieson, Jim McInnes, Fred Popplewell, George Naismith and a very young amateur Bruce Crampton.

The Age, 27 March 1951
Jack Harris / Martin Smith (2 up) were tied second in Yarra Yarra Open. Ossie Pickworth (5up) won. Other scores included Len Boorer (1up), Bob Bull (1 down), Ray Wright / Barry West (2 down), Alex Kynnersley (3 down), Denis Denehey (5 down) and Colin Campbell / Laurie Duffy (6 down).

The Age, 3 April 1951
Jack Harris / Kel Nagle (291) tied 3rd in the **£500 Adelaide Advertiser** tournament at Kooyonga GC. They shared the £75 and £50 third and fourth prizes. Eric Cremin (281) won and collected the £150 first prize. Ossie Pickworth (282) was second for £100. Other scores included Brian Crafter (293), Bob Stevens (301), Dick Foot (303), Bill Clifford / Len Boorer / Murray Crafter (304), Bill Rymill (305), Fred Thompson (306), Bud Russell (309), Bert Auld (310), Bill Ackland-Horman (312), Dick Destree (313) and Willie Harvey (315).

The Argus, 5 April 1951
Jack Harris / Ray Wright (1 up) tied 4th in the Peter Scott purse at Huntingdale GC. Len Boorer / Alec Kynnersley / Jack Beazley (4 up) tied first.

The Argus, 5 June 1951
Jack Harris (146) won the Penfold-Bromford purse at Kingston Heath GC on six under the card. Ossie Pickworth (149) was second and Viv Billings / Horrie Boorer / Bill Clifford (152) tied third. Other scores included Martin Smith / Ray Wright / (153), George Naismith / Alec Kynnersley (155), Bill Swabey / Ted Naismith / Len Boorer / Graham Cates (156), Denis Denehey / Jack Boorer (158), Bert Ferguson (160), Brian Huxtable / Ted Nelms (162), Alec Orr (164), Stan McGeorge (167) and Bill English (169).

The Argus, 21 June 1951
Jack Harris / Colin Campbell / Alwyn Whykes / Bill Smith / George Naismith (4 down) tied 14th in the professional purse at Kingswood GC. (course par 74). Ossie Pickworth (4 up) won and Denis Denehey / Martin Smith / Ted Naismith (square) tied second. Other scores included Bert Ferguson / Alec Kynnersley / Bill Clifford / Jack Boorer (1 down), Bill English / John Creen / Ray Wright (2 down) and Len Boorer / Jack Beazley (3 down).

The Sun, 7 July 1951
Jack Harris (314) was 20th in the £250 Lakes Open. Ted Naismith (296) won and collected £100. Jack Barkell / Jim Moran (300) tied second. Other scores included Sid Cowling / Norm Berwick / Bill Bolger (301), Harry Berwick (305), Bill Holder (306), Billy McWilliam (307), Fred Bolger (311), Reg Want / Alan Myers (313), Len Woodward (316), Keith Pix (317), Bill Duval (318), Harry Hattersley (319), Eddie Anderson (321) and Lou Kelly (324).

The Age, 27 August 1951
Jack Harris (74) was fourth in the £50 purse at Rossdale GC. Ted Naismith (69) won, Ossie Pickworth (71) was second and Martin Smith (73) was third. Also played Denis Denehey / Charlie Gorman (76) and Bill Swabey (77).

The Age, 6 September 1951
Jack Harris (147) was second in the £200 Slazenger purse at Woodlands GC. Ossie Pickworth (142) won and Peter Thomson (150) was third. Other scores included Jack Boorer / Alec Kynnersley / Len Boorer / Bill Swabey (154), Bud Russell (155), Martin Smith / John Creen (156), Ted Naismith / Denis Denehey (158) and Viv Billings / Bob Jamieson / George Naismith (159). According to the report, Thomson played extremely slowly. At one point he had more than two full holes clear in front of him and a big queue of golfers behind him.

The Age, 17 September 1951
Jack Harris (304) on level par was 4th in the **Victorian Close championship** at Commonwealth GC. Peter Thomson (288) won, Ossie Pickworth (296)

was second and Bill Higgins (303) third. Other scores included Bill Edgar (306), Denis Denehey (307), Viv Billings / Laurie Duffy (309), John Hood (310), Bob Jamieson / Eric Routley / Ted Naismith (312), Len Boorer / Jack Boorer (315) and Bob Brown (316).

The Age, 27 September 1951
Jack Harris (152) was second in the £200 Dunlop purse at Commonwealth GC. Ossie Pickworth (150) won and Ray Wright (153) was third. Other scores included Ted Naismith (155), Viv Billings (156), Jack Boorer (157), Jack Beazley (158) and Horrie Boorer / Martin Smith / Bud Russell (159).

The Age, 28 September 1951
Jack Harris (71) successfully defended the Amstel GC Show Day purse. Ted Naismith / Jack Boorer (72) were tied second. Ossie Pickworth / Martin Smith (73) tied fourth. Also played George Naismith / Horrie Boorer (75), Des Ferguson / Ray Wright / Bill Fowler / Denis Denehey (78), Jack Beazley / Bob Jamieson / Harry Jones (79) and Colin de Groot / Alwyn Whykes / Ted Nelms (80).

The Age, 3 October 1951
Jack Harris (75) was 10th in the £100 Metropolitan GC purse. Sid Cowling / Martin Smith (72) were joint winners and shared £75. Ray Wright / Ossie Pickworth / Denis Denehey (73) were tied third. Other scores included Eric Cremin / Billy McWilliam / Alf Toogood / Colin de Groot (74), Kel Nagle / Len Woodward / Ted Naismith / Ernie Wood / Bert Ferguson / Les Wilson (76) with George Naismith/ Norman von Nida / Malcolm Willis / Norm Berwick (77).

The Age, 4 October 1951
Jack Harris beat Kel Nagle 2 and 1 at Metropolitan GC to help Victoria win the **Vicars Shield** against NSW for the first time since 1939. Peter Thomson lost to Eric Cremin 3 and 2 and Ted Naismith was beaten 4 and 2 by Norm Berwick. But Ossie Pickworth beat Norman von Nida 2 up and Martin Smith just pipped Sid Cowling at the 19th hole.

The Age, 5 October 1951
Jack Harris (292) was 4th in the **Jubilee Australian Open championship** at Metropolitan GC. Peter Thomson (283) won his first of three Opens. He

equalled the previous best score in the Australian Open by an Australian golfer which was held by Billy Bolger in the 1934 event. The previous best score at Metropolitan by US golf legend Gene Sarazen in the 1936 Australian Open was of course 282. This was not equalled until Jack Harris shot 282 (14 under the card) in the Victorian Open in 1960 on that course. Only extremely bad weather stopped Jack from smashing the record on that occasion. After three rounds he was already 16 under the card but a howling gale and torrential rain thwarted him in the final round.

Norman von Nida (287) was second and Ossie Pickworth (288) was third. Other scores included Kel Nagle / Keith Pix (296), Eric Cremin / Norm Berwick (297), Doug Bachli / Bill Clifford / Ted Naismith / Sid Cowling (298), Jim Moran / Noel Weston (299), Peter Toogood / Len Boorer (301), Denis Denehey (302), Bill Edgar / Jack Boorer / Harry Berwick (304), Harold Knights / Peter Heard / Bill Gluth (306), Martin Smith (307), Viv Billings / Laurie Duffy (308), Mick Kelly / Harold Hattersley (309), George Naismith / Alf Toogood (310), Bob Brown / Eric Routley (311), Horrie Boorer (312), Alan Waterson / John Toogood (313) and Dick Payne (314). In reality this was a very weak Australian Open field. Twenty-six of the first forty-six finishers, over 56%, were amateur players.

The Age, 10 October 1951

Jack Harris / Sid Cowling / Len Boorer / Kel Nagle / Martin Smith / Jim Moran / Denis Denehey / Jack Boorer tied 9th in the **Australian PGA championship** at Metropolitan GC. Jack lost in match-play to Ted Naismith. Quarter-finalists were Peter Thomson, Ted Naismith, Bill Clifford, Ossie Pickworth, Norman von Nida, Harry Berwick, Harold Knights and Eric Cremin. Norman von Nida beat Ossie Pickworth 6 & 5 in the final.

The Argus, 15 October 1951

Jack Harris (156) was 8th in the £100 Major-General H W Grimwade purse at Peninsula GC. Martin Smith (144) won, Ernie Wood (147) was second and Ted Naismith (148) third. Other scores included Bill Clifford (149), Colin Campbell (153), George Naismith (154) and Arthur Le Fevre / Arthur Spence (158).

The Age, 18 October 1951
Jack Harris / JC Brown (297) tied 11th in the £500 Silver King tournament at Riversdale GC. Eric Cremin (277) won the £130 first prize. Ossie Pickworth (278) was second and Peter Thomson (281) third. Other scores included Norman von Nida (287), Billy McWilliam / Kel Nagle (293), Norm Berwick / Ted Naismith (294), Viv Billings / Les Wilson (295), Jim Moran / Ray Wright (300), Denis Denehey / Martin Smith (301), Sid Cowling / Brian Huxtable / George Naismith (302) and Bill Clifford (303).

The Age, 19 October 1951
Jack Harris / Peter Thomson / Eric Cremin / Bert Ferguson (156) tied 8th in the £400 purse at Kingswood GC. Norman von Nida (135) won by a remarkable 14 stroke margin. Ossie Pickworth / Kel Nagle / Ted Naismith (149) tied second. Other scores included Jack Boorer / Bill Clifford (153), Martin Smith (154), Norm Berwick (155), Bill Smith / Sid Cowling / Len Boorer / Denis Denehey (157) and Alec Kynnersley / Colin de Groot / Jim Moran (158). This may have been the only time when Jack played in the same field as Jimmy Grace who was about 46 years old at the time. Grace had been one of the early Australian golfers to work and play golf in America when he followed Victor East to the USA in the 1920s. Later he returned to Melbourne and was the professional at Royal Park GC in the 1940s when Peter Thomson was learning to play golf there. Jimmy didn't trouble the scorers on this occasion. And the player he mentored as a junior, Peter Thomson, just managed a tie with Jack Harris.

The Argus, 26 October 1951
Jack Harris / Ray Wright (152) tied 9th in Don Walker memorial purse at Heidelberg GC. Ossie Pickworth (142) won and Len Boorer / Noel Smith (149) joint second. Other scores included George / Ted Naismith / Denis Denehey (151), Alwyn Whykes (154) and Cliff Naismith / Bill English (155).

The Age, 14 November 1951
Jack Harris (150) was 7th in the **Victorian Provincial championship** at Ballarat GC. Peter Thomson (140) won, Ted Naismith (141) was second and Ossie Pickworth (142) third. Other scores included Martin Smith

(143), Bob Brown (148), Denis Denehey (149), Ted Nelms (151), Graham Cates / Ray Wright (154) and George Naismith / Jack Boorer (155).

The Argus, 21 November 1951
Jack Harris / Colin Campbell (157) were second in the **Victorian PGA foursomes championship** at Long Island GC. Martin Smith / Bill Clifford (152) won and Ossie Pickworth / Alec Orr and John Creen / Alec Kynnersley (159) tied third. Len Boorer / Bill Smith (161) also played.

The Age, 3 December 1951
Jack Harris / Denis Denehey (71) tied 3rd in the £100 purse at Rossdale GC. Jack Boorer / home professional Bill Swabey (70) were joint winners. Other scores included Alwyn Whykes / Arthur Spence (74), Ted Nelms (75), Ray Wright (77), and Bill Smith / Ted Naismith / Ossie Pickworth (78).

The Age, 8 December 1951
Jack Harris was knocked out of the last 16 by Ossie Pickworth in the match-play segment of the **Victorian PGA championship** at Southern GC and subsequently tied 9th. Ossie won 4 & 3. After the two stroke-play qualifying rounds, Jack (145) had qualified second best on one under par. Jack Boorer (143) was lowest qualifier and Ted Naismith / Martin Smith (146) tied third. Ossie Pickworth (151) had only qualified in seventh position. But as usual the match-play segment was not seeded, so Jack had to play the triple Australian Open winner in the first round! Ossie won that match 4&3 but was subsequently knocked out by Jack Boorer who eventually lost to Martin Smith 7&5 in the final.

The Age, 15 December 1951
Jack Harris / Ted Naismith played in a special challenge match on Royal Melbourne GC (West course) against Ossie Pickworth / Ray Wright. The proceeds went towards a sportsmen's ward at Sandringham Community Hospital. Over 300 people watched the match. Ossie and Ray won 2&1. Ossie shot 68, Jack 71 and Ted/Ray both shot 72.

The Argus, 7 March 1952
Jack Harris / Len Boorer / Alec Kynnersley (156) tied 7th in the £200 Spalding purse at Kingswood GC. Ossie Pickworth (143) won and Jack

Beazley / Viv Billings (151) tied second. Other scores included Martin Smith / Jack Boorer / Bill Swabey (154), Horrie Boorer / Bill Clifford / Brian Huxtable / Denis Denehey (157), Bill Smith (158) and Graham Cates / Ray Wright (159).

The Age, 31 March 1952
Jack Harris / Reigning British Open winner Max Faulkner (292) tied 4th in the £2500 **McWilliams Wines** tournament at the Australian GC, Kensington. The each received £132/10 prize money. Norman von Nida (281) won the £600 first prize. Ossie Pickworth (283) was second for £300. Peter Thomson (285) was third for £200. Next came Ryder Cup players Dai Rees / Harry Weetman and Eric Cremin (293) for £91 each. Other scores included Peter Heard (294), Dan Cullen / NZ player Ernie Southernden (295), Sid Cowling / Bill Bolger (296), Ryder Cup player Jimmy Adams (297), NZ Open winner Alex Murray (298), Bill Holder (299), Chris Porter (300), Martin Smith (302), Colin de Groot / Les Wilson / Reg Want (303), Jim McInnes (304), Doug Bachli / Harry Hattersley / John Collins / Sam Richardson (305), Jim Moran / Norm Berwick (306), Jack Boorer / Alan Myers (307), Murray Crafter (308), Ernie Chaplin / Neville Wilson (309), Bill Clifford (311) and Viv Billings (321). There was a big field of over 140 players. Some of the also-rans who didn't trouble the scorers included Bill Edgar, Bob Jennings, Eddie Anderson, Bob Jamieson, Dan Cullen, Graham Watson, Bill Duval, Billy McWilliam, Keith Clark, Jim Petterson, Charlie Cowling, Jack Brown, Harry Berwick, Ray Wright, Fred Bolger, Len Woodward, Jim Pettersen, Brian Crafter, Ted Bolger, NZ player Frank Buckler, Malcolm Willis, Alf Toogood, Alec Mercer, Don Spence, Tommy Tanner, Lou Kelly, Keith Pix, Bert Swabey, Fred Belle / son Graham Belle and a very young amateur called Bruce Crampton.

Brisbane Sunday Mail, 6 April 1952
Jack Harris (285) won the **£500 Adelaide Advertiser** tournament at Royal Adelaide GC with 11 under par despite missing a three-foot putt on the thirteenth and also three putting the 18th in the last round. Kel Nagle the 1952 NSW PGA champion was second and Dick Destree (290) was third. The 1951 winner of this event, Eric Cremin (298), was 13 shots back. This was Jack's first win in a big tournament and he received £150. Jack's four

under par 70 in the second round equalled the course record. But this was overtaken in round three when Destree shot a great 69.

Prize money was given to the first nine finishers and was distributed as follows £150, 100, 75, 50, 40, 30, 25, 15, 15. Other scores included Dick Foot (300), Billy McWilliam (301), Brian Crafter (306), Ray Wright (331) and Graeme Keane (337).

The Age, 10 April 1952
Jack Harris / Denis Denehey / Viv Billings / Ray Wright / Bill Clifford / Charlie Oliver (1 down) tied 4th in the £600 purse at Kingswood GC. Ossie Pickworth (2 up) won with Ted Naismith / Bill English (1 up) tied second.

The Age, 12 April 1952
Jack Harris / Ray Wright (4 up) tied in 1st place in four-ball £50 purse at Royal Canberra GC with Eric Cremin / Sam Richardson, Dan Cullen / B Jackson and Bill Holder / Jim Pettersen. As was Jack Harris's normal practice, he only arrived in Canberra from Melbourne just a few hours before the hit-off time and had never seen the course before he played it. Despite that they still shot under par.

Wagga Wagga Daily Advertiser, 15 April 1952
Jack Harris (218) was second in the ACT Open championship at Royal Canberra GC and third for £50 in the £450 professional purse. Eric Cremin (214) won the Open and the £150 first prize in the purse. Kel Nagle (217) was second in the purse for £75 but third in the Open. This was because the Open was decided on the first and third rounds and Jack's score for these rounds was less than Kel's.

The Age, 2 May 1952
Jack Harris / Ossie Pickworth (2 up) tied second in the 3AW Sportsman's Day at Kingswood GC. Denis Denehey (3 up) won. Australian cricket captain Lindsay Hassett and champion jockey Scobie Breasley also played. About £800 was raised for the Women's Hospital Appeal.

The Age, 2 August 1952
Jack Harris (146) won the £200 Penfold tournament at Metropolitan GC. He had five one-putt greens on the last nine. Ossie Pickworth (149) was

second and Denis Denehey / Jack Boorer (150) tied third. Other scores included Ray Wright / Ted Naismith (155), Horrie Boorer (156), Bert Ferguson (158), Harold Knights / Ted Nelms (160), Viv Billings / Bill Clifford (161), Jack Beazley / John Creen / Noel Smith (162) and Stan McGeorge / Brian Huxtable / Len Boorer (163).

The Age, 14 August 1952
Jack Harris (156) was second in the £200 Slazenger purse at Huntingdale GC. Ossie Pickworth (154) won and Ted Naismith (158) was third. Other scores included Jack Boorer (160), Len Boorer / Ray Wright / Horrie Boorer (162), Bob Jamieson / Bill Fowler / Noel Smith (166) and George Naismith (169). Conditions were bad with very high cross winds. There were several scratches before the tournament started and some players picked up their balls after just a few holes. The course par was 75 but only Ossie and Jack managed to break 80 for both rounds.

The Age, 26 August 1952
Jack Harris / Eric Cremin / Dan Cullen (286), at two under the card, tied fifth in the **£2000 Mobilco Machinery** tournament at Cottesloe GC, Mt Claremont, WA. Peter Thomson (278) won on 10 under. Kel Nagle / Ossie Pickworth / John Collins (280) tied second. Other scores included Norman von Nida (289), Ryder Cup player Jimmy Adams / Les Nichols (290), Jim Moran (294), Justin Seward (295), Billy McWilliam (296), Denis Denehey (299), Charlie Newman / Colin de Groot (300), Bill Fowler (302), Peter Toogood (305), Ted Naismith (312) and Ray Wright (316). Behind Wright were WA Open champion Kelly Rogers and West Australian amateur champion Larry Harke. Les Nichols was a great player, like Jack Harris, who did not travel much to play outside of WA. He won eight WA PGA titles and a WA Open and is well ranked on the all-time Australasian tour winners list.

The Age, 27 August 1952
Jack Harris 1 up beat Ryder Cup player Jimmy Adams at Lake Karrinyup GC, WA to help Victoria retain the **Vicars Shield** against the NSW team. Ray Wright lost 6 and 5 to John Collins and Denis Denehey lost 5 and 3 against Kel Nagle. However, Ossie Pickworth beat Eric Cremin 2 and 1 and Peter Thomson got the job done against Norman von Nida 3 and 2.

The Age, 27 August 1952
Jack Harris / Dan Cullen / Ray Wright / Jack Collins (77) tied 12th in the £100 Lake Karrinyup GC purse. Eric Cremin (70) won and Fred Thompson / Jimmy Adams / Denis Denehey (72) tied second. Norman von Nida / Ossie Pickworth shot 73 and Kel Nagle shot 75.

The Age, 30 August 1952
Jack Harris (286) tied fourth with Peter Thomson in the **Australian Open** at Lake Karrinyup GC. Norman von Nida (278) won, Ossie Pickworth (283) was second and Peter Toogood (285) third. Other scores included Ryder Cup player Jimmy Adams / Les Nichols (288), 1949 Australian Open winner Eric Cremin (290), John Collins (291), Peter Heard (292), Kel Nagle (294), Doug Bachli / Bob Stevens (296), Jim Moran (297), Keith Pix / Brian Crafter (298), Larry Harke (300), Ted Taylor (302), Denis Denehey (304), Justin Seward / Dan Cullen / John Toogood (305), Harry Hattersley / Alan Myers (306), Harry Berwick (307), Billy McWilliam (309), Bill Fowler (312), George Naismith (317) and Ray Wright (321).

The Argus, 1 September 1952
Jack Harris / Les Nicholls (3 up) were third in the four-ball best-ball 18-hole £200 purse at Mount Yokine GC, WA. Peter Thomson / D Westthorpe (6 up) won and Ossie Pickworth / V Analzark (5 up) were second. Other scores included Charlie Newman / Denis Denehey (2 up), Colin de Groot / D Fowler (1 up) and Frank Thompson / Eric Cremin (1 up).

The Age, 13 September 1952
Jack Harris (145) won the £200 Chesterfield purse at Riversdale GC. Ossie Pickworth (146) was second and Jack Boorer (148) was third. Other scores included Viv Billings (152), Bill Clifford (153), Len Boorer / Denis Denehey / Ray Wright (155) and Harold Knights / Brian Huxtable / Alwyn Whykes (156).

The Age, 20 September 1952
Jack Harris (149) won the £100 Don Walker Memorial purse at Heidelberg GC. Ossie Pickworth (150) was second and Len Boorer / Harold Knights (154) tied third. Other scores included Bob Furborough (155), Ray

Wright / Denis Denehey (157), Jack Boorer (158) and Alwyn Whykes / Brian Huxtable / Stan McGeorge (159).

The Argus, 26 September 1952
Jack Harris / Ossie Pickworth / Graham Cates / Alec Kynnersley / Noel Smith (75) tied in first place for the £150 purse at Amstel GC on four over par. Other scores included Harold Knights / Viv Billings / Bill Clifford / (76), Colin Campbell / Ted Nelms (77), Len Boorer / Horrie Boorer (78) and Bob Jamieson / Cliff Naismith / Denis Denehey (79).

The Argus, 4 October 1952
Jack Harris (149) was third in the £200 Dunlop Cup at Kew GC. Ossie Pickworth / Peter Thomson (141) tied first. Jack Boorer / Len Boorer / Horrie Boorer were all in the top ten.

Sydney Morning Herald, 7 October 1952
Jack Harris (149) was 4th best qualifier for the **Victorian PGA championship** at Victoria GC. Other stroke-play qualifiers included Peter Thomson (141), Eric Cremin (144), Ossie Pickworth (146), Len Boorer (150), Denis Denehey (151), Martin Smith (152) and Jack Boorer (153). Jack suffered a shock loss in the first round of the match-play format knock-out final to Alwyn Whykes and finished tied ninth in the event. Peter Thomson, with the big advantage of playing on his home course, beat Ossie Pickworth 2 & 1 in the final.

The Argus, 20 October 1952
Jack Harris (294) won the **Victorian Close championship** at Woodlands GC after shooting a course record five under par 68 in the third round. Bert Clay (300) was second and Bill Edgar (203) third. Other scores included Ted Naismith (304), Brian Huxtable (307), Eric Wishart / Jack Boorer (308), Viv Billings / Horrie Boorer (310), Denis Denehey (310), Laurie Duffy (313), John Hood (314), Bill Richardson / Bob Brown / Hartley Mitchell / Keith McPherson / Eric Routley / Ray Wright (316) and John Baillieu (317).

The Age, 28 October 1952
Jack Harris (312) tied 22nd with Ted Naismith / Murray Crafter / Bill Bolger and A Myers in the **£3500 Ampol** tournament at The Lakes GC.

US player Ed Oliver / Norman von Nida (288) tied in first place. US player Jimmy Demaret / Peter Thompson (292) were joint third. Other scores included US player Lloyd Mangrum (296), Ossie Pickworth (297), Dan Cullen (300), Sam Richardson (303), Kel Nagle (304), Colin de Groot (305), Len Woodward (306), Jimmy Adams / Eric Cremin (307), US player Jimmy Turnesa (310) and Reg Want (311).

The Argus, 29 October 1952
Jack Harris / H Thredgold (154) tied 13th in the **£1000 Advertiser** purse at Kooyonga GC. US player Lloyd Mangrum (137) won the £500 first prize, US player Ed Oliver (141) was second and US player Jimmy Demaret / Kel Nagle (143) tied third. Other scores included Ossie Pickworth (145), US player Jim Turnesa (147), Peter Thomson (149), Jim Moran / Dick Foot / Brian Crafter (150), Eric Cremin (151), Bert Auld (152) and C Westthorpe (153).

The Argus, 17 November 1952
Jack Harris / Dan Cullen / Martin Smith / Laurie Duffy / Bill Higgins (301) tied 16th in the **£3500 Ampol tournament** at Yarra Yarra GC. US player Lloyd Mangrum (281) won, Peter Thomson (282) was second and Norman von Nida / Kel Nagle (283) tied third. Other scores included US player Jim Turnesa (287), Ryder Cup player Jimmy Adams / Sam Richardson (294), Bill Clifford (295), Eric Cremin / Eric Wishart (297), Sid Cowling / Darryl Cox / Hartley Mitchell (298), Ossie Pickworth / Len Woodward (300), Bill Holder / Ted Naismith / Barry West (302), Jim Moran / John Collins (303), Peter Toogood / Jim McInnes / Colin de Groot (305), and Denis Denehey / Norm Berwick (306). US players Ed Oliver and Jimmy Demaret also played but were playing badly and did not finish. Oliver walked off after a clash with the fiery Norman von Nida.

The Age, 2 February 1953
Jack Harris (72) was second in the Patterson River GC purse on one under par. Martin Smith (70) won and Colin Campbell (74) was third. Other scores included Bob Furborough / Horrie Boorer / Bob Jamieson / Jack Boorer (75) and John Creen (76).

The Argus, 27 February 1953
Jack Harris (73) was second in the Albert Findlay Cup and Peter Scott purse at Kingswood GC. Martin Smith (72) won and Denis Denehey (74) was third. Jack Beazley / Ossie Pickworth (75) tied fourth.

The Age, 4 March 1953
Jack Harris / Denis Denehey (71) tied second in the professional purse at Cheltenham GC. Ossie Pickworth (68) won on two under par. Other scores included Martin Smith / Bob Furborough (73) and Ted Nelms / Alec Orr / Ernie Wood Jr (75).

The Age, 6 March 1953
Jack Harris / Alec Orr (147) were third in the **Victorian PGA foursomes championship** at Long Island GC. Bill Clifford / Martin Smith (145) won and Peter Thomson / Denis Denehey (146) were second. Other scores included Ossie Pickworth / Colin Campbell (149) with George Naismith / Ted Naismith and Viv Billings / Ken Loy (151).

The Argus, 9 March 1953
Jack Harris (77) tied second with Bob Jamieson in the Latrobe GC £50 purse. Ossie Pickworth (71) won. Other scores included Martin Smith / Bill Clifford / Charlie Oliver (78), John Creen / Denis Denehey (79), Ken Loy (80), Bill English (81) and Ray Wright (83).

Sunday Mail, 22 March 1953
Jack Harris / John Collins (301) was 22nd in the **£5000 McWilliams Wines tournament** at The Australian GC. Kel Nagle (277) won the £1100 first prize, Roberto de Vicenzo (284) was second and Harry Weetman (285) third. Other scores included Peter Thomson (286), Max Faulkner (290), Eric Cremin (291), Ugo Grappasonni (292), NZ player Ernie Southerden / Harry Berwick / Jim McInnes (294), Bob Jennings / Norman von Nida (295), Bill Bolger (296), Peter Heard (297), Ossie Pickworth / Alec Murray / G Thomson (297), Keith Pix (299), Dan Cullen / Len Woodward / M Behringer (300), Sid Cowling (302) and Ted Naismith / Peter Toogood (303).

The Age, 31 March 1953
Jack Harris (295) was 10th in the **£1000 Advertiser tournament** at Royal Adelaide GC, Seaton. Kel Nagle (279) won, Ossie Pickworth (280) was second and Peter Thomson (282) third. Other scores included Ugo Grappasonni (286), Larry Montes / Eric Cremin (287), Brian Crafter / Norman von Nida (288), Len Woodward (294), Bill Ackland-Horman (297), Mick Kelly (299), Bob Stevens (300), John Kelly (305), Dick Foot (307), Harry Thredgold (309), Gordon Westthorpe / Graeme Keane (312) and Fred Thompson (317).

The Age, 7 April 1953
Jack Harris (1 up) was second in the £150 Yarra Yarra Easter open. Peter Toogood (7 up) won and Hartley Mitchell / Ted Naismith / Bob Bull (all square) tied third. Other scores included Martin Smith / Darryl Cox (2 down), Ossie Pickworth / Horrie Boorer / Noel Smith (3 down), Denis Denehey (4 down) and Bill Richardson / Arthur Spence (5 down).

The Age, 14 April 1953
Jack Harris, square to the card, tied 4th with Bill Clifford in £150 Long Island GC purse. Ted Naismith won on 2 up and Ossie Pickworth / Martin Smith were tied second on 1 up. Jack Boorer was 1 down.

The Age, 3 June 1953
Jack Harris / Amateur Eric Wishart (2 up) tied in first place in 36-hole bogey event at Woodlands GC. Jack took home the £60 first prize. Barry West (square) was third. Other scores included Doug Bachli / Harold Knights / Noel Smith (2 down), Jack Boorer / Horrie Boorer / Ted Naismith (4 down) and Denis Denehey / Bill Clifford / Brian Huxtable (5 down).

The Age, 8 June 1953
Jack Harris (139) won the £100 **Victorian Provincial championship** at Ballarat GC and collected the £40 first prize. Bill Edgar (143) was second and Jack Boorer / Tom Crow (145) tied third. Other scores included Bill Clifford / Doug Bachli (147), Hartley Mitchell (148), Ted Naismith (149), Harold Knights (150) and Jack Beazley (151).

Gippsland Times, 15 June 1953
Jack Harris (66) set a new course record at Maffra GC with six under the card. This included a sensational 29 on the back nine. His three playing partners took, 72, 76 and 78.

The Age, 20 June 1953
Jack Harris (298) was 4th in the **Victorian Close championship** at Kew GC. Tom Crow (296) won and Doug Bachli / Bill Higgins (297) tied second. Amateurs occupied the first three places so Jack Harris picked up most of the dosh. Other scores included Peter Toogood (299), Bill Edgar (300), Hartley Mitchell (302), Eric Routley / Jack Boorer (303), Frank Gluth (305), Bob Bull / Barry West (306), Eric Wishart (307), Laurie Duffy / Bill Clifford (309), Denis Denehey (312), Dick Payne (314), Bill Richardson (315), Brian Huxtable (321), Max Nunn / Bill Smith (322), Ken Loy (323), Ted Naismith / Peter Speed (327) and Stan McGeorge (342).

The Age, 5 September 1953
Jack Harris (153) was 4th in the £200 Chesterfield purse at Yarra Yarra GC. Ossie Pickworth (143) won, Peter Thomson (149) was second and Ted Naismith (152) third. Other scores included Denis Denehey / Jack Boorer / Alec Kynnersley (155), Horrie Boorer / Bob Furborough / Len Boorer (157), Martin Smith (158) and Bill Fowler (159).

The Age, 12 September 1953
Jack Harris / Jack Boorer tied third in the **Victorian PGA championship** at Commonwealth GC. Peter Thomson beat Denis Denehey in the matchplay final.

The Age, 25 September 1953
Jack Harris / Viv Billings / Brian Huxtable (76) tied 11th in the £250 purse at Amstel GC. Peter Thomson (67) won on four under par. Ossie Pickworth (69) was second and Harold Knights (72) third. Other scores included Ray Wright / Jack Boorer / Noel Smith (73), Bob Jamieson / Brian Jones (74), Ted Nelms / Des Ferguson (75) and Martin Smith / Ken Loy / Denis Denehey (77).

The Age, 8 October 1953
Jack Harris / Bob Jamieson / Bill Smith / Ted Naismith / Eric McCutchan (75) tied fifth in £100 Don Walker Memorial at Heidelberg GC. Bill Fowler / John Creen / Ossie Pickworth / Bill Clifford (74) tied in first place. Other scores included Ken Loy / Jack Beazley / Jack Boorer / Bill Richardson (76), Bill English (77) and Alwyn Whykes / Ray Wright / Bob Furborough / Charlie Oliver / Horrie Boorer / Viv Billings (78).

The Argus, 19 October 1953
Jack Harris / Norman von Nida (297) tied in 8th place in the **Ampol** tournament at The Lakes GC and won £75 each. Ossie Pickworth (288) won for £600, Len Woodward (291) second for £300 and Peter Thomson / Bill Holder (294) joint third for £175 each. Also played Kel Nagle / Norm Berwick / Alan Myers (295) for £125 each, Eric Cremin / Jim McInnes (298) for £70 each, Ted Naismith / Les Wilson (299), John Kelly / Dick Carr (300), John Collins (302), Sam Richardson / Fred Bolger (303), Jim Moran (304), Sid Cowling (305), Bruce Crampton (307), Frank Phillips / Chris Porter / Bill Duval (308), Charles Booth (311), Bruce Devlin (317), Dan Cullen / Reg Want (310), Malcolm Willis / Neville Wilson (317), Lou Kelly / Bob Swinbourne (318), Mick Kelly / Vic Anlezark (319), Colin de Groot / Billy McWilliam (321), Viv Billings / Alice Bauer (322), Dave Mercer (325), Bill Fowler / Peggy Kirk / Jackie Pung (327)., Peter Bradley (328) and Marlene Bauer (330). Unusually for the era, the prize money went down past the first fifty placegetters. The visiting team of lady golfers from the USA (Jackie Pung, Peggy Kirk and the Bauer sisters) were also allowed to play in the tournament.

The Age, 21 October 1953
Jack Harris / Ossie Pickworth (75) tied 6th in the £100 purse at Royal Melbourne GC (East Course). Norman von Nida (70) won, Frank Phillips (72) was second and John Collins (73) third. Other scores included Denis Denehey, Kel Nagle / Peter Thomson (76) and Horrie Boorer / Bert Ferguson / Ted Naismith (77).

The Age, 21 October 1953
Jack Harris beat Bill Holder 4 and 2 at Royal Melbourne GC (East Course) to help Victoria win the **Vicars Shield** against NSW for the third year in

succession. Peter Thomson lost 2 and 1 to Kel Nagle and Jack Boorer lost 3 and 2 to Len Woodward. But Ossie Pickworth beat Eric Cremin 3 and 2 and Denis Denehey beat Les Wilson 3 and 1.

The Age, 26 October 1953
Jack Harris / Jim McInnes (298) tied 12th in the **Australian Open championship** at Royal Melbourne GC East Course. Norman von Nida (278) won, Peter Thomson (280) was second and Ossie Pickworth (286) third. Other scores included Kel Nagle (290), Bob Brown (292), Eric Cremin / Laurie Duffy / Len Woodward (294), Doug Bachli (295), Frank Phillips / Jim Moran (296), Eric Wishart (299), Viv Billings / Bill Clifford / Hartley Mitchell (300), Peter Toogood (301), Denis Denehey / Bill Edgar / Ted Naismith (303), John Collins / Bill Holder / Brian Huxtable / Alwyn Whykes (304), Sam Richardson (305), Les Wilson (306), Bob Bull / Bill Higgins (307), Norm Berwick / Martin Smith (308), Dan Cullen (309) and Bill Swabey (310).

The Age, 2 November 1953
Jack Harris lost to Peter Thomson 3 & 2 in the first match-play round of the **Australian PGA championship** at Royal Melbourne GC even though Jack was three under the card at the 16th hole. Jack finished tied 9th in the tournament. The quarter-finalists were Jim McInnes, Denis Denehey, Ossie Pickworth, Jim Moran, Peter Thomson, Ted Naismith, Kel Nagle and Bill Holder. Ossie Pickworth beat Peter Thomson in the final when he holed a 12-foot putt on the last hole to go one-up.

Hobart Mercury, 9 November 1953
Jack Harris (151) was 7th in the £225 purse at Riverside GC, Tasmania. Peter Thomson (140) won, Kel Nagle (143) was second and Eric Cremin (144) third. Other scores included Norman von Nida (146), John Toogood (147), Ossie Pickworth (150), Roy Stott (153), Bill Swabey (155), Roy Summers (156) and Len Nettlefold (157).

The Age, 16 November 1953
Jack Harris (137) won the **West-Victorian Open championship** at Horsham GC on five under par. Ted Naismith / Peter Toogood (147) tied second, ten strokes behind. Before Jack's record 69 and 68 scores, the best

rounds on this course had been by Ossie Pickworth (70) and Bobby Locke (71). Other scores included Jack Boorer / George Naismith (148), Doug Bachli (149), Tom Crow (150), Bill Edgar / Barry West (151) and Harold Knights / Martin Smith (152), Ray Wright / L Newlands (154), Lou Kelly / Bob Jamieson / Noel Smith (155) and Graham Cates (156).

The Age, 18 November 1953
Jack Harris / N McLane (3 up) tied 4th in the captains and professional's tournament at Cheltenham GC with George Naismith / G Patterson. Jack Boorer / T Spence (5 up) won and Ray Wright / T Crowle (4 up) were joint runners-up with Alwyn Whykes / T Garrett.

The Age, 7 December 1953
Jack Harris (65) won the £100 purse at Keysborough GC and beat the old course record by ten strokes. Martin Smith / Denis Denehey (72) tied second. Other scores included Ossie Pickworth / Jack Beazley / Bill Clifford (74), Bill Fowler (76), Bob Furborough / Ted Nelms / Ted Naismith / Ray Wright (77) and Bill Smith / Len Boorer / Noel Smith / Bert Ferguson (78).

The Age, 19 March 1954
Jack Harris (4 up) won the £50 Peter Scott purse and Findlay Cup at Kingswood GC. Ossie Pickworth (3 up) was second and Viv Billings (square) third. Other scores included George Naismith (1 down), Ray Wright / Denis Denehey / Jack Boorer (2 down), Noel Smith / Bob Jamieson (3 down), and Alwyn Whykes / Len Boorer / Bill Clifford / Bert Ferguson / Martin Smith (4 down).

The Age, 22 March 1954
Jack Harris (76) won the £75 purse at Williamstown GC on four over par in a gale force wind. Bill Smith / Martin Smith / Ray Wright / Alwyn Whykes / Bob Jamieson (78) tied second. Other scores included Ossie Pickworth (79), Charlie Oliver (80) and Bill Fowler / Denis Denehey / Ernie Wood / Jack Beazley (81).

The Age, 26 March 1954
Jack Harris / Alwyn Whykes / Martin Smith (75) tied third in the £100 Uncle Bob's purse at Kingswood GC. Denis Denehey / Ossie Pickworth

(74) tied first. Other scores included John Creen (76), Bill Fowler / Ray Wright / Colin Campbell / Noel Smith (78) and Jack Beazley / Bill Clifford (79).

The Argus, 23 April 1954
Jack Harris (142) won the Yarra Yarra Open by three strokes. Graham Wilson / Martin Smith (145) tied second. Ossie Pickworth / Jack Boorer (148) tied fifth.

The Age, 3 May 1954
Jack Harris / Charlie Oliver (72) tied 4th on one over par in the £100 purse at Latrobe GC. Ossie Pickworth (69) won and Len Boorer / Martin Smith (70) tied second. Other scores included Bob Jamieson / Jack Boorer (73), Denis Denehey (74), Bill Fowler / Ken Loy / Lou Kelly (75), Brian Huxtable (76) and Peter Bradley / John Creen / Bill Clifford (77).

The Age, 13 May 1954
Jack Harris / Ken Loy (35) tied second in the 9-hole tournament at £130 Peninsula GC. Jack Boorer (32) won. Ossie Pickworth had 38.
Jack Harris (73) was in a six-way tie for second in the 18-hole event which Ossie won on 71.
Jack Boorer (105) won the 27-hole event with Jack Harris (108) second and Ossie Pickworth (109) third. Ted Naismith (110) and Martin Smith (111) also played.

The Age, 23 May 1954
Jack Harris (291) was 4th in the **Queensland Open** at Gailes GC and won £20. Reg Want (287) won for £100, Eric Cremin (289) was second for £50 and Kel Nagle (290) third for £30. Other scores included Sid Cowling / Jack Brown (293), Frank Phillips (294), Doug Katterns / Jim Moran (296), Jim McInnes (300) and Darryl Welch (315). The course par was 75. Reg Want was 13 under par and Jack Harris was 9 under par. Reg Want and Jack Harris were the only two players in the field to shoot four consecutive sub-par rounds.

Sydney Morning Herald, 24 May 1954
Jack Harris / Ossie Walker / Mick Kelly / John Sullivan / John Kelly / Les Wilson / Sid Cowling (70) tied 5th in the £100 purse at Victoria Park

GC, Queensland. Kel Nagle (66) won the £40 first prize on three under par. Eric Cremin / Jim Moran (67) tied second. Other scores included Frank Phillips (69), Darryl Welch (71), Jim McInnes (72) and reigning Queensland Open champion Reg Want (76).

Sydney Morning Herald, 26 May 1954
Jack Harris / Reg Want / F Hayes (77) tied 6th in the £150 purse at Royal Queensland GC. Kel Nagle (72) won and Eric Cremin / Les Wilson (75) was second. Nagle was the only player to break the 75 course par. Other scores included Jim McInnes / Doug Katterns (76) and Sid Cowling / Alan Myers / Charlie Brown / J Downs (78). The legendary "One-putt" Charlie Brown had earlier won the Queensland Open and at one stage in his career also won four consecutive Queensland PGA championships.

The Age, 31 May 1954
Jack Harris / amateur Eric Routley (303) shot 3 over par to tie second in the **Victorian Close championship** at Huntingdale GC. Ossie Pickworth (289) won on eleven under the card with a fourteen stroke margin. Other scores included Bob Bull (307), Barry West / Denis Denehey (308), Archie Campbell (309), Noel Smith (310), Graham Wilson (311), Ian Syle (312), and Bill Higgins / David Joubert / Keith McPherson (313).

The Age, 15 June 1954
Jack Harris / Ossie Pickworth / Denis Denehey (152) tied first place in £150 Woodlands Open. This was six over par in high wind conditions. Amateur Tony Thomson (153), Peter Thomson's 18-year-old brother, tied fourth with Jack Boorer. Jack Harris three putted from 20 feet on the 17th but managed to redeem himself with a birdie on the 520 yards last hole. Other scores included Noel Smith (156), Brian Huxtable / Martin Smith (157), Viv Billings / Bob Brown (158) and Harold Knights / Tom Crow (160).

The Argus, 18 June 1954
Jack Harris (78) starting on plus 4 was tied 7th in the £100 professional handicap event at Commonwealth GC. Effectively he shot the course par 74 but the handicap was too much. Ossie Pickworth also suffered similarly

and finished 11th. Charlie Oliver / Harold Knights with a much lower penalty were joint winners.

The Hobart Mercury, 15 July 1954
Jack Harris (77) tied second with Charlie Oliver / Alec Kynnersley / Colin Campbell / Martin Smith in £150 Liquor Industry purse at Huntingdale GC. Ossie Pickworth (76) won on the par 75 rated course.

The Age, 9 August 1954
Jack Harris / Brian Huxtable / Denis Denehey (74) tied 4th in the £100 purse at Rossdale GC. Ossie Pickworth (70) won on two under par. Colin Campbell (72) was second and Martin Smith (73) third. Other scores included Jack Boorer (75), Bill Fowler / Bob Brown (76) and John Creen / Horrie Boorer (77).

The Age, 16 August 1954
Jack Harris was second in the **Victorian PGA championship** at Rossdale GC. Ossie Pickworth won the match-play event 5 and 4.

The Age, 31 August 1954
Jack Harris / Eric Cremin (74) tied 6th in the £100 purse at Kooyonga GC with a course par score. Ossie Pickworth (70) won on 4 under par and Billy McWilliam / Jim McInnes (72) tied second. Other scores included Bob Brown / Reg Want / Denis Denehey / Ted Nelms / Len Woodward / John Collins (75), Sid Cowling / Bruce Crampton / Norman von Nida (76), Ken Loy / Peter Bradley (77) and Jim Moran (78). This was the first ever appearance in a money event of a young Bruce Crampton. Jack played with Norman von Nida in this event. Von had an altercation with the starter before the match started. He insisted that when he was called to the tee he should be announced as " Mr " von Nida and not by his surname alone. The starter was an old experienced guy who defused the situation by calling up "Messrs Harris and von Nida" to the tee. Jack had a great 35 on the front nine but faded on the home stretch.

The Age, 1 September 1954
Jack Harris was beaten (3-2) by Kel Nagle in the final of the **Vicars Shield** as Shield holders Victoria came second to NSW (2-3). Ossie Pickworth beat Norman von Nida (2-1), Eric Cremin beat Denis Denehey (2-1), Jim

McInnes beat Ted Naismith at the 20th hole and Frank Phillips lost to Bob Brown (1 down).

The Age, 6 September 1954
Jack Harris / Dick Foot / Bill Gluth / Peter Toogood (300) tied 9th in the **Australian Open** at Kooyonga GC. Ossie Pickworth (280) won his fourth and last Open. Norman von Nida (288) was second and Kel Nagle (290) third. Other scores included Eric Cremin / Len Woodward (295), Denis Denehey / Frank Phillips (297), Bruce Crampton (301), Brian Crafter (302), Sid Cowling / Keith Pix (303), Bob Brown (304), Les Wilson / Billy McWilliam / Jim Moran / John Toogood (305) and Ted Naismith / Jim McInnes (306). Behind Big Jim came in no particular order were Dave Mercer, Mick Kelly, Alwyn Whykes, Sid Coogan, Eric Wishart, Bill Edgar, Harold Knights, Norm Berwick, Reg Want and Jack Brown.

The Age, 15 September 1954
Jack Harris / Noel Smith (155) tied 4th in the £200 Chesterfield purse at Kingston Heath GC. Ossie Pickworth (147) won, Bob Brown (149) was second and Ted Naismith third. Other scores included Len Boorer / Bert Ferguson (156), Denis Denehey (157), Ray Wright / Bill Clifford (159), Bob Furborough (160), Harold Knights / Viv Billings (161), Ken Loy (163) and Alwyn Whykes / Bob Jamieson (164).

The Age, 21 September 1954
Jack Harris (72) was third in the £100 ULVA purse at Geelong GC. Ossie Pickworth (70) won and Bob Brown (71) was second. Other scores included Harold Knights (73), Viv Billings / Noel Smith / George Naismith (74), John Clark (75), John Creen / Alwyn Whykes / Bill Clifford (76), Len Boorer (77) and Bill Smith / Bill Fowler / Ray Wright (78).

The Age, 23 September 1954
Jack Harris / Ted Nelms / Horrie Boorer / Ted Naismith / Denis Denehey (78) tied 6th in the £300 purse at Kingswood GC. Ossie Pickworth (66) won on 8 under par. Eric Cremin (74) was second and Viv Billings (75) third. Other scores included Jack Beazley / Len Woodward (77), Jack Boorer / Bert Ferguson / john Clark / Ray Wright (79), Bob Brown /

Bob Furborough (80), Alec Kynnersley / Bill Smith / John Creen / Alwyn Whykes (81) and Bob Jennings / Ken Loy (81).

The Argus, 1 October 1954
Jack Harris (72) tied first with Ossie Pickworth in the £300 purse at Amstel GC. Noel Smith (73) was third. Jack missed a 3-foot putt at the 15th and he also took a five at the 17th after going through the green in two. Other scores included Horrie Boorer / Harold Knights (74), Len Woodward / Martin Smith (75), Bob Brown / Denis Denehey / Eric Cremin / Bob Jamieson / John Creen (76), Viv Billings / Graham Cates (77), Colin Campbell / Ken Loy / Charlie Oliver / Bill Smith (79) and Ray Wright / John Clark / Peter Bradley (80). First prize was £100, second was £65 and third £45.

Williamstown Chronicle, 8 October 1954
Jack Harris (75) was 5th in the £75 purse at Williamstown GC. Ossie Pickworth (68) won, Bob Brown (72) was second and Brian Huxtable / Noel Smith (74) tied third. Other scores included Viv Billings / Martin Smith / Peter Bradley (76), John Clark / Bob Furborough / Bill Smith / Charlie Oliver (77) and Harold Knights (78).

The Age, 15 October 1954
Jack Harris / Len Woodward/ John Collins / Sid Cowling tied 5th in the **Australian PGA championship** at Royal Sydney GC. Jack lost one down in his quarter-final against Jim McInnes. Jim had earlier knocked out pre-tournament favourite Ossie Pickworth but lost in the final to Kel Nagle.

The Sun Herald, 17 October 1954
Jack Harris (77) was 6th in the £100 purse at St Michaels GC. Ossie Pickworth (71) won, Eric Cremin (72) was second and D Gray (74) third. Other scores included Bob Brown / Billy See Hoe (75), Len Woodward / Reg Want / Frank Phillips / Sid Cowling (78), Colin de Groot / Ian Alexander (79) and Billy Bolger / John Collins / Sam Richardson / Mick Kelly (80).

The Age, 25 October 1954
Jack Harris / Norman von Nida / Kel Nagle (297) tied third in the **Ampol** tournament at The Lakes GC. They each received £250 prize money. USA player Dutch Harrison (292) won the £750 first prize and second placed

Ossie Pickworth (293) won £450. Other scores included Ted Rigney / Sid Cowling (300), Frank Phillips (301), USA players Marty Furgol / Tommy Bolt (302) tied with Dan Cullen / Billy Bolger, Peter Thomson (303) in 13th place, Eric Cremin (304), Len Woodward / Mick Kelly / Reg Want (305), Bob Brown / John Kelly / Sam Richardson (308), Jim Moran / Colin de Groot (309) and Norm Berwick / Jim McInnes (310).

The Age, 1 November 1954
Jack Harris (141) was second in the **£150 West-Victorian Open** at Horsham GC. Barry West (140) won and Noel Smith (142) was third. Other scores included Bob Brown (148), Ray Wright / Viv Billings (149), Brian Huxtable (150), Bob Jamieson (151), Harold Knights / Ken Loy / Ted Naismith (152), Tom Crow (155) and Jack Boorer / Bob Furborough (156).

The Age, 3 November 1954
Jack Harris (145) was third in the £300 purse at Patterson River GC. Ossie Pickworth (138) won with eight under par and Eric Cremin (144) was second. Other scores included Noel Smith (147), Kel Nagle (149), Frank Phillips (150), Ted Naismith / Les Wilson (152), Peter Bradley / Harold Knights (153), Jim McInnes / Jack Boorer (155) and Bill Clifford / Denis Denehey / Brian Huxtable (156). The also-rans included John Clark, Bob Furborough, Ernie Wood Jr, Norm Berwick, George Naismith, Ray Wright, Ted Nelms, Bob Jamieson, Bill Smith, Colin Campbell, Martin Smith, Alec Kynnersley, Horrie Boorer, Bill Fowler, Bert Ferguson, John Creen, Len Woodward, Jack Beazley and Bob Brown.

The Age, 16 November 1954
Jack Harris (292) was sixth in the £1500 **Ampol** tournament at Yarra Yarra GC. Peter Thomson (282) won, Ossie Pickworth / Kel Nagle (288) tied second and USA Ryder Cup player Dave Douglas (289) was fourth. US superstar Tommy Bolt (293) tied with Eric Cremin in seventh place. Other scores included Barry West (294), Len Woodward / Bill Higgins (296), US PGA player Marty Furgol (297), Jim McInnes (299), Bob Brown / Mick Kelly (302), John Kelly / Martin Smith (303), Jack Boorer / Sid Cowling (304), Viv Billings / Jim Moran / Laurie Duffy (307), Denis Denehey / Frank Phillips / Norman von Nida / Bill Edgar (308), Len Boorer (310),

Dave Mercer (311), Colin Campbell / Eric Wishart (312), Les Wilson (314), Norm Berwick (315), Sam Richardson (317), Harold Knights (318) and Peter Speed (319).

The Age, 18 November 1954
Jack Harris / Bob Brown / Viv Billings / Peter Bradley / Bob Jamieson (73) tied 6th in the Don Walker Memorial purse at Heidelberg GC. John Kelly (67) won, Frank Phillips (68) was second and Ossie Pickworth (70) was third. Other scores include Eric Cremin / Len Woodward (72), Ted Nelms (74), Brian Huxtable / Bill Clifford (76) and Colin Campbell / Noel Smith (77).

The Age, 22 November 1954
Jack Harris (284) was 5th in the Riverside GC and Tasmanian Tyre Service £500 purse. Kel Nagle (273) won, Ossie Pickworth (274) was second and Norman von Nida (280) was third. Other scores included Peter Thomson (283), John Toogood / Eric Cremin (285), Bob Brown (287), Frank Phillips (288), Len Woodward (291), Alf Toogood / Jim McInnes (292), Peter Toogood (295), Len Bowditch (297), Peter Bradley (299), John Kelly (304), John Clark (321) and Ron Harris (326).

The Age, 29 November 1954
Jack Harris / Bill Clifford / Colin Campbell (77) tied 7th in the £200 purse at Long Island GC. Ossie Pickworth (70) won and Bert Ferguson / Ted Naismith (72) tied second. Other scores included Bob Jamieson / Martin Smith (75), Harold Knights (78) and John Clark / Bill Smith (79).

The Age, 6 December 1954
Jack Harris (68) won the £120 purse at Kew GC on three under par. Martin Smith (70) was second and John Clark (71) third. Other scores included Ossie Pickworth / Bob Brown (72), Jack Boorer (73), Bert Ferguson / Ken Loy / Ted Naismith / Bob Jamieson (75), Horrie Boorer / Bill English (76), Denis Denehey / Bob Jennings (77), Bill Smith / Viv Billings / Alec Kynnersley / Peter Bradley (78) and John Creen (79). Jack's 68 equalled the course record.

The Age, 4 March 1955
Jack Harris / Ossie Pickworth / Len Boorer / Ted Naismith (70) tied first in the £50 Peter Scott purse and Albert Findlay Cup at Amstel GC. Jack went on to easily win the six-hole play-off. The play-off scores were 21, 23, 24 and 25. Other scores included Ken Loy 971), Viv Billings / Bob Furborough (73), Jack Boorer / Ray Wright / Brian Jones (75), Bob Jamieson / Peter Bradley / Bob Brown / Denis Denehey (74), Barry Chapman / Lou Kelly / Peter Speed / Harold Knights / Bill Clifford (76), Horrie Boorer / Alec Kynnersley / Bill Fowler (77) and Peter Block / John Creen (78).

The Age, 31 March 1955
Jack Harris / Ted Naismith tied for first place in the £100 purse at Keysborough GC.

The Age, 9 April 1955
Jack Harris / Bob Spencer and John Clark / Bob Furborough (152) tied 5th in the **Victorian PGA foursomes championship** at Croydon GC. Bill Smith / Jack Boorer (142) won, Ossie Pickworth / Bert Ferguson (148) were second and Viv Billings / Ken Loy (150) third. Other scores included Horrie Boorer / Harold Knights (151) and Denis Denehey / Barry Chapman (153).

The Age, 12 April 1955
Jack Harris (142) was second in the Pro-Am scratch at Yarra Yarra GC. Ossie Pickworth (140) won and Denis Denehey (145) was third. Other scores included Kevin Hartley (147), Len Boorer (149), Bill Higgins / Jack Boorer (150), Hartley Mitchell (151), Bob Jamieson (152), Tony Thomson / Vic Sleigh / Jack Beazley / Brian Huxtable (153).

The Argus, 15 April 1955
Jack Harris / A McLean, Ossie Pickworth / H Cohen, Denis Denehey / W Clemens tied second in the Centenary Cup at Kingswood GC. Bill Fowler / D MacFarlane won on a count back after all four pairs had returned a score of 3 up.

The Age, 25 April 1955
Jack Harris was second in the **Victorian PGA championship** at Amstel GC. He lost 2 and 1 in the match-play final against Ossie Pickworth. Jack

was one up at the 29th hole and was on the 409 yards hole in two, 20 feet from the pin. Ossie hooked his drive and was 15 feet from the pin in three. Jack three-putted and Ossie made his putt and Jack had blown his chance to take a commanding lead.

The Age, 10 May 1955
Jack Harris / Bob Brown / Jack Boorer (70) tied first in the £100 purse at Latrobe GC. Other scores included Ossie Pickworth (71), John Clark (72), John Sullivan / Noel Smith (74), Denis Denehey / Brian Huxtable (75), Ted Nelms / Peter Bradley / Bill Smith (76), Ray Wright / Bob Spencer / Charlie Oliver (77), Bert Ferguson / Ernie Wood Jr (78), John Creen / Viv Billings / Cliff Naismith / Colin Campbell (79) and Stan McGeorge / Ken Loy / George Naismith (80).

The Age, 24 May 1955
Jack Harris / South African superstar Bobby Locke / former Australian Open winner Eric Cremin (73) tied fifth on level par in the £200 purse at Gailes GC and won £8/6/8 each. Ossie Pickworth (68) won the £75 first prize with a new course record. Frank Phillips (69) was second for £50 and Jim Moran (71) was third for £30. Other scores included Sam Richardson (72) for £15, Sid Cowling (74), Bob Brown / Norman von Nida / Charlie Cowling / Darryl Welch (75), Les Wilson (76), Len Woodward / Ken Loy / Kel Nagle (77), Ossie Walker (78), Len Boorer / Dave Mercer / Doug Katterns (79), Alan Myers (81) and Arthur Gazzard (82). A few days later Bobby Locke won the Australian Open on the same course and Norman von Nida was runner-up in a tournament which was ruined by a monsoon-like deluge that wiped-out half of the field including Jack Harris.

Sydney Morning Herald, 25 May 1955
After beating Queensland 3-1 in the **Vicars Shield** semi-final, Victoria lost to NSW in the final by 3.5 to 1.5. Kel Nagle beat Jack Harris (1up), Norman von Nida lost to Ossie Pickworth (4 and 3), Eric Cremin beat Bob Brown (4 and 3), Les Wilson halved with Len Boorer and Len Woodward beat Ted Naismith (1 up).

The Argus, 27 May, 1955

Jack Harris missed the cut in the **Australian Open Championship** at Gailes GC. It was the only time when Jack ever missed the cut in this event. The tournament was marred by a tropical downpour in the first round. Any player who was out on the course at the time of the downpour (and Jack Harris was one of them) had their tournament completely washed-out. At the peak of the storm the bunkers were full to the brim with water and " rivers of water " washed across the fairways. It was impossible to play proper golf but the organisers refused to suspend play. Bobby Locke was just finishing his first round on the 18th green when the deluge started. He eventually won his first and only Australian Open. Jack Harris never returned to play golf in Queensland.

The Age, 14 June 1955

Jack Harris / Bill Higgins (146) tied second in the £150 purse at Woodlands GC. Ossie Pickworth (139) won. Other scores included Bob Brown / Kevin Hartley (152), Denis Denehey / Dog Bachli / Keith McPherson (153), Jack Boorer / Ted Naismith (154), Barry West (155), Hartley Mitchell / Noel Smith (156), John Hood / Ken Loy (157) and Ray Wright (158).

The Age, 20 June 1955

Jack Harris / Jack Boorer (148) tied second in the **West-Victorian Open** at Horsham GC. Ossie Pickworth (145) won. Other scores included Tom Crow (149), Tony Thomson (151), Noel Smith / Bill Clifford (153), Doug Bachli / Colin Campbell (154), Brian Huxtable / Ken Loy (155), Viv Billings (158), John Sullivan (159), Peter Block (160) and Bob Brown / Ivan Cross (161).

The Argus, 19 July 1955

Jack Harris (72) won the £120 Liquor Industry purse at Victoria GC on one under par. Bob Brown (73) was second and Denis Denehey (74) third. Other scores included Len Boorer (75), Geoff Flanagan / Alec Kynnersley / John Clark (78), Bob Jamieson / Barry Chapman / Ossie Pickworth / Colin Campbell (79), Bob Jennings (80), Ken Loy / Brian Huxtable / Horrie Boorer / Bill Clifford / Viv Billings (81) and Des Martin / Noel Smith / Bill Smith / Ted Nelms (82).

The Argus, 21 July 1955
Jack Harris / Brian Huxtable (153) tied 5th in the £180 purse at Northern GC. Ossie Pickworth (146) won, Bob Brown / Denis Denehey (151) tied second. Other scores included Colin Campbell (152), Ken Loy (155), Horrie Boorer (159), Bob Jennings / Bill Smith / Noel Smith (162), Viv Billings / Len Boorer (163) and Peter Bradley (164).

The Age, 1 August 1955
Jack Harris (72) was runner-up in 200 Guineas purse at Long Island GC. Ossie Pickworth (71) won and John Sullivan (73) was third. Other scores included Denis Denehey / John Clark (75), Ted Naismith / Geoff Flanagan / Bob Brown / Ray Wright (76), Martin Smith / Ted Naismith Jr (78) and Horrie Boorer / Ted Nelms / Bert Ferguson / Bob Spencer (79).

The Age, 17 September 1955
The £2000 **Speedo** tournament at Bonnie Doon GC was one of very few tournaments where Jack Harris missed the cut. Uncharacteristically he shot 81, 76 and failed by five strokes to qualify for the last 36 holes. I suspect that it was one of those occasions when he played a course which he had never seen before and had no opportunity to have a practice round on it. Peter Thomson (288) won, Frank Phillips (290) was second and Bill Holder (291) was third. Other scores included Ossie Pickworth (292), Norman von Nida (294), Bruce Crampton (299), Kel Nagle (301) and Eric Cremin (306). Frank Phillips was very unlucky in this tournament. On the last day he hit a shot which struck a gutter over the out of bounds fence and the ball was bouncing back towards the green when a spectator caught the ball and threw it back over the OOB fence. It cost Frank a two shot penalty and ruined his chances of winning the tournament.

The Age, 19 September 1955
Jack Harris / Eric Cremin / Bill Bolger / Brian Huxtable / Alan Myers / Neville Wilson / Len Woodward (69) tied 7th in the £400 purse at Roselands GC. Frank Phillips / Terry Brady (67) tied first. Ted Bolger / Sid Cowling / J Summergill / C Barnes (68) tied third.

The Age, 27 September 1955
Jack Harris (71) was runner-up in the £100 purse at Williamstown GC. Ossie Pickworth (68) was the winner with seven one-putt greens. Bob Brown / Peter Block / Alec Kynnersley (75) tied third.

The Age, 30 September 1955
Jack Harris (74) was fourth in the £300 Amstel GC purse. Denis Denehey (72) won on one over par and collected £75. John Sullivan / Ken Loy (73) tied second. Ossie Pickworth (75) was fifth.

The Age, 3 October 1955
Jack Harris (1 down) was runner-up in the RSL tournament at Long Island GC Winner was Ossie Pickworth (2 up).

The Age, 17 October 1955
Jack Harris (70) was third in the £250 Lion's Club purse at Medway GC. Ossie Pickworth (67) won and Les Wilson (69) was second. Other scores included Eric Cremin (72), Bob Brown / John Sullivan / Bob Jennings / Ray Wright (75), Peter Block / Bill Smith / Ron Harris / Peter Mills (76), Brian Huxtable (77) and Bill Clifford / Colin Campbell / Bob Jamieson / John Creen (78).

The Age, 24 October 1955
Jack Harris / Mick Kelly (74) tied second in the £100 purse at Spring Valley GC. Len Woodward (73) won. Other scores included Les Wilson / Ossie Pickworth (76), John Sullivan / Peter Mills (77), Alan Heil (78), and Eric Cremin / Brian Huxtable / Martin Smith / Bob Jamieson (79).

The Age, 24 October 1955
Jack Harris / Denis Denehey (378) tied 5th in the £2500 **Pelaco** tournament at Commonwealth GC. This was despite a disastrous 81 which Jack shot in the fifth round. Peter Thomson (366) won and collected the £1000 first prize. Ossie Pickworth / Kel Nagle (371) tied second. Other scores included Len Woodward (376), Norman von Nida (380), Eric Cremin (383), John Kelly (384), Sid Cowling (386), Brian Huxtable / Murray Crafter (387), Jim Moran / Bob Furborough (394), Les Wilson (395), Bill Swabey / Brian Twite (397), Martin Smith / Mick Kelly (398), Jeff

Giles / Frank Phillips (400), John Sullivan (401), Charlie Oliver (402) and George Cussell (413).

The Age, 26 October 1955
Jack Harris (3 down) was runner-up in the Patterson River GC purse. Ray Wright (1 down) won and Denis Denehey (3 down) was third.

The Age, 31 October 1955
Jack Harris / Graham Campbell / Bob Jennings / Barry West (154) tied 13th in the **East Victorian Open** at Warragul GC. Jack Boorer (146) won and Ossie Pickworth / Ken Loy (147) were tied second. Other scores included Harold Knights (150), Bill Clifford (152), Bob Jamieson / Colin Campbell (156) and John Sullivan (157).

The Argus, 15 November 1955
Jack Harris / Bob Furborough / Jeff Giles / Bob Jamieson (76) tied 13th in the Don Walker Memorial at Heidelberg GC. Denis Denehey (70) won and Eric Cremin / Ken Loy (71) were tied second. Other scores included Len Boorer (72), Ossie Pickworth (73), Bob Brown / Ted Bolger / Charlie Oliver / Alec Kynnersley (74), Bob Spencer / Alwyn Whykes / Bob Jennings / Peter Speed (75), Bill Clifford (77) and Brian Huxtable / Bill Fowler / Bill English / Bill Smith (78).

The Age, 15 November 1955
Jack Harris / Billy See Hoe (298) tied 4th in the £3000 **Ampol** tournament at The Lakes GC. Eric Cremin (285) won the £1000 first prize. Ossie Pickworth (292) was second for £400 and Norman von Nida (295) third for £200. Other scores included Bruce Crampton / Len Woodward (299), John Sullivan (300), Reg Want / Sid Cowling (302), Bill Holder (303), Norm Berwick (304), Sam Richardson / Les Wilson (306), Jim Moran (308) and Kel Nagle / Bob Brown / John Collins / Frank Phillips (310). In the also-rans were Colin Campbell, Bert Auld, Peter Block, Charlie Earp, Malcolm Willis, Jeff Giles, John Clark, Col Johnston, Alan Heil, Ernie Wood Jr, Colin de Groot, Alan Myers, Jim McInnes, Billy McWilliam, Mick Kelly and Dave Mercer.

The Age, 16 November 1955
Jack Harris / Brian Twite (75) tied 8th in £200 Riversdale GC purse. Kel Nagle (69) won, Bill Edgar (71) was second and Ossie Pickworth (72) third. Other scores included Denis Denehey / Len Woodward / Ted Naismith (74), Colin Campbell / Bill Clifford / Alwyn Whykes / Bob Brown (76), Martin Smith / Viv Billings (77), Brian Huxtable / John Creen (78) and Graham Cates / Jeff Giles / Len Boorer / John Sullivan (79).

The Age, 19 November 1955
Jack Harris / Norman von Nida (150) tied 7th after R2 of the **£600 Riverside & Tasmanian Tyre** Service purse. Eric Cremin (141) was leading with Len Woodward (147) in second and Kel Nagle (147) in third. Frank Phillips (148) and Alf Toogood (158) also played.

The Age, 28 November 1955
Jack Harris (75) was second in the £150 purse at Cranbourne GC. John Sullivan (72) set a new course record on two under par and Ossie Pickworth (76) was third. Other scores included Brian Huxtable (77), Peter Block / Peter Mills (78), Bill Clifford / Colin Campbell (79), Des Martin (80), John Creen / Ted Naismith (82), Ken Loy (83) and Bob Jennings / Bill Smith (84).

The Age, 27 February 1956
Jack Harris / Ossie Pickworth / John Clark (74) tied third in the '£100 purse at Rossdale GC. Peter Mills (71) won and Brian Twite (73) was second. Other scores included Denis Denehey (75), Noel smith / Bob Brown / Peter Block (76), Ken Loy / John Sullivan / J Greenhill / Ray Wright / Horrie Boorer (77), Bob Jamieson / Jack Beazley / Jeff Giles / J Penn (78) and Harold Knights / Geoff Flanagan / Stan McGeorge (79).

The Age, 20 March 1956
Jack Harris (70) won the Peter Scott purse and Albert E Findlay Cup at Victoria GC on three under the card. This was a new course record since the 18th hole had only recently been lengthened by 30 yards. Ossie Pickworth (71) was second and Harold Knights / John Sullivan (72) tied third. Other scores included Brian Twite (73), Viv Billings (74), Denis Denehey (75), Ray Wright / Ted Nelms / Peter Mills / Graham Campbell

(76), Brian Huxtable / Bob Furborough (77), Geoff Flanagan / Alan Heil / Ken Loy (78), Bob Brown / Bill Clifford / Peter Speed / Peter Block / Alec Kynnersley (79) and Cliff Naismith / Colin Campbell (80).

The Argus, 27 March 1956
Jack Harris / Viv Billings and Brian Twite / John Young (6 up) tied in second place in the Four-ball best ball at Kingswood GC. Ossie Pickworth / Sir Dallas Brooks won (7 up)

The Age, 3 April 1956
Jack Harris / Ken Loy / Hartley Mitchell (148) tied 7th in the £150 Yarra Yarra Easter Open. Ossie Pickworth (142) won and John Sullivan / Eric Wishart (144) tied second. Other scores included Max Nunn / Charlie Roberts (145), Doug Bachli / Bob Brown (146), Colin Campbell (147), Keith McPherson (150), Denis Denehey / Peter Mills / Bob Bull (152), Bob Spencer (153), Peter Block / John Clark (154), John Kennedy / Len Boorer (155) and Brian Twite (157).

The Age, 9 April 1956
Jack Harris / Jim Moran / Bill Ackland-Horman (218) tied 6th in the **£1000 Advertiser** tournament at Kooyonga GC. Bill Shephard (211) won and Ossie Pickworth / Len Woodward / Sid Cowling / Eric Cremin (216) tied second. Other scores included Les Wilson (220), Billy See Hoe / John Sullivan / Bob Brown / Kel Nagle / Mick Kelly / Bob Stevens (221), Billy McWilliam (222) and Brian Twite / Jim McInnes (223).

The Age, 13 April 1956
Jack Harris (290) was runner-up in the **Victorian PGA championship** at Long Island GC. Ossie Pickworth (288) retained his title which he had won in 1955 under match-play format. This was the first year it had been played under stroke-play conditions since 1947. It was the last time Ossie beat Jack in this event. Ted Naismith (299) was third. With only two holes to go Jack was leading but Ossie pulled an 18-foot eagle putt out of his backside on the 17th hole to clinch the title. Other scores included Brian Twite (300), John Clark / Noel Smith (301), John Sullivan / Bob Brown (303), Ken Loy (307), Peter Mills (312), Viv Billings (315), Bob Jennings (323) and Barry Chapman (324). Further down the field came all the

usual suspects...John Creen, Bill Clifford, Bob Jamieson, Ray Wright, Jack Boorer, Denis Denehey, Jeff Giles, Alec Kynnersley, Brian Huxtable, Bill Fowler, George Naismith and Stan McGeorge.

The Age, 30 April 1956

Jack Harris / Brian Twite defeated Ossie Pickworth / Graham Campbell in a four-ball best ball match at Eastern GC. Jack / Brian shot 62 against the par 71.

The Age, 9 May 1956

Jack Harris / Ossie Pickworth (71) tied first in the £150 Liquor Industry purse at Kingston Heath GC. Denis Denehey (73) was third. Other scores included Len Boorer / Bob Brown (74), Noel Smith 975), Ted Nelms / John Clark (76), Ken Loy / Brian Twite / Bob Jennings / Jeff Giles (77), Bob Jamieson / Peter Block / John Sullivan (78) and Viv Billings / Alan Heil (79).

The Age, 14 May 1956

Jack Harris / NSW player Graham Campbell (72) tied first in the £100 purse at Latrobe GC. Ossie Pickworth / Ray Wright / Peter Mills (73) tied third. Other scores included Barry Chapman / Brian Huxtable (74), Ken Loy / Bob Brown / Noel Smith (75), Bob Jennings (76) and John Clark (77).

The Age, 5 June 1956

Jack Harris (144) won the Woodlands Open scratch event. Bill Higgins (146) was second and Ossie Pickworth (147) third. Other scores included Doug Bachli (149), Eric Wishart (150), Brian Huxtable / Ken Loy (151), Jack Boorer / John Clark / Jeff Giles (154), Peter Mills / Tony Thomson / Max Nunn (155), Ray Wright / Bob Brown (156) and John Sullivan / Barry West (157).

The Age, 11 June 1956

Jack Harris / Peter Mills (149) tied second in the £150 North-East Open at Yarrawonga GC. Bob Brown (147) won. Other scores included Terry Kennedy (151), Ken Loy (152), Mick Kelly (157), John Clark (159), Bob Jamieson (165) and Cliff Naismith (171). Jack had an unlucky two-shot penalty on the 13th in the last round when a ball rebounded from a tree and struck him.

The Age, 2 July 1956
Jack Harris / Ossie Pickworth / Murray Crafter (73) tied 4th in the Warracknabeal GC purse on sand scrape greens. Bob Brown (68) won the £45 first prize plus an extra £20 for breaking th course record. Ken Loy (70) was second and John Sullivan (71) was third. Other scores included Peter Mills / Harold Knights (74), Max Nunn (75), Ivan Cross / Peter Block / John Clark / Barry Chapman (76), Colin Campbell / Viv Billings (77) and Bill Clifford / Bob Jamieson (78).

The Age, 2 July 1956
Jack Harris (145) was 2nd in the West-Victorian Open at Horsham GC. Peter Mills (141) won and Ossie Pickworth / Ken Loy (147) tied third. Mills had spent one full week before the tournament at the course practising. Jack turned up on the day the tournament started and played with an injured finger heavily bandaged. Other scores included Peter Block / Max Nunn (150), Bill Clifford (152), Jack Boorer (153), John Clark (154), Bob Brown (155) and Viv Billings (156).

The Age, 30 July 1956
Jack Harris (78) was 3rd in the 200 Guineas purse at Long Island GC. Ossie Pickworth (75) won and John Sullivan (76) was second. Other scores included Jack Boorer / Ray Wright / Ken Loy / Ted Naismith Jr (79).

Sydney Morning Herald, 12 August 1956
Jack Harris / Noel Bartell / Ted Rigney / John Toogood / Hartley Mitchell / Alan Waterson (305) tied 15th in the **Australian Open championship** at Royal Sydney GC. Bruce Crampton (289) won, Kel Nagle (291) was second and Ossie Pickworth (295) third. Other scores included Alan Myers (298), Les Wilson / Jim McInnes (300), Len Woodward / Barry West / Frank Phillips / Eric Routley (302), John Clark / Sid Cowling (303), Billy McWilliam / Bob Brown (306), Eric Cremin / Norm Berwick (307), Harry Berwick (308), Peter Toogood / Peter Heard (309), Jim Moran / Keith Pix (310), Eric Wishart (311), Bob Bull (313), Colin de Groot (315) and Bert Ferguson (317).

The Age, 3 September 1956
Jack Harris (73) won the £100 purse at Williamstown GC. Peter Mills / John Kennedy (74) tied second. Other scores included Bob Brown / Ray Wright / Barry Chapman (76), John Sullivan / Ken Loy / Noel Smith / Viv Billings (77), Bob Jennings / Jack Boorer (78), Stan McGeorge / Peter Block / Jeff Giles (79) and John Clark (80).

The Age, 12 September 1956
Jack Harris (147) was 2nd in the £200 Chesterfield purse at Woodlands GC. Bob Brown (145) won on 1 under par and Ray Wright / Brian Twite / Bob Furborough / Denis Denehey (150) tied third. Jack Harris's 3 under par 70 in the last round was the lowest of the tournament but he had a poor 77 in the first round which spoilt his chances. Other scores included Alan Heil (152), John Sullivan / John Kennedy (153), Ken Loy / Graham Campbell (154), Peter Mills / Jeff Giles / Barry Chapman (155), Geoff Flanagan (156), Noel Smith / Alec Kynnersley (157), Bill Clifford / Bill Fowler (158) and Viv Billings / Jack Boorer / Colin Campbell (159).

The Age, 1 October 1956
Jack Harris / Ossie Pickworth / John Sullivan / South African Harold Henning (296) tied 10th in the **£2000 Speedo** tournament at Victoria GC. Twenty-one-year-old Bruce Crampton (278) won his first big tournament and collected the £400 first prize. Pre-tournament favourite Peter Thomson (282), who just two months earlier had won his third consecutive British Open, was second. Amateur Doug Bachli (289) was third. Crampton shot an eight under the card 65 in the final round to set a new course record. Jack Harris and Peter Thomson had earlier both shot new course record 68s in the first round. This was twice in one year that Jack Harris had created a new course record at Victoria GC. Other scores included Bob Brown (290), Sid Cowling / South African Gary Player (291), Bill Higgins (293), Kel Nagle (294), Brian Twite (295), Norman von Nida (297), Barry West / Len Woodward / Col Johnston / Harold Knights (298), Norm Berwick (300), South African Trevor Wilkes / Les Wilson / Tom Crow (301), Denis Denehey / Fran Phillips (304), Bill Bolger / Eric Cremin (305), Brian Huxtable (306), Alan Heil (308), Billy McWilliam (311), Colin Campbell (313) and Bob Bull (314).

The Age, 8 October 1956
Jack Harris (146) was 4th in the £200 purse at Croydon GC. He shot a consistent 73,73 for the two rounds. Ossie Pickworth (142) won, Harold Knights (144) was second and Bob Brown (145) was third. Other scores included Ted Naismith (147), Laurie Duffy / Viv Billings / Ken Loy (148), Peter Mills (149), Geoff Flanagan / John Clark (150), Jack Boorer (151) and John Sullivan / Bob Bull / Alan Heil (152).

The Age, 24 October 1956
Jack Harris (76) tied 6th in 18-hole Peninsula GC purse with Ted Naismith / Jeff Giles / Bob Jamieson / Bill Clifford / Alan Heil. Ossie Pickworth (69) won and Ken Loy (74) was second. Also played Brian Twite / Peter Mills (78) and Bob Brown / Colin Campbell (80).
In the 9-hole purse Jack Harris (36) was runner-up behind Ossie Pickworth (35).

The Age, 30 October 1956
Jack Harris / John Clark (229) tied second in the £300 purse at Amstel GC. Each received £46. Ossie Pickworth (228) won the £100 first prize. Other scores included Denis Denehey (230) for £22, Brian Huxtable / Peter Mills / Brian Twite (231), Bob Furborough (232), Bob Spencer (233), Ray Wright / Ted Naismith (234) and Ken Loy / Bob Brown / Harold Knights (235).

The Age, 12 November 1956
Jack Harris / Bob Brown (371) tied 11th in the **£2500 Pelaco** tournament at The Australian GC, Kensington. Peter Thomson (349) won the £1000 first prize and Frank Phillips (356) was runner-up. Kel Nagle / Len Woodward (358) tied third. Other scores included South African Gary Player / Norman von Nida (361), Bruce Crampton (362), Belgian champion Flory van Donck (364), USA player Bo Wininger / South African Harold Henning (366), USA player George Bayer / John Sullivan (372), Peter Mills (374), Jim McInnes (376), NZ player Ernie Southerden (377), Col Johnston (378), Bill Holder / Eric Cremin (379) and Billy See Hoe / John Clark / Graham Watson (379). Further down the field came NZ amateur player Bob Charles, Bill Edgar, Bill Bolger, Dan Cullen, Jeff Giles, Harry Berwick, Sam Richardson, South African Trevor Wilkes, Billy McWilliam,

Dick Carr, Alan Myers, John Kelly, Alf Toogood, Bruce Devlin, Norm Berwick, Jim Moran, Dave Mercer, Chris Porter, Barry Warren, Kevin Donohoe, Malcolm Willis and Ted Rigney.

The Age, 19 November 1956
Jack Harris / Ossie Pickworth / Belgian champion Flory van Donck (288) tied third in the **£10,000 Ampol** tournament at Yarra Yarra GC. They shared £1600 prize money. Gary Player (280) won first prize money of £5000 and American Bo Wininger (286) was second for £1000. Other scores included triple British Open winner Peter Thomson / Eric Cremin (289) sharing £650, Kel Nagle / Norman von Nida (290) shared £480, American George Bayer / South African Harold Henning (291) shared £365, Denis Denehey (293) for £150, Billy McWilliam / Barry Warren / Frank Phillips (294) shared £360, Tom Crow / John Sullivan (295), Bob Brown / reigning Australian Open champion Bruce Crampton (296), Len Woodward / Brian Crafter (298) and Bill Holder / Jeff Giles / Jim Moran / Bill Swabey / Harold Knights / Graham Watson (300). Further down the field were South African Trevor Wilkes, NZ player Ernie Southerden, Bill Higgins, Eric Routley, Chris Porter, Ken Loy, Les Wilson, Col Johnston, Brian Huxtable, Malcom Willis, Bill Bolger and a young amateur Bob Charles.

The Age, 21 January 1957
Jack Harris (105) was second in the £100 Oscar Mayer purse at Portsea GC. Ossie Pickworth (100) won and Brian Twite (108) was third. Two rounds were played over a 14-hole course. Other scores included Peter Mills / Geoff Flanagan / Bob Brown / Barry Chapman / Noel Smith (111) and Bert Ferguson / Bob Jamieson (112).

The Age, 21 January 1957
Jack Harris (70) was second in the professional purse at Anglesea GC. Ossie Pickworth (68) won and Bob Jamieson (71) was third.

The Age, 27 March 1957
Jack Harris / Bob Spencer (157) were 12th in the **Victorian PGA Foursomes** at Kew GC. Viv Billings / Ken Loy (151) won in a play-off with Ossie Pickworth / Bert Ferguson. John Clark / John Sullivan, Noel

Smith / Charlie Oliver and Bob Furborough / Brian Huxtable (152) were in a three-way tie for third. Other scores included Alan Heil / Bob Jamieson (153), Bill Fowler / Jack Beazley and Bob Brown / John Davis (154), Denis Denehey / Barry Chapman (155) and Bill Smith / Len Boorer and Brian Twite / John Greenhill (156).

The Age, 9 April 1957
Jack Harris (294) tied 12th with Bob Tuohy in the **Advertiser £1000** at Royal Adelaide GC, Seaton. Murray Crafter (282) won, Sid Cowling (286) was second and Kel Nagle (287) third. Other scores included Bob Stevens / Eric Cremin / Ossie Pickworth (290), Norman von Nida (291), Bob Brown (292), Frank Phillips / John Sullivan (293), Brian Twite (296), Peter Mills (297) and Len Woodward (298).

The Age, 23 April 1957
Jack Harris (139) won the Yarra Yarra Easter Open and set a new tournament record at seven under the card. He collected £100 prize money. Amateur Bob Bull shot a course record 67 in the first round but faded with 81 in the final round. Peter Mills / Hartley Mitchell (147) tied second. Mills collected the £40 second prize money and the next five professionals shared £60. Other scores included Bob Brown (148), Bill Higgins (149), Denis Denehey / Ossie Pickworth (151), John Clark / John Sullivan (152), Len Boorer / Doug Bachli (154) and Viv Billings / John Kennedy / Bill Clifford (155).

The Age, 1 May 1957
Jack Harris / Viv Billings (72) tied fourth in Rotary Club purse at Southern GC. Harold Knights won with a brilliant 66. John Kennedy (70) was second and Ossie Pickworth (71) third. Denis Denehey / John Sullivan (73) also played.

The Age, 7 May 1957
Jack Harris (278) won his second **Victorian PGA championship** at Croydon GC on 2 under par. There was a £100 purse plus gate money. Bob Brown (285) was second and four times Australian Open champion Ossie Pickworth (290) was third. Other scores included Viv Billings / Graham Campbell (293), Harold Knights (294), John Sullivan (296), John Clark

/ Geoff Flanagan (298), John Kennedy (301), Noel Smith / Bob Jennings (302), Brian Huxtable (303), Bob Furborough (304), Ray Wright / Brian Twite / Colin Campbell (306), Barry Chapman (308) and Bill Smith (309). In his final round 71, Jack had three three-putts on the front nine but came home with a four under par 30 on the back nine.

The Age, 20 May 1957
Jack Harris (75) was 7th in the £100 purse at Latrobe GC. Geoff Flanagan (72) won and Brian Twite / John Clark / Brian Huxtable (73) tied second. Other scores included Ossie Pickworth / Denis Denehey (74), Bob Brown / Ken Loy / John Sullivan / Harold Knights / Peter Speed (76), Viv Billings (77) and Ray Wright (78).

The Age, 18 June 1957
Jack Harris (142) was 3rd in the £200 purse at Woodlands GC. After an ordinary first round 75, Jack shot a 6 under par course record 67 final round. John Clark / amateur Barry West (141) tied in first place. John Clark collected the £70 first prize. Other scores included Ossie Pickworth (145), Max Nunn (147), Bob Brown (148), John Kennedy (149), Geoff Flanagan (150), Denis Denehey (151), Vic Sleigh / Viv Billings / John Sullivan (152) and Colin Campbell / Ken Loy / Brian Twite / Tony Thomson (153).

The Age, 24 June 1957
Jack Harris / John Sullivan (146) tied 6th in the **North-East Victorian Open** at Yarrawonga GC. Bob Brown (139) won, Ossie Pickworth (140) was second and Terry Kennedy / Peter Mills (142) tied third. Other scores included Geoff Flanagan (145), Bill Edgar (147) and Ken Loy / Bob Jamieson (149).

The Age, 1 July 1957
Jack Harris / Ossie Pickworth (206) tied 2nd in the inaugural **£700 South-West-Victorian Open** at Warrnambool GC. John Sullivan (204) won with a level par score. Jack Harris shot a new course record 65 in the second round. He missed a 12-inch putt on the 18th green in the last round when he piled up a double bogey on a par three to miss out on being joint winner or even outright second. Other scores included Bob Brown (207), Len

Boorer (210), Ron Hollingsworth (211), Colin Campbell / Les O'Shea / Geoff Flanagan (212), Bob Jamieson (213), Bill Edgar (214), Brian Twite (215), Viv Billings (215), Tom Crow (218) and Barry Chapman (220).

The Age, July 1957
Jack Harris (71) won the £122 Liquor Industry purse at Woodlands GC on two under par. This was the third consecutive year he won this event. Denis Denehey / Brian Huxtable / Bryan Smith (76) tied second. Other scores included Jack Beazley / Bert Ferguson / Harold Knights / Bob Jamieson / Ivan Cross 978), Bob Brown / Barry West (79) and Jeff Giles / Barry Chapman / Brian Twite (80).

The Age, 4 September 1957
Jack Harris (145) won the £200 Chesterfield purse at Spring Valley GC on 1 over par. Scoring was difficult in a strong blustery north wind. Denis Denehey (148) was second and Ossie Pickworth / Ken Loy / Bob Brown / John Sullivan (150) tied third. Other scores included Brian Twite / Barry Chapman (154), Martin Smith (155), Viv Billings / Peter Mills (157), Noel Smith (158), Harold Knights (159) and Alwyn Whykes / Bob Jennings (160).

The Age, 7 October 1957
Ossie Pickworth (282) won the inaugural **£250 Victorian Open** at Riversdale GC. Jack Harris, who according to *The Age* would have started tournament favourite with both Peter Thomson and Kel Nagle skipping this event to play in NZ instead, pulled out before the start because of " personal reasons ".

The Age, 4 November 1957
Jack Harris / Bruce Crampton (291) tied 11th in the **£2500 Ampol** at The Australian GC. Gary Player (281) won the £800 first prize, Welshman Dave Thomas (283) was second and South African Harold Henning (284) was third. Other scores included Peter Thomson / Les Wilson (286), Ossie Pickworth (287), Kel Nagle / John Sullivan (288), Eric Cremin / Chris Porter (290), Frank Phillips / Ryder Cup player Eric Brown (292), Ryder Cup player Peter Alliss / Len Woodward / Norman von Nida (293), Murray Crafter / Bill Holder (295), Sid Cowling (296), Bill Bolger / John

Collins (298), NZ player John Kelly (299), Billy Dunk / Billy McWilliam (302), Bill Duval (303), Dave Mercer (304) and Mick Kelly (305). Ten days later Frank Phillips won the first of his two Australian Opens when he beat Gary Player / Ossie Pickworth into second place at Kingston Heath GC. Jack Harris had the best final round of the tournament with a four under par 68.

The Age, 12 November 1957
Jack Harris / Ossie Pickworth (359) tied 6th in the £2500 **Pelaco tournament** at Victoria GC. Bruce Crampton (354) won the £650 first prize and Frank Phillips / Gary Player (355) tied second. Other scores included Peter Thomson (357), Norman von Nida (358), Eric Cremin / Kel Nagle (360), Peter Toogood (362), Ryder Cup player Peter Alliss (364), Brian Crafter / Col Johnston (365), Ryder Cup player Dave Thomas (366), Doug Bachli / South African Harold Henning (367), Barry West (368), John Sullivan / Bob Tuohy (369), Ryder Cup players Eric Brown / John Panton (370), Norm Berwick / Brian Huxtable (371), Denis Denehey / Len Woodward / John Clark (372), Les Wilson (374), John Collins (377), Graham Campbell (379), Chris Porter (380), John Kennedy (381), Ken Loy (384) and John Greenhill (390). Behind Loy in no special order were Bob Spencer, Jeff Giles, Colin Campbell, Dave Mercer, Bill See Hoe, Billy McWilliam, Geoff Flanagan, Jim McInnes, Brian Twite, Les Nichols, Les O'Shea, Bill Clifford, John Davis, Colin de Groot, Vic Sleigh, Alan Heil, Sid Cowling, Bob Jennings, Eric Wishart, Bob Jamieson, Martin Smith, Darryl Welch, Barry Chapman, Peter Mills, Ted Naismith, Bob Brown, Malcolm Willis, Bob Jennings, Ralph Judd and Charlie Cowling. Triple British Open winner Peter Thomson was of course the clear pre-tournament favourite. But in the end he just managed to beat week-end golfer Jack Harris by only two strokes over five rounds. Jack Harris shot the best round of the day in the second round and was the only player in the field to break 70.

Sydney Morning Herald, 17 November 1957
Jack Harris / Doug Bachli (295) tied 8th on 5 under par in the **Australian Open championship** at Kingston Heath GC. Frank Phillips (287) won his first Open and collected the £250 first prize. Ossie Pickworth / Gary

Player (288) tied second. Second prize was £125. Other scores included Peter Thomson (289), Kel Nagle / Harold Henning (290), Bruce Crampton (294), Murray Crafter / Eric Cremin (296), Ryder Cup player Dave Thomas / Barry West (298), Norman von Nida (302), Bill Edgar / Tom Crow (303), Ryder Cup player John Panton / Norm Berwick / Eric Routley / Bruce Devlin (304), Denis Denehey (305), John Clark / Sid Cowling (306), Malcolm Willis / Harry Berwick (307), Brian Huxtable (308), John Toogood (309), Brian Twite / John Sullivan / Eric Wishart (310), Peter Mills (311), Peter Heard (312), Billy See Hoe (314), Chris Porter (315) and Bob Tuohy (316). Behind Tuohy in no special order were Jim McInnes, Len Woodward, Brian Jones, Bob Swinbourne, Len Boorer, Les Wilson, Les Nichols, Bob Brown, Harold Knights, Billy McWilliam, Viv Billings, Colin de Groot and Ryder Cup player Peter Alliss who shot 79 in the first round. The last time the Australian Open had been played at Kingston Heath was in 1948 when Ossie Pickworth / Jim Ferrier tied on 289. Pre-tournament favourite was as usual Peter Thomson. He had practised his back-side off for this tournament but all to no avail. The big hitting man from NSW was just too good.

The Age, 18 November 1957
Jack Harris / Eric Cremin / Ossie Pickworth (74) tied 8th in the £200 purse at Spring Valley GC. Gary Player (66) beat the course record by four strokes to win. Kel Nagle (69) was second and Malcom Willis (70) third. Other scores included Ken Loy (71), Darryl Welch (72) and Peter Mills / Colin de Groot (73).

The Age, 20 November 1957
Jack Harris / Sid Cowling / Denis Denehey / Malcolm Willis / Norman von Nida / John Clark / Norm Berwick / Brian Huxtable tied 9th in the **Australian PGA championship** at Commonwealth GC. Jack lost in the first match-play round to Eric Cremin 2 & 1. South African Gary Player beat Peter Thomson in the final.

The Age, 25 November 1957
Jack Harris / Bob Brown / John Collins / Harry Berwick (74) tied 10th in £200 purse at Keysborough GC. Eric Cremin / Sid Cowling (70) were joint winners. Frank Phillips / Kel Nagle (71) tied third. Ossie Pickworth

(72) was fifth and Brian Twite / Denis Denehey / Harold Henning / Brian Huxtable (73) tied sixth.

Sydney Morning Herald, 27 November 1957
Jack Harris / Bob Brown (283) tied 7th in the **£1500 Lawn Patrol** tournament at Croydon GC. Kel Nagle (272) won the £400 first prize on 8 under the card. Bruce Crampton (273) was second and Doug Bachli (280) third. The leading 24 professionals received some prize money which included £500 worth of lawn mowers. Other scores included Ossie Pickworth (281), South Africans Gary Player / Harold Henning (282), 1957 Australian Open winner Frank Phillips (284), Norman von Nida (286), Barry West (287), Darryl Welch / Norm Berwick (288), Brian Huxtable / Ken Loy / Alan Heil / Harold Knights (289), Peter Mills / Denis Denehey (290), John Sullivan / Len Woodward / Eric Cremin / Sid Cowling (291) and John Clark (292). Peter Thomson also played but was well off the pace after two rounds and decided to pull out due to 'injury'. Down the field in no special order were Bill Cussell, Peter Speed, Bill Fowler, Bob Spencer, Noel Smith, Jeff Giles, Billy See Hoe, Geoff Flanagan, George Naismith, Ted Naismith, John Greenhill, Kel Llewellyn, Fred Thompson, Bob Jamieson, Viv Billings, John Kennedy, Bob Tuohy, Malcolm Willis, Brian Twite, Keith McPherson, Bob Jennings, Bert Ferguson and Les Wilson.

The Age, 20 January 1958
Jack Harris (68) shot a new course record to win the £100 purse at Anglesea GC. Ossie Pickworth (70) was second and Noel Smith / Len Boorer (73) tied third.

The Age, 17 March 1958
Jack Harris (286) was second in the **Victorian PGA championship** at Latrobe GC. Peter Mills (280) won on four under par. Ossie Pickworth (288) was third. Other scores included Jeff Giles (290), Barry Chapman (291), Brian Huxtable (292), John Clark / Bob Brown (294), John Kennedy (295), Geoff Flanagan (297), Brian Twite (300), Jack Beazley / Denis Denehey (302), Bob Jennings (304), Bryan Smith (305) and Bob Jamieson / Bob Spencer (307).

The Age, 25 March 1958
Jack Harris / John Kennedy (73) tied 7th in the £100 purse at Rossdale GC. Geoff Flanagan / Barry West (68) tied first. Bob Brown (69) was third. Other scores included Ossie Pickworth / Peter Mills (71), Bob Jamieson (72), Ivan Cross / Colin Campbell (74), John Clark (75), Jeff Giles / Noel Smith / Bill Clifford (76) and Viv Billings / Peter Speed (78).

The Age, 8 April 1958
Jack Harris (144) won the £200 Yarra Yarra Open. Ossie Pickworth (145) was second and Barry West (147) was third. Other scores included Brian Huxtable (148), Denis Denehey (151), Doug Bachli / Bob Brown / Geoff Flanagan / Bob Furborough / Bill Higgins / Peter Mills / Jeff Giles (152), Ray Wright (154), John Davis (156) and Viv Billings / John Kennedy (157).

Sydney Morning Herald, 13 April 1958
Jack Harris (287) was 6th in the **£1000 Advertiser** purse at Kooyonga GC. Kel Nagle (279) won, Murray Crafter (280) was second and Bob Tuohy (281) third. Other scores included Dick Foot (282), Eric Cremin (285), Sid Cowling / Barry West (290), Norm Berwick / Brian Crafter (296), Len Woodward (297), Bob Stevens / Bob Brown (298) and Alec Mercer / John Sullivan (299).

The Age, 5 May 1958
Jack Harris / Geoff Flanagan / Jeff Giles (73) tied 4th in the £100 purse at Green Acres GC. Assistant professional Brian Huxtable (70) won first prize on his home course. Jack Beazley / Denis Denehey (72) tied second. Other scores included Ray Wright (75), Brian Twite / John Davis / Bob Brown / Barry West (76) and Viv Billings (77).

The Age, 5 May 1958
Jack Harris / Ossie Pickworth / Bob Brown (72) tied first in the Testimonial tournament at Rossdale GC for Ossie's retirement from golf. Ossie was given a cheque for £250 as the ultimate winner on a countback. Other scores included Barry West (74), Bill Higgins (75), Ray Wright / Noel Smith (76) and Bill Edgar (79).

The Age, 18 June 1958

Jack Harris / Noel Smith / Barry West (149) tied 3rd in the £200 purse at Woodlands GC. Amateurs Bill Kellow (147) and Kevin Hartley (148) occupied the first two places. However, Jack Harris and Noel Smith were first professionals to finish and took home most of the loot! Other scores included Eric Routley / Barry Chapman (150), John Clark (151), Denis Denehey / Doug Bachli / Bill Higgins / Geoff Flanagan (152), Bryan Smith / Ray Wright (153), Bob Brown / Max Nunn (154), Viv Billings / Hartley Mitchell (156) and Ken Kilburn (157). Behind them came Peter Mills, Brian Huxtable, Bill Clifford, Bob Spencer, Jeff Giles, Ivan Cross, Len Boorer and Brian Twite.

The Age, 23 June 1958

Jack Harris (139) was second in the **£200 North-East Victorian Open** purse at Yarrawonga GC. Bob Brown (134) won and Brian Huxtable (140) was third. Other scores included Barry Chapman (144) and Viv Billings (147).

Sydney Morning Herald, 29 June 1958

Jack Harris (299) was 3rd in the **Lakes Open** in Sydney. Kel Nagle (290) won and Bruce Devlin (291) was second. Other scores included Len Woodward (300), Colin de Groot / Col Johnston (301), Neville Wilson / Chris Porter / Alec Mercer (302), Alan Murray / Jim McInnes (303) Kevin Donohoe / Harry Berwick (304) and Billy Dunk (306). Behind them came Eric Cremin, Billy See Hoe, John Sullivan, Barry Warren, Len Thomas, Norm Berwick, Sid Cowling, 1959 NSW Open champion Harry Kershaw, Bill Bolger, Dave Mercer, Billy McWilliam and Malcolm Willis.

The Age, 7 July 1958

Jack Harris / Barry West (210) tied 5th in the **£400 South-West Victorian Open** at Warrnambool GC. Bob Brown (203) won the £120 first prize. John Sullivan (204) was second and Len Woodward (206) third. Other scores included Barry Chapman (211), Brian Huxtable (212), Les O'Shea (214), Bob Jamieson (216), Bob Furborough / Harold Knights (218) and Brian Twite (219). Prize money went to the top ten finishers.

The Age, 13 August 1958
Jack Harris (71) won the £180 Liquor Industry purse on two under par at Woodlands GC. This was an excellent round in very poor weather conditions. No other player in the field came even remotely close to shooting par. Denis Denehey / Bryan Smith / Brian Huxtable (76) tied second. Other scores included Jack Beazley / Bob Jamieson / Harold Knights / Bert Ferguson / Ivan Cross (78), Barry West / Bob Brown (79) and Jeff Giles / Barry Chapman / Ted Nelms / Brian Twite (80).

The Age, 26 August 1958
Jack Harris / Frank Phillips / Len Woodward / Sid Cowling (145) tied 5th in the **£500 Ampol tournament** at The Grange GC. Amateur Bob Stevens (138) won and Kel Nagle / South African Harold Henning / Eric Cremin (144) tied second. Other scores included Ian Alexander (146), Dan Cullen / Alec Mercer (147), Billy See Hoe (148) and Col Johnston / Brian Crafter / Bob Brown (149).

The Age, 27 August 1958
Jack Harris / Eric Cremin / Bruce Crampton / Sid Cowling / Bob Brown (78) tied 13th in Kooyonga GC purse under very difficult gale-force conditions. John Sullivan (71) won, Harold Henning (72) was second and Gary Player / Frank Phillips (73) tied third. Also played Kel Nagle (75), Len Woodward / Billy Dunk / Jim McInnes / Colin de Groot (76) and Dan Cullen / Murray Crafter (77).

The Age, 31 August 1958
Jack Harris / Norman von Nida (293) tied 14th in the **Australian Open championship** at Kooyonga GC. Gary Player (271) won with a record 25 under par. Kel Nagle (276) was second and Frank Phillips (279) third. Other scores included Eric Cremin (286), Bruce Devlin / John Sullivan (287), Eric Routley (288), Harold Henning (289), Eric Wishart / Jim McInnes / Murray Crafter (291), Les Wilson / Barry West (292), Kevin Hartley (296), John Clark (297), Bruce Crampton (298), Len Woodward (300), Billy Dunk (301), Col Johnston (302), Alec Mercer (304) and Sid Cowling (306). Behind Cowling included Dan Cullen, Peter Toogood, Billy See Hoe, Billy McWilliam, Darryl Welch, Brian Jones, Harry Berwick,

Bob Stevens, Bob Tuohy, Colin de Groot, Harold Knights, Barry Warren, Bob Brown, Brian Crafter, Keith Macpherson and John Toogood.

The Age, 3 September 1958
Jack Harris / John Sullivan / Frank Phillips / Les Wilson tied 5th in the **Australian PGA championship** at Kooyonga GC in Adelaide behind Gary Player, Harold Henning, Kel Nagle and Eric Cremin. In the match-play format, Jack lost to Kel Nagle in the quarterfinals. Typical of the PGA tournament in those days the crowd attendance was very poor. Only 25 people watched superstar Gary Player's match and that was the biggest crowd of the day! Kel Nagle beat South African Harold Henning in the semi-final and Eric Cremin beat Gary Player. Kel Nagle went on to win the title.

The Age, 8 September 1958
Jack Harris (143) was 9th in the £400 Goulburn Valley Open at Mooroopna GC which was played on sand scrape greens. Gary Player (136) won, Bob Brown (138) was second with a course record 66 in the first round and Bruce Crampton / Alan Heil / Geoff Flanagan (139) tied third. Other scores included John Sullivan (141) and Norman von Nida / Bert Clay (142).

The Age, 29 September 1958
Jack Harris (223) was 4th in the **Ampol** professional purse at Bendigo GC. South African Harold Henning (209) won on 10 under par. John Sullivan (216) was second and Peter Mills (222) third. Other scores included Barry Chapman (225), Ivan Cross (226), Brian Huxtable / Bob Brown (227), Viv Billings / Colin Campbell (229), Bob Jamieson (231) and Geoff Flanagan (233).

The Age, 3 October 1958
Jack Harris / Barry West (68) shared the lead in the **Victorian Close championship** at Geelong GC after equalling the course record in the first round. After completion of this round, pre-tournament favourite Jack Harris dramatically withdrew from the event. Bob Brown / Barry West eventually tied first but Bob won the play-off.

The Age, 27 October 1958

Jack Harris (79) won the £100 purse at Northern GC on the very high score of six over par. This was not a bad score under the very high wind and rain conditions as Jack was the only golfer in the field to break 80. Brian Huxtable (80) was second and Barry Chapman / Ray Wright / Bob Jennings (81) tied third. Other scores included Alec Kynnersley / Brian Twite (82), Len Boorer / John Clark / Bill Fowler (83), Kel Llewellyn (84), John Davis / Geoff Flanagan (85), Bob Jamieson (86) and Viv Billings (87). Bob Brown also played but did not return a card.

Sydney Morning Herald, 9 November 1958
Jack Harris / Len Woodward (361) tied 10th in the **£2500 Pelaco tournament** over 90 holes at The Australian GC, Kensington. Peter Thomson (342) won the £650 first prize on 13 under par. Gary Player (348) was second for £325 and Bruce Crampton / Harold Henning (353) tied third for £200 each. Other scores included Frank Phillips (356) for £150, Kel Nagle / Barry Warren (359), Norman von Nida / Bob Tuohy (360), Bill Holder (363), Chris Porter (365), Col Johnston / Billy McWilliam (366), Ian Alexander (367), John Sullivan / Ryder Cup player Dave Thomas (368), Malcolm Willis (369), Jim McInnes (370), Darryl Welch (371), Alan Murray / Alec Mercer (375), Sid Cowling / Bob Swinbourne (376), Dan Cullen (378), Jeff Giles (383), Geoff Donald (385) and Len Bowditch (386). After that came Alan Myers, Ted Ball, Dave Mercer, Sam Richardson, Graham Watson, Viv Billings and Colin Campbell.

The Age, 14 November 1958
Jack Harris / Ted Nelms / D Pearce (74) tied 4th in the £100 Don Walker Memorial purse at Heidelberg GC. Sid Cowling / Kel Llewellyn (72) tied in first place and Jack Beazley (73) was third.

The Age, 17 November 1958
Jack Harris (74) was second in the £200 purse at Spring Valley GC. Alan Heil (73) won and Colin Campbell / Bryan Smith / Bob Brown (75) tied third. Other scores included Noel Smith / Bob Jennings (76) and Ted Nelms / Brian Huxtable (77).

The Age, 17 November 1958
Jack Harris (296) was third in the **£1000 Victorian Open** at Kingston Heath GC. Peter Thomson (289) won his first of three Vic Opens and took home the £500 *premio gordo*. Barry West (292) was second and collected £100. Jack Harris shot six under par for the last two rounds which was the best of any player in the tournament but his poor start had put him behind the eight-ball. Other scores included Barry Chapman (299), leading amateur Keith McPherson (301), Bruce Crampton / Norman von Nida (302), Doug Bachli (308), Brian Huxtable / Eric Routley (309), Tom Crow (310), Bob Brown / Denis Denehey (312), Len Boorer / Peter Mills (313), Kevin Hartley / Alan Heil / Harold Knights (314), Sid Cowling / Geoff Flanagan / Bryan Smith (315), Les O'Shea / Eric Wishart / Ray Wright (316) and Brian Twite (325).

The Age, 28 November 1958
Jack Harris / Geoff Flanagan (77) tied 7th in the Hawthorn Rotary Club's £50 purse at Riversdale GC. Brian Huxtable (72) won and Alan Heil / Jeff Giles (74) tied second. Other scores included Len Boorer (75) and Viv Billings / John Davis (76).

The Age, 22 December 1958
Jack Harris (70) won the £100 purse at Keysborough GC on three under par. Jack Beazley / Alan Heil (73) tied second. Other scores included Brian Huxtable / Ray Wright (74), Jeff Giles / Martin Smith (75) and Viv Billings / Barry Chapman (76).

The Age, 31 March 1959
Jack Harris (146) was 4th in the £200 open scratch event at Yarra Yarra GC. Despite taking a horrifying six over the card on the first nine in the morning round, Jack managed to pull his final score back to level par. Kevin Hartley (143) won, Jack Sullivan (144) was second and Max Nunn (145) third. Other scores included Alan Heil / Jack Beazley (147), Peter Mills / Graham Wilson (148), Bob Brown / Geoff Flanagan / Doug Bachli / Bob Bull / Keith McPherson (149) John Kennedy / Noel Smith (150)

The Age, 5 April 1959

Jack Harris (289) was 5th in the £1000 Advertiser tournament at Royal Adelaide GC. Murray Crafter (281) won, Kel Nagle (283) was second and Len Woodward (287) third. Other scores included amateur Bill Shephard (288), Eric Cremin / Frank Phillips / John Sullivan (290), Darryl Welch (291), Dick Foot (293), Billy Dunk / Bob Stevens (294), Sid Cowling / Mick Kelly (295), John Collins (299), Bob Brown / Brian Crafter (300), Alan Murray (302), Bryan Smith (303) and John Clark / Alan Heil (305).

Adelaide Advertiser, April 1959

Jack Harris and Kel Nagle (62) tied in first place in the £150 Mt Lofty GC purse with a record six under par score. It beat the previous record by six strokes. Jack shot a record 28 on the back nine and 34 on the front nine. The latter included one three-putt. Kel shot 31/31. Other scores included John Sullivan (63), Murray Crafter (64), Frank Phillips (65), John Collins / Mick Kelly (66), Len Woodward / Bob Brown / Billy Dunk (67), Darryl Welch (68), Alan Heil / Bruce Auld (69) and Alan Murray (70).

The Age, 11 May 1959

Jack Harris (70) won the £100 professional purse at Green Acres GC on three under par. Brian Huxtable (72) was second and Viv Billings (73) third. Other scores included Peter Mills / John Davis / Bryan Smith / Ray Wright (74), Jack Beazley / Jeff Giles (75), Bob Brown (76), Bob Spencer (77) and Alan Heil (78).

The Age, 25 May 1959

Jack Harris / Kel Llewellyn / John Kennedy (75) tied 5th in £100 purse at Kooringal GC. Bob Brown / Don Walker (72) were joint winners. Jack Beazley (73) was third. Also played Barry Chapman (74), Noel Smith (77) and Viv Billings / Brian Huxtable (79).

The Age, 8 June 1959

Jack Harris (285) won the **Victorian PGA championship** at Medway GC by five strokes. Bob Brown (290) was second and Brian Huxtable (297) third. Other scores included Barry Scott / Bob Furborough (301), John Davis / Jeff Giles (303), Barry Chapman / Jack Beazley (304), Bryan Smith

(305), Ray Wright / Noel Smith (306), Geoff Flanagan (307), Viv Billings (308), Alan Heil (310) and Ted Nelms (311).

The Age, 16 June 1959
Jack Harris / Bruce Devlin (143) tied first in £200 Woodlands Open. John Clark / Kevin Hartley (148) were tied third and John Davis / Alan Heil / J Leith (149) tied fifth. Other scores included Bill Higgins / Eric Routley / Tom Crow (152), Max Nunn / Barry Chapman (153), Tony Thomson / Jeff Giles (154), Brian Huxtable (155) and Eric Wishart (156).

The Age, 22 June 1959
Jack Harris (147) won the £200 Yarrawonga Open. Brian Huxtable / Geoff Flanagan (149) tied second. Other scores included Bob Brown (152), John Davis / Bryan Simpson (156), John Clark / Kel Llewellyn (157) and R Croxford / Ted Naismith / Viv Billings (159).

The Age, 6 July 1959
Jack Harris (201) was second in the South-West Victorian Open at Warrnambool GC. Bob Brown (200) won and Kevin Hartley (203) third. Other scores included Bill Edgar / Bruce Devlin (206), Alan Toe / Dick O'Shea (209), Ralph Judd / Jeff Giles (213), Brian Huxtable (214), Viv Billings (215) and Graham Campbell / Les O'Shea (216).

The Age, 9 September 1959
Jack Harris / Bob Brown (77) were 9th in the **Australian foursomes championship** at The Australian GC, Kensington. Sam Richardson / John Sullivan (72) won on level par. Kel Nagle / Norm Berwick and Frank Phillips / Sid Cowling (73) tied second. Other scores included Norman von Nida / Billy Dunk (74), Billy McWilliam / Malcolm Willis (75) and Mick Kelly / Darryl Welch (76).

Sydney Morning Herald, 13 September 1959
Jack Harris / Bruce Devlin / Sid Cowling (295) tied 8th in the **Australian Open** championship at the Australian GC, Kensington. Kel Nagle (284) won his one and only Australian Open. Vic Bulgin / John Sullivan (291) tied second. Other scores included Len Woodward / Norman von Nida / Peter Thomson (291), Billy See Hoe (293), Ted Ball / John Clark / Murray Crafter (297), Frank Phillips (298), Les Wilson / Peter Heard /

Eric Wishart (300), Norm Berwick (301), Billy Dunk / Dan Cullen / Bob Touhy (303), Jim McInnes / Bill Holder (304) and Darryl Welch / Kevin Hartley (305).

The Age, 16 September 1959
Jack Harris was one of the 16 qualifiers for the Australian PGA championship at La Perouse GC but elected not to play. Tied 9th would have been his worst possible finish had he not withdrawn. Kel Nagle beat Peter Thomson in the final. In the semi-finals Thomson had been lucky to beat Sid Cowling on the 38th hole and Nagle had also been lucky to beat Len Woodward on the 39th hole.

The Age, 5 October 1959
Jack Harris / Harold Knights (225) tied 15th in the **£300 Victorian Close championship** at Geelong GC. Amateur Bruce Devlin (213) won and amateur Doug Bachli (215) was second. Jeff Giles (217) was third and collected the £100 first prize as first professional to finish. This was the biggest prize Jeff had ever won up to that point. Other scores included Kevin Hartley / Barry Chapman / John Hood (218), Bob Brown (220), Alan Heil / Brian Huxtable (221), Noel Smith / Len Boorer (222), Bill Edgar / Bill Clifford (224) and Neil Titheridge (227). Behind Neil came Bill Fowler, Brian Twite, Bob Jennings, Ray Wright, Ted Nelms and Geoff Flanagan. Jack had the absolute horrors with his putter in this tournament. He lost count of the number of putts less than four feet he missed.

The Age, 12 October 1959
Jack Harris and Mrs. R D smith were runners-up in the Sir Dallas Brooks Mixed Open at Metropolitan GC. Winners were Len Murphy / Elizabeth Jones with a 2& 1 performance.

The Age, 19 October 1959
Jack Harris (74) shot level par to win the £110 purse at Cranbourne GC. Home professional Alan Heil (76) was second and Len Boorer / Bryan Smith / Bill Clifford (77) tied third. Other scores included Ivan Cross / Barry Chapman / Jeff Giles (79). These were the only players in the field to break 80 in very bad weather conditions.

The Age, 8 November 1959
Jack Harris / Bob Tuohy (292) tied 6th in the **£1000 Victorian Open** at Yarra Yarra GC on level par. Gary Player (275) won the £500 first prize with 17 under par. Harold Henning (280) was second for £500 with Peter Thomson (281) third. Other scores included Frank Phillips (284), Kel Nagle (289), Len Woodward / George Mitchell (293), Norman von Nida (294), John Davis (296), Alan Heil (298) and John Clark / Eric Routley (299).

The Sporting Globe, 14 November 1959
Jack Harris / Billy See Hoe / Chinese Canada Cup player Chen Ching Po / Italian Canada Cup player Alfonso Angelini (224) tied 21st in the **£3000 Ampol** tournament at The Australian GC. South African Canada Cup player Gary Player / Australian Canada Cup player Kel Nagle (212) tied in first place and collected £600 each. Australian Canada Cup player Peter Thomson (213) was third. Other scores included Jim McInnes (214), Bruce Crampton / Ryder Cup player Bernard Hunt / Peter Alliss (217), Canada Cup players Canadian Stan Leonard / Egyptian Said Moussa / Argentinian Leopoldo Ruiz / Spaniard Angel Miguel (218), Welsh Ryder Cup player Dave Thomas (219), Italian Canada Cup player Ugo Grappasonni / Norman von Nida / Len Woodward (220), Les Wilson / South African Canada Cup player Harold Henning (222), Canadian Canada Cup player Al Balding / Ryder Cup player Eric Brown / John Sullivan / Canada Cup players Argentinian Fidel de Luca / Japanese Pete Nakamura (223), Ryder Cup players Dai Rees and Christy O'Connor / Belgian Canada Cup player Flory van Donck / Alan Murray (225), Eric Cremin / Frank Phillips / Ryder Cup player John Panton / Brazilian Canada Cup player Mario Gonzales (226), Bob Swinbourne / Darryl Welch / Sid Cowling (227), Colombian Canada Cup player Miguel Sala / Belgian Canada Cup player Donald Swaelens (228), Dan Cullen / British Open winner Roberto de Vicenzo (229), German Canada Cup player Herbert Becker (230), Norm Berwick / German Canada Cup player Freidrich Becker / Swiss Canada Cup player Jacky Bonvin (231), Sam Richardson / Dutch Canada Cup player Gerard de Wit (232), Bill Holder / Mick Kelly / Billy McWilliam / Chinese Canada Cup player Yung Yo Shieh (233), Colombian Canada Cup player Pablo Molina / Chilean Canada Cup player Enrique Orellana /

Filipino Canada Cup player Larry Montes (231), Swiss Canada Cup player Otto Schoepfer (236) and David Mercer (238).

The Age, 25 November 1959
Jack Harris / Brian Huxtable (67) tied 2nd in the £250 purse at Keysborough GC on six under par. Bill Dunk (66) won but just failed to equal the course record 65 held by Jack Harris. Other scores included Filipino Canada Cup player Larry Montes (69), Barry Coxon (70), NZ Canada Cup player Frank Buckler (71), Noel Smith / John Davis / Len Woodward / John Sullivan / Ryder Cup player John Panton / Alan Murray (72) and Jack Beazley / NZ Canada Cup player John Kelly / Dutch Canada Cup player Gerard de Wit / Bob Spencer / Barry Chapman (73). Irish Canada Cup player Harry Bradshaw, 1957 Australian Open champion Frank Phillips and Spanish Canada Cup player Angel Miguel were further adrift.

The Age, 30 November 1959
Jack Harris / Frank Phillips (353) tied 5th in the **£2500 Pelaco** tournament at Victoria GC. Peter Thomson (339), with the massive advantage of playing on his home course where he had played dozens of pennant matches, won the £650 first prize. Jack shot 12 under par for the five rounds but Peter shot 26 under par. Having said that Jack's 66 in the second round was lower than any of Peter's rounds. Kel Nagle (346) was second and Spaniard Angel Miguel / Welshman Dave Thomas (348) tied third. Other scores included Ryder Cup captain Dai Rees (354), Ryder Cup player Peter Alliss / Len Woodward / Murray Crafter (356), Ryder Cup player John Panton / Norman von Nida (358), Ryder Cup player Harry Bradshaw (360), Sid Cowling / Belgian champion Flory van Donck (362), Canada Cup players Egyptian champion Cherif Said / Filipino champion Larry Montes (364), Brian Huxtable / Tom Crow / Jim McInnes (365), Belgian Canada Cup player Don Swaelens / Eric Cremin / Alan Murray / Geoff Flanagan / Bryan Smith (366), Egyptian Canada Cup player Mohammed Said Moussa / John Sullivan (367), Eric Routley (368) and Danish Canada Cup player Henning Kristensen (380). Behind Kristensen in no particular order were Bruce Crampton, Bill Dunk, Bob Brown, Brian Twite, Colin de Groot, Jeff Giles, Barry Coxon, Bob Tuohy, Alwyn Whykes, Canada Cup players Gerard de Wit / Carl Poulson / Harry Karlsson / Frank Buckler, Denis

Denehey, George Naismith, Ivan Cross, Billy McWilliam, Ray Wright, Noel Smith, Len Boorer, Alan Heil, John Clark, Col Johnson, Brian Simpson, Harold Knights, Ted Nelms, Alec Mercer and Bob Spencer.

The Age, 30 November 1959
Jack Harris (78) was 13th in £250 purse at Northern GC. Egyptian Mohammed Said Moussa / Jim McInnes (71) were joint winners. Billy Dunk (72) was third. Other scores included Harry Bradshaw / Frank Phillips / Jack McKinnon (73), Cherif Said (74) and Frank Buckler / John Kelly / Jeff Giles / Len Woodward (76).

The Age, 7 December 1959
Jack Harris / Len Woodward (291) tied 3rd in the **£3000 Coles Stores** tournament at Huntingdale GC at nine under par. Peter Thomson (282) won the £650 first prize and Kel Nagle (288) was second. Other scores included Norman von Nida (293), Billy Dunk (294), Canada Cup player Angel Miguel / Ryder Cup player John Panton / Alan Murray / Murray Crafter (295), Geoff Flanagan / Ryder Cup player Dai Rees (297), Frank Phillips / Bob Tuohy (298), Sid Cowling (299), Jim McInnes (301), Canada Cup player Cherif Said (302), Bob Furborough (303), Dutch Canada Cup player Gerard de Wit / Colin McGregor / Eric Routley (304), Alan Heil / Eric Cremin / John Clark / Norm Berwick (305), Jack Beazley (306), Bruce Crampton / John Sullivan (307) and Bryan Smith / Barry Coxon (310). Jack Harris's 70 was the lowest score in the last round. Other players after Coxon in no particular order included Canada Cup players Peter Alliss / Harry Bradshaw / Carl Poulson / Henning Kristensen / Mohamed Said Moussa / John Kelly / Frank Buckler, Bob Spencer, John Davis, Len Boorer, Brian Crafter, Bill Clifford, Bob Jennings, Viv Billings, Brian Simpson, Alec Mercer, Jeff Giles, Dave Mercer, Ray Wright, Brian Twite, Denis Denehey, Bob Brown, Ted Nelms, Bill Fowler, Ivan Cross, Tom Crow, Harold Knights, Bob Jamieson, Bob Jennings and Colin McGregor.

The Age, 14 December 1959
Jack Harris / Alan Murray (287) tied 6th in the **£1000 Coca Cola** tournament at Royal Hobart GC. John Sullivan (282) won the £225 first prize. Frank Phillips / Barry Coxon / Len Woodward (284) were tied

second. Eric Cremin (286) was fifth. Behind Jack Harris were Billy Dunk, Jim McInnes and Geoff Flanagan.

The Age, 8 March 1960
Jack Harris (283) won the **£1200 Victorian PGA** championship at Cranbourne GC. It was his fourth win in this event and he collected £400 first prize, Ken Nagle (284) was second and Alan Heil (287) was third. Other scores included Billy See Hoe / Bob Tuohy (289), Peter Thomson / Bob Brown / Billy Dunk / Frank Phillips (290), Colin McGregor (293), John Sullivan (295), John Clark / Mick Kelly (296), Walter Gale / Denis Denehey / Darryl Welch / Bob Brown (298), John Davis (300) and Barry Coxon (306). A few months later Kel Nagle won the British Open at St Andrews and Peter Thomson was in a six-way tie for ninth.

The Age, 11 March 1960
Jack Harris / Bob Spencer (144) won the **Victorian PGA Foursomes** at Croydon GC to complete their hat trick in this event. Bob Brown / Denis Denehey (146) were second and Barry Chapman / Bob Davis (148) were third. Other scores included Ivan Cross / Colin Campbell (149) tied with Geoff Flanagan / Bryan Smith, Harold Knights / Bob Furborough (151) tied with Viv Billings / Brian Huxtable, Ray Wright / Brian Twite (152), Jeff Giles / John Kennedy (154) tied with Ted / George Naismith and Graham Campbell / Kel Llewellyn (155). This was Jack's sixth **Victorian PGA Foursomes** title. He had already won this event three times with Colin Campbell in the 1940s.

The Age, 19 April 1960
Jack Harris / amateur Kevin Hartley (139) tied first in the £200 Yarra Yarra Easter Open on 7 under par. Amateur Eric Routley (140) was third. Jack collected £100 as leading professional. Other scores included John Sullivan (144), Barry Chapman (146), Bill Higgins (147), Les O'Shea / Bob Brown (148), Bill Edgar (149), John Clark (150), Ted Naismith (151), Denis Denehey / Kel Llewellyn (151), Ray Wright / Jeff Giles (152) and Tony Thomson (154).

The Glasgow Herald, 6 June 1960

Jack Harris / Irish Ryder Cup and Canada Cup player Norman Drew (279) tied 11th in the **£4000 Penfold Swallow** tournament at Copt Heath GC, Birmingham. Winner of the £1000 first prize was Ryder Cup player Harry Weetman (271) and tied second were five times British Open winner Peter Thomson / Ryder Cup player Christy O' Connor Sr, AKA "Himself" (273). Other scores included George Low (274), South African Harold Henning (275), Ryder Cup players Ralph Peter Mills / Eric Brown / Jimmy Martin (276), M Kennedy (277), Ryder Cup player Ken Bousfield (278), British Close champion Arnold Stickley / Ryder Cup player Peter Butler (280), Australian Murray Crafter / British PGA champion Brian Bamford (281), RA Smith / Ryder Cup players Syd Scott & Jimmy Hitchcock / Canada Cup player Angel Miguel / British Open player Brian Allen (282), British Open winner Henry Cotton / British Match-play champion David Snell / Ryder Cup player Peter Alliss / G Johnson / B Hutchinson / British Open player Fred Boobyer (283), Ryder Cup players Bernard Hunt & Dave Thomas / British Open player WD Smithers (284), British Open winner Max Faulkner / Ryder Cup players Neil Coles & Lionel Platts (285), Spanish World Cup player Ramon Sota / British Open player Robert Mandeville (286), A J Harman (287), Frank Jowle who was third in 1955 British Open behind Peter Thomson (288), C Stowe (289) and Ryder Cup player Ralph Moffitt / John Sharkey (289). Notable "also-rans" included triple Dutch Open winner Sewsunker Sewgolum, Ryder Cup players Harry Bradshaw / Dai Rees / John Panton / Jack Hargreaves, World Golf Hall of Famer John Jacobs, Bill Hector and British Open players Hugh Lewis / South African Ken Redford.

Glasgow Herald, 12 June 1960

Jack Harris and Murray Crafter both missed the cut in the **£2750 Daks** tournament at Wentworth GC played over both the East and West courses. This was a rude introduction for both of them to the infamous "Burma Road" fairways which were so hard that almost every shot bounced over head height on the first bounce and kept rolling for 50 yards or more. It was certainly a course where local knowledge was essential and Jack/Murray had never experienced those kinds of conditions previously. Peter Thomson who had ten years' experience at that point of playing such courses (279) won the £1000 first prize. Tom Haliburton / Jimmy Hitchcock (281) tied second. Other scores included Dai Rees (282), Bernard Hunt (283), Peter Alliss (284), Christy O'Connor (285), Kel Nagle (286), Roberto de Vicenzo / Sebastian Miguel (288), Ramon Sota / Harold Henning / Harry Weetman / Lionel Platts (288), Dave Thomas / Guy Wolstenholme (290), John Panton (291), Norman Drew / Brian Huggett (292) Ralph Peter Mills (293), Neil Coles (294), Syd Scott / Angel Miguel (295), Peter Butler (297) and Fred Boobyer (298). Jack Harris and Murray Crafter were not the only ones to struggle on this concrete-like course. Four-times British Open winner Bobby Locke also missed the cut! The week before the Daks and the week after Jack played many of these players on decent tracks and beat most of them.

It has to be said however, that Jack had certainly did not have a hectic playing schedule in the five-month period leading up to his departure from Melbourne on May 19, 1960. In fact, he hardly played at all! He played his last 72-hole tournament in 1959, the Coca Cola Classic, on December 14/15. In the five months to follow he played just one more 72-hole tournament and a couple of 36-hole events. These were the Victorian PGA, the Yarra Yarra Open and the Victorian PGA Foursomes. He won all three. In the Victorian PGA he beat Peter Thomson / Frank Phillips / Billy Dunk by seven strokes and Kel Nagle by one stroke. Of course, he did cut back his teaching and normal club duties during that period from 70 hours per week to about 50 hours per week so that he could step up his practice time and be razor sharp for his Open campaign! The English tournament season had been in full swing for over one month by the time Jack arrived in England. Most of the British professionals were tournament-sharp by the time he arrived. Kel Nagle and Peter Thomson had been playing in the USA just prior to the Penfold Swallow tournament so they were also very well prepared.

The Wentworth golf course had enjoyed a notorious reputation long before Jack Harris played it in 1960. When Peter Thomson played in the Daks on one of his first UK trips in 1952, he shot a 78 in the first round. According to the *Adelaide Advertiser*, 27 June, he compared the West course to a typical Australian bush course and complained bitterly that it was an insult to be asked to play on such a course. He did make the cut on that occasion though and finished tied eighteenth. The reigning British Open champion, Max Faulkner, was not so lucky. He missed the cut.

The Glasgow Herald, 18 June 1960
Jack Harris / Ryder Cup player Ralph Peter Mills / WCA Hancock (288) tied 16th in the **£1750 Yorkshire Evening News** tournament at Moortown, Leeds. Peter Thomson (268) won the £500 first prize, Bernard Hunt (273) was second and Eric Lester (277) third. Other notable scores included Ryder Cup player Peter Alliss (279), Sewsunker Sewgolum (281), Kel Nagle / Angel Miguel (283), Tony Coop / Ryder Cup players Norman Drew / Peter Butler / Geoffrey Hunt (284), Ryder Cup players Eric Brown / Max Faulkner / Ken Bousfield (286), South African Ken Redford (287), Spanish champion Ramon Sota / John Player Trophy winner Ross Whitehead (289), Six-times Argentinian PGA champion Leopoldo Ruiz (290), Sebastian Miguel (293) and Ryder Cup player Neil Coles (293). There were some very big scalps for Jack Harris in the "also-rans". These included Ryder Cup players Christy O'Connor Sr / Dai Rees / John Fallon, British Match-Play champion David Snell, British PGA champion Brian Bamford, Mexican Canada Cup player José Gonzales, Argentinian Canada Cup player Fidel de Luca, Murray Crafter, News of the World Match-Play semi-finalist Hedley Muscroft, South Africans Harold Henning / Brian Wilkes, former Yorkshire Evening News runner-up Walter Lees, Bill Hector who had won the 1960 Martini Foursomes playing with South African Brian Wilkes, British Open qualifiers Fred Boobyer/ Bob Halsall and World Cup / Ryder Cup players Hugh Boyle / Brian Waites.

Glasgow Herald, 21 June 1960
Jack Harris (143) was 30th in the **£3000 Bowmaker** purse at Sunningdale GC, Berkshire, UK. Peter Thomson (132) won and collected the £350 first prize. Bernard Hunt (133) was second and Harry Weetman / Peter Butler (135) tied third. Other scores included Tom Haliburton (136), Peter Alliss / Eric Lester / Sid Scott (137) and Harry Bradshaw / Ken Bousfield / Neil Coles / David Snell (138). Kel Nagle (140) was 18th and two weeks later went on to win the 1960 Centenary British Open at St Andrews GC.

Glasgow Herald, 7 July 1960
Jack Harris and Murray Crafter both failed to qualify for the **British Open Championship** at St Andrews in the Centenary Open. Out of 410 entrants the qualifying mark was set at 147 for two rounds. Murray played the Old Course first and shot a good 72 but on the New Course he shot 76 and missed the mark by just one stroke. Jack shot a disappointing 77 on the New Course in the first round which included four five-foot lip-outs and then failed to make 70 in the second round on the Old Course thus also eliminating him from the tournament. The second qualifying round was played in atrocious weather conditions. The day's play ended at 9.40 pm in torrential rain and a very strong wind. Only three players in the field of 410 broke 70 in the second qualifying round. There were many famous names who also failed to qualify. These included multiple British Open winner Henry Cotton and former British Open winner Max Faulkner. The 1960 individual Canada Cup champion Flory van Donck also missed out. So too did Ryder Cup players Harry Bradshaw / John Panton / Dave Thomas / Lionel Platts, Canada Cup player Mario Gonzales, US PGA superstar Dick Metz and US player Frank Stranahan who had twice won the British Amateur championship and twice been runner-up in the British Open. Only 74 of the 410 entrants made it to the start line for the Open tournament proper. After two rounds of the final tournament a further 27 players were cut and only 47 competed for the Claret Jug. Among those cut were triple Dutch Open winner Sewsunker Sewgolum, Ryder Cup players Peter Alliss / Norman Drew and David Snell. Kel Nagle who had just crept into the 147-qualifying mark with a 145, went on to win the Open by one stroke from Arnold Palmer. Only three Americans qualified for the 1960 British Open and of those three only Arnold Palmer was in contention. There had been some notable scratchings from the tournament even before the qualifiers started. These included all-time US PGA record holder and former British Open winner Sam Snead, four times British Open winner Bobby Locke, Italian Canada Cup players Alfonso Angelini and Ugo Grappasonni, Philippines champion Larry Montes and US star Johnny Bulla who had been second in the British Open twice, runner-up in the US Masters and third in the US Open.

Jack was gutted not to have at least qualified for the Open. Of the players who finished in the top 14 places there were only two players he had not beaten previously in other tournaments. There were two players he had never played before and ten players he had beaten. In fact, he had beaten the winner, Kel Nagle, before they left Australia that year to play in Europe and also former four times winner Peter Thomson. He beat them both again when they returned to Australia after the Open later that year. His total lack of overseas playing experience no doubt did not help his cause.

Glasgow Herald, 14 July 1960 / Tennis et Golf No 472 August-September 1960
Jack Harris (143) was going well in the **French Open championship** at St Cloud GC, Paris. After two rounds he was three shots behind Peter Thomson (140) and four shots better than fellow Australian Murray Crafter. However, Jack Harris (294) shot 77 and 74 in the final two rounds and dropped down the field finishing tied 24th with José Gonzales. Jack played with Murray Crafter in the last round and saw him shoot a sensational new course record 63 to finish sixth. The old record of 64 had been held by Ryder Cup player Jimmy Adams who Jack Harris had beaten by two strokes in the 1952 Australian Open at Lake Karrinyup, WA.
Argentinian Roberto de Vicenzo (275) won and US player Bill Johnston / Argentinian Leopoldo Ruiz (278) tied second. Other scores included Peter Thomson / Sebastian Miguel (279) tied fourth, Murray Crafter (280), Fidel de Luca / Henri de Lamaze / South African P Verwey (281), Ryder Cup players Bernard Hunt / Ken Bousfield (282), Ryder Cup player Harry Weetman (283), South African Denis Hutchinson (284), Jean Garaïalde (285), US player Dick Metz / Angel Miguel / José Gallardo (286), South African Sewsunker Sewgolum / Ryder Cup player Dave Thomas (287), Belgian Donald Swaelens (292), South Africans Brian Wilkes / John Hayes (295), former Belgian Open winner Albert Pellisier (296), US players Dick Chapman / Sam Friedman (299) and US player Kyle Burton / four times Grand Prix PGA France winner Jean Baptiste Ado (302). US player Stan Dudas who in 1958, 1959 and 1960 had tied 27, 49 and 38 in the US Open withdrew after two rounds on 147. Dick Metz had ten US PGA tour wins and seventeen top ten finishes in majors. Dick Chapman was a former US and British Amateur champion. Peter Alliss also played but pulled out half-

way through round three. The exiled Duke of Windsor (formerly King Edward VIII who abdicated the British throne in 1936) was in the gallery to watch this event. No mention of Mrs Wallis Simpson!

Glasgow Herald, 18 July 1960 / Official Publication of the Dutch Golf Committee 24th Volume No 8, 15 August 1960 p278
Jack Harris / A Moore / South African Bobby Verwey (300) tied 14th in the **Dutch Open championship** at Eindhoven GC. South African Sewsunker Sewgolum (280) successfully defended his title and collected 2000 Dutch Guilders. South African Denis Hutchinson (283) was second for 1500 Dutch Guilders and UK Ryder Cup player Brian Huggett (286) was third. Australian Murray Crafter (290) was fourth. Other scores included Gerard de Wit (291), Major SL Friedman (USAF) (296), Belgian Donald Swaelens / Sookdeo Maharaj from Trinidad and Tobago (298) and German Canada Cup player Herbert Becker (309). Jack had been accepted into the tournament only to replace former champion Alfonso Angelini who had been a late withdrawal. Mysteriously, even though Sewsunker won, his name was not mentioned in the official programme. Black South Africans in the terrible apartheid days were generally *persona non grata*. Within a few years both Swaelens and Verwey became German Open winners. Much later, in 1991, Bobby Verwey at 50 years of age, won the Senior British Open Championship at Royal Lytham GC. He beat Sir Bob Charles and Tommy Horton by one stroke.
In 2018 at the German Seniors tournament at Nettetal they held the first Super-Seniors event when twelve players over 60 years of age competed. One of the players who competed was 78 years old "Sooky" Maharaj from Trinidad who Jack Harris had played against in 1960!

Glasgow Herald, 26 July 1960 / Golf 12 (1960) No 8, p10
Jack Harris / Italian Alfonso Angelini / German Hans Heiser / Swiss Karl Koch (306) tied 21st in the **German Open** golf tournament played at Cologne Refrath GC, Golf and Country Club Cologne. At the time it was said to be the most difficult course in Germany and was designed by Bernhard von Limburger. There were 140 players in the starting field. Only 50 made the final cut. Seventeen withdrew after the first round and a further 73 missed the halfway cut. Peter Thomson (281) won the 3000 Deutsche

Marks first prize and French PGA champion Jean Garaïalde / Roberto de Vicenzo (283) tied second. Other scores included Flory van Donck (286), Denis Hutchinson (287), Peter Butler (288), South African Bobby Verwey (290), George Low (293), Angel Miguel (294), Australian Murray Crafter (295), John Jacobs (296), Dai Rees (301). Ralph Moffitt (303), Dick Metz (307), Sam Friedman / Herbert Becker (308), Kyle Burton (311) and Mexican José Gonzales (312). This was the last event Jack played on his one and only venture overseas. He didn't play his best golf. He was terribly homesick and the bitter disappointment of not qualifying for the British Open was still fresh.

The Age 15 August 1960
Jack Harris (147) was third in the £150 Border Open at Barham GC. Alan Heil (139) won and Bob Brown (144) was second.

The Age, 15 August 1960
Jack Harris / Jeff Giles (74) tied second in the £50 purse at Cohuna GC. Viv Billings (73) was the winner.

The Age, 22 August 1960
Jack Harris / Les Nicholls (72) tied fourth in the £200 purse at Royal Freemantle GC. Norman von Nida (68) won and John Sullivan / Frank Phillips (71) tied second. Other scores included D Waterman (73), Alan Murray / Bob Tuohy (74), Dan Cullen / Alec Mercer / Len Thomas (75), Stan Peach (78) and South African Brian Henning (81).

The Age, 22 August, 1960
Jack Harris / John Hood / Kevin Hartley (292) tied 11th in the **Australian Open championship** at Lake Karrinyup GC. Amateur golfers took the first three places. Bruce Devlin (282) won, Ted Ball (283) was second and Tom Crow (285) was third. Other scores included Eric Routley / Kel Nagle (286), Viv Billings / Doug Bachli (288), Kevin Donohoe (289), Bob Stevens (290), John Sullivan (291), Len Thomas / Norman von Nida (293), Brian Crafter (294), Bill McPherson / Peter Toogood (295), Brian Henning / Les O'Shea / Frank Phillips (296), Bob Tuohy (297), Alec Mercer (298), Dan Cullen (300), Keith Drage (301), Murray Crafter / Alan Murray (304), Harry Berwick / Bill Edgar (305), Dick Foot (308)

and Roy Draddy (310). Jack Harris was third professional to finish so he collected his best ever prize money in this event.

The Age, 23 August 1960
Jack Harris was third best out of 16 qualifiers for the **Australian PGA championship** at Royal Fremantle GC and Kel Nagle was best qualifier. Both elected not to play in the tournament. John Sullivan, who had been second best qualifier, won the title. He beat Frank Phillips in the semi-final and Norman von Nida in the final.

The Age, 16 September 1960
Jack Harris (73) won the 3AW purse at Kingswood GC. Harold Knights (74) was second and Noel Smith (75) third.

The Age, 11 October 1960
Jack Harris (295) was 5th in the **£2000 Standard Triumph** tournament at Commonwealth GC. Frank Phillips (284) won the £500 first prize with a new course record. Kel Nagle (290) was second and Peter Thomson (291) was third. Other scores included Norman von Nida (293), Alan Murray (296), Colin McGregor (297), Bruce Crampton (300), Bill Dunk (302), Sid Cowling / Bob Tuohy (303), South African Brian Henning / Denis Denehey (304), John Sullivan / Eric Cremin (305), Bob Brown / Peter Mills / Harold Knights (306), Geoff Flanagan (309), Barry Coxon (313), Alan Heil / Eric Wishart (314), Tom Crow (315), Len Thomas / Brian Simpson / Doug Bachli / Kel Llewellyn (316), Bob Spencer (318) and Brian Twite / John Kennedy (319). Jack was unlucky in this event. It was originally scheduled to be run at his home course of Keysborough where he would have been very difficult to beat. However, bad weather caused a last-minute change of venue which was bad for Jack but a big slice of luck for all the other competitors.

The Age, 24 October 1960
Jack Harris (70) won £100 purse at Kooringal GC and shot a new course record in the process. Bob Tuohy (71) was second and Ray Wright / Harold Knights (74) tied third. Other scores included Peter Mills / Kel Llewellyn / Bryan Smith (75), Jeff Giles (76), Bob Brown / Bob Jennings (77), Noel Smith (78), South African Brian Henning (79), Len Boorer /

Brian Huxtable (81) and Bill Swabey / Brian Simpson / Colin Campbell (82).

The Age, 31 October, 1960
Jack Harris / Kel Nagle (294) tied third on six under par in **£5000 Coles** tournament at Huntingdale GC. Len Woodward (292) won the £1500 first prize and Darryl Welch (293) came second for £750. Other scores included former US PGA winner Jim Ferrier / Frank Phillips (299), Col Johnston / Peter Thomson (301), Norman von Nida (302), Eric Cremin (303), Bruce Crampton (306), Alan Heil (307), John Sullivan / Colin McGregor (308), Peter Mills (309), Bob Tuohy / Bryan Smith / Brian Huxtable / Harold Knights (310), John Clark (311), John Kennedy / Barry Coxon (313), Brian Henning / Ivan Cross (314), Denis Denehey (317) Geoff Flanagan / Bill Swabey (319) and Noel Smith (321). Two months earlier Kel Nagle had won the British Open at St Andrews beating Arnold Palmer by one stroke.

The Age, 15 November 1960
Jack Harris (282) on 14 under par, won the **Victorian Open** at Metropolitan GC and the £525 first prize. He equalled the course record set by the legendary American golfer Gene Sarazen in the 1936 Australian Open. After three rounds Jack was already on 16 under par and was on track to absolutely demolish Sarazen's record. However, torrential rain and gale force winds during the last round ruined his chances. He had to settle for a hard fought 76 two over par in the final round which tied him with the record. Even then he three-putted the 18th by missing a four-foot putt which would have been enough for a new record. Billy Dunk (286) was second and Alan Murray (287) was third. Other scores included Frank Phillips / Bob Tuohy / Darryl Welch (290), Harold Knights / Norman von Nida (293), Bob Brown / Doug Bachli (295), Len Woodward / Bruce Crampton / Geoff Flanagan (297), John Sullivan / John Clark / Kevin Hartley (299), Tom Crow (300), Bill Higgins (303), Len Thomas (304), Bill Edgar (308), Brian Simpson (309), Bob Spencer (312) and Denis Denehey (316).

The Age, 24 November 1960
Jack Harris (69) won the £100 purse at Keysborough GC on four under par. He was level par on the first nine and four under on the back nine. Bob Furborough (73) was second and Ivan Cross / Denis Denehey / Len Boorer / Peter Mills / Barry Chapman / John Davis / Harold Knights / Barry Scott (74) tied third.

The Age, 28 November 1960
Jack Harris (203) was second in the **£300 Victorian Close championship** at Midlands GC, Ballarat. Ballarat amateur champion Neil Titheridge (200) won on 7 under par. Jack Harris collected first prize of £100. Four times British Open winner Peter Thomson (204) was third. Other scores included Alan Toe (210), John Clark (212), Peter Mills / Doug Bachli (214), Bob Brown (215), Don Moir (216), and Bryan Smith (217).

The Age, 12 December 1960
Jack Harris (73) shot level par to win the professional purse at Northern GC. Bob Jennings (74) was second and Bob Brown / Peter Mills (75) tied third. Other scores included Denis Denehey / Ivan Cross / Brian Twite (77) and Barry Chapman / Jeff Giles (79).

The Age, 28 February 1961
Jack Harris shot 6 under par 67 to win the Victoria GC purse. John Clark / Len Boorer / Brian Simpson were tied second on 71. Other scores included Alan Heil (74), Harold Knights (75) and Ray Wright (76).

The Age, 6 March 1961
The amateurs beat the professionals by 8 matches to 7 at Yarra Yarra GC but Jack won his match against the State Amateur Champion, Eric Routley by 2 and 1.

The Age, 10 March 1961
Jack Harris / Bob Spencer (149) were third in the **Victorian PGA foursomes championship** at Croydon GC. John Clark / Barry Chapman (142) won and Harold Knights / Bryan Smith (143) were second. Other scores included Bob Brown / Denis Denehey (150), Bob Jamieson / Alan Heil (154), George Naismith / Ted Naismith, Viv Billings / John Davis and Brian Simpson / Graham Campbell (156), Brian Huxtable / B Scott

and Ray Wright / Bert Ferguson (158) and Ivan Cross / Colin Campbell and Bob Furborough / Jack Beazley (159).

The Age, 4 April 1961

Jack Harris / Graham Wilson / Peter Mills / Alan Heil (146) tied 4th in the Yarra Yarra Open. Amateur John Hood (139) won, Bryan Smith (144) was second and Bill Edgar (145) third. Other scores included Brian Huxtable (147), Bill Higgins / John Clark / John Kennedy (149), Dick O'Shea (150), Eric Routley (151), Doug Bachli / Kevin Hartley / Alan Toe (152), Ken Loy / Bob Brown (153), Eric Wishart / Hartley Mitchell (154), Ivan Cross / Denis Denehey (155), Bob Jennings / Bob Spencer (146) and Ray Wright / Les O'Shea / Graham Campbell (158). Bryan Smith won the £100 first prize.

The Age, 8 May 1961

Jack Harris (71) was runner-up in the £60 purse at Green Acres GC. Viv Billings (70) was first and Bob Spencer / Jeff Giles (72) tied third. Also played Ray Wright (74) and Bob Jennings / Brian Simpson (75).

The Age, 13 June, 1961

Jack Harris (142) won the £200 Woodlands Open for the fourth time after shooting a course record 69 in the first round. Eric Routley / John Clark (145) tied second. Other scores included Ralph Judd (147), B Coleman / Peter Mills (148), John Davis / Tom Crow / Ray Wright (149), Barry Chapman (150), Kevin Hartley / Hartley Mitchell (151) and John Hood / Les O'Shea / Dick O'Shea / Denis Denehey (153).

The Age, 19 June 1961

Jack Harris / Colin McGregor (149) tied third in the £300 Yarrawonga Open. Alan Murray (144) won and Billy Dunk (146) was second. Other scores included Peter Mills / Len Thomas (150), Bob Brown / John Clark / Dan Cullen (153), Alan Heil (154) and Brian Huxtable (156).

The Age, 28 June 1961

Jack Harris (73) won the £100 Liquor Industry purse at Keysborough GC on level par. John Kennedy (74) was second and Noel Smith (75) third. Other scores included Bryan Smith / Barry Chapman / John Davis / Bob Brown (76), Bill Clifford / Peter Mills / Ray Wright (77), Viv Billings /

Ivan Cross / Harold Knights (78), Bob Jennings / Ivan Dummett / Brian Simpson / Alan Heil / Denis Denehey / Jeff Giles (79).

The Age, 3 July 1961
Jack Harris / Bob Brown / Kel Llewellyn (207) tied second in the £200 **South-West Victorian Open** at Warrnambool GC. Peter Mills (198) won. Other scores included Dick O'Shea (208), Kevin Hartley / Barry Chapman (210), Ron Hollingsworth / Doug Bachli (212), Tom Crow / Les O'Shea (213), John Yelland (214) and Brian Huxtable / Bob Spencer / Ralph Judd (216).

The Age, 4 September, 1961
Jack Harris (280) won the **£500 Henderson** tournament at Rosebud GC. The 1960 Queensland Open champion, Alan Murray (281), was second and later went on to bigger and better things. Billy Dunk / Len Thomas (285) tied third. In 1962 Billy won the first of his five Australian PGA titles.
Frank Phillips / Bryan Smith (287) tied fifth. Just a few weeks later Frank went on to win his second Australian Open at Victoria GC beating Jack by eight strokes.
Other scores included Colin McGregor / Bob Tuohy / John Davis (290), Peter Mills (291), Alan Heil (293), Jack Bennett (296), Barry Chapman (297) and Noel Smith (300).
The course record 70 held by Jack Heil was broken thirteen times. Jack Harris briefly held the new record with his third round 68. Eventually Billy Dunk pipped this with a 67.

Canberra Times, 19 September 1961
Jack Harris / 45-year-old Viv Billings, Graham Watson / Bob Swinbourne and Mick Kelly / Chris Porter (156) tied 10th in the 36-hole PGA Jubilee Foursomes at Royal Sydney GC. Darryl Welch / Eric Cremin (144) won. Bob Tuohy / Jim McInnes (145) were second and Alan Murray / Colin McGregor (150) third. Other scores included Len Wilson / Neville Wilson and Frank Phillips / T Moore (152), Len Woodward / Dave Mercer (153), Dan Cullen / T Kelly, Bruce Devlin / Ted Ball and Peter Mills / Barry Coxon (155), Len Thomas / Billy Dunk (158), Billy See Hoe / Ian Alexander, K

Willis / Billy McWilliams, Sam Richardson / John Sullivan, Sid Cowling / Norman von Nida and Graham Belle / Jack McKinnon (159).

The Sydney Morning Herald, 21 September 1961

After R2 Jack Harris / Colin Johnston (149) were tied in 10th place in the PGA Jubilee Open Championship at La Perouse GC.
Alan Murray (137) was leading with Frank Phillips / Len Woodward (142) joint second. Ted Ball / Bob Tuohy / Eric Cremin were on 150 and Norman von Nida on 153.

The Sydney Morning Herald, 22 September 1961

Jack Harris / N Chant (6 up) tied second with Eric Cremin / D Turner in the Massey Park GC Pro-Am Four Ball. V Richardson / N Hardy (8 up) won. D Mercer / J Mercer (5 up) tied fourth with Len Woodward / Kevin Donohoe, Alan Murray / K Abrahamsen and Peter Mills / Vic Bulgin. Len Thomas / P Langham (4 up) tied with Frank Phillips / L Roy.

The Age, 2 October 1961

Jack Harris (295) was third in the **£1000 Victorian Open championship** at Commonwealth GC. He won £75. Alan Murray (290) won the £500 first prize. Peter Thomson (294) was second. Other scores included reigning Australian Open champion Bruce Devlin / Frank Phillips (297), 1960 British Open champion Kel Nagle / Len Woodward (298), four times Australian Open champion Ossie Pickworth (299), Billy Dunk (300), Bill Edgar / Peter Mills (301), Tom Crow / Eric Routley / Darryl Welch / Ted Ball (303), John Hood (304), Barry Coxon (305), Bob Brown / Ralph Judd (306), Kevin Hartley / Brian Huxtable / Colin McGregor (307), Len Thomas / Bob Tuohy (308), Bruce McClure (309), Bob Jennings / Alan Toe / former Australian Open winner Eric Cremin (310), Viv Billings / Ivan Cross (312), Alan Heil (313), Dick O'Shea / Barry Chapman (314), Colin Campbell / Don Moir / Hartley Mitchell (315), Eric Wishart (318), Bruce Hiam / Brian Twite (320) and Bob Bull (325).

The Age, 31 October 1961

Jack Harris (298) was 13th in the £3000 WD and HO Wills tournament at The Lakes GC. Gary Player (286) won the £800 first prize. Eric Cremin (289) was second for £400. Peter Thomson / Bruce Crampton (290) tied third. Other scores included Kel Nagle / Sid Cowling / Bruce Devlin (293), US superstar Arnold Palmer (294), Bob Tuohy (295), Ted Ball / John Sullivan / Len Woodward (296), Billy Dunk / Alan Murray (299), Frank Phillips (301), Norman von Nida (302), three-time US PGA tour winner Canadian Stan Leonard / Murray Crafter (304), Les Wilson (308), Stan Peach (309), Peter Mills (310), Jim McInnes / Bill Holder (311), Bob Brown (313), Viv Billings (315), Brian Huxtable / Bob Jennings (321), Doug Katterns (323) and Ivan Cross (329). Kiwi Mike Busk withdrew after round three on 246 (84, 79, 83). A few weeks after this tournament Frank Phillips won his second Australian Open. Superstar Arnold Palmer who only beat Sunday golfer Jack Harris by four stokes was the reigning British Open champion. He had won his fourth major championship at Royal Birkdale GC , Southport only three months earlier.

The Age, 28 November 1961
Jack Harris (283) on 9 under the card was sixth in the **Australian Open** at Victoria GC. Frank Phillips (275) on 17 under won his second Open and the £400 first prize. Kel Nagle (277) was second and Bruce Devlin / Gary Player (279) tied third. Other scores included Peter Thomson (281), Daryl Welch (284), Bruce Crampton (286), Kevin Hartley (287), Eric Cremin / Canadian Stan Leonard / Alan Murray (288), Billy Dunk (290), Norman von Nida / Col Johnston (291), Bob Brown / Dan Cullen / Les Wilson (293), Bob Tuohy / Tom Crow (294), Jim McInnes (296), Ted Ball / Bryan Smith (297), NZ player Walter Godfrey / John Clark (298), Len Woodward / Peter Mills (300), Barry Coxon (301), Les O'Shea / Brian Huxtable / John Sullivan (302) and Mick Kelly (304). Players who missed the 151 half-way cut mark were Eric Routley, Bob Spencer, Bob Jennings, Sid Cowling, Barry Chapman, Alan Heil, Billy See Hoe, John Davis, Brian Twite, Len Boorer, Jeff Giles, Ted Naismith and George Cussell.

The Age, 29 November 1961
In the **£500 Victorian PGA** Championship at Keysborough GC it was a very tight affair after the first two rounds. Jack Harris (136), the defending champion, who was going for three in a row, was tied with Frank Phillips. Only the week before Frank had won his second Australian Open title so he was obviously in very good form. Both had shot course record 8

under par 65's in the first round. Despite this, Billy Dunk (138) and 1960 British Open champion Kel Nagle / Len Woodward (139) were hanging in there. They were closely followed by Col Johnston / Alan Murray (140) and Peter Thomson (141), who had already won four of his five British Opens. After them came former Australian Open winner Eric Cremin (142) tied with Bryan Smith / Bob Tuohy, Mick Kelly (143), Stan Peach / Les Wilson / Darryl Welch (144), John Kennedy / Colin McGregor / Len Thomas (145), Peter Mills / Ted Ball / John Clark / John Davis / Jim McInnes (146), Noel Smith / Alan Heil (147), Ivan Cross / Bob Jennings / Barry Chapman (147), Bob Brown / Brian Twite (149), Bob Furborough / Ray Wright / J Klatt (150), Bob Spencer / Brian Simpson / Viv Billings (151), Colin Campbell / Brian Huxtable (153), Len Boorer / J Borthwick / Jeff Giles (154), John Collins / Charlie Cowling (155), Charlie Earp (157) and Harold Knights (157). After round three Peter Thomson had slipped from five to eight shots off the pace. He had turned up late twice for his tee-off times and complained about hay fever at the start. When he discovered after three rounds that his 70, 71, 71 (212) seven under the card was uncompetitive he decided to pull the plug!

Jack Harris (276) won the tournament on 16 under the card and a new course record for 72 holes. He completed a hat trick of Victorian PGA wins. Only the great Ossie Pickworth had equalled this feat. Australian Open winner Frank Phillips (278) was second and the 1960 British Open winner, Kel Nagle (280) was third. Other scores included Alan Murray (282), Billy Dunk / John Clark (283), Eric Cremin / Bryan Smith (285), Les Wilson / Colin McGregor (286), Stan Peach / Bob Tuohy / Alan Heil / Col Johnston (287), Ted Ball (289), Peter Mills (291), John Davis / Len Thomas (292), Jim McInnes / Mick Kelly (292), Bob Brown (295), Bob Furborough (299), Ivan Cross / Bob Jennings / Brian Huxtable / John Klatt (302).

Even though the Victorian PGA didn't offer big prize money, the fields in those days always had plenty of stars. At the time this tournament was played the collective field already had amassed five British Opens, seven Australian PGAs and five Australian Opens between them. Before they packed up golf, members of this field went on to win another British Open, ten more Australian PGAs and two more Australian Opens!

This tournament highlighted what Jack Harris could do when he played on a level playing field. Normally he only ever did a tiny fraction of the tournament preparation that players like Peter Thomson or Kel Nagle did. However, playing on home course of Keysborough, where he often played lots of holes with club members, he left the superstars Thomson and Nagle for dead.

The Age, 29 November 1961
Jack Harris / Bryan Smith / Stan Peach / Darryl Welch / Bob Tuohy / Col Johnston / Dan Cullen / Jim McInnes tied 9th in the **Australian PGA championship** at Rossdale GC. In the semi-finals Frank Phillips beat Peter Thomson and Alan Murray beat Bob Brown who had earlier beat Jack Harris. Alan Murray went on to win the title.

The Age, 4 December 1961
Jack Harris (199) won the **£300 Victorian Close championship** at Midlands GC, Ballarat after shooting a new course record 62 (31,31) in round two. Former Wattle Park player Dick O'Shea (205) was second and four times British Open winner Peter Thomson (206) was third. Other scores included Tom Crow / Kevin Hartley / defending champion Neil Titheridge (207), Alan Heil / John Yelland (208), John Hood (209), Vic Sleigh (210), Brian Huxtable (211) and Doug Bachli / Bob Jennings (213).

The Age, 14 December 1961
Jack Harris / Bob Spencer / John Davis (70) tied third in the Don Walker Memorial purse at Heidelberg GC. John Clark (68) won and Brian Simpson (69) was second. Other scores included Barry Chapman (71) and Alan Heil / Bryan Smith (72).

The Age, 14 February 1962
Jack Harris (72) on two under the card was second in the £100 purse at Kingston Heath GC. Geoff Flanagan (69) won on five under par and Peter Mills (73) was third. Also played, George Cussell (74) and Brian Simpson (75).

The Age, 24 April 1962
Jack Harris (148) was 3rd in the £400 Yarra Yarra Open. Peter Thomson (140) won and received £150 with Kevin Hartley (142) second. Other

scores included Ossie Pickworth (153), Bob Spencer (155) and Alan Heil (156).

The Age, 28 April 1962
Jack Harris / Mrs S Gaskell (152) were third in the £150 mixed foursomes tournament at Keysborough GC. Peter Mills / Mrs A Blazey (149) won and Ray Wright / Mrs D Towt (151) were second. Other scores included Bob Brown / Mrs C Whitehead and Ivan Cross / Miss Pam Tompkins (154), Alan Heil / Miss D McDonald (155), Barry Chapman / Mrs N Broadbent (157), Geoff Flanagan / Mrs W Hebb (158), Bob Jennings / Mrs Joan Fisher and Brian Simpson / Miss Barbara Coulson (159), Viv Billings / Mrs P Simpson (160), Bob Furborough / Mrs M Evans (161), Bob Jamieson / Miss Margaret Masters (162), Bob Spencer / Mrs j Dwyer (164), Harold Knights / Miss M Munster (166), Bert Ferguson / Miss G Carr (168) and Denis Denehey / Miss d Dehnert (179). Margaret Masters went on to be the first Australian lady to play in the USA on the LPGA Tour and paved the way for later stars such as Jan Stephenson and Karrie Webb.

The Age, 5 May 1962
Jack Harris / Bob Spencer (144) were second in the **Victorian PGA foursomes championship** at Croydon GC. Peter Mills / Bryan Smith (141) won. Denis Denehey / Bob Brown and Brian Huxtable / Viv Billings (149) tied third. Other scores included Ivan Cross / Bob Jennings (154), Ray Wright / Bert Ferguson and Geoff Flanagan / Graham Howroyd (155).

The Age, 5 June 1962
Jack Harris / Brian Simpson / John Hood / Harry McGain (150) tied 7th in the £200 Woodlands Open. Peter Thomson (141) won, Kevin Hartley (147) was second and Brian Huxtable / Don Moir (148) tied third. Other scores included J Black / Alan Toe (149), Harold Knights / Ralph Judd (151), Ivan Cross / Tom Crow / Max Nunn (152) and Bob Furborough / Bob Spencer / Brian Twite (153).

The Age, 18 June 1962
Jack Harris (155) / Bruce McClure tied 9th in the Yarrawonga Open. Peter Mills (144) won, Ted Ball (145) was second and John Yelland (147) third. Other scores included Len Woodward (151), Eric Cremin (152), Stan Peach / John Davis (153), Brian Simpson (154), Harold Knights (156), Alan Heil (157), Brian Huxtable / Ivan Cross (158) and Viv Billings (160). Very heavy rain fell during the last round. Luckily Mills had completed most of the first nine before it started.

The Age, 9 July 1962
Jack Harris (197) won the **South Western Victorian Open championship** at Warrnambool GC and in the process broke the event record held by Peter Mills. Les O'Shea (198) was second and Kevin Hartley (206) third. Other scores included John Sullivan (206), Peter Mills / Alan Toe / John Yelland (208), Harold Knights / Ron Hollingsworth (209) and Kel Llewellyn (210).

The Age, 28 August 1962
Jack Harris / Alan Heil (77) tied 4th in the Fairway Club £100 purse at Keysborough GC. Winner was Bob Brown (73), runner-up was Bryan Smith (75) and third John Clark (76).

The Age, 8 October 1962
Jack Harris / Ted Ball / Bob Stevens / Peter Mills (301) tied 12th in the **£1000 Advertiser tournament** at Kooyonga GC. Kel Nagle (280) won, Peter Thomson (286) was second and Len Woodward (288) third. Other scores included Alan Murray (290), Bruce Devlin (291), Billy Dunk (295), Murray Crafter (296), Darryl Welch / South African Alan Brookes / Frank Phillips (298), South African Brian Wilkes (299) and Eric Cremin (302).

The Age, 24 October 1962
Before the start of the **Wills Classic** at the Australian GC, Kensington, forty-years old Jack Harris played a practice round with Jack Nicklaus, Gary Player and Bruce Devlin. Jack Harris and Gary Player both shot six under par 66s. Player had 33 on each nine. Harris had a sensational 30 on the front nine and par 36 on the back nine. Jack Nicklaus shot 72.

The Age, 29 October 1962

Jack Harris / Brian Huxtable / Norman von Nida (296) tied 13th in the **£4000 WD and HO Wills tournament** at the Australian GC. Bruce Devlin (281) won the £800 first prize. Ted Ball (287) was second for £400 and Gary Player (288) was third. Other scores included Len Thomas (289), Jack Nicklaus (290), Bruce Crampton / Frank Phillips / Jay Herbert / Billy Dunk (292), Alan Murray / Barry Coxon (294), Colin McGregor (295), Darryl Welch (297), Col Johnston / Stan Peach / Len Woodward / Eric Cremin (298), Bob Swinbourne (299), Jim Pettersen / John Sullivan (300), John Davis (303) and Colin de Groot (304). This was a superb performance by "Sunday golfer" Jack Harris against the likes of full time tour professionals Jack Nicklaus, Gary Player and Jay Herbert. At the time Nicklaus was the reigning 1962 US Open champion, Player was the reigning 1962 US PGA champion and Herbert had beaten Player in the 1961 American Golf Classic with six other US PGA tour wins before that.

The Age, 5 November 1962
Jack Harris / Billy Dunk / Darryl Welch / Brian Crafter / Alec Mercer / Col Johnston (295) tied 12th in the **Australian Open championship** at Royal Adelaide GC. Gary Player (281) won, Kel Nagle (283) was second and Peter Thomson / Bob Charles (285) tied third. Other scores included Jack Nicklaus (286), Jay Herbert (287), Alan Murray / Bruce Devlin / Len Woodward (288), Frank Phillips / Norman von Nida (289), John Sullivan (290), Bruce Crampton (292), Doug Bachli (293), Bob Tuohy (294), Ted Ball (297), Kevin Hartley (298), Stan Peach (299), Eric Cremin (300), Bob Stevens (301), South Africans Alan Brookes / Brian Wilkes (302), Brian Huxtable / John Clark (303), Mick Kelly / Barry Coxon (304), Colin de Groot / Randall Vines (305), Murray Crafter (307), Mike Wolveridge (308), Bob Mesnil (309) and Bob Brown (315). Billy Dunk was the reigning 1962 Australian PGA champion. Col Johnston won the Australian PGA in 1963 and 1964.

The Age, 7 November 1962
Jack Harris (77) was 15th in the £100 purse at Amstel GC. South African Brian Wilkes (70) won, Brian Huxtable (71) was second and Stan Peach (72) third. Other scores included South African Alan Brookes / Bob Brown / Peter McGee / Noel Smith / Ray Wright (73) tied fourth and

Geoff Flanagan / David Graham / Bob Furborough (74) tied ninth. Ex UK player Mike Wolveridge didn't return a card.

The Age, 9 November 1962

Jack Harris (72) was 4th in the £200 purse at Southern GC. South African Alan Brookes (68) won. South African Brian Wilkes (69) tied second with Peter Mills. Other scores included Ray Wright / Stan Peach / John Clark (73), Ivan Cross / Bob Tuohy (74) and Bill Cussell / Brian Simpson / Noel Smith / Brian Huxtable (75). Bob Tuohy was the course record holder with 67 shot in 1961.

The Age, 19 November 1962

Jack Harris / Bruce McClure (299) tied 5th in the **£1500 Victorian Open championship** at Huntingdale GC. Bruce Devlin (293) won and took the £650 first prize money. Billy Dunk (295) was second and South African Brian Wilkes / Frank Phillips (297) tied third. Other scores include Ralph Judd / Don Moir (300), Bob Brown / Darryl Welch / Len Woodward (301), Norman von Nida (302), John Davis (303), Barry Coxon / Kel Llewellyn / Brian Huxtable (304), Alan Heil (305), Peter Mills / Max Nunn / Ted Ball (306), Harry McGain / Bryan Smith (307), Ivan Cross (308), John Hood / Les O'Shea / Bob Tuohy (309), Ken Kilburn (310), Mike Wolveridge / Vic Sleigh (311), Eric Routley / Tom Crow / Barry Chapman (313) and John Yelland / Stan Peach / Bill Cussell (314). Behind them were Doug Bachli, Alan Murray, Neil Titheridge, Viv Billings, Colin McGregor, Bob Jennings, Eric Cremin and David Graham.

The Age, 20 November 1962

Jack Harris / Peter Mills / Ivan Dummett / Len Woodward / Bob Tuohy / Barry Coxon / Bryan Smith / Charlie Cowling tied 9th in **the Australian PGA championship** at Rossdale GC. Jack lost one-down to Ted Ball in the first round of match-play. Billy Dunk easily beat Eric Cremin 8 & 7 in the final. This was the first of five Australian PGA wins for Billy Dunk.

The Age, 11 December 1962

Jack Harris (212) won the **Victorian Close championship** at Traralgon GC. Alan Heil (215) was second and Kel Llewellyn (219) third. Other scores included Viv Billings (220), Peter Mills (221), Doug Bachli / Bruce McClure (222), Geoff Donald (223) and John Kellaway (227).

The Age, 24 December 1962

Jack Harris / Alan Murray (291) tied 6th on 5 under par in the **£500 Victorian PGA** at Patterson River GC. Kel Nagle (286) won and Frank Phillips / Bob Tuohy (287) were tied second. Other scores included Peter Mills / Peter Thompson (290), Alan Heil (293), South African Brian Wilkes (300), John Clark / Ivan cross / Kel Llewellyn / Mike Wolveridge (304), John Kennedy (305), Bryan Smith (309), Geoff Flanagan (310), a young David Graham (315) and Bob Spencer (317).

The Age, 27 February 1963

Jack Harris (72) was second in the Pro-Am at Commonwealth GC. Elsternwick pro, Bob Spencer (71) won with a great three under par. John Clark (73) was third. Also played Bob Jennings (74) and Noel Smith (76).

The Age, 6 March 1963

Jack Harris / Bob Spencer and Denis Denehey / Bob Brown (154) tied 5th in the **Victorian PGA foursomes championship** at Croydon GC. John Clark / Noel Smith (147) won and collected £50 each. Bert Ferguson / Ray Wright (149) were second and Viv Billings / Brian Huxtable (151) third. Other scores included Don Walker / John Bassett (153), Ivan Cross / Bob Jennings, Bob Jamieson / Alan Heil and Alec Kynnersley / Brian Simpson (155), Bryan Smith / Bill Clifford (156) and Harold Knights / Bill Smith, George Cussell / Geoff Donald and Geoff Flanagan / Graham Howroyd (158).

The Age, 21 March 1963

Jack Harris tied first with professionals Noel and Bryan Smith in a Pro-Am at Keysborough GC.

The Age, 16 April 1963

Jack Harris / Peter Mills (145) tied second in the Yarra Yarra Open. Peter Thomson (144) won. Jack Harris shot a three under par 70 in the final round, which was the lowest of the tournament, but his poor first round 75 was just too much to pull back. Other scores included Kevin Hartley (147), Vic Sleigh (149), Neil Titheridge (152), John Clark (154), John

Kennedy (155), George Cussell / Bob Spencer / Noel Smith (156), Bob Brown / Bob Jennings / Bill Smith / Ray Wright (157) and Viv Billings / Colin Campbell / Bob Furborough (158).

The Age, 24 April, 1963
Jack Harris (74) tied with Peter McGee in 4th place in the £100 purse at Metropolitan GC. Bob Brown (70) won the £40 first prize and John Clark / Brian Twite (73) were joint runners-up. Brian Twite was on his own course and had been the club professional at Metro for about 7 years at that stage.

The Age, 15 May 1963
Jack Harris / Peter Mills / John Clark (70) tied second in the £100 Yarra Yarra Pro-Am with three under the card. Un-attached professional Noel Smith (68) won from 106 entries on five under the card. Bob Brown (73) was fifth.

The Age, 5 June 1963
Jack Harris (67) won the Victoria GC pro-am with six under the card. He was already six under after 11 holes and parred the last seven holes. Peter Mills (69) was second and G Howroyd (71) third. Other scores included John Clark (72) and George Cussell / Bob Brown (73).

The Age, 11 June 1963
Jack Harris / Kevin Hartley (148) tied third in the £250 Jubilee tournament at Woodlands GC. Peter Mills / Peter Thomson (147) tied first. Jack Harris and Kevin Hartley both had "Mick Jaggers "(lip-outs) on the last hole to miss out on a joint win. Other scores included Eric Routley (149), Ray Wright / Bob Jennings (153), Dick O'Shea / Geoff Donald / Ralph Judd (154), Alan Heil / Bill Bosley / Brian Twite / Doug Bachli (155), Peter McGee / Bryan Smith (156), John Kennedy (157), Bill Higgins / Peter Block (158), Tony Thomson (159), John Clark / Harry McGain (160), Bob Spencer (161) and Neil Titheridge (162).

The Age, 17 June 1963
Jack Harris (145) was second in the £390 Yarrawonga Open on five under the card. Peter Mills (138) won after shooting a course record 65 in the final round. Bob Tuohy (146) was third. Other scores included Darryl

Welch (147), Stan Peach / Don Moir / Roger Cowan (148), John Davis (149), Alan Heil / Bruce McClure (150), Mick Kelly / Colin McGregor (151), Ivan Cross / Les O'Shea / Bill Bosley (152), Bob Brown (153), Barry Chapman / Brian Huxtable (154) and Noel Smith (156).

The Age, 25 June 1963
Jack Harris / John Clark (75) tied third in the Pro-Am event at Rossdale GC. Peter Mills / Bob Brown (73) won on one over par. Bob three-putted the 18th to miss out on an outright win. Bryan Smith / Bob Spencer (76) also played.

The Age, 20 August 1963
Jack Harris (139) won the Border Open at Barham GC. Peter Mills (143) was second and Bob Brown (146) third. Don Douglas (145) won the amateur section.

The Age, 6 November 1963
Jack Harris / Bob Chapman / Bob Spencer (78) tied 7th in the £100 Amstel purse. Jeff Giles (72) won, Peter Mills (73) was second and George Naismith / Geoff Flanagan (76) tied third.

Sydney Morning Herald, 12 November 1963
Jack Harris (319), in what for him was a very poor tournament, was 30th in the £4000 Wills Masters tournament at The Lakes GC. Arnold Palmer (285) won, Jack Nicklaus (287) was second and Kel Nagle (292) third. Other scores included Gary Player / Colin McGregor (295), Bruce Devlin (296), Bob Charles (297), Frank Phillips / Len Thomas (300), Alan Murray (301), Mick Kelly / John Sullivan / Peter Mills (302), Peter Thomson (305), Bob Brown / Ron Howell / Bruce Crampton / Norman von Nida (307), Col Johnston / Bob Tuohy (308) and Bill Holder / Billy Dunk / Billy See Hoe (309). Only Palmer and Nicklaus beat par 288. Most of the field shot over 300.

The Age, 17 November 1963
Jack Harris (298) was 5th in the **£1500 Victorian Open Championship** at Kingswood GC. Bruce Devlin (286) won the £650 first prize. Peter Mills (291) was second and Frank Phillips (293) third. Other scores included Peter Thomson (294), Kel Nagle / former wattle Park player and leading

amateur Les O'Shea (301), Eric Cremin / Len Thomas (302), Ted Ball / Darryl Welch / Bob Brown (303), Alan Murray (304), Japanese player Hideyo Sugimoto (305), Eric Routley / Bryan Smith (305), US player Ron Howell / Ken Kilburn (307), Barry Chapman / Brian Huxtable (308), Bob Jennings (311), Noel Smith (313), Alan Heil / John Clark (314), Mick Kelly / Kel Llewellyn (316), Harold Knights / Peter McGee (319) and Frank Stobie / Bruce Hiam (325). Also played Brian Simpson, Ken Loy, Bill Edgar, Ray Wright, Doug Bachli, Ivan Cross and Stan Peach.

The Age, 18 November 1963
Jack Harris / Brian Huxtable / Alan Heil (141) tied third in the professional purse at Latrobe GC. John Davis (137) won and Peter Thomson (140) was second. Other scores included Ted Ball (142), Stan Peach / Bruce Devlin (143), US player Ron Howell / Len Thomas (144), Bruce Hiam / Bryan Smith (145), Bob Brown / Japanese player Hideyo Sugimoto / Mick Kelly / Doug Bachli (146).

The Age, 27 November 1963
Jack Harris / Mick Kelly / Darryl Welch (154) tied 16th in the £800 Liquor Industry purse at Kingswood GC. Alan Murray (144) won, Len Thomas (145) was second and Bob Brown / Ivan Cross / George Cussell (149) tied third. Other scores included Ron Howell / Stan Peach / Ted Ball (150), Peter Mills / Frank Phillips / Peter Thomson (151), John Clark / Colin McGregor (155), Jeff Giles (155) and Kel Llewellyn / John Kennedy (156).

The Age, 16 December 1963
Forty-one-year-old Jack Harris (273) won the **£520 Victorian PGA** Championship at Long Island GC for a record sixth time. He was nineteen under the card! USA player Ron Howell (277) was second and Darryl Welch (280) third. Thirty-four-year-old Peter Thomson (285) had been the almost unbackable pre-tournament favourite. In Don Lawrence's pre-tournament write-up Jack Harris never even rated a mention. Peter started well with a 67 and was leading Jack by five strokes after the first round. But when Jack turned up the heat, he couldn't cut the mustard. Although Peter turned in a creditable performance with seven under the card, he was still 12 shots off the pace at the finish. Peter Thomson had already won four

British Opens at that stage and arguably his best British Open was still to come in 1965.

Other scores included Peter Mills (291), Bob Brown (293), Brian Huxtable (294), John Clark (295), Eric Cremin / Geoff Donald (297), Bryan Smith (299), Bob Spencer (300), Jeff Giles / Stan Peach (302), Ivan Cross (306), John Kennedy (307), Kel Llewellyn (308), Noel Smith (310), Graham Howroyd (312), Viv Billings (314), Peter McGee (315), Stan McGeorge (318), Bill Clifford (319), Frank Stobie (319), Bob Jamieson (323) and Brian Twite (325).

The Age, 4 March 1964

Jack Harris / Bob Spencer and Brian Twite / Graham Campbell (153) tied 5th in the £150 **Victorian PGA foursomes championship** at Croydon GC. Alan Heil / Brian Huxtable won, Viv Billings / Geoff Donald (146) were second and Bob Jennings / Bryan Smith (150) third. Other scores included Peter McGee / Frank Stobie (155), Bert Ferguson / Ray Wright (156), John Clark / Geoff Flanagan (158) and Alec Kynnersley / Brian Simpson (160).

The Age, 31 March 1964

Jack Harris (149) tied 8th in £250 Yarra Yarra Open with Peter Thomson / John Kennedy / Bryan Smith / Jeff Giles. Amateur Harry McGain (143) won from Ken Loy (144) and John Davis / Eric Routley / Peter Mills (146). Other scores included John Clark (147), Max Nunn (148), Brian Huxtable / Kevin Hartley (150), Tony Limon / Alan Heil (151), Bob Brown (152) and Geoff Donald / Stan Peach (153).

The Age, 24 April 1964

Jack Harris / Ivan Cross / John Kennedy / Bob Jennings (78) tied 8th in the £200 Colvan tournament at Green Acres GC. John Clark (69) won and Bob Brown / Brian Huxtable (73) tied second. Other scores included Geoff Flanagan (74) and Peter Thomson / Bert Ferguson (77).

The Age, 16 June 1964

Jack Harris / amateur Kevin Hartley (149) tied first in the Woodlands Open. Ralph Judd (151) was third. Other scores included Alan Toe / Alan Reiter (152), John Hood (154), John Davis / John Clark / Roger Cowan

(155), Harold Knights / Bryan Smith / Barry Chapman / Peter Block (156), Jeff Giles / Colin McGregor (157) and Don Reiter / Dick O'Shea / Les O'Shea / Harry McGain (158).

The Age, 22 June 1964
Jack Harris / Bryan Smith / Bill Bosley (151) tied 13th in the Border Open at Yarrawonga GC. Peter Mills (143) won and Darryl Welch / Geoff Flanagan (145) tied second. Other scores included Bill Britten (146), Alan Heil / Roger Cowan / Brian Simpson / Kevin Donohoe (147), Eric Cremin (148), Brian Huxtable / Kevin Hartley (149) and John Davis / Colin McGregor (152).

The Age, 15 July 1964
Jack Harris (74) won the Liquor Industries purse at Commonwealth GC. Brian Huxtable / Bob Jennings (75) tied second. Also played Harold Knights / Bob Brown (76), George Cussell (77), Ray Wright (78) and Alan Heil / John Kennedy / Brian Twite / John Clarke (79).

The Age, 21 July 1964
Jack Harris (148) won the £100 purse over Royal Melbourne's West course. Bryan Smith (151) was second and Harold Knights / Bob Brown (153) tied third. Geoff Donald / John Clark (155) also played.

The Age, 18 August 1964
Jack Harris (145) was 3rd in the Barham GC £250 Border Open. Winner was Kel Llewellyn (139) and Bob Brown (144) was runner-up.

The Age, 28 September 1964
Jack Harris / South African Cobie LeGrange (291) tied 8th in the £1500 **Victorian Open championship** at Victoria GC. Frank Phillips (278) won, Kel Nagle (281) was second and Ted Ball (283) third. Other scores included Harry McGain / Peter Thomson (284), Bruce Devlin (286), Roger Cowan (289), Bob Tuohy / Walter Godfrey (292), Alan Heil (294), Bill Britten / Eric Cremin / Les O'Shea (296), Billy Dunk (297), Len Thomas / US player Ron Howell / South African Cedric Amm (298), John Hood / Bob Brown / South African Barry Franklin / Don Moir (299), Kevin Donohoe / South African John Hayes (300), Brian Huxtable (301), John Davis (302), Geoff Donald (307) and Geoff Flanagan / Bryan Smith (308).

The Age, 28 September 1964
Jack Harris (290) was 8th in the **Victorian PGA championship** at Latrobe GC. Bruce Devlin (277) won on 11 under par. Ted Ball (284) was second and Geoff Flanagan (285) was third. Other scores included Peter Thomson (286), South African John Hayes (287), Kiwi Walter Godfrey / South African Cobie LeGrange (289), John Davis / Bob Tuohy / Mike Wolveridge (292), Bob Brown (293), Colin McGregor (294), Brian Huxtable / Alan Heil (295), Geoff Donald (296) and Ray Wright / South African Cedric Amm (297).

The Age, 5 October 1964
Jack Harris (65) won the £250 Van Cooth Celebrity tournament at Box Hill GC on five under par. Peter Thomson (69) was second and Geoff Flanagan (70) third. Other scores included Bob Jennings / Alan Heil (71), Harold Knights / Brian Huxtable / Frank Stobie (72), Geoff Donald / Brian Twite / Bryan Smith / Bob Brown (73) and John Kennedy / Ivan Cross / Bill Cussell / Bob Jamieson (75). Twenty-two years old Miss Barbara Coulson, in her first professional event, shot 75 off the men's tees and beat 11 professionals.

The Age, 19 October 1964
Jack Harris / Bob Brown / Jim Moran (150) tied 5th in the £300 Medway Open. Geoff Flanagan (144) won, Stan Peach (145) was second and Bryan Smith / Harry McGain (149) third. Other scores included Harold Knights / Bob Spencer (151), Brian Huxtable / Guy Wolstenholme / Don Moir (152) and Peter Thomson / John Clark (154).

The Age, 27 October 1964
Forty-two years old Jack Harris (298) tied 17th in **£4000 Wills Masters** at Victoria GC with Les Wilson, Bryan Smith and South African Denis Hutchinson. Cobie Le Grange (277) won £1000 first prize. Jack Nicklaus / Bruce Devlin (280) tied second for £400 each. Other scores included Arnold Palmer / Kel Nagle (282), Ted Ball (288), NZ players Walter Godfrey / Bob Charles (291), Frank Phillips / Peter Thompson / Cedric Amm / Billy Dunk (292), South African John Hayes (294), Bruce Crampton (296), Darryl Welch / Col Johnston / Stan Peach / Peter Mills (299), John Sullivan (302), Billy See Hoe (304), US player Ron Howell

(306), British Canada Cup player Guy Wolstenholme (305) and Colin de Groot (313).

The Age, 3 November 1964
Jack Harris / S Davies (304) tied 28th in the **Australian Open Championship** at The Lakes GC. Jack Nicklaus (287) beat Bruce Devlin in a play-off. Ted Ball (288) was third. Other scores included Alan Murray (290), Bruce Crampton (291), Bob Mesnil (292), Col Johnston / Frank Phillips (293), Peter Thomson / Darryl Welch (294), Len Thomas (295), Bob Charles / John Sullivan (296), Bob Swinbourne (297), Bob Tuohy / Malcolm Willis (298), Bill Holder / Billy Dunk (301), Colin McGregor / John Kelly / Eric Cremin / Guy Wolstenholme / Doug Fearns / Jack Coogan (302), Les Wilson (303), Kiwi Walter Godfrey / South African Denis Hutchinson (305), Colin de Groot / Tim Woolbank (307), Vic Bulgin (312) and South African John Hayes (314). Behind Jack Harris also came South African Barry Franklin, Jim Moran, US player Ron Howell, Billy See Hoe, Sam Richardson, Harry Berwick, Dan Cullen, South African Cedric Amm, Stan Peach, Sid Cowling and South African Cobie le Grange.

The Age, 23 November 1964
Jack Harris / Bill Britten / Don Moir (222) tied 6th in the 54-hole **Victorian Close championship** at Shepparton GC. Brian Simpson (217) won, Bryan Smith (219) was second and John Yelland / Kevin Donohoe (220) tied third. Other scores included Geoff Flanagan (221).

The Age, 13 January 1965
Jack Harris / Bob Spencer (75) tied 4th in the Commonwealth GC Pro-Am. John Clark (70) won and Brian Twite / Alan Heil (73) tied second. Other scores included Geoff Flanagan / John Kennedy (76) and Len Boorer (77).

The Age, 26 January 1965
Jack Harris / Bob Brown / Alan Heil / Bob Spencer (75) tied second in the Metropolitan GC Pro-Am. John Kennedy (73) won.

The Age, 5 March 1965
Jack Harris (70) was second in the Colvan Pro-Am at Green Acres GC. Brian Huxtable (68) won on thee under par. Jeff Giles / Bob Jennings / Alan Heil (71) tied third.

The Age, 20 April 1965
Jack Harris (118) tied 18th with Max Nunn and John Davis in the £250 Yarra Yarra Open after the event was reduced to 27 holes because of bad weather. Kevin Hartley (112) won with Peter Thomson / Geoff Flanagan (113) tied second.

The Age, 18 May 1965
Jack Harris / Geoff Flanagan (76) tied 4th in very bad weather in the £100 Liquor Industries purse at Keysborough GC. Viv Billings (72) won on level par and George Cussell / Brian Huxtable (75) tied second. Other scores included Bryan Smith / Alan Heil (77), John Clark / Ray Wright / John Kennedy (78) and Harold Knights / Alby Woodhouse (79).

The Age, 15 June 1965
Jack Harris (140) won the £250 Woodlands Open on six under par. Kevin Hartley (145) was second and John Davis / Harry McGain (147) tied third. Other scores included John Hood (148), Tim Woolbank (149) and Stan Peach / Kel Llewellyn (150).

The Age, 21 June 1965
Jack Harris / Peter Mills / Brian Huxtable (149) tied 7th in the £390 Border Open at Yarrawonga GC. Bob Stanton (142) won and W Robinson (145) was second with Eric Cremin (146) third. Other scores included Alan Heil (147), Ivan Dummett (148), G Kramer (150) and R Shaw (151).

The Age, 14 September 1965
Jack Harris (143) was runner-up in the £100 Victoria GC purse at three under the card. Alan Heil (142) won and Bryan Smith / Bob Brown (148) tied third. Other scores included Geoff Flanagan (150), Brian Huxtable (154), John Kennedy (157) and Viv Billings (158).

The Age, 22 September 1965
Jack Harris / Peter Mills (295) on three over par, tied second in the **£500 Victorian PGA championship** at Woodlands GC. Forty-three-year-old Harris was leading the tournament on 144 after two rounds despite carding a double bogey six on the 18th. Then, after a very bad round of 82 in round three, when he looked as if he had bombed out, he shot the best round of the tournament with a four under par 69 in the last round. This would have

given him seven wins in this event. His record six wins has still not been seriously threatened by any player even up to 2016...over 50 years later. Alan Murray (293) won. Other scores included pre-tournament favourite Ted Ball (296), Bob Stanton (298), Bob Brown (299), Tim Woolbank (300), Frank Stobie / Geoff Flanagan (303), Alan Heil / Bryan Smith (304), Brian Huxtable (305), Stan Peach (306), and Brian Simpson / Bob Spencer (307).

The Age, 27 September 1965
Jack Harris / Geoff Donald / Geoff Flanagan / Bob Brown (305) tied 14th in the **£1500 Victorian Open championship** at Royal Melbourne GC. Alan Murray (291) won the £400 first prize. Veteran Eric Cremin (295) was second and Frank Phillips / Kevin Hartley (296) tied third. Other scores included NZ player Walter Godfrey / amateur Neil Titheridge / Colin McGregor (298), Eric Routley (300), Bob Stanton (301), Peter Mills (302), Roger Cowan / Ken Kilburn (303), Barry Coxon (304), Ted Ball (306) and Doug Bachli / Brian Huxtable (307). Behind them in no particular order came Kel Llewellyn, Bob Shearer, Ian Stanley, Stan Peach, John Davis, John Clark, Bob Furborough, Tim Woolbank, Jeff Boyle, Harold Knights, Ivan Cross and Bill Edgar.

The Age, 7 October 1965
Forty-three-years-old Jack Harris (71) won the £150 purse at Keysborough GC on two under par which was four strokes better than his nearest rival. Tied second were Bob Jennings / Geoff Flanagan / Bryan Smith / Brian Huxtable / Alan Heil (75). Other scores included Colin Harrington / Jeff Giles / John Kennedy (76) and Harold Knights (77).

The Age, 15 October 1965
Jack Harris (77) tied 12th with Dutch player Martin Roesink / Frank Stobie / Bryan Smith in £200 pro-am at Southern GC. Ted Ball / Paul Connell / Bob Brown (72) were joint winners at one under the card. Also played Geoff Flanagan (73), Barry Coxon / Brian Huxtable (74), Bob Stanton / Viv Billings (75), Alan Heil / Ray Wright / Harold Knights (76) and Geoff Donald / Brian Twite / Colin McGregor / John Kennedy (78).

The Age, 25 October 1965
Jack Harris (76) tied 22nd with Dutch player Martin Roesink, Alan Murray and Guy Wolstenholme in the Medway Open. Joint winners were Kevin Hartley / Paul Connell (69) and Ted Ball / Bob Stanton tied third (70) with Barry Coxon / Col Johnston (71).

The Age, 25 October 1965
Jack Harris / Murray Crafter (291) tied 11th in the £2500 **Australian PGA championship** at Riversdale GC. Kel Nagle (276) won the £600 first prize, Frank Phillips (277) was second and Peter Thomson (278) third. Other scores included Bruce Devlin (279), Barry Coxon (287), Col Johnston / Brian Crafter (289), Alan Murray / Ted Ball / Bob Stanton (290), Geoff Donald (292), John Sullivan / Brian Huxtable / Darryl Welch (293), NZ player Ross Newdick / South African Cedric Amm (294), Guy Wolstenholme / Colin McGregor (295), Geoff Flanagan (296), Alan Heil / Billy See Hoe (297), Cobie LeGrange (298) and John Davis (299).

The Age, 22 November 1965
Jack Harris (219) was 3rd in the **Victorian Close championship** at Sale GC. Alan Heil / Bob Brown (218) tied first but Heil won the three-hole play-off. Jack missed a three-foot putt on the 16th to force a three-way play-off. Other scores include Roger Cowan (221), Don Moir (228), Don Reiter / Bryan Smith (229) and Alan Reiter (230).

The Age, 3 March 1966
Jack Harris /Spencer / Len Boorer (73) tied third in the £1000 Colvan tournament at Green Acres GC. Mike Murfitt (71) won and Brian Huxtable (72) was second. Jeff Boyle was unlucky. He also shot 71 but was penalised eight strokes for having 16 clubs in his bag.

The Age, 12 April 1966
Jack Harris and Brian Simpson (151) tied 8th in the $500 Yarra Yarra Easter Open. Kevin Hartley (145) won, John Davis (147) was second and Brian Huxtable / Bob Jennings / Bob Brown (149) tied third. Other scores included Stan Peach / Geoff Flanagan (150), Roger Cowan / Ray Wright (152), Eric Routley / Neil Titheridge / Eric Wishart (153), Kel Llewellyn

/ Howard McHutchison / Don Reiter (155) and Alan Heil / Brian Twite (156).

The Age, 25 May 1966
Jack Harris / Len Boorer (75) tied third in the $352 Liquor Industry purse at Kingswood GC. Geoff Flanagan (72) won and Harold Knights (74) was second. Other scores included Bob Brown / Brian Huxtable (76), Viv Billings (77), Geoff Parslow / Ivan Cross (78), Mike Murfitt / John Kennedy (79) and Alan Heil (81).

The Age, 14 June 1966
Jack Harris / R Presnall (152) tied 6th in the $500 Woodlands Open. Geoff Flanagan (143) won, Brian Huxtable (144) was second and Kevin Donohoe (148) third. Other scores included Kevin Hartley (149), Ralph Judd (151), Bob Jennings / Harry McGain (153), Don Moir / Brian Twite / John Davis (154) and John Clark / Alan Heil / Peter Block / Bill Britten (155).

The Age, 23 August 1966
Jack Harris (153) was 6th in the $300 Victoria GC purse. Winner was Kel Llewellyn (147), second was Alan Heil (149) and third Harold Knights (150). Bob Brown (151) and Geoff Flanagan (152) also played.

The Age, 26 September 1966
Jack Harris / Neil Titheridge / Don Reiter (300) tied 21st in the $2000 Victorian **Open championship** at Riversdale GC. Frank Phillips (284) won the $600 first prize, Barry Coxon (288) was second and Alan Murray (289) third. Other scores included Eric Cremin (291), NZ players Walter Godfrey / Dennis Clark (292), Tim Woolbank / Frank Conallin (294), Geoff Flanagan / Randall Vines (295), Stan Peach / Bruce Devlin (297), Bill Britten / Eric Routley / Eric Wishart / Kevin Donohoe (298), Kevin Hartley / Bob Jennings (299), Frank Stobie / Bob Brown / Bill Bosley / Brian Huxtable (301), Geoff Donald (302), Roger Cowan / Ivan Dummett (303) and Geoff Parslow / Bill Kellow (304). Behind Geoff Parslow in no special order were Ian Stanley, Ivan Cross, Bob Spencer, Brian Boys, Len Thomas, Dough Bachli, Malcolm Willis, Viv Billings and Brian Twite. Bruce Devlin, who finished just three strokes ahead of forty-four -year-old

Jack Harris, had been the hot pre-tournament favourite. At that stage in his career Devlin already had amassed six top-ten finishes in majors, including all four major tournaments. He also had three US PGA tour wins to his credit.

Sydney Morning Herald, 24 October 1966
In only his second four-round tournament of the year, 44 years old Jack Harris / Alan Heil / Billy McWilliam (300) tied 34th in the **$8000 Wills Masters** at Victoria GC. Jack had resigned his pro job at Keysborough GC at the end of April, 1966 and was very busy setting up his St Kilda golf school. His preparation for this tournament had been just about zero. Despite this he only finished 7 shots behind Billy Casper, the 1966 reigning US Open champion. Casper was eight or nine years younger than Jack and won 51 PGA tour events.

Kel Nagle, who was even two years older than Jack, won this tournament on 278 and picked up $2012.50 first prize money. Argentinian Roberto De Vicenzo (280) was second and collected $1012.50 with Frank Phillips (283) in third place.

Other scores included John Sullivan (284), Alan Murray (285), Peter Mills / Peter Thomson (287), Bruce Devlin (289), Les Wilson (290), Ted Ball / Billy Casper / Barry Coxon / Geoff Flanagan / Norman von Nida / Ryder Cup player Clive Clark (293), Geoff Parslow / Guy Wolstenholme / Murray Crafter / Darryl Welch (294), Randall Vines / Martin Roesink (295), John Davis / Col Johnston / Stan Peach / Mike Murfitt / Billy See Hoe (296), Geoff Donald / Len Woodward (297), Brian Simpson / Jim Moran (298) and Walter Godfrey (299). Behind Jack Harris in no particular order came NZ player Brian Boys, Jim Pettersen, Bob Spencer, Brian Twite, Frank Conallin, David Graham, Ray Wright, Len Thomas, Jeff Boyle, Frank Stobie, Viv Billings, Harold Knights, Mike Wolveridge, Alby Woodhouse, Bryan Smith, Bob Mesnil, Doug Fearns, Walter Gale, Alec Mercer and Ivan Dummett.

The Age, 15 November 1966
Jack Harris (72) was third in the Waverley GC Pro-Am. John Davis / Bob Brown (70) were joint winners. Bryan Smith / Peter Mills (73) tied fourth.

The Age, 26 November 1966
Jack Harris (314) was 10th in the **$500 Victorian PGA championship** at Huntingdale GC. After resigning from Keysborough earlier that year and starting up his St Kilda Golf School he had played very little golf in 1966. Geoff Flanagan (289) won, Brian Huxtable (293) was second and Peter Mills (294) third. Other scores included Alan Heil (300), Kel Llewellyn (309), Bob Brown (310), Jeff Boyle (312) and Ivan Cross (313). Behind Jack Harris in no particular order came Brian Simpson, Howard McHutchison, Geoff Parslow, Harold Knights, Denis Denehey, Bob Jamieson, Jeff Giles, Mike Murfitt, Brian Twite, Bob Spencer, George Cussell, Ray Wright, Bob Jennings and Viv Billings.

The Age, 6 February 1967
Jack Harris / Randall Vines / John Davis / Peter Thomson (290) tied 10th on 2 under par in the **$5000 Victorian Open championship** at Yarra Yarra GC. Kel Nagle (283) won, Guy Wolstenholme (284) was second and Ryder Cup player Tony Jacklin / Bob Stanton (287) tied third. Other scores included Barry Coxon / Alan Heil / Don Reiter (288), Ted Ball / Frank Phillips (289), Peter Mills (291), Brian Huxtable / Rick Shaw (293), Kevin Donohoe (294), Tim Woolbank / Eric Routley (296), Dutch World Cup player Martin Roesink (298), Alan Murray (299), Doug Fearns / Norman von Nida (300). Behind Von in no particular order were Bryan Smith, David Graham, Geoff Parslow, Ted Stirling, Jeff Boyle, Bill Bosley, Bob Jamieson, Roger Cowan, Tom Linskey, Howard McHutchison, Stan Peach, Len Thomas and Harry McGain.

The Age, 7 March 1967
Jack Harris and Viv Billings / Brian Huxtable and Alan Heil / John Davis and Colin Harrington (146) tied second in the **Victorian PGA foursomes championship** at Croydon GC. Brian Simpson and Geoff Donald (138) won on six under par. Other scores included Ivan Cross and Harold Knights (148), John Kennedy and Bob Spencer (149), Peter Mills and Cyril Trist (150), Brian Twite and Mal McLennan (151), Jeff Boyle and Howard McHutchison / Ray Wright and Bert Ferguson (152) and Barry Chapman and Frank Connallin (153).

The Age, 10 March 1967
Jack Harris / Geoff Donald / Jeff Giles / Brian Huxtable (72) tied second in the $750 Colvan tournament at Green acres GC. Peter Mills (69) won on two under par. Other scores included John Davis / Ray Wright (73), Bob Spencer / Ivan Cross / Geoff Parslow / Jeff Boyle / Bob Jennings (74) and Brian Simpson / Brian Twite / Frank Connallin (75).

The Age, 28 March 1967
Jack Harris / John Lindsay (150) tied 10th in the Yarra Yarra Open. Roger Cowan (144) won after beating Kevin Hartley in a play-off. Randall Hicks (145) was third. Also played Don Reiter (146), Geoff Flanagan / Neil Titheridge (147), Geoff Parslow / Bob Jennings (148), Jeff Boyle (149) Eric Routley / Peter Mills (151) and Bill Simpson (152).

The Age, 13 June 1967
Jack Harris / Bob Jennings (152) tied 12th in $500 Woodlands Open. Peter Mills (144) won. Max Nunn (145) was second and Bill Bosley / Alan Reiter (146) tied third. Also played Randall Hicks / Kevin Hartley (147), Geoff Donald / Geoff Parslow / Alan Heil (150) and Howard McHutchison / Stewart Ginn (153).

The Age, 19 June 1967
Jack Harris (149) was 5th in the $1000 Yarrawonga Open. Jim Moran / Geoff Donald (143) were joint winners and Tom Linskey (145) was third. Peter Mills (147) was fourth. Other scores included Geoff Parslow (150), Bob Shearer / Len Woodward (151) and Roger Cowan / Ray Wright (152).

The Age, 14 August 1967
Jack Harris / Peter Mills (145) tied third in the $500 purse at Barham GC. John Davis (142) won on four under the card and Jeff Boyle (143) was second. Other scores included Kel Llewellyn (146), Ray Wright / Brian Simpson (150).

The Age, 31 October 1967
Forty-five-years-old Jack Harris / Geoff Flanagan / Kevin Hartley / Geoff Donald / Alan Murray (303) tied 17th in the **Australian Open championship** at Commonwealth GC. Peter Thomson (281) won the $1600 first prize. Col Johnston (288) was second and Harry Berwick /

British Ryder Cup and World Cup player Peter Townsend (292) tied third. Other scores included Bert Yancey (294) 7 PGA tour wins, Kel Nagle / Ted Ball / Guy Wolstenholme (295), Billy Dunk / Randall Vines (296), Frank Phillips / South African Bobby Cole (297), Stan Peach (298), NZ player Walter Godfrey (299), Eric Routley / Barry Coxon (301), Les Wilson (304), Peter Mills / Colin McGregor (306), Bob Shearer / NZ World Cup player Brian Boys / John Davis / Dennis Ingram (307), Len Woodward / Roger Cowan (308). Ryder Cup player Maurice Bembridge / Bob Stanton / Don Reiter (309), Tim Woolbank (310), Bill Britten / British Walker Cup player Dudley Millensted (311), Ted Stirling (315) and Tom Linskey (316). The also-rans included Graham Marsh, Clive Clark, Norman von Nida, David Graham, Kel Llewellyn, Len Thomas, George Cussell, Darryl Welch, Bill Bosley, Jeff Boyle, Brian Twite, Alan Heil, John Hood, Harold Knights, Billy See Hoe, Peter Clutton and Walter Gale. Superstar Bruce Devlin walked off the course in disgust after a horror first 27 holes. At that stage in his career he was 30 years old and at the peak of his powers. He already had three wins on the PGA tour and 10 Tour of Australasia wins under his belt!

The Age, 9 November 1967

Jack Harris (68) was second in the $1000 purse at Southern GC shooting five under par. He was pipped by Barry Coxon (67) who won on six under par. Queensland player Walter Gale (71) was third. Other scores included Len Thomas / Billy Dunk / Brian Huxtable (72) and NZ player John Lister / Stan Peach / Peter Mills / Tom Linskey (73). Gale later tied with Peter Thomson in the 1973 Australian Open comfortably beating Greg Norman / Jack Newton who tied well down the field.

The Age, 14 November 1967

Forty-five years old Jack Harris / Walter Gale / Alan Heil / Tom Linskey / Darryl Welch (294) tied 11th in the $5000 **Australian PGA championship** at Metropolitan GC. Peter Thomson (282) won on 14 under par. Col Johnston / Frank Phillips (283) tied second. Phillips blew his chance to win the title when he missed an 18-inch putt on the last hole. Other scores included Ryder Cup player Peter Townsend (286), Tim Woolbank / Ted Ball (289), Billy Dunk (291), Kel Nagle / Ryder Cup player Maurice

Bembridge (292), Randall Vines (293), Walker Cup player Dudley Millensted (295), Stan Peach / Len Thomas (296), Walker Cup player Clive Clark (298), Norman von Nida / Kiwi Brian Boys / South African Bobby Cole (300), David Graham / Kiwi John Lister (301), Geoff Donald (304), Peter Mills / Bruce Green (305), Bruce Devlin / Brian Huxtable (306), Ivan Cross (310), Barry Coxon (312), Frank Stobie (314) and South African Alan Brookes (315).

The Age, 27 November 1967
Jack Harris / John Davis (221) tied 11th in the **$1000 Victorian Close championship** at Croydon GC. Peter Mills (213) won and Bill Britten / Alan Heil (214) tied second. Other scores included Kel Llewellyn (219), Ivan Cross (220), Harry McGain (222), Bruce Green (224) and Jack Westmore (225).

The Age, 11 December 1967
Forty-five years old Jack Harris / John Davis (290) tied fourth in the **Victorian PGA championship** at Waverley GC. Bruce Green (284) won, Alan Heil (285) was second and Peter Mills (287) was third. There were only four rounds under 70 shot during the whole tournament. Jack Harris's last round of 69 was one of them. Other scores included Brian Huxtable (292), Ted Stirling / Kel Llewellyn (296), Jeff Giles (298), Brian Twite / Ivan Cross (301) and Bob Spencer / Brian Simpson (302).

The Age, 5 March 1968
Forty-six years old Jack Harris / Colin Campbell (142) tied for first place with Brian Twite / Ivan Cross in the **Victorian PGA foursomes** at Croydon GC but they finished runners-up after a sudden death play-off. Jack and Colin, despite their combined age of 100+ years, had an impressive first round five under par 67. However, two rounds in one day proved a bit too much for old codgers like them and they slumped to a 75 in the afternoon round. Alan Heil / Brian Huxtable and Peter Mills / Kel Llewellyn (143) tied third. Brian Simpson / Geoff Donald (149) also played.

The Age, 6 March 1968
Jack Harris / Colin Harrington / Frank Conallin (72) tied third in $1000 Colvan tournament at Green Acres GC. Peter Mills (70) won and Ivan

Cross (71) was second. Other scores included Bruce Green / Geoff Donald (73), Ray Wright / Bob Jennings / Howard McHutchison (74) and Bill Swabey / Alan Heil / John Kennedy (76).

The Age, 11 June 1968
Jack Harris / Ivan Cross / Bill Bosley / Harry McGain / B Stuart / D Hale / G Wills (154) tied 11th in the $500 Woodlands Open. Alan Heil (149) won, Roger Cowan (150) was second and J Webb (151) was third. Due to poor conditions caused by heavy pre-tournament rains, it was the first time in 30 years in this event that not a single player broke par. Other scores included Bruce Green / Geoff Donald / Ken Kilburn (152), John Hood / John Davis / Ray Wright / Les O'Shea (153), Stewart Ginn (155), Peter Mills (156), Brian Simpson / Ian Stanley / Jeff Boyle / Brian Huxtable / Bob Jennings (157).

The Age, 17 June 1968
46 years old Jack Harris (149) was 4th in the $1000 Yarrawonga Open. Peter Mills (145) won, Eric Wishart (147) was second and Geoff Donald (148) third. Other scores included John Davis (151), Geoff Parslow / Bruce Green / Brian Huxtable (152), Brian Simpson / Glen McCully (153) and Kel Llewellyn / Ray Wright (155). The scoring was good considering that the par 74 rated course was fully water-logged and fog reduced visibility to less than 50 yards.

The Age, 3 September 1968
Jack Harris (146) was second in the Royal Melbourne purse. Glenn McCully (142) won and left-hander John Davis (147) was third. They played the East course (par 74) in the morning and the West course (par 73) in the afternoon. Jack's one under the card for two rounds was not a bad effort for a 46-year-old golfer who had more or less retired from tournament golf two years earlier. Other scores included Brian Huxtable (149), Peter Mills (150), Harold Knights (152) and Bob Shearer / Alan Heil / Ray Wright / Kel Llewellyn (153). This was 18-year-old McCully's first ever senior win. Jack Harris won his first Victorian title, the 1946 Vic PGA Foursomes, four years before McCully was even born!

The Age, 11 September 1968
Jack Harris (73) was third in the $500 Liquor Industries purse at Kingswood GC. Winner was John Davis (70) and runner-up was Peter Mills (72). Also played Geoff Parslow (74) and John Kennedy / Ivan Dummett (75).

The Age, 2 November 1968
Jack Harris / South African Bobby Cole / Brian Huxtable / Col Johnston / Dan Cullen / John Kennedy / Harold Knights / NZ player John Lister / Graham Marsh / Japanese player H Suzumura / Bryan Smith / Guy Wolstenholme / Ryder Cup player Peter Townsend (76) were tied 38th after R1 of the **Australian PGA championship** at Metropolitan GC. Billy Dunk (67) was leading on 7 under par. Len Woodward / Kel Nagle (69) were tied second. Other scores included Arnold Palmer / Darryl Welch (70), Jack Nicklaus / Randall Vines / John Sullivan (71), Frank Phillips / Ron Howell / South Korean Han Sang Chan / Bob Jennings / Gary Player (72), Maurice Bembridge / Brian Boys / Errol Hartvigsen / Tim Woolbank (73), Ryder Cup player Clive Clark / Bruce Devlin / Mick Kelly / T Murakami / Howard McHutchison / Tony Mangan (74), Ted Ball / John Davis / Alan Heil / Colin McGregor / Peter Mills (75), Viv Billings / David Graham / South Korean Lee Ahn / Geoff Parslow (77), Kel Llewellyn / Stan Peach / Les Wilson / Alan Murray (78) and Frank Conallin / Peter Thomson / Bruce Green / NZ player Terry Kendall / Japanese player Haruo Yasuda (79).

The Age, 2 November 1968
Forty-six years old Jack Harris / Peter Thomson / New Zealand World Cup player Dennis Clark / Japanese World Cup player Haruo Yasuda / Ivan Cross / Bob Jennings / Howard McHutchison / Kel Llewellyn (156) were tied 49th after R2 in the **Australian PGA championship** at Metropolitan GC. Tournament leaders were Kel Nagle (136), Jack Nicklaus (138) and Billy Dunk (141). Other scores included Ryder Cup player Clive Clark (142), Gary Player / David Graham (145), Graham Marsh (146), Arnold Palmer / Maurice Bembridge / Frank Phillips / Ron Howell / Len Woodward (147), Randall Vines / Bruce Devlin / Errol Hartsvigsen / Peter Mills (148), Ted Ball (149), Bruce Green / John Davis / Mick Kelly (150), Guy Wolstenholme / Peter Townsend / Geoff Parslow / Col Johnston

(151), South African Bobby Cole / Dan Cullen / Bryan Smith / Alan Heil (152), South Korean Lee Ahn / Geoff Donald / Walter Godfrey / Brian Huxtable / Alan Murray / Les Wilson (153), NZ player Brian Boys / Paul Hart (154), Walter Gale / NZ player Terry Kendall / John Kennedy / NZ player John Lister / Alex Mercer / Dave Mercer / Tim Woolbank (157), Viv Billings / Harold Knights / Brian Twite (158) and South African P Matkovich (159)

The Age, 9 December 1968 (Ken Knox)
Jack Harris (289) was runner-up in the **Victorian PGA** championship at Waverley GC. Alan Heil (282) won and Brian Huxtable (290) was third. Jack shot an eagle on the final hole to sneak into second position. Other scores included Peter Mills (291), Harold Knights / John Davis (293), Ray Wright / Kel Llewellyn (298), John Kennedy (299), Ivan Cross (300), Bob Spencer / Bruce Green (302), Frank Conallin (305), Jeff Boyle / Trevor Horne (307), Viv Billings / Brian Simpson (308) and Geoff Flanagan (310). Bringing up the rear in no particular order were Brian Twite, Jeff Giles, Bryan Smith, Bob Jamieson, Howard McHutchison, Graham Howroyd, George Cussell and Ivan Dummett.

Sydney Morning Herald, 10 February 1969
Forty-seven years old Jack Harris (304) was 55th in the **Victorian Open** at Kingston Heath GC. Kel Nagle (279) won and Peter Thomson / Billy Dunk (282) tied second. Other scores included Frank Phillips (284), Maurice Bembridge / Walter Godfrey / Stan Peach (286), Glenn McCully (287), John Sullivan (288), Alan Murray (289), Col Johnston (291), Jack Newton / John Davis (292), Stewart Ginn / Alan Heil (293), John Lister / Terry Kendall (295), Ian Stanley (296), Guy Wolstenholme / Randall Hicks / Doug Bachli (297), Geoff Parslow / Randall Vines / Tim Woolbank (298), Ted Ball / Bob Shearer (299), Bruce Green (302) and Tom Linskey (303).

The Age, 24 March 1969
Jack Harris / Kel Garner / George Cussell (144) tied 7th in the first Sunshine GC Open. Peter Mills (136) won, Jeff Boyle (138) was second and Geoff Parslow / Brian Huxtable (142) tied third. Other scores included Glenn McCully / Geoff Donald (143), Bob Spencer (145), Mike Cahill (146) and Geoff Flanagan / Kel Llewellyn (149).

The Age, 20 May 1969
Jack Harris / Bruce Green / Charlie Oliver / Jeff Boyle / Brian Huxtable (152) tied 5th in $300 purse at Victoria GC. Colin Harrington / Peter Mills (144) were joint winners. Glenn McCully (148) was third. Also played Alan Heil (150) and US player Gerry Stolhand / Geoff Flanagan (153).

The Age, 26 September 1969
Forty-seven-years old Jack Harris / Jeff Boyle (145) tied 15th in the Eastwood Open. Amateur Randall Hicks (140) beat Ivan Cross / Bruce Green in a play-off. Other scores included Brian Simpson (141), Geoff Flanagan / Ian Stanley / Kel Llewellyn (142), L Moore / A Ephraums (143), Charlie Oliver / Bob Spencer / Peter Mills (144) and Geoff Parslow (146). Behind Parslow in no special order came Brian Huxtable, Peter Block, Jeff Giles, Alan Heil, Ray Wright, Colin Harrington, Doug Horne, Ivan Dummett, Bob Jennings, Trevor Horne and Viv Billings.

Sydney Morning Herald, 3 November 1969
47-year-old Jack Harris / Les Wilson / 19-year-old amateur Jack Newton / NZ player Walter Godfrey (301) tied 44th in the **$25,000 Dunlop International** tournament at Yarra Yarra GC. Bruce Devlin / American superstar Lee Trevino (276) tied first on 16 under the card, but Devlin won the sudden death play-off. Grand Slam champion Gary Player (278) was third. Other scores included British Open champion Tony Jacklin (280), Ryder Cup player Maurice Bembridge / 4 times Victorian Open winner Guy Wolstenholme (281), Bob Stanton (285), reigning US Open champion Orville Moody (284), Graham Marsh (285), Ryder Cup player Clive Clark / Geoff Parslow (286), Alan Heil (287), Zambian champion Simon Hobday (288), Ryder Cup player Malcom Gregson / Ted Ball / Glenn McCully (289), David Graham (290), Japanese player Tadashi Kita / John Sullivan / Peter Thomson (291), Kel Nagle / Taiwanese player Mr Lu (292), Tim Woolbank (293), Geoff Donald / Errol Hartsvigsen (294), Ryder Cup player Peter Oosterhuis (295), Bryan Smith / Billy Dunk / Terry Kendall (297) and Darryl Welch / Tom Linskey / Col Johnston / Bruce Green / Thai champion Sukree Onchum (299). Behind Jack Harris came former double Australian Open winner Frank Phillips, Alan Murray, Formosan player Kuo Chi Hsiung, Jeff Boyle, Ivan Cross, John Kennedy,

Japanese player Teruo Suzumura, former Australian Open winner Eric Cremin, Len Woodward, Barry Coxon, Kel Llewellyn, Stan Peach and Jeff Giles. Two years later Jack Newton turned professional and in 1975 was runner-up to Tom Watson after a play-off in the British Open at Carnoustie GC. Newton won the Australian Open in 1979 and had a great career before it was tragically curtailed in July 1983 when he walked into the spinning propeller of a Cessna light plane and lost both an eye and an arm.

The Age, 17 November 1969
Jack Harris / Brian Huxtable (219) tied 9th in the **Victorian Close championship** at Rossdale GC. Twenty-year-old Glenn McCully (208) won on eight under par and collected $225 first prize. Geoff Parslow (211) was second Geoff Donald / Bill Britten (214) tied third. Other scores included Ian Stanley (216), Kevin Hartley (217), Bob Shearer / Ivan Cross (218), Bill Bosley (220), Alan Heil / Rick Wines (222), Trevor Horne (224), Bryan Smith / Kel Llewellyn / Mike Cahill / John Kennedy / Viv Billings (225), Charlie Oliver (227), Stewart Ginn / Harold Knights / Trevor McDonald (228), Doug Horne / Brian Simpson (229) and Howard McHutchison (230). Jack Harris was 27 years older than the winner but he still shot the same one under par score of 71 in the final round.

The Age, 2 December 1969
Just a few days before his 47th birthday, Jack Harris / Alan Heil (145) tied in first place in the $300 Niblick-Corfam tournament at Riversdale GC. Jack shot a six under par 67 in the first round which was the lowest score of the tournament. However, it pissed down throughout the last round and scoring slipped. Jack and Alan both finished on one under the card. Other scores included John Kennedy / John Davis (146), Bryan Smith / Bruce Green / Howard McHutchison / Col Harrington / Harold Knights / Trevor Horne (148).

The Age, 8 December 1969
Jack Harris / Geoff Parslow (292) tied in first place in the **Victorian PGA** at Waverley GC. They split the first / second prize money for $250 each. Parslow easily won the 18-hole play-off for the title. Brian Huxtable (293) was third. Other scores included Kel Llewellyn (295), John Davis (297), Alan Heil (298), Howard McHutchison (298), Ivan Cross (301), Jeff Boyle

(302), Bob Spencer (303), Bruce Green (306), John Kennedy / Charlie Oliver (307), Harold Knights / Viv Billings (313) and Geoff Flanagan (317).

The Age, 5 February 1970

Jack Harris (69) tied 7th in the Riversdale Pro-Am with John Sullivan / NZ player Terry Kendall / Billy Dunk and US player J Vaughan. Winner with a super score of 61 was NZ player John Lister. Runner-up with a personal best was Randall Vines (65) and third was Kel Llewellyn (66). Tied 4th were Peter Thomson / Kel Nagle / NZ player Brian Boys (68). Behind Jack Harris were Peter Harvey / David Graham / Mick Kelly / Tim Woolbank / Tony Mangan (70) and Alan Heil / Bruce Green / Guy Wolstenholme / Tom Linskey / Graham Marsh / Stan Peach (71). Two very good scalps for Jack Harris at the age of 48 were Marsh and Graham. In fact, David Graham went on to win the Victorian Open which was also played at Riversdale the day after. Lister's score was twelve under the card and Vines was eight under. Forty-seven years old Jack Harris was four under par!

The Age, 9 February 1970

Forty-seven-year-old Jack Harris / Don Reiter / Rick Wines (288) tied 31st on four under par in the **$12500 Victorian Open championship** at Riversdale GC. David Graham (273) won on what had been his home course when he first turned professional. Kevin Hartley / Guy Wolstenholme / Kel Nagle (277) tied second. Other scores included Alan Heil / Peter Thomson (278), Geoff Parslow (280), Graham Marsh / Geoff Donald (281), NZ player Terry Kendall / Ted Ball / Tim Woolbank / Glenn McCully (282), Billy Dunk / NZ player Walter Godfrey / Randall Vines / Peter Harvey (283), C Pettit (284), Mick Kelly / Vic Bennetts / Jeff Boyle / NZ player / John Lister / S Vernon / Stan Peach (285), Barry Coxon (286), Jerry Stolhand / John Lindsay / Eric Routley / Ian Stanley / Bruce Green (287), John Sullivan / Tony Mangan / John Davis)289), Frank Phillips / B Moran / player Brian Boys (290), Doug Fearns / Col Harrington (291), Ryder Cup player Maurice Bembridge / Tom Linskey / Bob Shearer (293), Howard McHutchison / Alan Lehner (296) and Bob Jennings (299).

The Age, 31 March 1970
Jack Harris / Don Reiter / Eric Routley (147) tied 6th on one over the card in the $750 Yarra Yarra Easter Open. Kevin Hartley (139) won. 1968 Victorian amateur champion John Lindsay (140) was second and Bill Britten (141) third. Other scores included Harry McGain (144), Alan Heil (145), Bob Shearer (148) and John Hood / Kel Llewellyn / John Kennedy / Ken Kilburn (149). Due to the prevalence of amateurs in this tournament, 47-year-old Harris still collected second place prize money behind leading professional Alan Heil.

The Age, 16 April 1970
Jack Harris / Ivan Cross (74) tied 7th in the pro-purse at Medway GC. Frank Conallin (69) won and Jeff Boyle / Trevor Horne (72) tied second. Other scores included Doug Horne / Alan Heil / Geoff Parslow (73), Geoff Flanagan (75) and Brian Simpson / Charlie Oliver (76).

The Age, 15 June 1970
Jack Harris / Mike Cahill (152) tied 6th in the $750 Woodlands Open. Kevin Hartley (147) won, Ken Kilburn (148) was second and John Davis / Geoff Parslow (149) tied third. Also played Glen McCully (154), Brian Simpson (155), Jeff Boyle (156) and Bob Spencer / Brian Huxtable / Bill Britten (157). This was quite good scoring on a par 72 course that was in a completely water-logged condition. With amateur players featuring strongly in the top positions, Jack Harris picked up third place prize money.

The Age, 11 November 1970
Jack Harris / Jeff Sandford (78) tied 7th in the Pro-Am at Patterson River Country Club. Ken Kilburn (70) won on three under par for a new course record. Peter Mills / Bob Jennings (71) tied second but took home the bulk of the prize money as first professionals to finish. Other scores included Bob Spencer / Ian Stanley (76), John Zwirs (77) and Alan Heil / Brian Huxtable / Kel Llewellyn / Ivan Cross (80).

The Age, 23 November 1970
Forty-eight years old Jack Harris / Kel Llewellyn / South African John Stokoe / Randall Hicks / Larry Moore (220) tied 9th in the **Victorian Close championship** at Northern GC. Kevin Hartley / Garry Mansfield (217)

tied first on 2 under the card. Kevin won the sudden death play-off. Brian Langsford / Bob Jennings / Alan Heil / Bill Britten / Peter Mills (218) tied third. Other scores included L Tomholt (219), John Davis (221), Trevor Horne (222), Geoff Parslow / Stewart Ginn (224) and Ian Stanley / Mike Cahill (225).

The Age, 3 December 1970
Jack Harris / Charlie Oliver / Howard McHutchison (73) tied 6th in the $1500 Rothmans Pro-Am at Long Island GC. Ivan Cross (71) won on level par. Bruce Green / Harold Knights / Geoff Parslow / John Davis (72) tied second. Other scores included Brian Twite / Alan Heil / Frank Conallin / Peter Mills / Bob Spencer (75). Some of the amateurs playing included boxer Johnny Famechon, footballer Ted Whitten, jockey Roy Higgins, tennis player Frank Sedgman and cricketer Ian Meckiff.

The Age, 5 December 1970
Jack Harris / Alan Heil (290) tied 4th in the **Victorian PGA championship** at Long Island GC. Bob Jennings (286) won, Geoff Parslow (288) was second and Geoff Flanagan (289) third. Other scores included Peter Mills (293), Bob Spencer (299) and Ivan Cross (303).

The Age, 13 April 1971
Jack Harris / J Barton (146) tied 4th in the Yarra Yarra Open. Kevin Hartley (144) won in a playoff against Rick Wines. Geoff Parslow (145) was third and won the professional purse just one stroke ahead of forty-nine years old Harris.
Other scores included Bob Shearer / John Davis (147), Jeff Boyle / Bruce Green (148), Stewart Ginn / Ian Stanley (150), Alan Heil (154), Kel Llewellyn (156) and Ray Jenner (156).

The Age, 13 July 1971
Jack Harris / Bob Shearer / Kel Llewellyn (154) tied 9th in the $300 purse at Victoria GC. Alan Heil (146) won, Peter Mills (147) was second and Jeff Boyle (150) third. Other scores included Trevor Horne / Bob Spencer (152), Bruce Green / Ron Wood (153), Harold Knights (155) and Ian Stanley / Tim Ward (156).

The Age, 23 September 1971
Jack Harris / Bruce Hiam / Alan Lehner (152) tied fifth in $600 Eastwood Open. Jeff Boyle (144) won, Peter Mills (147) was second and Ron Wood (148) third. Other scores included Tony Limon (150), Bob Shearer (153), Alan Heil / Bruce Green / John Davis (154), Ken Kilburn (155), Randall Hicks (156), Charlie Oliver / Trevor MacDonald (157) and Stewart Ginn (158).

Sydney Morning Herald, 22 October 1971
Forty-nine-year-old Jack Harris / Trevor Horne / Jeff Boyle / former US Open winner Gene Littler / Thai World Cup player Pradana Ngarmprom / South African Dale Hayes / five times British Open winner Peter Thomson / John Kennedy / Charlie Oliver (74) tied 31st after R1 of the **$20,000 Wills Classic** tournament at Victoria GC. Not a bad effort for Jack, who had essentially retired from serious golf over five years earlier, to stay with Gene Littler who had tied 4th in the US Masters in 1971 and had been runner-up in the US Masters in 1970.
Dennis Ingram / David Graham (68) were leading and US superstar Dave Stockton (69) was second. Other scores included Guy Wolstenholme / Billy Dunk / Thai player Sukree Onchum / Geoff Parslow / Bruce Crampton (70), Tom Linskey / Glenn McCully / Barry Coxon / Roberto de Vicenzo (71), US player Martin Bohen / Tim Woolbank / US player Dave Hill (72), Walter Godfrey / Tony Mangan, Frank Phillips / Vic Bennetts / Peter Harvey / Randall Vines / Harold Henning / Kel Nagle / Alan Murray / NZ player Alan Snape (73), Bob Tuohy / Ron Howell (75), Jack Newton / Graham Marsh / Stan Peach / Ted ball (76) and Ian Stanley (77).

The Age, 25 October 1971
49-year-old Jack Harris / NZ player Terry Kendall / South African Harold Henning / Doug Maggs (301) tied 33rd in **$20,000 Wills Classic** at Victoria GC. Bruce Crampton (281) won on 7 under par. Ryder Cup player Maurice Bembridge (284) was second and US player Dave Stockton (285) was third. Other scores included Roberto de Vicenzo / Kel Nagle (287), David Graham / Glenn McCully / Thai player Sukree Onchum (288), NZ player Walter Godfrey (290), Guy Wolstenholme / Peter Thomson / Alan Murray (291), Stan Peach / US player Gene Littler (292), US player

Martin Bohen / Tom Linskey (293), Peter Oosterhuis / Barry Coxon (294), reigning Australian PGA titleholder Billy Dunk / US player and 1970 US Open runner-up Dave Hill (295), Randall Vines / Geoff Parslow / Frank Phillips (296), South African Dale Hayes (297), Graham Marsh / Dennis Ingram (298), Jerry Stolhand / Jeff Boyle (300), Ian Stanley / Tim Woolbank (302), World Cup player Pradana Ngarmprom / NZ player Alan Snape / Bob Tuohy / Ted Ball (304), Japanese player M Mizuno (304) and Doug Horne / WA Open champion G Johnson (307). Bringing up the rear was twenty-one-year-old Jack Newton who, as a nineteen-year-old, had tied with Jack Harris in the 1969 Dunlop International. However, he couldn't manage to keep up with the old boy on this occasion.

Also behind G Johnson were US player Ron Howell, Vic Bennetts, Colin McGregor, Bob Tuohy, Paul Hart, and Alec Mercer.

The Age, 22 November 1971
Forty-nine years old Jack Harris / Garry Mansfield (234) tied 26th in the **Victorian Close** at Waverley GC. Peter Mills (210) won with Frank Conallin / Geoff Parslow (221) joint runners-up. Also played John Davis (222), Stewart Ginn / Kevin Hartley / Randall Hicks / Russell McLennan (223), Glen McCully (224), Ian Stanley (226), Alan Heil (228), Bob Spencer (229), Geoff Flanagan (230) and Ivan Cross / Bert Ferguson (236).

The Age, 29 November 1971
Forty-nine years-old Jack Harris / Alan Lehner / Viv Billings / Frank Conallin (150) tied 12th in the $500 Heidelberg Open. Stewart Ginn (142) won and John Davis / Peter Mills (144) tied second. Ginn was still on 12 months' probation so Davis / Mills shared the prize money. Other scores included Noel Beattie / Rob McLennan (145), Ted Stirling (146), Ian Stanley / Bob Shearer (147), Colin Harrington (148) and Brian Huxtable (149).

The Age, 2 December 1971
Just a few days before his 49th birthday, Jack Harris (74) tied 5th with G Powell and Colin Harrington in the Rothman's Pro-Am at Long Island GC. Peter Mills (68) won and Ted Stirling (72) was second. Ian Stanley / Derek Cabrin (73) tied third. Some of the celebrities playing were England

pace bowler John Snow, boxer Johnny Famechon, footballer Jack Dyer and tennis legend Frank Sedgman.

The Age, 4 December 1971
Jack Harris (297) was 8th in the **$1000 Victorian PGA championship** at Long Island GC. He shot a par 71 in the first round but for a 49-year-old to play 36 holes of gruelling tournament golf on consecutive days was very tough and he faded in later rounds. Peter Mills (288) won the $225 first prize. Bob Jennings (291) was second and Geoff Parslow (292) was third. Other scores included Alan Heil (294), John Davis / Bruce Green / Ted Stirling (296), Colin Harrington (298), Glenn McCully (299) and Ron Wood / Tim Ward (300). Behind Tim in no special order came Doug Horne, Ivan Cross, Geoff Flanagan, Howard McHutchison, Trevor Horne, Frank Conallin and Charlie Oliver.

The Age, 7 February 1972
Forty-nine years old Jack Harris / Mark Tapper / Paul Hart / R Beel (306) tied 30th in **Victorian Open** at Commonwealth GC. NZ champion Walter Godfrey (283) won and Peter Mills / Kel Nagle / Japanese superstar Isao Aoki (290) tied second. Other scores included Ian Stanley (291), Vic Bennetts (292), Frank Phillips / Billy Dunk / NZ player Terry Kendall / US player Martin Bohen (294), Japanese player N Takasu (295), Geoff Parslow / Kevin Hartley / Alan Heil / Dennis Ingram (296), Randall Vines / Bob Tuohy (297), Peter Thomson (298), John Davis (299), Stan Peach / Bob Shearer / Jerry Stolhand / Eric Routley (300), Stewart Ginn / Bob Jennings (302), Mike Cahill (303), Ken Kilburn / Alan Reiter (307), Don Reiter (308), Barry Coxon / Bill Britten / Derek Cabrin / John Lindsay (309), Geoff Smart (311) and Ron Wood (312). In the also-rans were Kel Llewellyn, US player J Vaughan, Ron Howell, Jack Newton, Tim Woolbank, Col Harrington and Trevor McDonald. Guy Wolstenholme was disqualified for signing an incorrect card but would have scored 288 and been a clear runner-up.

The Age, 2 May 1972
Jack Harris / George Cussell (153) tied 5th with Brian Simpson / Laurie McConnell in the **Victorian PGA Foursomes** at Croydon GC. John Davis / Geoff Parslow (147) won. Jeff Boyle / Ivan Cross (150) were

second and Ron Wood / Peter Mills (151) were third. Colin Harrington / Kel Llewellyn (152) were fourth.

The Age, 29 September 1972
Fifty-year old Jack Harris / Noel Beattie (144) tied second on level par in the $750 Eastwood Open. This was despite Jack dropping three shots over the last three holes. On the 16th he had a superb drive but a shocking bounce on his second shot cost him a double bogey. Then he three-putted the 18th. Geoff Parslow (142) on the other hand had a great finish and snook in to win. Other scores included Glenn McCully (145), Peter Mills (147), Peter Croker / Jack Westmore (148), Kel Llewellyn (149), Geoff Flanagan (151) and Ron Wood (152). Behind these players in no special order were Brian Simpson, Laurie McConnell, Bob Spencer, Colin Harrington, Alan Heil, Bruce Green, Ivan Cross, Ken Kilburn, Charlie Oliver, Bob Jennings, Randall Hicks, Viv Billings and Bob Jamieson.

The Age, 4 November 1972
After the first round of the **$25000 Dunlop International** tournament at Yarra Yarra GC, fifty-year-old Jack Harris / Peter Croker / Stan Peach / Egyptian Mohammed Moussa / Bob Tuohy / Tim Ward / Tim Woolbank (76) were tied in 52nd place. At that stage, the eventual winner, Ryder Cup player Tony Jacklin, was tied on 74 with South African Dale Hayes / Guy Wolstenholme. Just one stroke ahead of Jack Harris were Jerry Stolhand / Bryan Smith / Vaughan Sommers / John Davis / Jack Newton / Bruce Devlin / Ryder Cup player Guy Hunt (75). Behind Jack Harris were Vic Bennetts / Stewart Ginn / Alan Heil / Randall Vines / (77), Ivan Cross / Alec Mercer / Ron Howell / Walter Gale / Viv Billings / Bob Swinbourne (78) and Jim Moran / Glenn McCully / Col Johnston / Ian Stanley / NZ player Simon Owen (79). This was not a bad effort from Jack Harris considering that he had effectively been winding down from tournament golf for the previous seven years.

The Age, 9 December 1972
Fifty-years-old Jack Harris / Bruce Green (309) tied 6th in the **Victorian PGA Championship** at Long Island GC. John Davis (297) won, Charlie Oliver (301) was second and Bob Spencer / Peter Mills (304) tied third. Other scores included Bob Jennings (306) and Brian Huxtable (311).

Behind them came Laurie McConnell, Colin Harrington, Ron Wood, Tim Ward, Brian Simpson, Trevor Horne, Viv Billings, Graham Howroyd, Alan Heil and Kel Garner.

The Age, 16 October 1973
Jack Harris / Peter Croker / Geoff Parslow (74) tied 12th in the Victorian qualifying round for the $50000 **Chrysler Classic** at The Lakes GC in November 1973. Bob Shearer (66) led the qualifiers, Jeff Boyle (69) was second and Howard McHutchison (70) was third. Other scores included Rob McNaughton / Charlie Oliver (72), Frank Conallin / Guy Wolstenholme / Darryl Welch (73), Alan Heil / Jeff Giles / Laurie McConnell / Bob Swinbourne (75), Ian Stanley (76) and Doug Horne / Viv Billings / Kel Garner / Ivan Cross (77). Jack Harris, Charlie Oliver and Jeff Giles all comfortably met the qualifying 76 score but chose not to go to Sydney.

The Age, 6 December 1973
Jack Harris / Peter Mills (74) tied 8th in the $2000 Rothman's Pro-Am at Long Island GC. John Davis (68) won the $380 first prize on 3 under par. Trevor McDonald (69) was second and Bruce Green / Guy Wolstenholme / Rob McNaughton / Doug Horne (72) tied third. Other scores included G Hoskins (73), Bryan Smith / Noel Beattie / Charlie Oliver / Bob Spencer / Trevor Horne (75) and Harold Knights / Ray Wright (76).

The Age, 23 September 1974
Fifty-two years old Jack Harris (84) was 29th in the Seymour Pro-Am. Michael Cahill (71) won and Ron Wood / Geoff Parslow / Glen McCully (73) tied second. Also played Alan Heil (74), Brian Huxtable (75), John Davis / Howard McHutchison (76), Bert Ferguson (77) and Viv Billings / Ivan Cross (86).

This was a good score by Cahill because the course was in appalling condition with 60% of the course under two inches of water, covering another two inches of mud!

The Age, 4 February 1975
53 years old Jack Harris (76) was tied 13th in the qualifying tournament at Metropolitan GC for the **Victorian Open** with Geoff Parslow, Kel

Garner and four others. 28 years old Bruce Green (68) won, Alan Heil (69) was second and 24 years old Rodger Davis (70) was third. Other scores included Peter Mills (75), Noel Beattie / Bryan Smith (77), Bob Spencer / Jerry Stolhand / Ted Stirling / Brian Huxtable / Tim Ward / Kel Llewellyn (78), Colin Harrington (79) and Doug Horne (80)

The Age, 21 February 1977
Fifty-five years old Jack Harris played in the $5000 pro-am tournament at East Malvern public golf course. I couldn't find his score but in this tournament, he crossed pathways with a future superstar of world golf, 22 years old Greg Norman.
Norman only tied 8th in this event with Alan Heil, Geoff Parslow, John Davis and Terry Gilmore on 67. Randall Vines won with a course record 64 and Paul Hart / Mark Tapper (65) tied second. Ian Stanley was tied in 4th place on 66.

The Age, 8 March 1977
Fifty-five years old Jack Harris / fifty-three years old George Cussell (147) were second in the **Victorian PGA foursome's championship** at Croydon GC. They shot an under-par round of 70 in the morning round but ran out of puff in the afternoon round when their combined age of 108 caught up with them. Peter Mills / Jeff Sandford (145) won and Geoff Parslow / John Davis (149) were third. Other scores included Laurie McConnell / Brian Simpson and Guy Wolstenholme / Trevor McDonald (150).

The Age, 10 March 1977
Fifty-five years -old Jack Harris / Howard McHutchison (74) tied 4th in the $200 purse at the Colvan Charity Day Pro-Am at Green Acres GC. Colin Harrington (69) won on two under par. Terry Hulls (72) was second and Bob Spencer (73) third. Other scores included John Davis / Peter McGrath (75) and John Furze / Bruce Green / Duncan Moodie / Alan Heil / Bruce Milgate (76).

The Age, 8 October 1979
Fifty-seven-years-old Jack Harris (225) was 11th in the $25000 **Citizens Watches Australian Seniors championship** at Manly GC. Former US Open winner Tommy Bolt (214) won the $5000 first prize. Former US

Open winner Jack Fleck (215) was second and former Irish Ryder Cup / Canada Cup player Jimmy Martin (217) was third. Other scores included US PGA tour winner George Bayer / former US PGA champion Dow Finsterwald (218), former British Open winner Kel Nagle (219), former US Masters winner Art Wall Jr / Japanese superstar Tomoo Ishii (221), former Irish Ryder Cup / Canada Cup player Christy O'Connor (223), all-time record US PGA tour winner Sam Snead (224), Harry Berwick / Don Sharp (226), Keith Pepper (227), Dan Cullen (228), Japanese Open winner Yoshimasha Fujii (229), former British Open winner Bobby Locke (230) and former Japanese Open & PGA winner & Canada Cup player Torakichi Nakamura / John Kelly / US player and Hawaiian Golf Hall of Famer John Kalinka (231). Behind Kalinka were Denis Denehey, Jim McInnes and Reg Want.

Only four players in the whole tournament managed to shoot a sub-70 round. Fifty-seven years old Jack Harris was one of them! Jack had the great pleasure of playing this tournament with Art Wall Jr. It was also the one and only time Jack had the thrill of playing in the same field as the great Sam Snead. Although Sam was about ten years older than Jack Harris, he was still playing excellent golf at age 67. That year Sam was the oldest man ever to make the cut in the US PGA championship when he finished T42 on 288 which was six strokes ahead of 39 years old Jack Nicklaus who was already a fifteen-times major tournament winner by that time. It was the last time Sam made the cut in a major championship although he did appear in two more US Masters in the early 1980s. Aficionados will also be aware that the 1979 US PGA championship was a very significant year for Australian golf because it was won by ex-Wattle Park player David Graham! In the **Citizens Watches** Sam just pipped Jack Harris by one stroke but of the three rounds played Jack Harris outscored Sam in two of them! When both Jack Harris and Tommy Bolt were playing at their peaks in the 1950s, Jack Harris had beaten Tommy several times when Bolt visited Australia to play in the Ampol sponsored tournaments. Jack Harris had essentially been retired from tournament golf for about 15 years when he played in the **Citizen's Watch** tournament and had already survived two heart attacks. For him to come out of a long retirement and hold his own in this kind of company when he didn't have a long history of Tour Golf on his résumé is simply astounding.

Appendix I

Norman von Nida
(14 Feb 1914 – 20 May 2007)

Life Member of Australian PGA

'Dear Jack, I've never during my career as a golfer, met a professional golfer who was as dedicated to teaching the game, as you. The people who were fortunate enough to have been the recipient of the knowledge of how to play our game would be unanimous in using the words "Thank you Jack"! Your contribution to the game will be long remembered by the pleasure they have derived from that knowledge! You will long be remembered as a wonderful contributor to the game of golf, and as a friend of Norman von Nida, who wishes all the best to you on your retirement; you were always the perfect gentle man. Von'

Norman & Elva von Nida

Dear Jack, 17 June

I've never during my career as a golfer, met a professional golfer who was as dedicated to teaching the game, as you.

The people who were fortunate enough to have been the recipient of the knowledge of how to play our game, would be unanimous in using the words "Thank you, Jack".

Your contribution to the game will be long remembered by the pleasure they have derived from that knowledge.

You will long be remembered as a wonderful contributor to the game of golf, and as a friend of Norman von Nida, who wishes all the best to you in your retirement, you were always the perfect gentleman.

Norm

Above letter received from Norman von Nida at the time of Jack Harris's retirement.